NUCLEAR POWER AND NON-PROLIFERATION

The remaking of U.S. policy

This book is dedicated to my wife, Mounira

Nuclear Power and Non-Proliferation

The remaking of U.S. policy

MICHAEL J. BRENNER

University of Pittsburgh

CAMBRIDGE UNIVERSITY PRESS

Cambridge
London   New York   New Rochelle
Melbourne   Sydney

Published by the Press Syndicate of the University of Cambridge
The Pitt Building, Trumpington Street, Cambridge CB2 1RP
32 East 57th Street, New York, NY 10022, USA
296 Beaconsfield Parade, Middle Park, Melbourne 3206, Australia

© Cambridge University Press 1981

First published 1981

Printed in the United States of America

Library of Congress Cataloging in Publication Data
Brenner, Michael J.
Nuclear power and non-proliferation.
Includes index.
1. Nuclear nonproliferation. 2. Atomic power –
Law and legislation – United States. I. Title.
JX1974.73.B73   327.1′74   80–28561
ISBN 0 521 23517 0   AACR1

Contents

Preface

NUCLEAR power has been an absorbing subject for more than a generation. The peril created by weapons of mass destruction has riveted the attention of governments and peoples. The peaceful atom, too, has exercised an exceptional hold on the imagination. Neither of atomic energy's two sides has lacked for critical examination. They have received constant and sober scrutiny from political leaders, scholars, concerned citizens, and moral philosophers.

Familiarity has dispelled some of the mystery that surrounds nuclear power. We have come to understand much about the way it can and does affect our lives. In certain respects, we have accommodated ourselves to its presence. Yet it remains a source of recurrent anxiety. Few people feel fully confident that "the bomb" is under adequate restraint. Worries about the safety of electric generating plants are pervasive. Most recently, concern has been aroused by the troubling prospect of nuclear arms spreading around the world as a direct consequence of expanding civilian nuclear programs. The mounting proliferation danger has revived latent fears and focused them on the disquieting link between the military atom and the peaceful atom. The prospect of nuclear armed states appearing at all points of the compass has unsettled a good deal of conventional government thinking about national security and international stability.

As nuclear proliferation moved toward the top of problem lists in Washington in the mid-seventies, it became evident that the issue posed an exceptional challenge to the U.S. government. There were many pieces to the puzzle, pieces strewn all across the administrative and political landscape. Obviously the problem did not lend itself to solution by conducting government business as usual. This study set out to recount how the United States has moved to compose these pieces into a coherent policy. It is at once a historical narrative and a work of policy analysis. My main objective is to explain why policies took the shape they did. A subsidiary goal is to assess their significance for global nuclear relations. Although the work does not purport to be a comprehensive chronicle of events during the period it treats, I believe that it represents a fair and reasonably detailed account of the principal decisions taken and policies executed. As for the mode of analysis, I have tried to make it as straightforward as the subject allows. Like all social scientists, I must struggle to suppress the impulse to formalize and to catalogue. I hope that I have succeeded in sparing the reader the distractions of a too elliptical style. At the same time, I trust that enough of an analytical frame has been provided to aid in making sense of the events described and to say something worthwhile about the way U.S. government behaves.

The book's structure is intentionally a simple one. A short introduction plays the proliferation issue against the backdrop of postwar nuclear history. It calls attention to the dual personality of atomic power, noting the steady divergence of military and civilian programs (and of the imagery each created) until a series of stunning events in 1974 forced an effort to bring them into single focus. The ensuing chapters center on three crucial episodes in the making of U.S. policy on nuclear exports and weapons proliferation. Chapter 2 deals with the crisis of nuclear enrichment services that came to a head in June 1974 with major implications for the international nuclear market and its regulation. Chapter 3 concentrates on the Ford administration's rethinking of established attitudes and programs, which laid the basis for the more drastic reforms of President Carter. The latter are the subject of Chapter 4. Chapter 5 follows with an account of how the Carter administration's initiatives fared. The concluding chapter offers an overall assessment of the United States' performance during this critical period when it sought to restore a greater measure of national and international control over the growth and extension of nuclear power worldwide.

The completion of this book has depended on the support and cooperation of many people and institutions. A grant from the Arms Control and International Security Program of the Ford Foundation made it possible for me to conduct the study on which it is based. Portions of the research were done in Washington at the Brookings Institution, where I enjoyed the hospitality extended me as a Guest Scholar during the spring and summer of 1977. As a second-time beneficiary of its generous assistance, I am especially appreciative of the encouragement to scholarly enterprise offered by the Institution's atmosphere of dedication, diligence, and good cheer. At the University of Pittsburgh, I am indebted to John Funari, Dean of the Graduate School of Public and International Affairs, who gave the project his fullest support throughout. The late Carl Beck, Director of the University Center for International Studies, also provided valuable assistance.

A work of policy analysis requires, above all, that government officials willingly make available their knowledge and experience. Without the ready help of those who are the actors in the policy dramas described herein, it would have been impossible to write this critical account. In some respects, it is a remarkable act of bravery to speak with the frankness that characterized most of my interviews, for an official can never know with certainty if his responses will be handled conscientiously, and himself treated fairly. I hope that nothing in this book violates that implicit trust.

A special word of gratitude and appreciation goes to two men who played an active role in the non-proliferation policies of the Carter administration: Joseph S. Nye, Jr., Professor of Government at Harvard University and former Deputy to the Undersecretary of State for Security Assistance, Science and Technology; and Albert Carnesale, Professor of Public Policy in the Kennedy School of Government at Harvard University, who acted as the United States Representative of the Technical Coordinating Committee of the International Fuel Cycle Evaluation. They contributed greatly to my effort to understand the processes and policies of the administration they so ably served. Any lapses of fact or interpretation that may be discovered in this work should in no way reflect on their ability as tutors. Both embody the virtues of the scholar-statesman whose talents are a unique strength of U.S. government.

Many others gave freely of their time and knowledge. Among those who have held positions in the Atomic Energy Commission (AEC) and its successor agencies are AEC Commissioners William O. Doub, Clarence E. Larson, John G. Palfrey, and James T. Ramey; John Erlwine, General Manager of the AEC; Nuclear Regulatory Commission (NRC) Commissioner Victor Gilinsky; Nelson F. Sievering, Assistant Administrator for International Affairs, Energy Research and Development Administration (ERDA); Myron B. Kratzer, Assistant General Manager for International Activities, AEC, and later Deputy Assistant Secretary of State for Nuclear Energy and Energy Technology Affairs; Gerald Tape, U.S. Ambassador to the International Atomic Energy Agency (IAEA); Peter N. Brush, Assistant General Counsel, ERDA; Julius Rubin, Production Division, ERDA; Robert Ritzman, Production Division, ERDA; Gerard Helfrich, International Program Implementation, ERDA; Vance Hudgins, International Security Affairs (ISA), ERDA; Jamed Hanrahan, Division of Planning, Evaluation and Forecasting, ERDA; Jeremiah Kratz, ISA/ERDA; and Fred McGoldrick, Deputy Director for Nuclear Affairs, Department of Energy.

Officials in the State Department and the Arms Control and Disarmament Agency were equally helpful. They included Donald Tice, Office of the Undersecretary of State; Jerome Kahan, State Planning Office (SP) and Bureau of Political–Military Affairs (PM); Louis V. Nosenzo, Deputy Assistant Secretary of State for Nuclear Energy and Energy Technology Affairs; Herman Pollack, Director, Bureau of International Scientific and

Technological Affairs; Dixon Hoyle, Acting Deputy Assistant Secretary for Energy and Technology Affairs and, previously, Acting Director, International Affairs, ERDA; Harold D. Bengelsdorf, Office of the Administrator for International Affairs, ERDA, and Office of Oceans and International Environmental and Scientific Affairs (OES – State); Marvin Humphries, PM; Charles van Doren, Assistant Director for Non-Proliferation, Arms Control and Disarmament Agency (ACDA); Robert Einhorn, ACDA; John Boright, ACDA and OES – State.

I benefited as well from conversations with officials in the Executive Office of the President, among whom were James Connor, Secretary to the Cabinet under Gerald Ford, and previously Assistant Director for Planning and Analysis, AEC; Glenn Schleede, Office of Management and Budget and the Domestic Council; David Elliott, Senior Staff Member for Scientific and Technical Affairs, National Security Council (NSC), and Office of the Science and Technology Adviser to the President (OSTP); Benjamin Huberman, NSC Deputy Director for Analysis, NRC Staff, and OSTP; Gustave Speth, Council on Environmental Quality; Peter Zimmerman, NSC; Gerald Oplinger, NSC; and Ted Greenwood, OSTP.

On the legislative side, I had the opportunity to talk with Craig Hosmer, former Joint Atomic Energy Committee member; Warren Donnelly, Senior Specialist in Energy, Congressional Research Service, Library of Congress; Maury Canfield, General Accounting Office; William Anderson, Staff of Congressman Clarence E. Long; Edward Bauser, Staff of the House Committee on Science and Technology; Len Weiss, Staff of the Senate Government Operations Committee, Subcommittee on Non-Proliferation.

Finally, there were discussions with David Burnham of the *New York Times*; James M. Cubie, legislative representative for New Directions; Lincoln Gordon, Resources for the Future; and Herbert Scoville, Jr., former official with ACDA and AEC.

Officials in private industry were also receptive to my inquiries. I wish to thank George L. Wilcox, Ralph Simpson, Dwight Porter, A. L. Bethel, Dr. Daniel Berg, and Joseph Bader of the Westinghouse Electric Corporation; Arnold Fritsch of Gulf, Inc.; Kenneth Davis and Ash O'Donnell of Bechtel, Inc.; Edward A. Wiggin, Vice-President, and Frank Graham, Manager for Special Studies, of Atomic Industrial Forum; and Donald Couchman, Vice-President, N.U.S., Inc.

The task of bringing coherence to a narrative work is an arduous one. I was fortunate in benefiting from the critical comments and sympathetic advice of two exceptionally knowledgeable readers, Professor Irvin C. Bupp of the Harvard Business School and Professor Lawrence Scheinman of Cornell University. Professor Scheinman brought his considerable knowledge of nuclear affairs into government service, first in the office of the Administrator for International Affairs at ERDA, and then as Senior Adviser to the Undersecretary for Security Assistance, Science and Technology. I also received the able counsel of my editor, Walter Lippincott of Cambridge University Press, whose support helped to keep patience and confidence from wavering. I am especially grateful to Janis Bolster, who applied all her skill to grooming an unruly manuscript.

I received assistance in preparation of materials for the study from two exceptionally able graduate assistants at the University of Pittsburgh's Graduate School of Public and International Affairs, Donald Orr and Getachew Felleke, who deserve more than the conventional word of thanks. I am similarly grateful to Mrs. Barbara Wells of the Graduate School, who had the formidable, but by no means thankless, chore of arranging the manuscript's typing, and of serving as principal cryptographer. My typists, Mrs. Betty Watson, Kathy Roper, Dolores Rosepink, and Maryann Welsh, brought to the task rare skill and a great capacity to bring order out of chaos. My thanks go as well to Henrietta Moss of the Center for International Studies, who also gave the manuscript's preparation her sympathetic attention.

My greatest debt is to my beloved wife, Mounira, to whom this book is dedicated.

M.J.B.

1

Introduction: postwar nuclear history

TWO VISIONS OF ATOMIC POWER

WHEN nuclear power was demonstrated for the first time at Alamogordo, Robert Oppenheimer reverted to the apocalyptic language of the Bhagavad-Gita to express his feelings of awe. The sensation was one of wonder tinged with dread. Supernatural metaphors have always seemed best suited for evoking the specter of unimagined force and for showing deference. Magic inspires atavistic respect and caution.[1]

But display of the atom's power was also a source of pride and confidence. Alamogordo was not the doing of a mysterious and unknowable spirit. Human ingenuity and skill were the instigators. Confident and hopeful men saw in the successful achievement of a chain reaction and release of the atom's power confirmation of man's technical prowess. They also foresaw an enormous potential good in the power that stood ready to be harnessed and put to peaceful uses. If this was magic, it was neither wholly alien nor entirely frightening. Nuclear power's dual personality, as threat and as promise, has been the hallmark of its short social history. The contradictions and strains it engenders are visible in the policies that for thirty-odd years have sought to mitigate the threat and to realize the opportunity.

Military use of nuclear energy has been the paramount concern dominating the thinking of governments and publics. Hiroshima left no doubt that atomic weapons were something new under the sun. Any sensible person could see that they posed a unique threat to the survival of nations. The postwar era in international politics is, in large measure, a record of the great powers' efforts to come to grips with the quantum jump in the destructiveness of armaments. However strong the inclination to put new technologies to military advantage, however artful the strategic improvisations to make nuclear arms fit for traditional military purposes, the states

1

possessing the military atom have felt compelled to treat it as something very special. There is a practical recognition that nuclear arms are ill-suited to performing any of the classic roles of weaponry: compelling behavior, extracting concessions, or subduing an opponent. Their primary and probably sole function is to deter other states similarly endowed. Their very existence has instilled a prudent caution about all manner of great-power conflict, out of respect for the intolerable consequences were hostilities to get out of hand. The nuclear powers could not fail to concede their mutual interest in restraining the impulse toward conflict.

An appreciation that nuclear explosives pose a unique danger has also been reflected in the U.S. and Soviet aversion to the spread of atomic arms to other countries. The nuclear powers' common stake in stability, and in the prudent management of nuclear arsenals, has made them sensitive to the menace of proliferation. Atomic weapons are something to be contained, guarded, and restricted. The United States, despite its global system of alliance commitments, never yielded control of nuclear warheads to other states. In NATO, it devised painstaking procedures centering on Permissive Action Links to ensure that the thousands of nuclear weapons on foreign soil could not be detonated without explicit approval and physical action by U.S. officers under instruction from their political leaders. It has steadfastly resisted the temptation to meet recurrent NATO anxieties over the credibility of the U.S. commitment to its defense by sharing the control of nuclear weapons. In support of this principle, Washington has been prepared to incur the rebuke of a France aggrieved by U.S. refusal to assist in the building of its *force de frappe*. It also has suffered British charges that the United States reneged on a wartime agreement with the United Kingdom to share in the fruits of the Manhattan Project, to which the latter made a substantial intellectual contribution. Moscow has been even stricter, if anything, in keeping its nuclear arms to itself.

In the United States, steps also were taken early on to prevent bomb-making materials and critical technology from being transferred to other countries. The Atomic Energy Act of 1946 embodied the belief that nuclear power contained within it the seed of great harm, which global welfare, as well as U.S. national interest, dictated should be kept from spreading. The legislation contained a sweeping prohibition against the participation by U.S. government agencies or private individuals in any way, "directly or indirectly," in the fabrication abroad of fissionable material – for example, plutonium or enriched uranium, the two elements that in certain isotopes are the stuff of nuclear explosives. The act not only put under tight reign material transfers and technical aid; it inhibited exchanges of scientific knowledge as well. This extremely restrictive policy, which governed the United States' dealings with other countries until Atoms for Peace (see Appendix A) and the amended Atomic Energy Act of

1954 loosened regulations, testified to the intensity of the belief pervading official government circles after Hiroshima that nuclear power warranted special attention and exceptional control.

That was the prevailing belief where U.S. images of the atom were colored by lingering visions of its fearful destructiveness. From the outset, though, there was another, competing vision of atomic power as a bountiful supplier of many wondrous and beneficial things. Like other, less dramatic marvels of modern science, the atom exercises an attraction that mixes the fascination of the forbidden with the appeal of extraordinary beneficence. The promise of nuclear energy as a cheap and abundant source of electricity is the key element in this positive image. Fostered by the Atomic Energy Commission (AEC), the idea of nuclear energy's latent power to do good has been a secondary theme in counterpoint to the predominant military theme.[2] These motifs have aroused very different sentiments, while contributing to the sense of nuclear power's magical properties. There was always something remarkable about the limitless benefits that would flow from uncovering the atom's secrets. It was by no means a conventional prospect to contemplate. Everything nuclear has a touch of the dramatic. Certainly President Eisenhower's proclamation of Atoms for Peace had an adventurous and romantic ring to it. Yet the very notion of a peaceful atom removed that aura of the forbidden that initially surrounded all nuclear matters. Programs to tame the atom, to tap its energies for benign ends, and to commercialize the means for doing so could not fail to make nuclear power seem less exceptional, if not quite mundane.

From the mid-fifties onwards, the military and civilian themes moved wider apart. Civilian nuclear power proceeded steadily along one path, guided by more and more conventional standards and routines for the commercialization of a new technology. Weapons programs and strategies, in their own arena of discourse, still were dominated by early fears and anxieties. Those in government and industry who were custodians of the civilian programs followed a course that only intermittently crossed that of the military planners and weapons analysts. Organizationally, the AEC had responsibility both for perfecting nuclear warheads and for promoting power-generating facilities; and there was some movement of personnel from one sphere to the other. But in spite of the common institutional roots and, in some important respects, technical lineage, military and civilian programs drew upon basically different sets of attitudes. The divergence became more pronounced as civilian power development passed into the jurisdiction of the private corporations whose task was to make it technically reliable and financially profitable. To be sure, part of the impetus behind the civilian program came from a calculated decision of the AEC to attenuate the gruesome image of nuclear weapons (and thereby to neutralize visceral antibomb sentiment by calling attention to nuclear energy's more favorable side). But as civilian programs grew and matured, they acquired a meaning and character of their own.

The support structure that emerged in the AEC was an empire within an empire – with its own sense of mission, its own organizational interests, and bureaucratic modes of conduct. Measures of success were simplified: expansion of domestic power-generating capacity and the opening of foreign markets. Procedures became less exceptional as the prohibitions and proscriptions associated with nuclear technology gradually weakened and gave way to more conventional forms of management and regulation. The civilian program became the preserve of the technocratic managers whose approach was attuned more to the engineer's penchant for displaying technical virtuosity, and the bureaucrat's yen for expanding institutional scope, than to the political leader's cautious and apprehensive attitude toward nuclear power. They acted on the confident assumption that the framework of safeguards and limits built into transfer agreements (and later incorporated in the International Atomic Energy Agency [IAEA]) constituted a *cordon sanitaire* that keep at a comfortable distance the dreadful dangers of atomic power.

Those engaged in the generation and dissemination of nuclear information and technology for peaceful purposes viewed their activity as technically safe and politically desirable. The prevailing mood was not of trafficking in dangerous technologies, but rather of carrying out the United States' altruistic mission. They claimed a mandate to provide nuclear technical assistance deriving from a solemn national undertaking (circa 1954) to share with the world the fruits of the atom. That feeling of obligation added a gloss of righteousness to the promotion of nuclear power, and imparted a feeling of certitude to the labors of civilian atomic power's promoters. In this sense, the civilian program, too, has acknowledged the singularity of its subject. Yet the grand trappings in which the power program was wrapped masked the reversion to very ordinary ways of managing a very exceptional technology.[3]

The cardinal truth of the civilian nuclear energy program, with profound implications for the proliferation of weapons, is that its basic outlook was at variance with that which guided the thinking of those in charge of weapons. For the men with ultimate responsibility for deploying and commanding atomic (or hydrogen) weapons, nuclear power retained its essential horror. It was to be addressed with the utmost respect. It was to be handled physically and politically with extreme care. Whatever weakness some in the U.S. defense establishment may have had for "conventionalizing" nuclear doctrines, the power of control and decision has lain with a political leadership imbued with a keen apprehension about the lethal arsenal in its charge. The critical difference is that those who "domesticated" nuclear power for nonmilitary ends received only occasional, and far less conscientious, direction from political leaders, who might be expected to dilute the enthusiasm of nuclear technocrats for internationalizing the peaceful atom with a large measure of concern for the proliferation risks.

Only on those occasions when the U.S. government addressed the framework question of a world regime for civilian nuclear power was political attention clearly focused. The Baruch Plan, Eisenhower's Atoms for Peace, creation of the IAEA, negotiation of the Non-Proliferation Treaty – these were the points in the postwar development of a global system for managing peaceful nuclear energy at which a conscious effort was made to impose a political frame on the technical and institutional arrangements for developing and transferring civilian technology. Great care was taken that the IAEA be endowed with powers to exercise surveillance over national nuclear facilities of member states. The Non-Proliferation Treaty (NPT) elicits a pledge from nonweapons states to deny themselves the right to manufacture or to obtain nuclear armaments (see Appendix B).[4] And the battery of U.S.-sponsored bilateral exchange programs with recipients of American nuclear assistance contained conditions of use, including provision for safeguards and inspection by external parties, the U.S. government, and/or the IAEA.

These arrangements were meant to embed civilian nuclear power in a safe wadding of protective limitations and controls. Their practical effectiveness has been substantial, if not total. But they also accomplished the inadvertent end of encouraging an exaggerated faith in the power of legal and organizational formats to keep the civilian and military applications of nuclear power in watertight compartments. This faith allowed technicians, industrialists, and bureaucrats to demystify the "white magic" while believing that society was safeguarded against the "black magic" of the nonpeaceful atom. The agreements of cooperation between the United States and nations receiving technical aid or purchasing nuclear products were the purest expression of this confident dualism. Drafted in accordance with the twin principles of weapons abstention and maximum feasible exploitation of civilian nuclear powers, the agreements were highly successful vehicles for channeling skills and technology. They were less obviously a success in neutralizing the danger of civilian facilities' being exploited for military ends. Events would demonstrate the falsity of the basic premise that a crisp line of demarcation could be drawn between civilian and military programs.

THE NEW CONSCIOUSNESS

Evidence that the magic of civilian power had not been wholly domesticated, and the evil nuclear genie exorcised, came with stunning effect in

1974 when India exploded a rudimentary atomic bomb. That act forced new awareness of the unbreakable bond between the pacific promise and the military threat of nuclear power. It reminded the Nixon White House and its successors that the incomplete non-proliferation regime inherited from previous administrations, which the Nixon leadership had done little to expand or strengthen, carried a serious risk of weapons spread. It roused Congress to launch a round of critical investigations of the United States' nuclear export policies and nuclear diplomacy. It gave cause to those on the regulatory side of AEC (soon to be reincarnated as the Nuclear Regulatory Commission [NRC]) who were campaigning for the tightening of conditions on shipments of nuclear fuel and technology. And it opened the way to critical reexamination of the confident assumptions of the AEC officialdom that underlay the promotion of civilian nuclear energy internationally.

For India had used its civilian facilities as the technological base and fuel source for its bomb. In the process, it had neatly sidestepped the safeguards that were supposed to prevent the exploitation of civilian operations for military purposes. The New Delhi government had used a Canadian-supplied (Candu) research reactor, moderated with U.S.-supplied heavy water, to partially irradiate natural uranium (of Indian origin), and then made use of a nonsafeguarded, independently built reprocessing plant to separate the plutonium that served as the fissile material. A nonsignatory of the NPT, India technically had not violated an international treaty in producing its bomb (euphemistically called a nuclear device). The test officially was declared a peaceful nuclear explosion and as such was not prohibited by existing agreements. India's safeguards agreements with the United States, as well as those with Canada, were so loosely written as to leave unclear whether the letter, as opposed to the spirit, of those accords had been contravened.

The implications of the Indian explosion went far beyond the question of India's respect for legal and diplomatic niceties. Most worrisome was that the key critical technology employed, spent-fuel reprocessing, and the key material, plutonium, were on the point of entering the commercial market. If the then-current practice of closing the nuclear fuel cycle by the recycling of plutonium were to continue, a host of countries would move to the nuclear weapons threshold. Although the critical facilities would remain under safeguards so far as U.S.-supplied technology was concerned, other suppliers were less strict. Moreover, safeguards themselves had suffered a blow to their credibility with the explosion in India's Western Desert. In the future their adequacy for meeting a renewed proliferation threat would be in question.

Consternation about the implications of India's explosion was deepened with the coincidence of other events. One of these, President Nixon's pledge to sell reactors to Egypt and Israel, with unspecified controls, raised the distressing picture in many minds of an experience like India's being repeated in the tinderbox of the Middle East. Another development, the great oil crisis created by the Arab embargo and OPEC price rise some months earlier, had sensitized states to the costs of energy dependence while providing strong economic and political incentives for them to develop independent, nuclear-based energy programs. Finally, the burgeoning world market in nuclear power was being populated by new sellers, as well as new buyers, who gave every indication that they would set less-demanding terms for the sale of conventional reactors. Most important, they were prepared to sell the sensitive technologies for reprocessing and uranium enrichment.

This concatenation of developments brought an appreciation, keener in some official circles than in others, of how virile and independent the civilian offspring of military nuclear programs had grown – and, along with it, an uncomfortable sensation that there could be no assurance of that offspring's good behavior. The tame genie of nuclear power let out of the bottle on a leash was now mischievously gamboling about the room. Worries about the bomb once again were rife – not about the Russian, American, and Chinese bombs, whose power to terrorize the minds of government and public had been dulled by familiarity and the years of assiduous efforts to hold them in check – but about the still conjectural bombs of prospective candidates to the nuclear club located at all points of the compass. Starting in the spring of 1974, the issue of nuclear weapons proliferation was making rapid progress to the top of Washington's problem lists.

The ensuing attempt by the U.S. government to divert the current running in the direction of proliferating capability (if not, immediately, of bombs) is the principal subject of this book. It deals with how official Washington has struggled to get its house in order on nuclear energy and proliferation. The study is organized around three crucial episodes in recent policy-making history:

1. The United States' closing of the order books on enrichment services for civilian nuclear fuel in 1974, an action with far-reaching repercussions for the global market in nuclear energy and for Washington's power to control the spread of sensitive fuels and technologies

2. The landmark rethinking of the U.S. policy on plutonium fuels in the last months of the administration of President Gerald Ford, which established the connection between domestic, civilian nuclear power and the military applications of atomic energy

3. The promulgation of President Jimmy Carter's aggressive new non-proliferation strategy and the launching of a diplomatic campaign in its behalf

My account of these episodes is at once a narrative of events and an examination of how the U.S. government works when faced with an exceptionally complex and delicate problem of policy innovation. The three administrations that successively addressed the issue differed in philosophy and leadership style. They represented phases in the evolution of national policy and in dealings with the rest of the world. In each, ideas, personalities, and the givens of nuclear life combined to give a particular shape to attitudes and programs. Together, they reveal how the U.S. political system functions under stress and how its government conducts the country's public business on matters of international consequence.

A MATTER OF GOVERNMENT

The study of U.S. nuclear policy making confronts the most deep-seated and stubborn issues of contemporary government. Above all, there is the question of competence. Leonardo's obsessive marginalia, "Di mi se mai fu fatta alcuna cosa [Tell me if anything has ever been accomplished]," too often seems the refrain of rueful commentators on the performance of our public institutions. There is rampant pessimism about the ability of government to surmount the internal obstacles of bureaucratic politicking and divided authority in order to fashion a coherent policy that is executed with consistency and a modicum of finesse. So tangled is the institutional underbrush, so cumbersome is the process of deliberation, and so apparently well adapted are officials to the cramped ways of thinking and acting that the shaping of a multifaceted policy and the orchestration of a campaign for its implementation seem the most improbable of undertakings. Yet it is just such an effort that is demanded by an issue as intricate, contentious, and unyielding to formula answers as is nuclear non-proliferation. It has been singularly resilient to piecemeal approaches or doctrinal analyses.

The issue is distinctive in intersecting conventional boundaries drawn between domestic and international spheres of policy, between economic affairs and national security management. Nuclear energy straddles normally separate spheres of political discourse, of popular interest, of clientele, and of jurisdiction. Today it is taken for granted that non-proliferation is inexorably linked to what the United States does with its domestic nuclear programs. The reliance placed on nuclear power in its national energy strategy; the judgments reached about the economies and safety of reprocessing plutonium and operating the fast-breeder reactor; the speed with which uranium enrichment capacity is expanded; the dispatch with which secure waste-disposal facilities are made available – these are all matters of nominally internal policy with profound implications for the nature and extent of international nuclear developments. These factors also figure critically in the equation of nuclear weapons incentives and costs as viewed by other states.

Consequently, there are an exceptionally large number of pieces to this particular puzzle. These are programs to be meshed, organizational interests to be handled, technical assessments to be made, and trade-offs among diverse policy objectives to be decided. Multidimensionality also means that political backing must be built, and congressional support won, for policies with no natural constituencies, whose legislative fate is parceled out among a plethora of legislative committees (with additional complications introduced by the actions of semiautonomous regulatory bodies). Evidently, making the connections among the several parts of the proliferation issue has been an *intellectually* daunting task. As a matter of practical policy, it would have been difficult to act on even the most incisive and systematic analysis of the problem in the confined political space and under the institutional constraints that now characterize U.S. government.

Another cardinal feature of policy making in the nuclear energy field is the subject's large technical quotient. The prominence of technical considerations carries the obligation for officials to incorporate reasonably knowledgeable analyses of recondite engineering and resource questions into their policy judgments. Evaluations must be made, however roughly, of matters such as the design and performance standards of sophisticated technology for enriching uranium, for generating electricity, and for reprocessing plutonium; the resource and time requirements for bomb manufacture; the confidence margins of safeguards; the requirements for safe disposal of irradiated reactor waste; and the medium- and long-term availability and projected costs of natural uranium. In this respect, nuclear power is the quintessential problem of *technology assessment*, and of technology management: how technical expertise can be brought into the service of political judgment, and technological invention kept consonant with broad public objectives.

Contemporary societies are chronically fretful about their reliance on mechanical devices and the technical know-how they incorporate. In recent years, the breast-beating has sounded a steady accompaniment to the debate over the scale of values that should guide collective efforts to perfect and apply the fruits of our technologically fecund civilization. The broader cultural consequences of unbridled technological innovation are for the psychologist and social critic to evaluate. However, it is a proper, indeed unavoidable, responsibility of government to consider the full implications of refining and disseminating important new technologies. Too often arrangements for spreading nuclear technologies have tended to insulate technical from value concerns in public policy. Officials must take pains to assure that the value of non-proliferation bears its proper weight in cost-effective analyses of alternative nuclear technologies and fuel-cycle arrangements, as well as seeing that the economic costing and technical forecasting themselves have been done with all possible rigor.

In looking at the United States' performance in adjusting to the new realities of global nuclear energy, I am asking how the task of technology assessment is performed at the highest levels of government. How do non-expert officials get a grip on technical options and their possible meaning for policy goals? What formulas, or rules of thumb, have they used in making the crucial reconciliations of technical effectiveness, economic efficiency, and political need? And does the organization and style of government affect its ability to make these judgments intelligently and within a time frame suitable to slowly maturing problems?

Related to the theme of technology assessment is that of *technology transfer*. Rapid diffusion of conceptual knowledge, hardware, and know-how is a feature or today's tightly configured global economy. The great corporations in particular act as highly efficient transmission belts for moving innovation from country to country. Whether acting through multinational subsidiaries, joint ventures, or licensing arrangements, industrial firms have effectively surmounted the commercial and political barriers that previously served to restrict the movement of new methods and technologies. Governments, too, play the role of transfer agency, by sponsoring the exchange of knowledge and boosting technical cooperation as an instrument for building international goodwill and winning friends.

In the nuclear field, both industry and government – independently or, often, in tandem – have made available to the world a significant portion of the civilian nuclear skills and technology in the U.S. repertoire. U.S. business corporations have assisted in the maturing of fledgling nuclear industries elsewhere, some of which, once taking flight, have become purveyors of nuclear facilities and skills in their own right. For its part, the U.S. government has assiduously sponsored the development and use of nuclear science, engineering, and industry abroad – a policy that since 1969 has been reinforced by a treaty obligation (Article 4 of the NPT) to make the fruits of nuclear research available to other signatory states. Much of this activity does not seem always to have been undertaken in full cognizance of possible implications for weapons development. Or, at least, it failed to appreciate how the proliferation threat was changing. Clandestine use of plutonium for military purposes by semiindustrialized countries had become the main danger. Directing the outflow of specialized nuclear technology and skills along public and private channels became a central, if still elusive, aspect of nuclear energy policy, as awareness of proliferation dangers sharpened.

The closer one looks at the intricate and varied terrain of the proliferation issue, the more one appreciates the requirements for an unusually high degree of policy integration across an exceptionally broad range of issues. Easy tolerance of a disjointed approach to nuclear energy questions can expose proliferation concerns to the vagaries of domestic energy politics, or to the parochial behavior of executive agencies. The peculiar complications thus raised by nuclear energy are not merely a puzzle for academic commentators biased toward orderly categories and neat distinctions. They are at the heart of the dilemma that has been faced by the United States (and other concerned governments). It is my contention, and a basis for evaluating policy performance, that an effective nuclear energy cum nonproliferation strategy has placed exceptional demands of policy integration on successive Washington administrations. Their ability or inability to meet these demands has been a measure, and a cause, of their policies' successes or failures. A major policy is a revealing document because it bears all the imprints of the government that produced it. To anticipate our conclusions: Nuclear policy has too often showed the U.S. government failing to achieve adequate synchronization of policies, or even understanding of how they intersect.

PLANNING

To paraphrase Mark Twain, "Everyone talks about planning, but nobody plans," especially in the U.S. government. Public agencies in Washington regularly demonstrate how uncongenial they find such otherwise commendable tasks as defining objectives with reasonable clarity, choosing among positions that have been critically assessed, preparing coherent strategies to implement the preferred approach, and assuring that the actions taken by members of an administration bear at least a family resemblance to one another. The chronic failure to perform these tasks is one of the great secular mysteries of the age. It is a phenomenon that seemingly defies the norms of rationality and logical control that pervade the society. Yet the disjointed and often incoherent performance of those who conduct the public business is widely accepted as natural, and even inevitable.

Much ink has been spilled in recent years by students of government, and some reflective practitioners, expounding on the government's penchant for functioning with only the barest suggestion of design and coordination. Significantly less effort has been expended on determining the practical consequences of the unplanned course of public affairs (itself indicative of an unhealthy, and I believe indefensible, fatalism, rather than a witness to the irresistible power of the explanations offered). A good portion of this copious literature has appeared under the heading "bureaucratic politics," a label revealing of the central notion that animates much of the writing about public policy making.[5] This is the compelling idea that government is best understood not as a unitary body, but as a congeries of semiautonomous and self-willed organizational parts. Around this core idea revolve a cluster of satellite propositions: that each unit of government is moved by an overriding interest in protecting its institutional territory and controlling key missions; that elected officials and their senior appointees do not have the political power, attention span, or substantive interest in policy outcomes to override the bureaucratic parochialisms; and that in any event, central policy makers lack the will, conviction, technical knowledge, and breadth of experience to fashion comprehensive policies and to see that the strands of policy are pulled into unison.

Analysts quarrying this rich theoretical lode have struck nuggets of hard empirical truth about modern U.S. government. The same bureaucratic structures that have vastly increased the organizational capacity of modern government are an impediment to systematic policy making and to responsive, coordinated execution. Admittedly, public officials are not born problem solvers who come equipped with the knowledge and finely honed intellect that would make them exemplary systems analysts and master political generals. But, that said, there is no irrefutable evidence or logic that forces us to accept the generous standard for evaluating the performance of government implied by so much contemporary commentary. Before resigning ourselves to the inadequacies and limitations of the process they depict (and whose naturalness their models confirm), we should seek answers to three crucial sets of questions:

1. What are the inclinations and incentives for political leadership to bring intellectual discipline, and logical process, to policy making? Do a president and his senior deputies find it impossible to review policy rigorously and to maintain its coherence, *or* do they make a calculated judgment that the costs and difficulties of doing so are not warranted by the interests at stake and the expected benefits?

2. Is "synoptic" policy thinking (i.e., thinking that is rational, highly self-conscious, and well informed) always synonymous with an integrated, comprehensive policy approach? Are there circumstances when a political leader intentionally defines a problem and his response to it narrowly and treats it segmentally, accepting adverse secondary effects as an acceptable cost of doing what he most wants to do? What role is played by ideological and philosophical factors (as well as personal idiosyncrasy) in developing ways of thinking that are logically consistent but do not produce cost-effective policies? In other words, what exactly is the relationship

between the range and span of policy thinking, on the one hand, and on the other, the policies actually chosen and followed?

3. How much does the rampant incrementalism behavior readily observed in government offices reflect the inescapable logic of bureaucratic institutions and their codes of conduct, and to what extent is it encouraged inadvertently, or perhaps even intentionally, by political leadership unsure of its objectives and lacking the will or knowledge to assert itself?

The turbulent policy fields encountered by elected officials, along with the intricacy of the issues with which they must grapple, increase the odds favoring policy failure. That uncomfortable truth, however, cannot properly be used as an all-purpose excuse in defense of ineptitude or misjudgment. This review and analysis of three episodes in the making and reformulation of policy on nuclear exchanges and non-proliferation should offer a fair basis for one estimate of what the actual limits imposed on our government leaders are, and what measure of their effectiveness or ineffectiveness is ascribable to factors beyond their control.

2

The impasse on enrichment services

ON JULY 2, 1974 – with Washington absorbed by the drama of President Nixon's political demise and government offices easing into the long Independence Day weekend – the United States Atomic Energy Commission announced a suspension in the signing of long-term enrichment contracts.[1] The decision to close the order books on uranium enrichment services was a profoundly important act that belied the dry administrative language in which it was cast. The supplier of nearly all the low-enriched uranium (LEU) needed to fuel the light-water reactors (LWRs) outside the Communist world was declaring its capacity filled for the foreseeable future. The United States was making an official statement that it could no longer be counted upon as a reliable fuel supplier for the burgeoning civilian nuclear power industry it had promoted globally, most of whose reactors and technology were of U.S. manufacture or inspiration.

The event marked a milestone in the history of atomic power. For it showed the U.S. government as unable and perhaps unwilling, to fulfill its responsibilities as the paternalistic overseer of the existing international regime for managing the transfer and use of peaceful nuclear technology. From a non-proliferation standpoint, the effects were uniformly bad and quickly observable. Yet they were largely unanticipated and underestimated. Above all, the action irreparably damaged Washington's credibility in the world's nuclear marketplace. Failure to provide the services required to meet projected demand, and, equally damaging, the absence of any warning to customers of the shortfall, displayed a callousness to the interests of foreign governments that soured them on the United States as nuclear patron. It encouraged them to lessen their dependence on the United States for critical nuclear materials, and it offered good reason to accelerate purely national efforts to achieve a measure of self-sufficiency in nuclear fuels. The outcome was to weaken U.S. leverage on the nuclear programs of other states while offering those states a rationale for acquiring

14

technology that would substantially lower the barriers to weapons manufacture. Beyond the immediate issue of the United States' position as an assured source of LEU, the stunning – and, as was later proven, unwarranted – decision to accept no new enrichment orders engendered a pervasive skepticism about subsequent U.S. proposals and initiatives. The effect was to burden U.S. nuclear diplomacy, just when the Indian explosion was prompting efforts to tighten rules governing nuclear exchanges in the interest of non-proliferation. With doubts about its nuclear purposes and commitments rife, the United States would struggle to get its policies considered on their merits. Suspicion about U.S. intentions, as well as reliability, would bedevil three administrations as they sought to gain control over spreading nuclear fuels and technology.

THE EFFECTS OF THE IMPASSE

One consequence of the U.S. action was to give new impetus to Western Europe's and Japan's programs for developing their own fuel-producing technologies and merchandising them abroad. These technically proficient states were already expanding their technical and financial commitments to projects for construction of enrichment plants (there were two joint European efforts – Eurodiff and URENCO); for reprocessing spent reactor fuel so as to utilize more fully the energy value of LEU and to extend the life of natural uranium resources; and for moving toward commercialization of the light-metal fast-breeder reactor (LMFBR), which promised eventual energy self-sufficiency (and thereby an end to dependence on external sources of natural uranium, as well as enrichment services). All now appeared more attractive, both to developers and to possible customers. Uncertainty about U.S. intentions did not affect the direction of these programs: They were already off the drawing board and into the bricks-and-mortar stage. However, it could and did help to determine their shape and the pace at which they were implemented.

The greater weight now accorded nuclear self-reliance served to mute doubts about technical feasibility, and anxiety over the sometimes onerous financial requirements of these capital-intensive projects. Heavy investment demands and the protracted amortization period, in turn, underscored the need for a market larger than that provided by nuclear establishments of participating governments. The commercial incentive to find customers abroad was a powerful one. It sharpened the competitive edge of the challenge to the dominant U.S. reactor manufacturers. Most disturbing, in the hunt for markets Europeans showed themselves ready to sell sensitive enrichment and reprocessing technologies to sweeten the terms of reactor deals or simply to satisfy consumer wants. Within the short span of a few months in early 1975, France revealed plans to sell reprocessing plants to South Korea and Pakistan, and Germany entered into a massive deal with Brazil for the transfer of enrichment as well as reprocessing technology. All three purchasers (most vocally Brazil) cited the bottleneck on U.S. enrichment services as a reason for seeking their own nuclear fuel sources. These transactions were made even more disturbing by the European suppliers' seeming reluctance to impose strict conditions of sale – especially the requirement that all of the recipients' nuclear facilities be placed under safeguards to preclude a surprise, Indian-style detonation.[2] (However they did place stringent safeguards on the technology that was transferred.)

The United States did not bear exclusive responsibility for the emergence of this disturbing commercial pattern, but it had set a bad example by its high-handed behavior on enrichment contracts. If the United States was prepared to take a hard-nosed mercantile line on enrichment services (the political costs be damned), why should its commercial rivals feel constrained by the fine points of non-proliferation thinking? And why should the buyers of nuclear materials deny themselves the opportunity to gain greater independence from a supplier now shown to be indifferent to their interests? The swiftness with which this sequence unfolded owed much to the aftereffects of the oil crisis of 1973–4, which had left most governments with a keen desire to obtain access to new energy sources. Every state had been sensitized to its energy needs and vulnerabilities by the embargo and price rise from which all were still reeling in mid-1974.[3] Both the incentive to sell and the disposition to buy nuclear plants reflected a common interest in reducing reliance on external parties (whether for conventional fossil or nuclear fuels), an inclination strengthened to some immeasurable degree by the developments culminating in the AEC announcement of July 1974.

How could an action with such far-reaching implications for the United States' international nuclear position have occurred? Is it conceivable that the policies that forced the cutoff of enrichment contracts passed the muster of an internal governmental review? Are the policy-making processes so insular, the lack of oversight so complete, that a chain of consequences this damaging could be overlooked or disregarded? Or was the truth even more distressing? Had the Nixon administration made a calculation, in awareness of the risks entailed, that these risks were an acceptable price to pay for achieving another, to the administration, more vital end, such as moving the government out of the enrichment business and opening it to private interest? If so, what manner of thinking led them to view that goal as so compelling?

The answer is not a simple one, for the story of how the United States reached the impasse on enrichment services is threaded through the labyrinth of high-level Washington policy making. It has several themes: the difficulties of bringing political criteria to bear on nominally technical and commercial judgments; the characteristic inadequacy of mechanisms for interagency collaboration; the failure of responsible department heads to guard against the danger of immersion in policy minutiae at the expense of a wider view of national interests; the political reward structure at the upper echelons of government; and, not least, the limited vision of political leadership that, for all its vaunted pragmatism, is peculiarly receptive to the blandishments of ideology and prone to monomania. A close look at how the United States got itself into the enrichment bind reveals much of what has gone wrong in the way the federal government has discharged its responsibilities for the safe development of civilian power, abroad and at home.

BACKGROUND

The Nixon administration that took over the reins of government in 1969 held to two articles of faith that would shape official U.S. thinking about the government's responsibility for managing civilian nuclear power. One was an unbending commitment to a free-enterprise philosophy. Its guiding precept in the energy field was the virtue of reducing the federal government's role in the commercialization of energy sources. Its aim was to put on a businesslike footing those activities it could not readily shed (such as the operation of existing enrichment plants). The truest believers resided in the Domestic Council and the Office of Management and Budget (OMB), where ideological predilection and organizational mission neatly coincided. The second touchstone of policy was the conviction, shared equally by the president and his national security adviser, Dr. Henry Kissinger, that nuclear proliferation in the long run was pretty much inevitable. It followed that the United States should think twice before hazarding diplomatic capital in attempts to prevent other states from preparing to commit acts that it was in their nature to commit. Arms make the state; any self-denying injunction on weapons acquisition was unlikely to endure. The latter postulate of realpolitik wisdom would gain ascendancy at the upper echelons of the foreign policy bureaucracy as Kissinger's personal star rose. The two beliefs reinforced each other. Together, they fostered an atmosphere for nuclear policy making in which the preoccupation with setting civilian energy programs on a commercial foundation could proceed with scant regard for international ramifications. Those with political responsibilities disparaged the very danger (that of weapons proliferation) whose importance might have forced a critical look at the overall effects of the campaign to alter the AEC's role in curbing nuclear power. Lacking that awareness, the responsible parties could leave unresolved the ensuing problems of enrichment capacity and unmet customer contracts, without fear of dire consequence. Hence proliferation considerations did not figure prominently in reviews and assessments of enrichment practices and policies. These considerations were treated as quite another matter, to be dealt with elsewhere by other people.

The Nixon administration's tough attitude on AEC programs, domestic format and external dealings alike, gradually made itself felt on a clutch of thorny issues with which nuclear officials were grappling. Most prominent and trying were (1) expansion of the United States' existing enrichment facilities and the question whether new plants would continue to be owned by the government or whether private corporations should be encouraged to assume the responsibility; (2) the technology to be employed in new plants – whether the established gaseous diffusion or the innovative centrifuge technology; (3) the extent and form of appropriate cooperation with the West Europeans and Japanese, if joint ventures in the enrichment field were deemed desirable; and (4) the terms of sale for U.S. enrichment services. The four issues were intertwined, although only exceptionally treated as a package and never composed into a coherent set of policy alternatives.

By the late 1960s there was a general recognition in the nuclear establishment that the growing number of atomic reactors coming on line or projected would require a volume of fuel beyond what could be provided by the three giant diffusion plants at Paducah, Kentucky; Portsmouth, Ohio; and Oak Ridge, Tennessee.[4] Numbers of reactors, fuel loads, processing efficiencies, and therefore threshold dates were imprecisely known. But there was no denying that the time had come to plot future expansion.[5] The AEC's demand projections foresaw an enrichment squeeze developing by the mid-eighties, a date moved closer with the push given nuclear energy by the oil crisis. According to these calculations, there would be a global need (the Communist bloc excluded) for twelve to fifteen new enrichment plants (with a capacity of 8.75 million separative work units [SWUs]) by the end of the century. It was a formidable undertaking that called for the preparation of elaborate design plans and construction schedules.

The AEC, understandably, was staunchly committed to maintaining its monopoly over the enrichment program. Its Production Division, which exercised authority over the enrichment of uranium for both military and civilian purposes, had had exclusive custody of the program since its inception. The large, expensive facilities first built to produce material for warheads were later adapted to meet civilian needs for low-enriched uranium fuels. They were key components in the network of laboratories, production plants, and test facilities that was the commission's domain. AEC officials were loath to cede control over new facilities to commercial enterprises, to curb the growth of their own organization, and to weaken its hold over enrichment policy. They made the simple equation, as one seasoned official explained, that "what's good for Oak Ridge is good for the country." They believed it with complete conviction.[6]

Commission people knew, though, that they had a battle on their hands, and would have to fight to protect their monopoly. Government-run commercial ventures go against the American political grain. Uranium enrichment, having become a largely civilian activity, was a natural candidate for regularization, that is, transferral to the private sector. Since the Atomic Energy Act's amendment in 1964 to permit private ownership of sensitive nuclear materials, planning for expanded enrichment capacity had pivoted on the question of private versus public ownership. Under a Republican administration, it was wholly predictable that pressures would mount for private ownership of new facilities, and for putting existing operations on a more commercial basis. Stated in these terms, the issue was freighted with ideological significance that guaranteed a political clash along liberal–conservative lines.[7]

By 1970, with its first reviews of domestic nuclear policy completed, the Nixon administration had committed itself to the path of privatization. It is easy to underestimate the heavy political and ideological weight borne by the privatization plan. For the Nixon people in the early 1970s, the nuclear energy issue did not mean reactor safety, or the environmental dangers of poorly planned waste disposal, or the threat of terrorist seizure, or the proliferation of weapons states. It meant getting the enrichment business off the back of the federal government. Right up until the Indian explosion, and in some significant respects beyond it, this paramount idea took precedence over other aspects of nuclear policy and strongly colored White House thinking about them.

The campaign to open the enrichment field to private industry runs right through the Nixon and Ford administrations, with many battle episodes to be chronicled. Its importance in explaining how the U.S. government wound up subverting its own credibility as a reliable supplier of essential reactor fuel is basic. The bitter and prolonged political struggle set off by the Nixon privatization initiative effectively blocked the expansion of existing facilities for five years. Political maneuvering in support of it led directly to the apparent shortfall in enrichment capacity that was the immediate reason for the 1974 decision to close the order books. What is most instructive about this saga is not the single-mindedness of the crusaders in the cause of private ownership, but rather the tunnel vision and one-dimensional thinking that afflicted other major participants as well. The actors in this protracted political drama – the White House, the AEC (commissioners and bureaucracy), the Joint Committee on Atomic Energy, the nuclear power industry – all staked out positions that were logical enough, given their philosophical preferences and institutional interests. Their overall effect was to disregard and to damage more basic nuclear interests of the United States.

THE PATH TO PRIVATIZATION

The strongest push toward commercialization came from OMB. With sanction from the president, and support from the Domestic Council staff, OMB was the administration's standard-bearer on the enrichment front. The office instigated the move to commercialization, and was the driving bureaucratic force behind the privatization effort. Exerting its influence mainly from the financial sidelines, it was nonetheless a constant presence that kept the administration locked into an uncompromising position. The Office of Management and Budget, perhaps Washington's most powerful body, is also one of the least visible. Certainly, it is the most under-studied. Its abiding concern is fiscal restraint, a mission that is the counterpart in the financial sector of the institutionally defined prudence of the Federal Reserve Bank in the monetary domain. OMB plays the tightwad in every administration. To other agencies, it gives the impression of being obsessed with trimming programs and putting a lid on expenditures. Its high-powered cost analysis and program evaluation techniques are geared to-ward this end. In its better moments, it can present succinct critical reviews of program effectiveness and institutional performance in the manner of sophisticated systems analysis. During less imaginative and less ambitious times, it tends toward an inveterate negativeness, and wraps itself in a blanket of conservatism from which it casts a jaundiced eye on all proposals for public spending.

Under Nixon, OMB did more than strict fiscal planning. It was imbued with a sense of mission to redress a perceived imbalance between the public and the private sectors. The office was stocked with principled free-enterprisers who saw only virtue in getting the government out of things the private sector might be able to handle. What the latter might handle was defined very liberally. The guiding principle was simplicity itself: Save the federal government money by cutting back budgetary outlays. Enrichment was a very big item. Indeed, it was potentially a forty-billion-dollar item, according to AEC estimates of what it would take to meet enrichment demand by the year 2000. Fiscal prudence dictated getting out from under that burden, if at all feasible. The political philosophy of the Nixon administration stretched the bounds of what was feasible.

OMB Director Roy Ash took a personal hand in the campaign for privatization. Under his direction, an active group of officials with budgetary responsibilities in the energy field were set the task of overcoming AEC opposition and winning congressional approval. They were led by Frank Zarb, assistant director for nuclear materials (and later head of the Federal Energy Agency). Associated with the effort was James Schlesinger, then responsible mainly for defense procurement within the bureau but soon – in August 1971 – to be promoted to head the commission itself. Among the group members were several persons destined to play prominent roles in the contracting crisis and subsequent events: Glenn Schleede, later a Domestic Council staffer for President Ford; James Connor, who moved to the AEC as deputy director for planning and evaluation; and old nuclear hand Fred Schuldt, who with expertise acquired during years of battles over the nuclear budget and with sympathy for the new commercial approach, provided both bureaucratic energy and rare familiarity with the issues and institutions.

Not surprisingly, OMB looked on privatization as a prime opportunity for shedding financial responsibility. As an ancillary matter, the decision to put all nuclear energy transactions on a pay-as-you-go basis would provide the Treasury an added dividend while creating conditions more attractive to private entry. The same principles of budgetary restraint and limited government dictated both privatization and commercialization. They would be threatened by compromising either. Financially, the short-term perspective predominated. Long-term cost recovery of public outlays involved a time horizon beyond that conveniently accommodated by the terms of the presidents, or the fast-moving careers of officials. The watchword was to get the nuclear program on a secure financial footing, curb expenditures, and move government out of the enrichment business. This was the philosophy nurtured in OMB by Ash, and applied unremittingly on the enrichment question.

The initial corporate response to the opening of enrichment to private enterprise was disappointing. Industry had to be prompted and enticed. Official encouragement to commercial enrichment eventually bore fruit in the form of two private consortia prepared to venture a serious stake. One was Uranium Enrichment Associates (UEA), composed of Union Carbide (component hardware), Westinghouse (nuclear technology), and Bechtel (architectural engineering). The other was Cengex, the joint effort of Exxon (unlimited capital, unlimited self-confidence) and General Electric (component hardware and nuclear technology). From the outset, they were fragile unions, susceptible to fissioning in the presence of pessimistic financial forecasts or congressional slowness in satisfying necessary preconditions. The industrial consortia were hesitant about rushing headlong into this brave new world.

For one thing, the partners were not equal in enthusiasm or interest. Bechtel, with its engineering hubris and strong commitment to rapid corporate growth, was the prime mover of UEA and was most optimistic about the commercial prospects. Westinghouse never entirely resolved its doubts about the formidable financial and organizational obstacles to making a success of private enrichment. Its participation was predicated on the expectation that an enrichment plant would utilize the engineering experience and components Westinghouse had developed through its manufacture of light-water reactors. As the actual plans began to take shape and, in particular as attention shifted from the established gaseous diffusion to the unproven centrifuge technology, the opportunities for adaptation and application of Westinghouse's existing engineering and manufacturing resources began to slip away – and so did corporate interest. Attitudes of Exxon and General Electric in the other consortium were analogous. The great oil concern was irresistibly drawn to nuclear power as the next great energy source. The chance of getting into it at the production stage appealed to appetites whetted on oil. GE shared much of Westinghouse's circumstances and outlook. For even the more enthusiastic corporations, there were disturbing uncertainties over finances, obtaining the necessary electric power (for a diffusion plant), unresolved antitrust issues, and the pricing structure (especially possible competition from existing government plants with surplus capacity). Throughout the fight over privatization, the White House had to act simultaneously as morale booster and hand holder for its corporate fledglings, as well as political entrepreneur. It was a task that would test the most devout apostle of free enterprise. Nixon administration officials never faltered.

In order to overcome corporate hesitation, and to make private entry a credible alternative to continuation of the government monopoly, the White House had to remove several obstacles. The first, at the international level, took the form of emerging plans for Europe to build its own enrichment facilities under the sponsorship of multigovernment consortia. Second was the AEC's closely guarded monopoly of crucial technology, which had to be broken open to give industry a fair crack at launching a technically proficient private venture.[8] Finally, the enrichment business, under the current pricing arrangements, was not so obviously profitable as to be an attractive area for investment. Although the administration took deliberate steps to clear away each of these impediments, it was no easy task to open the road to privatization. For one thing, the administration did not have the luxury of tackling each problem separately, nor was it entirely free to choose when to act. The intrusion of external events, the demands of program schedules, the constraints created by the entrenched bureaucracy of the semiautonomous AEC, and the shackles imposed by an unaccommodating Congress assured that the White House strategy would leave much to improvisation. Consistency of objective, however, was never lacking.

The European connection

There was always more than one game going on in the enrichment field during this period. While the administration was beginning to make its push for privatization and preparing its first steps for reforming AEC operating procedures, it was confronted with European plans to enter the enrichment business. Europe's proclaimed intention to break the U.S. monopoly complicated the task of plotting a strategy for expansion of U.S. facilities.[9] Not only would the existence of foreign rivals make more difficult the estimation of market demand, lead times, and the scaling of projected plants, their presence in the marketplace would also reduce the incentives to private industry.

From the time that a European Community report pronounced itself in 1968 in favor of a European enrichment capability, a number of serious steps had been taken toward its achievement. In March 1970 the United Kingdom, the Netherlands, and the Federal Republic of Germany signed the Treaty of Almelo, which inaugurated a cross-national industrial–governmental consortium to build, run, and commercialize for external markets an enrichment plant using centrifuge technology. The tripartite agreement announced the formation of URENCO, Ltd., a corporation that would unite the three countries' technical resources and development programs. France, for its part, was proceeding with design plans for Eurodiff, another joint project, to which Spain, Italy, and Belgium (and, later, Iran) would lend financial backing, in return for a guaranteed share of the product.

The U.S. response was negative. As Edward Wonder correctly notes, Washington followed a consistent policy of "discouraging . . . the construction of foreign enrichment plants for sound security and commercial reasons."[10] A U.S. monopoly of LEU fuels assured critical leverage over the nuclear programs of other states; curbed the spread of the sensitive technology that could, with modification, produce weapons-grade material; and provided a financial return, however small, on the investment represented by U.S. gaseous diffusion plants. It always had been the deliberate aim of the U.S. government to use discount prices and easy terms to keep others out of the business. For the State Department, in particular, low prices meant high influence. For AEC officials, low prices meant encouragement of civilian nuclear power. So long as its domestic monopoly was assured, and political backing secured, unprofitable operations associated with concessionary rates could not be used to challenge the commission's organizational control. Impressive advances by the British, French, Germans, and others in building a technical base and industrial infrastructure for entering the fuel-production field now raised the prospect of unwelcome company in the enrichment business. The active interest being evinced abroad in plans for commercial enrichment forced a review and some rethinking of both past U.S. policy and future strategy. Was the old, liberal approach to the selling of services compatible with the administration's push toward a more commercial operation? How would the outlook for domestic privatization be affected by the appearance of foreign competition? Was there some way – perhaps multilateral development – of reconciling the multiple objectives of U.S. policy?

The drafting of a U.S. position revealed an untidy field of crosscutting organizational and political interests. The AEC resisted any approach to foreign governments that called into question its commercial and technological dominance. The State Department was sympathetic to collaboration, in principle, while mildly anxious about the release of sensitive technology. The White House, including the Domestic Council and OMB, was prepared to consider cooperative arrangements as long as they did not inhibit privatization. The least common denominator of these diverse positions, in the end, was agreement on a strategy aimed at neutralizing, or at least containing, the Europeans' threat to erode the U.S. enrichment monopoly. An effort would be made to draw them into joint projects on U.S. terms. That failing, the United States would go its own way and let the Europeans do their worst (that is, their commercial best).

Non-proliferation considerations figured hardly at all in this analysis. Only at the State Department was there a sensitivity to the issue's political dimensions. Represented principally by the Office of Science and Technology (backed by the political bureaus), State took a mildly internationalist position. On balance, it was inclined to look favorably on a collaborative enrichment program as a useful exercise in collective institution building, one that could remove a point of friction in relations with Western Europe and solidify the Atlantic Alliance. Support was conditioned on the proviso that the plants be adequately safeguarded, in no way undermine commitments and principles of the Non-Proliferation Treaty, and avoid serving as an unwitting, imperfectly regulated method of transmitting sensitive nuclear technologies to third parties. (The State Department did have the further preference, by no means insignificant, that centrifuge be excepted from any technology-transfer arrangements. Because of a centrifuge plant's smaller size and lower capital entry costs, it was seen as carrying a higher proliferation risk than the conventional gaseous diffusion technology.) State's attentiveness to the security factor was exploited by opponents in the AEC and Congress, who focused their criticism on the danger of releasing information about centrifuge, diminishing whatever small chance there was of an agreement with the Europeans.

State's attitude was matched by that of the AEC's own International Programs Division (IPD), whose responsibilities for regulating nuclear exports made it far more aware of the international aspects of policy than any others in the agency. Among AEC agencies, IPD was odd man out. In contrast to the operating divisions, International Programs had no organizational stake in protecting the enrichment monopoly. The division's performance was measured by other standards, namely, success in deepening the network of cooperation programs elaborated under Atoms for Peace and maintaining the United States' position at its center. Officials there shared State's fretful assessment of a future in which the United States had lost its position as exclusive purveyor of enrichment services. For this reason, the division was prepared to view favorably the idea of embedding the emerging European enrichment program in a collective institution upon the policies of which the United States could exert some influence. The International Program Division differed from State in that it felt less compunction about the spread of peaceful nuclear power, even while exercising its mandate to see that civilian facilities were not used in support of military programs.

The prevailing AEC attitude in the early 1970s was becoming increasingly insular and defensive. Threatened by the White House with the loss of exclusive control over U.S.-based enrichment facilities, it was all the more sensitive about being shoved into a multinational arrangement by which it would have to divulge critical information to foreigners, especially when it became apparent that the White House envisioned the proposed joint enterprises as cases of other governments buying into U.S.-led private ventures. The AEC's displeasure with the proposed joint enterprises was most pronounced in its dominant Production Division, which managed the commission enrichment facilities. Officials there steadfastly opposed releasing information about key technologies and resisted all pressure to relinquish the division's "benign monopoly" over the production of low-enriched uranium – whether to U.S. private companies or to foreign countries.

Cherishing their position as guardians of the United States' unique nuclear know-how, and fearful, in the bureaucratic manner, of losing control over their central function, officials turned a deaf ear to arguments pointing up the wider benefits of international cooperation and staunchly resisted a forthright approach to the Europeans. The AEC's dominant organizational interest also pointed to a tough position on the terms of compensation for U.S.-supplied technology. On the neighboring privatization front, they were just as unmoved by the ideological appeal made by White House staffers on behalf of private enterprise. This unyielding attitude won the Production Division people the epithet "old-time government monopolists, insensitive to the broader issues" – an uncomplimentary reference heard on the lips of both the boosters of privatization and the diplomatic backers of cooperation with the Europeans.

Yet, in fighting to squeeze every possible advantage out of any joint enrichment venture, the commission found itself on the same side as the White House. The result was policies aimed at achieving parallel interests, not open collaboration. This tacit alliance would reappear when the administration moved to reform the rate structure for enrichment services. In that latter instance, the White House and commission officials would hit upon the same means of pursuit of conflicting objectives.

The White House, for its part, felt no compelling reason to resolve interagency differences. State and the international-minded offices in the AEC could make their voices heard but were in no position to set the tone of discussions with the Europeans. As far as the activists at OMB and the Domestic Council were concerned, it would be nice if the Europeans put some money, minority money, into private U.S. enrichment enterprises. Any other arrangement could only get in the way of the administration's privatization plans. The overt approach could not be quite so blunt. Diplomatic tact dictated more circumspection. So did the seriousness with which the political departments took the multilateral idea. Besides, the alliance of convenience with the AEC's production people was too tacit and tenuous to withstand avowals of ultimate purpose.[11]

Hence the United States presented itself as earnestly interested in collaboration. The main ploy was a presidential offer of U.S. participation in construction and ownership of a common facility that would serve to meet both parties' (and the world's) growing demand for LEU. This initiative, boldly proclaimed in the president's annual foreign policy statement in spring 1971, appeared to herald a dramatic departure in U.S. nuclear policy.[12] It would acknowledge the end to the United States' monopoly on commercial enrichment, open its treasure trove of nuclear technology to outsiders for the first time, and introduce the radical idea of a multinationally owned and operated facility. This vision of a grand new day in Atlantic collaboration was rather swiftly dissolved in the protracted and progressively acrid discussions that occupied atomic energy officials on both sides of the Atlantic through 1971 and into 1972. At a Washington conference called in November for preliminary discussion of cooperative modes, the Europeans quickly discovered that the U.S. proposal was as hedged around with qualifications as a porcupine with quills.

The new, and potentially superior, centrifuge technology was to be excluded from any consideration whatsoever. Its transfer was declared out of the question. The proposed joint plant would be constrained to using diffusion technology. The AEC also revealed that its Domestic Access Program contained a restrictive provision discriminating between foreign governments and those U.S. corporations that would be granted access to the AEC store of technology and know-how. On White House insistence, privatization on the U.S. side had been built into the proposal from the start. In keeping with the priority the administration accorded a domestic reorganization of the enrichment industry, it was made clear that existing contracts with the United States for enrichment services would on no account be transferred onto the books of the conjectured enterprise. Protecting the commercial position of existing AEC plants would take precedence over the cultivation of a market for the new joint enterprise. This hard-line position both satisfied the commission's interest in guarding its privileged position and kept open U.S. options on how to handle the distribution of contracts between existing (government) and projected (private) plants, pending settlement of the internal U.S. debate. To top things off, compensation for transfer of U.S. technology was set at a level the erstwhile European partners found unacceptably high. What the U.S. administration was giving away with one hand it seemed to be taking back with the other.

In short, the discussions about a collaborative enrichment program foundered on the U.S. strategy of setting such severe conditions on technology transfer as to secure the United States a controlling position in any organization that might emerge. The keystone of administration nuclear policy was that future demand for enrichment capacity should be met by facilities owned and operated by private industry (even if technically buttressed by the federal government). If the Europeans wanted a share of the action, fine; they would be welcome as subsidiary builders, minority stockholders, and junior partners. The U.S. government would discuss terms for the transfer of technology to a collective private enterprise so organized that the transfer of technology would be on a purely commercial basis. The commitment to private development would not be compromised to accommodate European participation. As a tactical matter, the AEC's loathness to let go of its enrichment monopoly would be used by the White House to toughen the terms on foreign involvement (but the agency would be brought to heel when its bureaucratic imperialism appeared to the Nixon White House to be getting in the way of private development). When it soon became apparent that the Europeans would not swallow the administration's bait, privatization and all, there was a steady loss of interest in the whole idea.

Not surprisingly, the talks ground to a halt in March 1972. There was no rupture, just a petering out of interest on both sides. A brief revival activated by Henry Kissinger in early 1974 against the backdrop of the oil crisis was only a reminder of opportunities lost.[13] In the end, the AEC and the administration had joined hands to kill an idea in which neither had its heart. For the commission, the issue had been how U.S. leadership in the enrichment field could be preserved, and how the threat of a technically proficient, independent European capability might be warded off. For the White House, it was how to advance the goal of privatization. The question that never got serious attention was how Europe's entry into the enrichment field might enhance its ability to compete in export markets, and what that meant for the United States' domination of the world trade in nuclear technologies, including enrichment services. The problem was never defined in this way at the AEC or the White House, each of which had other fish to fry.

Domestic cooperation

The serious effort to clear the commercial ground for privatization got underway in late 1971 and early 1972, with visions of multinational projects fading into memory. The first issue to be dealt with was private industry's lack of commercial experience and limited technological capacity in enrichment. To remedy the situation, the AEC – under White House prodding – set up two programs designed to give industrial parties a look inside the enrichment business. They could familiarize themselves with the technology and get a grasp of the commercial opportunities. The first of these, the Domestic Access Program, provided for regular exchanges between commission and industry technical personnel in order to strengthen the technological foundation of participating corporations. Two years later, in 1973, the Access Permit Program carried the transfer process one step further, by giving industry access to classified AEC technology. In theory, the programs would open the AEC technical treasure chest to U.S. industries, putting them in a position to design plants as efficiently and knowledgeably as the AEC. Collaboration was anything but smooth, however.

The AEC moved grudgingly to implement the agreements under which it was to tutor its potential rivals. It created protracted delay by dickering with the industry consortia over the exact terms of technical cooperation: What categories of technological know-how would be transferred, what licensing and royalty conditions would govern their use by industry, and – most sensitive of all – what would be the commercial relationship between the proposed private and the established AEC enrichment plants? Discussions on the last matter disclosed the basic conflict of interest. The AEC was unprepared to make concessions on market access or to enter into market-sharing arrangements for the sake of private interest. Industry, for its part, sought an understanding that it would find ample demand for the enrichment capacity it would be building and that its market position would not be undercut by competition from an AEC able to discount its selling price and in possession of a privileged relationship with customers. Strategically placed officials in the AEC Production Division were only too ready to contribute to those doubts in ways that the amorphous situation permitted and that political deference to superior authority did not prohibit outright. They were less than keen about taking down boundary fences around their domain, inviting outsiders into the neighboring pasture land, donating prize studs, and sharing their select market. Faced with industrial concerns made tentative by internal divergences, the inescapable uncertainties of nuclear economics, and a Congress that was proving reluctant to provide necessary guarantees, the AEC barons could move at their own deliberate pace and so postpone the point of decision on privatization.

Congress

For the White House, Congress was at times an even bigger stumbling block than a recalcitrant AEC officialdom. There, nuclear matters were the preserve of the Joint Committee on Atomic Energy (JCAE). The JCAE was cast in the grand mold of the legislative barony, with a dominating chairman, "Chet" Hollifield of California; a like-minded membership animated by strong convictions about what was in the nation's best nuclear interest; and a finely honed sense of jurisdiction and prerogative. The prevailing committee view on expansion of enrichment capability was composed of three principal points.

First, the committee was an unrelenting promoter of nuclear power. It saw its mission as ensuring the American people's stake in fully realizing the promise of the peaceful atom. As self-declared guardians of the public's welfare, the committee members felt called upon to keep a watchful eye on all those who might subvert the nation's nuclear future. The threat could come from any one of several directions: (1) an Atomic Energy Commission hierarchy so absorbed with its scientific experimentation and the display of technical virtuosity as to be unconscionably slow in pushing for the commercialization of new power-generating technologies; (2) dubious critics of nuclear power, in Congress or the country at large, who opposed schemes for its rapid, large-scale development; or (3) a White House leadership that might disrupt progress along the path of atomic power either by neglecting things that should be done to clear the ground for development, such as making sure that adequate enrichment services would be available when needed, or by introducing extraneous political considerations, for example, enlisting foreign governments in a precarious scheme for multilateral enrichment.

Second, the JCAE was protectionist. To a man its members were guardians of the United States' exceptional competence in the applied science and engineering of nuclear power. Distrusting programs for technology transfer and sharing, the committee stoutly fought to maintain for the United States a benevolent monopoly of critical nuclear materials. Committed to the virtuous goal, enunciated in Atoms for Peace, of opening to the peoples of the world the wonderous fruits of the atom, JCAE members were equally firm that the United States should not subsidize other countries' nuclear programs by concessionary rates on enrichment services. Partaking of the populist paranoia that envelops Congress on diplomatic questions, the committee was ever alert to protect the United States in its dealings with foreign governments and innately suspicious of State Department internationalists. It made increasingly vocal demands that the AEC charge whatever the traffic would bear, adding to the weight building behind a businesslike approach to enrichment. This conviction that purchasers of U.S. nuclear services should get no special favors coincided with the commercial approach of the administration. Where the JCAE and the administration parted company was over the virtues and incentives of joint undertakings with the Europeans. Whereas the White House was prepared to drive a hard bargain (one so hard in fact as to make the deal impossible), the JCAE found the very notion of cooperation unpalatable. The latter's distaste for the multinational approach was reinforced by its distrust of privatization, which the White House insisted be the basis for collaboration.

The third precept guiding committee thinking about the preferred arrangements for increasing enrichment capacity was that the AEC, having proven itself an able builder and manager of sensitive fuel-producing facilities, should retain responsibility for the expansion program.[14] So long as the commission applied commercial standards in its rate structure (so as not to be a burden on the taxpayer), it was more practical to keep these critical facilities under direct government control. The JCAE was prepared to fight a war of attrition against the administration scheme. The committee realized that the struggle was likely to be a long one. Members also were aware that a standoff with the White House meant delays in getting new facilities on line. To compensate in part for any shortfall this slippage in the schedule might create, the committee, acting in conjunction with the AEC (where the Production Division was a ready collaborator), devised a program for increasing the productive capacity for existing plants at Portsmouth, Ohio; Oak Ridge, Tennessee; and Paducah, Kentucky. It had two parts: a Cascade Improvement Program (CIP) to provide an addition to present facilities, and a Cascade Upgrading Program (CUP) to modernize them. Once completed, it was estimated that capacity (measured in SWUs) could be raised by up to 60 percent. The programs won congressional approval in early 1972.

White House officials understandably saw the CIP as posing a clear threat to the privatization program (as well as sealing the lid on any multinational approach – an idea being kept alive for political convenience). The presidential response was the same one made to other inconvenient expressions of congressional independence that went against the grain of administration policy: Nixon impounded CIP funds appropriated by Congress. He thereby effectively killed the program, kept up the pressure to act on privatization, and incidentally helped to assure an enrichment bottleneck.

In retaliation, the JCAE persuaded Congress to withhold sanction for the Domestic Access Program that would enable the AEC to transfer technology to private industry. By denying the administration this essential inducement to corporate participation, the committee hit a sensitive nerve. Nixon backed down. In his energy message of June 1972, he pledged to release CIP funds (and thereby won back his hostage from Congress).[15] By devising the CIP–CUP plan, the Joint Committee felt that it had fulfilled its obligation to the nation. Now, with its honor restored, it was even less inclined to be blackmailed into a favorable action on privatization by any White House threat.

The unfelicitous trialogue among the Joint Committee, the AEC, and the White House thus succeeded in achieving a stalemate on the enrichment issue. For cooperative ventures, it meant terms too onerous to be accepted by the Europeans, yet still capable of raising hackles in Congress. For conclusive action on the private construction of new enrichment plants, it meant interminable delay. For additions to AEC plants, it meant funds dribbled out. For customers of U.S. enrichment services, it meant mounting concern over the supply of essential LEU fuels. What it did not mean – regrettably – was that the U.S. government would take steps to prevent any shortfall in enrichment or, if one did materialize, to avert the collapse of the network of understandings on which the system of safe civilian atomic energy was built.

THE WHITE HOUSE STRATEGY

Confronted by the tenacious opposition of the JCAE, which was abetted by a balky AEC establishment, the White House felt the need for strong action. A way had to be found to force Congress's hand on the privatization legislation and to galvanize the industry consortia. If the 1982 target date for the delivery of new enrichment services was to be met, the pace had to be quickened. Because a lead time of ten years for building new plant was generally assumed, 1972 loomed as the critical planning year. Yet there still was no agreement on industrial contractors, on the technology to be transferred to and incorporated in the privately built plants, or on the principle of privatization itself. The administration was in a hurry. Its concern was not a possible enrichment shortfall. The worry was rather that this cherished project might die of atrophy while Congress, AEC officials, and industry – each for its own reasons – moved at a dilatory pace.

Certain things were in the administration's province to control. It could revamp the AEC's commercial enrichment operation to remove all vestiges of subsidy, and thereby hope to improve the market outlook enough for industry to pick up its option on privatization. It also could move to build up demand for enrichment services in ways that would both attract industry and force action on an expansion program.

Commercial normalization

With the enabling legislation for privatization still receiving searching and deliberate congressional scrutiny, the administration, using its inherent executive authority, set about restructuring the AEC's contracting and procedures. Charged with laying down the new rules of the game at the AEC was James Schlesinger, appointed chairman of the commission in the summer of 1971. The message he delivered was simple and unequivocal: "Make money on nuclear sales." As for enrichment: "We provide a service; our customers should be grateful and prepared to accept charges commensurate with its value."[16] And the United States was the one best able to judge what that value was. Expectations were high that overseas nuclear transactions could make a hefty contribution to righting the swollen U.S. payments deficit.[17] The AEC, ever ready to paint a rosy picture of the nuclear future, foresaw an annual market of $3.5 billion for reactors and ancillary equipment within a decade. Enrichment services were calculated as bringing in an additional $1 billion as early as 1980. Total revenues from enrichment services provided to foreign customers would top the $20 billion level by the end of the century.[18] Nuclear power was to be the wave of the future, with the technologically superior U.S. industry riding its crest. (The AEC barons were happy to include private reactor manufacturers in the rhetorical flourish, but in their own minds they excluded them from the enrichment field.) The hard-nosed Yankee traders in the White House and the self-assured technocrats in the AEC could make common cause in boosting civilian nuclear energy as the answer to the country's balance-of-payments ills – and as the solution to growing energy needs.

The rate structure

A meeting of minds between the White House and the AEC officialdom, now represented by the highly visible Chairman Schlesinger, seemed less likely on the proposed new rating structure. Traditional agency thinking favored low enrichment prices as an inducement to utilities to purchase nuclear power reactors, and to keep down foreign competition. However, there was less friction than might be predicted, and less than most expected. The year 1972 was one of transition for the agency in more than one respect. Having seen the organizational armor pierced by the appointment of administration political operatives to policy and management positions previously reserved for career officers, the mandarins of the nuclear establishment realized that some habits, and some cherished practices, had to be abandoned in the interest of institutional survival. Low SWU rates were a candidate for sacrifice. The agency no longer could afford the luxury of downplaying commercial considerations. In order to counteract the OMB argument that a continued governmental monopoly of enrichment would put an intolerable burden on the federal budget, the AEC had to show that it could meet some significant portion of investment costs out of current income. A new rate structure would generate revenues to finance expansion and support research and development of new technologies; it would also lay the basis for accelerated amortization of the capital invested in new plant. Accordingly, commission officials joined with the new chairman to devise a rate formula keyed to the replacement cost of the three diffusion facilities inherited from the military (and constructed after World War II at a fraction of their current value).

Both parties had more in mind than a simple rate increase. A thoroughgoing overhaul of AEC enrichment contracts was called for. In December 1972, the commission temporarily suspended contracting while it set about reexamining contractual arrangements. The AEC took time out from deliberating the exact form of those arrangements long enough to announce a rate increase in February, a puff of smoke hinting at the direction in which policy was headed. The process of reorienting agency policy was labored and by no means free of conflict. It involved commission staff studies, formal analyses and informal strategy sessions, debates among the commissioners, and brainstorming sessions at the White House. Staff reports engaged the energies of agency officials seeking a way to derail privatization while remaining loyal to the political command hierarchy. White House sessions brought together the promoters of private entry. As for the meetings of the commissioners, they provided the forum in which all elements contended under the guise of a sober deliberation of the distinterested yet concerned overseers of the public good.

As of early 1973, the commission consisted of one old-line supporter of the government enrichment monopoly, James T. Ramey, who had served since 1962; one independent advocate of a quasi-public corporation, Clarence Larson; and three Nixon administration appointees pledged to the privatization cause: William O. Doub, a political associate of Spiro Agnew from Baltimore; Dixy Lee Ray, the pugnacious biologist who succeeded Schlesinger when he moved to the Pentagon in January; and William E. Kriegsman, a former official in the AEC Inspection Division who had been recycled through the Domestic Council under William Rumsfeld and John Erlichman, whence he had been released to the commission for the avowed purpose of pushing privatization. The arithmetic favored the administration. Sanction of a less generous rate structure was assumed. For that very reason, the commissioners' deliberations were less important than the discussions at the White House or the calculations made in the AEC's operating divisions.

Within the administration, officials at the Domestic Council had the political running on the issue. Their paramount interest was to find the means for forcing favorable action on privatization. The review of the AEC's enrichment contract terms and format provided the key. A basic restructuring of contract procedures, along lines being discussed in the agency, would increase nominal demand for enrichment services and strain supply. If acute enough, the conditions thereby created would serve a dual purpose: Prospective private enrichers would be given unimpeded access to a seller's market, and the exhaustion of available capacity would produce a sticky political situation demanding an expeditious congressional response. The White House had become convinced that without a saturated order book for existing capacity, the administration would be unable to get a definite commitment from private industry. Customers waiting in the wings made the venture look viable. There was the additional very practical consideration that buyer credit was expected to be an essential source of investment capital for the enterprise. Little of it would be forthcoming as long as the utilities saw the opportunity to satisfy their needs at AEC facilities. From the administration perspective, drastic action was called for to avoid the calamity represented by the construction of another AEC plant, using old-fashioned diffusion technology, and saddling the federal treasury with its building costs.

The principal architect of the strategy was James Connor, a lawyer who recently had left the Domestic Council to become deputy administrator of AEC's Office of Planning, Evaluation and Analysis, where he served as one of the administration's proconsuls helping to keep the agency officialdom honest. His team of White House and loyal AEC staffers acted under express presidential direction. The 1973 decision to introduce "fixed commitment contracts" was the strategy's centerpiece. A changeover from "requirements contracts" to fixed contracts had profound implications. This seemingly bloodless alteration in the terms of contract was to lead directly to the abrupt closing of the order books, with the profound proliferation consequences that followed in its train.

The essential feature of the old requirements contract was that it promised to provide utilities with all the fuel they wanted, for the life of the reactor, to be delivered when and in the quantities needed. The sole condition was that the customer give the AEC 180 days' notice of any changes in the volume and delivery date of individual orders. This was a highly attractive arrangement with obvious advantages to consumers. It guaranteed the utility operator LEU as dictated by fluctuating demand patterns for electricity, without locking him into inflexible commitments or tying up operating capital as security.

The fixed requirements contracts decreed by the commission in January 1973 changed all that. They demanded that buyers commit themselves "to purchase specified amounts of enriched uranium at specified dates" and, accordingly, "to deliver the required natural uranium feed," which they obtained from other parties on the international market, on an appropriate schedule.[19] The contracts would be long-term, involving a rolling ten-year commitment beginning with the enrichment of fuel for the initial core. Contracts would have to be made eight years in advance of the delivery date, entailing an overall planning time for the utilities of eighteen years! Large deposits were also required. Penalties of from 50 to 75 percent of the value of the contracted services attached to any failure to place the scheduled order. In practice "utilities must pay for and accept enrichment even if cancellation or slippage in the commercial service date for a reactor makes the delivery of enriched fuel on schedule unnecessary."[20]

In sum, the changed terms of contract meant minimum flexibility and maximum obligation for the consumer. Whereas previously the AEC had assumed the risk of uncertainty in estimating future enrichment requirements, now all the risk was shifted to the customers. Those seeking LEU from the period June 10, 1978, to June 30, 1982, were asked to tender contract applications by June 30, 1974. (To drive home the point that the U.S. government was no longer going to be Mr. Nice Guy on the nuclear block, a few other changes were made. Enrichment rates were hiked to thirty-seven dollars per SWU [they had been twenty-six dollars in 1966], with a built-in escalator of 1 percent biannually. Foreign buyers found that the new contracts deleted provisions tying SWU rates to those set for U.S. utilities – and thereby opened the possibility for discriminatory rate setting.)

This radical alteration in enrichment contracts was stated in dry administrative language and presented as an administrative modification to conform to the tightening enrichment situation: "The Atomic Energy Act requires that the AEC periodically promulgate Uranium Enrichment Services Criteria."[21] A seemingly routine restatement of rules and procedures was the occasion taken for announcing the shift to fixed commitment contracts. Customers were reminded at the same time that U.S. law did not permit the AEC to contract "in excess of available capability."[22] This was the sleeper, because, as would become apparent the following June, a system of fixed commitments contracts would greatly inflate demand and fully subscribe available capacity. In a public explanation of the reasoning behind the contracting decision, the administration claimed that it was a "move toward contracts that are firm and business-like and toward reliable planning for supplying enrichment services on a long-term basis." It was also admitted that the change would assist the private industrial consortia as they assumed "this major production activity."[23] The commission's annual report, *The Nuclear Industry*, reiterated the administration's conviction that "a more businesslike method of contracting should be adopted to make possible for private industry to plan future enrichment capacity increases or increases in contractual relationships rather than on forecast projections."[24] (The prose style suggests that the AEC bureaucracy was responsible for the language in which the policy was clad, if not the content.)

The officially stated purpose of this drastic action, then, was stabilizing the international enrichment market and ensuring that capacity met projected demand, that is, that new plants constructed would not create a capacity in excess of reasonable estimates of customer requirements. This logic was less than compelling. If market stabilization was indeed the paramount objective, then the administration chose a curiously inappropriate method of reaching it. For the introduction of fixed contracts succeeded very swiftly in distorting relations between the United States, as seller of enrichment services, and its dependent customers – especially those abroad.

The logic of what happened next was elementary. Consumers were told they had nine months in which to sign contracts for enrichment services required prior to June 1982. Because the United States was the only sure source for LEU (the USSR being politically unreliable, URENCO and Eurodiff still paper enterprises), any reactor operator who wanted to assure himself of adequate fuel supplies hastened to inscribe himself on the order books. The great enrichment rush began. Utilities at home and abroad did rough calculations and then sought a place near the front of the line forming at the doors of AEC headquarters in Washington. A prudent utility could do only one thing: make the most generous estimate of prospective needs and get a lien on a share of the finite AEC enrichment capacity. The tendency toward exaggeration was strong and inevitable. By June, available capacity for the period to 1982 would be subscribed, and oversubscribed.

RESPONSIBILITY FOR THE CRISIS

The most commonly heard explanation of this singular episode in nuclear policy making interprets it as a particularly stunning example of AEC misfeasance. Absorbed with adjusting its procedures and operations to contracting principles set down by the White House, this analysis goes, the agency – acting in the manner of great bureaucracies – executed orders with relentless disregard for consequences. For the failure to foresee the wider implications of forcing fixed contracts on customers, the finger is pointed at the political departments of government, above all the State Department. These departments are also held accountable for not having forced upon the attention of government leadership the points of intersection between technical programs and political interest. The White House, in turn, is said to have been preoccupied with defending itself against charges of "high crimes and misdemeanors" and, in any event, not unduly concerned about overseas reaction.

The truth of the matter was otherwise. Contrary to the popular interpretation, this outcome was neither wholly unexpected nor unwanted. The White House strategists had in mind a sequence of developments not very different from that which unfolded. The AEC officialdom, too, for reasons of its own, did not find the result entirely unwelcome. Key administration officials were aware that their push for commercialization of enrichment services would ripple through the international nuclear market. They knew that there could be a political price to pay, that it was likely to be substantial. They were prepared to accept it. Misguided and shortsighted though they might have been, they were not wholly ignorant of what they were doing. Responsibility for the crisis should properly be placed on the doorstep of the White House. *The crisis that flared in June 1974 with the blocking of enrichment orders was in fact planned.* As we shall argue, though, this truth does not exculpate the AEC entirely. The agency abetted the administration plan in important respects. Moreover, the internal structure of the commission made it possible to obscure from outsiders – the State Department and Congress – exactly what was happening.

James Connor and his associates intended to fill the order books, as the administration stated publicly. The plan's authors knew, too, that the result of fixed requirements contracts would be exaggerated demand, something that was not openly publicized. Moreover, some of the international political repercussions were foreseen. In their single-minded devotion to the privatization cause, administration officials claim that they did not overlook the political factors, but rather devalued them. By the testimony of at least one of the plan's architects, the external response was recognized, analyzed, and discounted. Would an enrichment crisis harden European resolve to pursue independent fuel programs? The Europeans were locked into that course of action anyway, and nothing the United States did or did not do could dissuade them. Would it create incentives for other parties, such as Brazil, to seek their own facilities? Brazil had a long-term program for national closure of the full cycle of which enrichment was a small part, and to which it was already committed in principle. Reaction to a closing of the U.S. order books would not bring into being any enrichment plant that was not already in the works (with the exception of a privately owned U.S. one). Would the tightening of fuel supplies encourage other states to obtain reprocessing plants in order to extend the life of available fuel?

Reprocessing was sanctioned by the U.S. government so long as it was properly safeguarded, and there was no reason to question that policy in 1973 or early 1974. It was a matter of national policy in each country, one that was too far removed from the immediate enrichment issue to have any bearing on it.[25] Having satisfied themselves that the political effects would be manageable, and in any event could not be so adverse as to outweigh the importance of reaching the administration's major objective, the strategists for privatization proceeded with their plans to provoke an enrichment crisis.

A possible fly in the ointment was the AEC bureaucracy. Agency officials who divined the real reason for the change in contracting procedures, and who were just as ardent in their opposition to the privatization initiative, conceivably could either (1) sound the alarm about the risk of oversubscription so early in the game as to embarrass the White House and give congressional opponents a shot at winning overwhelming support for expansion of publicly owned facilities or (2) manipulate the order books in such a way as to mask the fact that, according to the accounts, capacity was exhausted. The latter possibility was a particular cause of anxiety to some White House officials, despite the legal restriction on the AEC's contracting in excess of available capacity. It was suspected that commission officials might pass the word to buyers abroad that the apparent shortfall was on paper only and thereby slow the expected flood of orders.

A critical bureau for any administrative finagling (or counter-finagling) was the Office of Planning and Analysis. Out of this office came the estimates of demand and projections of supply scheduling that were the data base for such market analysis as went into contracting decisions and assessment of future needs. Its director at the time was Roger LeGassie. The division's activities had been conducted in the past with the independence from political direction characteristic of most AEC offices. Although LeGassie's loyalty to the administration would be established, the division's operation naturally came under suspicion at the beginning of Schlesinger's reign as chairman. The importance of the information it generated for evaluating the administration's case for privatization and commercialization was recognized early on. For that reason, James Connor had been brought in to take the responsibility for planning and analysis in 1973. His job was to supervise the division's work, to make sure that it played the already sharp rise in enrichment demand straight, and generally to keep a weather eye out for any bureaucratic chicanery. The White House emissary did succeed in planting the flag of privatization. Whether through his efforts or not, no statistics emanated from the division to embarrass the administration as it moved to exploit the emerging crisis in its intramural and congressional tussle. The "enrichment gap" was duly registered as the inflated orders were entered on the books. Indeed, the crisis was somewhat magnified, and appeared somewhat sooner than expected, thanks to the sharp upturn in reactor bids spurred by the oil embargo of that fall and winter.

The key to understanding what happened with enrichment contracts between 1972 and 1974 is thus a plan devised in the White House to force compliant action on privatization. With that said – and with proper appreciation noted for the tactical ingenuity displayed, if not for prescience in predicting the eventual outcome – a number of important questions remain unanswered. They are ones that bring our attention back to the issues of institutional behavior within the executive branch. First, how did AEC officials respond to the White House strategy? Did they have any intention or means of counteracting it? Second, were the commissioners entirely passive, or accomplices to the shuffling of agency procedures to achieve an enrichment outcome in keeping with the administration's orthodox free-enterprise philosophy? Third, what role, if any, was played by the AEC general manager? Did he have the unbiased information and authority to make independent assessments of the crisis that was brewing over the enrichment bottleneck? Fourth, why were other AEC divisions so acquiescent in permitting a situation to develop that could result in their loss of dominion over the enrichment business? And, finally, what efforts were taken by the political departments and offices – State, the National Security Council (NSC), AEC's International Programs Division – to forestall a policy with serious consequences for international interests, and to mitigate anticipated consequences once the White House strategy was put into motion? Were there mechanisms for interagency coordination, and if so, how were they used?

AEC: COMMISSIONERS, OFFICIALS, AND GENERAL MANAGERS

The great irony of the 1972–4 period, and the key to understanding the relationship between the administration and AEC officialdom, is that while they were in a standoff on the question who would own the next increment of enrichment facilities, *both were maneuvering to seize the same weapon to use in support of their conflicting ends.* Reorganizing the government's enrichment business on a commercial basis was the instrument. Depending on how it was designed and executed, and on the assessments made of political effect, it could be exploited by either side, or both. Increasing revenues, shifting to fixed commitment contracts, and altering the operating procedures of AEC plants came to be seen as in the commission's organizational interest.

Especially for the Production Division, headed by dyed-in-the-wool government monopolist Frank P. Baranowski, a change in rate structures and contract terms was an essential element in the resistance movement against privatization. The way this division assessed the situation, anything that made retention of government ownership look credible was ammunition for the AEC's allies, especially those in Congress. A profitable enrichment operation could do just that. A profit-minded approach corresponded to the dominant attitude in the Production Division which, unlike the more promotionally oriented parts of the agency, was always inclined to charge as much as the traffic would bear. To the extent that the AEC could finance proposed expansion out of current and projected revenues, government ownership could be cast in a more favorable economic light. The progressive rise in SWU prices with the termination of the concessionary rate structure could be earmarked "to recover costs associated with gas centrifuge research and development."[26] Advance payments made in conformity with long-term fixed commitment contracts, which would amount to $224.7 million, was a tidy sum to help defray the capitalization of new construction. Finally, the argument made by the White House that long-term consumer commitments were a precondition for intelligent market planning and for cutting equity risk to acceptable levels could be made just as effectively in support of an expansion of AEC-owned plants. This perspective was well understood at the top of the agency: Both General Manager Robert W. Hollingsworth and Assistant General Manager George Quinn had previously served as heads of the Production Division.

This revised attitude toward the commercial criteria for marketing enrichment services also manifested itself in thinking about plant operations. A stubborn problem for the Production Division had been the buildup of a big stockpile in LEU, owing in part to uncertainties about demand under the old requirements-contract arrangements. The stockpile had created a backup right through the system. At the upstream end, miners and millers of natural uranium were encountering a saturated market for feed. AEC policy was sympathetic to the producers, who were deemed in need of encouragement and assistance if the industry were to stay healthy. Its well-being was of interest to the agency because active exploration and development of natural uranium deposits was essential for countering arguments of energy competitors that nuclear fuel might soon be in short supply. One way to reduce the LEU stockpile, and to cure the depressed uranium business, would be to have buyers commit themselves to large long-term purchases (which would have the further benefit of giving miners and millers, like enrichers, something to plan against). A related proposal was to run the enrichment plants at a "high tails assay," which would lower the yield in LEU per unit of natural uranium feed. In effect, uranium feed would be exchanged for separative work. The consequence of this latter measure would be reduction in overall capacity.

In the atmosphere of fateful confrontation with the administration, the Production Division cast a benign eye on both steps. Fixed commitment contracts, desirable for the revenues they would yield, had the further effect of earmarking increased amounts of LEU for buyers and loosening the upstream market. As far as a higher tails assay was concerned, there was an undeniable danger of reducing the AEC's ability to meet its obligations to customers by lowering total LEU production. But that no longer was the priority issue. Agency officials were first tempted and then hooked by the idea that an enrichment bottleneck might work to their advantage. They were now silent partners with the White House in letting the rigged enrichment market do its worst. Where they differed was in their calculations of whether a crisis would work to the advantage of privatization or of a continued public monopoly.

Room at the top

A recurrent question for many who have observed or studied the workings of the AEC in its later years is, Who's in charge there, anyway? It was asked most pointedly during the period of the enrichment crisis, but it has also been raised in response to the agency's mishandling of waste management, its oversight of reactor safety and security, its export licensings, and its negotiation of bilateral exchange agreements. In each area, there have been chronic lapses in execution, failures to anticipate the secondary consequences of actions seemingly taken in isolation, a disposition to compartmentalize issues so that their deliberation seems impervious to views and interests other than those of the officials immediately involved, and a weakness for programs pursued with a single-mindedness that conceals their inherent shortcomings. When an agency conducts its affairs in this manner there is good reason to suspect that it suffers from a rigid, segmented organizational structure, and that little direction or control is being exercised by its head. In the AEC's case the internal structure was nearly feudal, built as it was around semiautonomous divisions; and the head was plural.

The commission

At the apex of the commission was a five-person board, under the loose leadership of its chairman. This board was the AEC's collective policy-making executive, with responsibility for policy guidance and oversight. Plural executives are characteristically prone to factionalism. Lack of unity and the dynamics of collective policy making encourage a tendency to defer difficult issues or to seek consensus through least-common-denominator agreements, either pitched at the level of vague principle or focused on very narrowly defined and highly specific actions. Weak collective leadership of this sort leaves central purposes unformulated; devolves operational responsibilities onto permanent officials, enhancing the power of estab-f67lished organizational fiefs; and strengthens the inertial force of existing programs and ideas. These tendencies are accentuated when the chairman is only first among equals, and when no coherent philosophy guides policy decisions. During the period under review, the AEC commissioners did not function as a collective executive, a board of directors. They were a baronial court, each of whose members had pet projects, cherished notions, and acknowledged spheres of primary influence. It was a less-than-functional division of labor.

Two relationships were organizationally critical: that between the chairman and his or her fellow commissioners, and that between the commissioners as a body and the corps of permanent officials. The cardinal feature of the former, as demonstrated under James Schlesinger and his successor, Dixy Lee Ray, was the "selective dominance" of the chairman. Neither imposed a coherent philosophy on the other commissioners or managed to forge them into a unified executive – the former for want of sufficient authority and shortness of tenure, the latter for excess of zeal and immersion in minutiae. Chairman Schlesinger did not rule. But neither was collegiality the hallmark of the commission under his stewardship. The chairman had the power to set the commission's agenda, to shape its public image, to deal with Congress, and above all to bring the weight of the White House to bear on these relationships. Yet he could not easily instruct the staff on matters of substance without approval of his associates; and the resolution of major questions required the support of a majority of commissioners. (A commission wholly congenial to the Nixon administration would not appear until 1974, with the departure of Commissioners Ramey and Larson.)

In a situation of shared authority, much depends, of course, on the degree of convergence in the attitudes and philosophies of the principals, as well as the compatibility of temperaments. In the early 1970s there were marked differences in the thinking of commissioners on many of the outstanding matters before them – namely, ownership of new enrichment plants and the level and nature of government support for development of new reactor types. Only exceptionally did these differences engender direct conflicts. Confrontation on issues and personality clashes were normally avoided. The generally temperate tone of deliberations owed something to measured self-restraint and something to the issues' complexity, which discouraged the formation of polar positions. However, it would be a mistake to conclude that compromise was an accomplished art on the commission. Rather, the atmosphere was one of peaceful coexistence, maintained by the practice of parceling out areas of primary responsibility according to commissioner interest. Division of authority, rather than the sharing of policy responsibility, was the system's modus operandi.It was built on the idea of the "lead commissioner," according to which each commissioner informally "represented" the board in dealing with the staff of those AEC divisions and offices whose work fell within his purview. He served as monitor and communications link. This division of responsibility neatly matched the delegation of authority among agency bureaucracies. When a matter was seen as warranting attention and possible action by the commissioners, its analysis and the preparation of a position paper were entrusted to a lead division. The designated office then would prepare a report, usually incorporating a recommendation, which would be discussed with both the general manager and the lead commissioner before being laid before the commission as a whole. Staffers from the appropriate office would make a formal presentation to preface a general debate kicked off by the appropriate commissioner.

Individual commissioners had substantial influence on the shaping of issues, but they could in no way control outcomes. By virtue of their specialized and concentrated interests, however, they could do much to prevent outcomes they found personally distasteful. Technically knowledgeable and strong-minded James Ramey devoted the greater portion of his energies to pushing for rapid development and early commercialization of breeder technology, while opposing privatization. Clarence Larson, a former director of Union Carbide's Nuclear Division, who had managed the Paducah, Kentucky, facility for the AEC, occupied himself with questions of enrichment financing and the program's organizational structure, while pushing his favored utility consortium plan. William Doub was concerned, above all else, with the regulatory side of the AEC's work. He directed his attention, and considerable political skills, to streamlining licensing procedures and inspection practices so that manufacturers and operators of nuclear facilities could make planning decisions in a more predictable regulatory environment. Dixy Lee Ray, appointed to the commission in August 1972 and then elevated to the chairmanship the following year, at first busied herself with the use of radiation in biomedical research, a major sector of AEC activity. With her promotion, Ray quickly became an activist on civilian power issues and an arch supporter of privatization.

As for James Schlesinger, his powers as chairman through 1972 were primarily at the disposal of the White House for use in advancing its program in the nuclear energy field; they were used, secondarily, to assure him an influential voice on policy matters of personal interest – including military questions of warhead design. Heading the list of presidentially mandated goals were putting the AEC fuels policy on a commercial basis and meeting the mounting environmental challenge to the growth of civilian nuclear power. With his OMB background, he not surprisingly took a personal hand in shaping the administration's privatization strategy. His

attendance, in company with his family, at the widely criticized under-
ground test at Kamchatka in the Aleutians in November 1972 was em-
blematic of both a keen sense of duty and an earnest belief in the probity
and safety of AEC nuclear programs, military and civil. Among his individual concerns was his deep involvement in issues of nuclear armaments
and strategy. A prime task was overseeing the perfection of "mininukes"
for battlefield use. Much time was spent winning political backing for this
new class of atomic arms and arguing the doctrinal case for their incorporation into the military inventory. Toward this end, he had himself appointed to the National Security Council's Undersecretaries Committee,
which orchestrated high-level policy making. These activities were arduous
and time-consuming, limiting his involvement in more prosaic policy
areas, such as assessing long-term nuclear fuel needs.[27]

The need for commercialization of the AEC's fuels program, and for
clearing the way for entry by private business, were not matters of deep
conviction to Schlesinger. He supported commercialization, counseled on
tactics, and acted as point man for the project within the commission. But
he was not numbered among the apostles whose free-enterprise faith had
its spiritual roots in the White House Domestic Council. Schlesinger was
President Nixon's agent for nuclear energy, a role with very precise job
specifications. It was less policy making than policy execution – at least
with respect to the commercial side of AEC operations. He was to build
backfires against the environmental activists who were threatening to
stymie the president's energy program; to get the government out of the
enrichment business; and to deal firmly with the Europeans, among other
foreigners, in commercial transactions. The chairman performed loyally
and ably. He also gave no indication of appreciating the wider political
implications of this single-minded pursuit of economic virtue.

It may be that he fully agreed with the estimates of marginal cost made
by Connor and his fellow strategists. It may be that his preoccupation with
several other demanding issues left him little opportunity for reflecting on
what is euphemistically, and somewhat disdainfully, called "the big picture"
in Washington political circles. It may be that he intentionally chose to be
ignorant of some of the technical arcana that were charged with political
meaning – although that seems unlikely for a man of studied intellectualism
with a liking for detail. Or, quite the opposite, perhaps Schlesinger's technocratic pride in the mastery of practical knowledge led him to be so
absorbed with cost analyses, comparative advantage of technical alternatives, and the contractual terms of technology transfer from the AEC to
private industry that he lost the forest for the trees. Whatever the combination of factors influencing his personal outlook, there was no evading
the political instruction he was under. The irony remains that notwithstanding Schlesinger's subsequent reputation as a reflective statesman sen-

sitive to the United States' global obligations, he gave little evidence as AEC chairman of perceptiveness about the international effects of the policies he pushed. The later secretary of defense, whose finely tuned antennae picked up the faintest signals of allied unease produced by minute shifts in the strategic balance between the United States and the USSR, never seemed to hear the rumbles of protest from the same quarters over the cavalier treatment being given their energy interests.

Hewing to the line drawn by the White House on enrichment was made all the easier by the ambivalence and inattentiveness of Schlesinger's fellow commissioners. Not until very late in the day, in the climactic weeks of May and June 1974, did they, as a group or individually, probe very deeply into the workings of the enrichment market for clues about how foreign consumers would respond to a contract change. More important, neither did they seek a systematic review of how a tightening of enrichment supplies would affect the delicate balance in the international atomic energy regime nurtured by successive U.S. administrations. Although there were many long meetings devoted to discussion of fixed requirements contracts, and much informal communication between commissioners and senior agency officials, at no time did they focus on the question of a possible enrichment bottleneck. The latter issue was within the range of collective commission responsibility, but were not the stipulated concern of any one member. They were faint objects in the background of narrowly focused debates on segments of the domestic program and AEC operating procedures. Political matters simply did not bulk very large in the commission vision of civilian nuclear power. Given the prevailing work style, there was little time for commissioners to ruminate over the grand issues of international order and stability. They occupied themselves with housekeeping chores at the expense of deliberate policy making and judicious oversight of the agency's overall operations. Their conduct, hence, ran counter to what normally is expected of a board of directors.

A commissioner straining to master the particulars of a recondite matter like the technology of centrifuges was the person most likely to fall victim to information overload and to be negligent of wider policy considerations. Thus, when the enrichment crunch became official in June 1974, the commissioners were almost as much surprised by the closing of the order books as they were taken unaware by the severe reaction to it. They were not briefed about the buildup of orders until weeks before the crisis began, and at that point they had done little more than open a rambling debate about the proper administrative response to an exhaustion of capacity. None felt compelled to sort out the full political implications. Without a preexisting appreciation of what an oversubscription of capacity would mean internationally, the commissioners could neither appreciate nor avert the full dimensions of the crisis.[28]

The general manager

In theory, the general manager's office could do much of the guiding and shaping that the commissioners neglected or were unable to do themselves. In fact, it did not serve as a central policy-making and coordinating body. The loci of power lay in the operating divisions that concentrated technical talent, dominated budget decisions, and were seen as the source of nuclear miracles. Their directors constituted a council of barons who conceded to the general manager the right to represent them before outside bodies, that is, the White House, Congress, and the commissioners. They were no more inclined to yield authority to their own agency head than to bend before political authority. Only on selected matters where the chief executive knew his mind, and had a sympathetic commission behind him, could the general manager bring the weight of his office to bear to circumvent a major bureaucratic interest.

As chief executive officer of the AEC, the general manager could *in principle* perform an essential mediation function between the policy-making executive – the commissioners – and the functional offices – the bureaucratically structured divisions. In the best of government worlds, the general manager's office might have been the synthesizer of agency policies. It could and in fairness probably should have made certain that a probing and comprehensive assessment of the new enrichment rate structure was made, and that its conclusions were laid before the commissioners. Roger LeGassie's planning office was never asked to conduct such a review. It should have been more aware of the obligation to maintain open communication channels with those executive branch offices, such as the State Department, exercising complementary responsibilities, and to moderate any undue tendencies toward organizational insularity with a measure of concern for the government's wider political interests.[29] In the dense institutional world of the AEC, with its tightly configured political space at the top, there was scant room for this type of enlightened leadership. The role of the AEC general manager had evolved in such a way that he was an expediter and facilitator, who maintained internal organizational solidarity, rather than a governor.

For most of the period under review, the AEC general manager was Robert W. Hollingsworth. He was succeeded by his deputy, John Erlwine, in February 1974, when Hollingsworth left the AEC to become a vice-president at Bechtel, Inc., the world's largest architectural engineering firm in the nuclear field, and the moving force in the UEA private enrichment consortium. Enjoying a reputation as an able administrator, Hollingsworth was generally acknowledged to be an effective manager of the commission's multifarious activities. In keeping with AEC tradition, he was more an organization man than a policy maker. His highest priority was maintaining the integrity of the AEC's institutional domain. He looked first at an issue's meaning for the organization, and only then at the policy implications. This conception of the chief executive officer's role gave little place to planning and prospective analysis. It meant, rather, accommodating the nominally central functions of budgeting, program development, and political liaison to the interests of the agency's component divisions. Above all, the general manager needed finely honed political skills in order simultaneously to hold the loyalty of his division heads, who were powers in their own right; to keep the commissioners at bay; to retain the sympathy of Congress; and to satisfy the chairman and the administration that he was a good soldier obedient to their policy wishes. It was a job for a pacifier and fence mender, not an activist.

There was no reason to expect that Hollingsworth's voice would be heard calling attention to the adverse international consequences of the emerging enrichment bottleneck, or revealing the dubious basis for the overabundance of contracts. He did not surprise anyone by so doing. On the privatization issue, Hollingsworth walked a narrow diplomatic line. He could not afford estranging powerful AEC officials by joining the White House in arguing for private entry; indeed, he was wholly sympathetic to their position. Yet he could not afford to be seen by the administration as an enemy of privatization and suspected saboteur of their plans. The only acceptable course was to assume a low profile, to present the agency case discreetly in private forums, to make suitably favorable comments about the president's program in public, and to concentrate on less delicate agency operations. Hollingsworth's success in keeping on the right side of the administration is attested by the subsequent tender of the offer to join Bechtel, the outstanding industrial backer of privatization. His success in retaining the respect of the Production Division people threatened by privatization is evidenced by the absence of charges that he sold out their interests to advance his personal career. Some executive chairs can be used only to straddle fences.

THE MISSING LINK

The international dimension

The enrichment issue was suffused with political meaning. Yet the crucial administration decisions slighted or ignored the international consequences of a shortfall in capacity. In discounting the effects abroad of its strategy to force Congress's hand on the privatization measure, the White House was treating nuclear energy primarily as a matter of domestic policy. It was the Domestic Council that had the action. Connor and his collaborators at OMB did not welcome the participation of foreign policy officials whose outlook and priorities were known to be at variance with their own. Enjoying a presidential mandate to take charge and to push ahead with privatization, they were only too happy to keep the play to themselves. The constant jousting between Kissinger's NSC (from which he shifted to State in June 1973) and the domestic affairs people, which was a staple of life in the Executive Office of the President, gave the Domestic Council extra incentive to guard its jurisdictional boundaries against any trespass by the national security adviser cum secretary of state. The threat from that corner never materialized. Kissinger was only too willing to leave the running on so technical and politically charged an issue to his colleagues in the other wing of the White House. Excessive anxiety over non-proliferation was a charge that could not be leveled against any part of the Nixon administration.

As for the State Department, officials there regarded the proliferation risk more seriously; they opposed the commercial-minded, get-tough stance on the sale of enrichment services. State was also known as a notorious political weakling within the administration. Formal responsibility for representing the State Department's interest in the international aspects of civilian nuclear power, and for tracking nuclear export programs, lay with the Office of International Scientific and Technological Affairs (SCI). It was headed by Herman Pollack, a competent and knowledgeable State official. In previous years, the office had collaborated actively with the AEC's International Programs Division in the negotiation of bilateral agreements of cooperation and the building of the IAEA-centered safeguards system. But as the sides were being drawn up on the enrichment battle, SCI was gradually squeezed out of the action and cut off from the communications flow. State was suspect in the eyes of both the White House and its appointees on the commission for being too internationalistic and overly sympathetic to the concerns of foreign governments. The AEC officials also felt that the department attitude could interfere with their own plans. They always were keen to keep other bureaucratic actors off their territory. The international offices' loss of influence to the Production Division on enrichment questions simply made interagency relations that much less hospitable.

The relegation of SCI to a spoiler's role on the margins of policy was the logical culmination of the virtual severing of relations on nuclear energy questions between the AEC leadership – both the dominant Production Division and the commission itself, acting under White House instruction – and the State Department. There were organizational reasons for the separation, there were difficulties rooted in fundamentally different perceptions of the problems, and there were personal antipathies to be taken into account. During James Schlesinger's tenure as AEC chairman, the estrangement was heightened by Schlesinger's general lack of respect for the State Department (an attitude widely shared in the administration and confirmed by the shift of responsibility for U.S. foreign policy to Henry Kissinger's National Security Council). Schlesinger was especially dubious about State's expressed sympathies for the European interest in multinational enrichment, and skeptical of what he saw as a pronounced tendency to place undue weight on non-proliferation as a U.S. national security objective. (The latter stricture applied even more strongly to the Arms Control and Disarmament Agency, which, on the matters under discussion here, was generally treated by all influential parties in the AEC as an institutional nonperson.)

Although kept at arm's length, SCI officials had a rough idea of what was going on. They realized how a failure to ensure enrichment capacity would damage the United States' position as the supplier of critical services. Later on, they came to appreciate the implications of the fixed commitment contracts for the order books. They also knew that the State Department had no hope of forcing a redirection of policy by carrying the issue to the White House. Under the stewardship of the newly promoted Secretary Kissinger, there was little sympathy at the highest level either.[30] SCI's muted voice had been heard but not really listened to as the policy took shape in 1972 and early 1973. So long as no high-placed State official was ready to take the non-proliferation issue under its wing, there was little for SCI officials to do except keep a watchful eye on the unfolding of the White House strategy and the counter-strategy of Production Division officials.

Dixy Lee Ray

The ostracism of the political offices from nuclear energy policy making was consolidated by the January 1973 appointment of Dixy Lee Ray to succeed James Schlesinger as chairman. Ray, a biologist by training, with limited government experience, was even less prepared than Schlesinger to appreciate the political dimensions of enrichment contracting, and even less inclined than he to give State's opinions much weight. Schlesinger had been in on the construction of the administration's program, even if he was not one of the policy's principal designers, and he was experienced in national security matters. Ray lacked both the background and the credentials of a foreign affairs specialist. She was appointed to spearhead the administration's privatization cause. Ray was an aggressive, outspoken advocate of nuclear power, a principled believer in private development, and someone whose bombastic personality would attract the public spotlight. She arrived on the scene with faith in the White House's hard-nosed commercial approach to AEC operations. She shared its free-enterprise philosophy, and accepted the proposition that foreign customers had been getting an unwarranted subsidy on enrichment services. She felt no discomfort at lending her full support to the campaign. She also was blissfully unaware of the international implications of a mercantile approach to nuclear exports.

The new chairman's personality did much to ensure that her faith in the new course of policy would not be disturbed by self-doubt or the skeptical analyses of others. A feisty individual of abundant self-confidence and boundless energy, she has been referred to by colleagues as "tyrannical," "petulant," and "abrasive." Whatever the most apt adjectives for describing her personality, Ray has never been accused of excessive subtlety or known to suffer from feelings of inadequacy. In particular, she was not disposed to seek political enlightenment from alien bureaucratic quarters.

One of the most pronounced traits of her vivid public personality was an abiding hostility to the State Department. Her animus toward State colored her judgment of views coming from that corner, and made her averse to any association with it. It succeeded in sealing off the commission from any political reporting and advice more completely than at any time in the AEC's insular history.[31]

If the State Department was disqualified as a source of political instruction, so were the agency's own international offices. Under Myron Kratzer, International Programs had been a force to be reckoned with on all questions of nuclear transfer. His departure to become scientific counselor in Tokyo, prompted by a personality conflict with James Schlesinger, enabled the White House to neutralize the division as a possible internal foe of its privatization strategy. Abraham Friedman, his successor, was more a planner than a bureaucratic games player. For the office to keep its influence under this difficult circumstance, it needed aggressive leadership. Without it, the office was systematically disregarded while the critical decisions were made between 1972 and 1974. Predictably, neither Ray nor the commissioners found any memos in their in-baskets anxiously pointing out the damaging international repercussions of the emerging enrichment crisis. The administration had taken steps that, together with the AEC's cultivated insularity from external views, ensured that there would be none. But Ray cannot be entirely absolved of responsibility for the crisis (much less for her handling of it when it erupted). For not long into her tenure of office, evidence was brought to her attention that serious trouble lay ahead – evidence that was summarily rejected.

The first suggestion that something was awry came in December 1973. At that time, the association of European nuclear utilities, which had been collaborating with France and its governmental partners in planning for Eurodiff, made an overture to the United States to discuss a possible pooling of technology and joint construction. The initiative was inspired by a combination of concern about the viablilty of the French-led venture and awareness that the United States (and the world) was getting into an enrichment bind, a situation that might soften administration opposition to collaboration. Included in the proposal was a suggested transfer of a certain number of contracts from the AEC to the conjectured project, to their mutual benefit. The State Department, having received advance word of the demarche from its diplomatic missions in Europe, dutifully informed the AEC of what was coming. Their message carried the counsel that Washington take a serious look at what the Europeans had in mind (an attitude reflecting State's hopes for a revival of schemes for multilateral nuclear cooperation).

Staffers in Chairman Ray's office responded sympathetically. Though they were largely unmoved by multilateral schemes, some had gotten the first inkling of the meaning of the new enrichment supply–demand equation. As the orders began to stream into the AEC, spurred by the September decree, the quicker minds in the commissioners' office needed only to do a bit of arithmetic to sense a problem in the offing. Unsure whether existing capacity would manage to cover the cumulative demand building up through 1982 (and to be contracted for by June 1974), they realized it would be a close thing. Not being party to the White House strategy, or to the calculations of the Production Division, they did not view the prospect with equanimity. So it was only sensible for the staff to draft a reply to the European utilities' overture that expressed cautious interest in pursuing the matter of load sharing. This budding interest was short-lived. Once Ray became apprised of the situation, she stopped the idea dead in its tracks. Piqued at the unauthorized exercise of independent judgment by subordinates, annoyed at State's meddling, and chary of entering into any joint deal with the Europeans (one that at this late date would have the irritating effect of further complicating the lagging privatization move), the chairman rejected any positive word on the proposal for an enrichment consortium. The diplomatic response – intended to dampen French interest – took the form of an AEC letter specifying terms for U.S. participation that simply reiterated the United States' 1971 offer, ones that already had proven unacceptable to the Europeans.

DENOUEMENT

For the next six months the pieces for the "great enrichment crunch" moved into place. Orders flowed in steadily, gradually filling the order book. Demand was strong but not immediately overwhelming. For a time it even looked as if the June 30 deadline would be reached without a subscription of all available capacity. Commissioner Larson was quoted as saying that it appeared likely that sufficient enrichment capacity would be available to permit long-term contracting through the end of 1974.[32] It was a deceptively optimistic forecast. Larson's statement, and others made in a similar vein by AEC officials, fostered the mistaken notion that there was no threat of an enrichment bottleneck after all. Those inclined to disbelieve reports of an imminent crisis anyway (among whom were numbered most foreign governments, and U.S. reactor manufacturers) had their confidence bolstered. When the crunch came, the shock was all the more severe for those verbal attempts at dissolving the sense of impending crisis.

In May and June, a flood of orders sent accumulated demand brimming to the top of the enrichment canister, and over it. One cause for the sudden rush was a backup on applications to URENCO and Eurodiff, which had attracted a considerable number of long-term orders from utilities hedging their bets against unpredictable U.S. policies by diversifying their sources of supply.[33] The Soviet Union, which also had begun to offer enrichment services, coincidentally had to slow the acceptance of orders. The main reason for the strong surge, however, was simply the utilities' procedural delay in getting their plans made and their contract applications prepared. In any event, the last-minute demand produced a shortfall that exceeded the expectations of the most devoted administration crisis monger. At the end of June the AEC signed the last batch of thirty-nine enrichment contracts, fifteen of them with foreign buyers. These signings were held off until the last moment while enrichment plant administrators struggled to reach a precise determination of how much capacity was available. The estimated ceiling was raised, with qualifications, from 290,000 megawatts to 320,000 megawatts, permitting the acceptance of the enlarged block of orders. Nevertheless, the July 2 announcement of a suspension in signing new enrichment contracts "declined" applications from another twenty U.S. and seventy-eight foreign "nuclear power units." *Nucleonics Week* reported that the "AEC showed no inclination to clarify immediately the situation of those left in limbo."[34] No commissioners appeared, as scheduled, before the JCAE hearings organized as a stock-taking exercise to coincide with the contractual deadline. The only straw customers had to latch onto was a phrase in the official commission statement declaring that the suspension was made "pending a review of the relationship between total contract requirements and the AEC's available productive capacity."[35]

The silence was not a sign of serenity and self-satisfaction. Behind the calm facade, the AEC and the U.S. government were in turmoil. The worst had happened, and the real world was ungraciously intruding upon the confined world of administration and AEC games players alike. As the commission inched toward the June 30 dénouement, those principals not committed to privatization became increasingly upset about cresting enrichment demand. Larson was active in instigating a lively, if fruitless, debate among the commissioners. The JCAE insisted that the AEC make clear its intentions, and that they conform to the committee's own principles, including observance of the legal prohibition on contracting for enrichment services in excess of stipulated capacity.[36] The protagonists in the battle over privatization were inclined to watch the countdown with knowing expectation and were ready to move to exploit the crisis when it came. Both sides miscalculated. When the storm broke, all parties quickly were drawn into a wide-ranging exercise of damage limitation and crisis management that transcended, if it did not entirely suppress, their self-interested maneuvering. White House operatives and AEC bureaucrats alike were reminded that there was another world out there, moved by considerations quite different from their own.

The bearer of bad tidings, if any were required against the backdrop of foreign government protests and the distressed cries of U.S. utilities, was the pariahed State Department. Through the spring, SCI had come to see the brewing enrichment crisis with ever greater unease as a major threat to U.S. interests abroad. Through its ties to the technical ministries of foreign governments, SCI picked up mounting signs of concern abroad about the future enrichment situation in the United States. Herman Pollack and his colleagues, acting on what were still mainly private expressions of disquiet, set out to get the State leadership involved in the enrichment question. They knew full well that their own pleadings to the AEC would be discounted by Chairman Ray. Bureaucratic weight had to be brought to bear against bureaucratic weight, to avoid a full-blown crisis if possible (it was not) or to mitigate the effects when it came (which it did).

By degrees, they pushed their cause up the organizational ladder. Memos detailing the situation and calling alarm reached first Joseph Sisco, undersecretary for political affairs, and then Robert S. Ingersoll, deputy secretary of state. Sisco had been brought into the nuclear power field a couple of weeks earlier when the Indian explosion forced non-proliferation a few rungs higher on Kissinger's worry list. The secretary deputized him to oversee State's involvement in the issue. Sisco was lead officer dealing with the AEC, under Ingersoll's direction, when the enrichment crisis broke.

One of Sisco's responsibilities was to oversee a National Science Foundation study of proliferation questions (National Security Study Memorandum 202) that had been commissioned earlier in the year in preparation for the NPT Review Conference scheduled at year's end. The study had been limping along, suffering from lack of urgency and handicapped by an uncooperative AEC. Dixy Lee Ray had demonstrated her distaste for the State Department and reinforced the commission's own well-developed territorial sense by proclaiming the department's lack of authority in the area. It was her constant refrain that the AEC had legal responsibilities (stipulated in the Atomic Energy Act) that could not be contravened by anyone, certainly not by so dubious a personage as the secretary of state.[37] That was also her immediate reaction when, in the first week in July, Ingersoll led a State Department deputation across town to lay its concerns about the enrichment crisis before the AEC and to argue for a concerted effort to make sure all foreign customers requiring enrichment services somehow got them.

The State officials were coolly received in Ray's office. They pressed their suit no less ardently for the lack of a warm reception, making three key points. They argued above all that a blunt announcement that the United States could not satisfy consumer needs for enrichment services would gravely damage its position as a reliable supplier of nuclear fuels. That reputation as a benevolent, sympathetic, and predictable source of civilian nuclear materials was the keystone of the U.S. policy on controlling the spread of nuclear power built over a twenty-year period. Erosion of confidence in Washington would subvert the entire structure of bilateral and multinational agreements on which the non-proliferation regime was grounded.

Second, as a consequence of disruption in LEU fuel deliveries, the United States would be providing an incentive for other states to acquire their own fuel-producing facilities (thereby gaining direct access to weapons-grade fissile materials). This was directly counter to U. S. non-proliferation policy and security interests. Moreover, the United States would be put on the defensive in its diplomatic efforts to dissuade the governments of nonweapons states from approaching a decision on weapons manufacture. As the State officials explained, a prospective proliferator might readily rationalize the acquisition of critical technology as a necessary, and therefore irreproachable, response to the U.S. failure to meet its specific, bilateral treaty commitments, as well as its general obligations under the Non-Proliferation Treaty to assist signatories to benefit from the peaceful applications of the atom. These remonstrances were strongly backed by the Arms Control and Disarmament Agency (ACDA) officials who had been brought temporarily out of political exile and into the discussions to corroborate the seriousness of the proliferation implications of an enrichment cutoff.

Finally, State pictured darkly the aggravating effect of such an action on already tender relations with friends and allies. The calculated U.S. policy of taking a more self-centered approach to international economic issues over the last few years had produced some particularly disagreeable episodes. The closing of the gold window in 1971, coupled with devaluation of the dollar, had opened a new era of instability and conflict in global monetary affairs. A major crisis had barely been overcome in the spring of 1973 when extreme disorder on the world's exchange markets brought a temporary closing of the money markets. The subsequent U.S. decision

not to defend the dollar when it plummeted against other leading curren-
cies had engendered considerable bitterness in European capitals. Close on
the heels of the drama of the dollar came the embargo on soybean exports
in the summer of 1973. The precipitate decision of the Agriculture Department to halt all foreign sales, owing to an unforeseen rise in demand
and a production decline, had been a shock to the Japanese (for whom soya
is a staple source of protein), and a cause of further dismay to other buyers
who had relied on the United States as the principal producer. (The soybean episode bears many similarities to the enrichment affair in the technical misjudgements of officials, the lack of planning and close monitoring
of programs, the nonexistent political oversight, and the casual disregard
of international considerations when drastic cutoffs were imposed.) The
United States, in the State Department's view, could not afford to tarnish
its reputation as a dependable economic partner in yet another critical area,
especially at a time when premiums were being placed on interallied cooperation in the wake of the Yom Kippur War and the oil crisis.

To the chairman, this political soul-searching might as well have been
Greek. Ray was unmoved by the foreign affairs lesson. She frankly declared
herself unprepared to make any changes in either contracting procedures or
operation of existing plant to accommodate overseas customers. This unbending attitude in the face of direct State Department opposition voiced at
senior levels was exceptional, even for the strong-willed head of one of
Washington's most powerful and independent-minded agencies. There was
more to it than Ray's crusty independence and strong convictions. The
White House Domestic Council, and its allies on the commission, were
silent players in this interagency tussle. They remained staunchly opposed
to accommodating the "internationalists." Although they, along with AEC
officials, had been taken aback by the intensity of the reaction to the decli-
nation of contracts, administration strategists were not yet ready to take
expedient actions that could jeopardize privatization. The testing time for
their policy had arrived. They would not willingly admit error or defeat.
With the White House presumably still at their back, privatization strategists would stand unflinching in the face of foreign outrage, and before the
representatives of Kissinger's State Department. Dixy Lee Ray was just the
person to handle their challenge. She had been given the AEC chairmanship
because her views passed muster at the White House. She had a touch of
xenophobia in her makeup. And she looked upon the State Department as a
natural enemy, while cultivating a personal feud with the secretary.

Ray could be all the more adamant in dealing with State officials knowing that she had powerful friends next to the Oval Office. Joe Sisco had
been reminded of this home truth about the pluralism of influence in the
administration when he approached his own patron, Henry Kissinger, for
backing on initial approaches to the AEC. Support was too qualified and

equivocal to provide much hope that State could carry the bureaucratic day. The secretary was slow to be convinced that proliferation posed a serious, immediate danger. He was aware of the depth of President Nixon's feelings about his program for restructuring AEC programs, averse to entering into new squabbles with White House staffers, and too uncomfortable with the subject to be tactically prepared to force a confrontation. For Sisco, and his colleagues at State, damage limitation became the goal. The department's belated entry into the enrichment issue had won it, if nothing else, a place at the policy table and a grudging right to be heard on ways and means of handling the moratorium on enrichment contracts. Some method of mollifying the outrage of customers and silencing the chorus of protest had to be found. Everyone, or nearly everyone, recognized that need. If for no other reason than commercial self-interest, some conciliatory gestures were in order. For the next month, AEC and State officials fought over what should be done, and how much should be done. Other elements of the executive branch joined in as the growing political void at the White House lowered inhibitions and lessened the authority of administration appointees within the commission.

LIMITATION OF DAMAGES

Entangled in the dispute were technical and legal questions of enrichment plant operations, the future of privatization, and the reprocessing of fuel at the back-end of the fuel cycle, as well as issues of political priority. Legislative statutes enjoined the AEC from contracting for enrichment services beyond available capacity. But there was no cut-and-dried formula for determining what constituted capacity. Earlier in 1974, commission officials had calculated the figure as 290,000 megawatts, based on operation of the enrichment plants at a 0.3 percent uranium-235 tails assay. That assay had been set in accordance with the LeGassie formula when the objective was to run down the LEU stockpile and to improve the market for natural uranium producers. Plants, however, could be run at a lower assay to increase the SWU rate – in effect increasing capacity. The commission, led by Dixy Lee Ray, and prodded by OMB, had resisted modification of operating modes to satisfy customers' needs at the expense of uranium interests and of what the AEC believed were economically the most efficient work levels. The marginal adjustments agreed to in June to raise capacity had been accepted with great reluctance. Further modifications would be strenuously opposed.

Also at issue in determining the ceiling was the time frame. Long-term needs depended in part on the date at which the commercial reprocessing of plutonium fuel would begin, thereby relieving some of the demand for enriched uranium. The AEC was wedded to plans for the recycling of plutonium into light-water reactors (LWRs). It had provided the technical know-how, and much encouragement, to the commercial-sized facility being built at Barnwell, South Carolina, by an industrial consortium. There already had been some slippage in the schedule, and the target date was likely to be pushed further ahead because the project faced licensing challenges on environmental and safety grounds. By making available an increment of fuel for LWRs beyond the LEU provided by enrichment plants, an operative Barnwell could ease the demand squeeze toward the end of the period in question. The AEC was ready to barter concessions on the enrichment contract ceiling for pledges of political support for the uncontested development of commercial reprocessing.

Third, and most crucial for the White House, Chairman Ray sought to forge an indissoluble link between flexibility on contracts and private entry into the enrichment business. Provisional contracts, it was suggested, could be offered to customers on the waiting list, conditioned on the shift of some unspecified portion of demand to the yet-unbuilt private plants (for which ground had not been broken or licenses granted). Providentially, United Energy Associates chose the month of July to send potential customers its preliminary contract terms, conditions, and estimated prices.[38] Less providentially, one of its members, Union Carbide, chose the same time to quit the consortium. Westinghouse was reported as thinking of following. The two companies had simply come to the conclusion that there was no money to be made in the venture. Without firm price guarantees by the government (and, vitally important, legal limits on accident liabilities), the enormous investment costs made profit unlikely. On the other hand, Bechtel, which would get its return on the construction, needed to be less mindful of ultimate market realities. Bechtel stayed with UEA to the end. The consortium, without Union Carbide, was being held together tenuously as much by governmental will as by entrepreneurial spirit. It gave every appearance of a jerry-built business enterprise that evoked little confidence from its prospective customers.

Throughout July, the hauling and pulling between the bureaucratic protagonists dragged on while utilities, foreign governments, and concerned officials grew increasingly exasperated. The unseemly delay in drafting a U.S. policy, or even issuing a clarifying statement, was due in large measure to the relatively equal weight of the contending forces, as well as to the intricacy of the problem with which they were struggling. In addition, prolonged indecision owed much to the disintegration of presidential authority, as the House impeachment proceedings took the political life out of the White House. The pressure to break the deadlock came from the State Department. Officials there saw every day that passed without a forthcoming U.S. response as adding to the hemorrhage of U.S. nuclear influence abroad. Blocked by an inflexible AEC chairman, and unaided by an indifferent secretary of state, Ingersoll and Sisco appeared stymied until they discovered their ace in the hole.

Staffers unearthed an executive order signed by President Dwight D. Eisenhower in 1955 (no. 10841), issued in conjunction with the plans setting in motion Atoms for Peace, which stipulated the State Department's primacy over the Atomic Energy Commission on matters affecting the country's national security interest. While acknowledging the AEC's status as an independent government agency, the order declared it nonetheless "necessary for any government agency, whether or not nominally empowered to take actions affecting other countries, to obtain the concurrence of the State Department whenever an action directly involves questions of U.S. foreign policy."[39] The order's appearance from Sisco's briefcase surprised and irritated Ray and her fellow commissioners. This stunning piece of one-upmanship triggered a bitter row and set the chairman fulminating against State Department machinations. The commissioners, Ray foremost among them, were incensed over the claim that they were subordinate to the inferior bureaucratic breed over at State. Heaven knows no wrath like that of demigods who discover archangels closer to the divine power than themselves. Outrage notwithstanding, there was now no choice but to concede a share of authority and to compromise with State's politically minded position.

Sisco's legalistic ploy was made, fortuitously, at the moment when President Nixon was about to be indicted by the House of Representatives – hardly a propitious time for officials to reject the claim of law over political power and institutional prerogative. Working out a face-saving formula was still difficult. It would not have been easy with the best of intentions and the clearest presidential lead. Neither was present. Only with great strain and elaborate maneuvering were the participants able to reach an understanding. The key element in the eventual plan was the creation of a special category of "conditional contracts." Included would be all those applications received before July 1, 1974, and not as yet entered on the order books. Signed and pending contracts in this category amounted to 44,000 megawatts above the previously established 320,000 limit.

How would the difference be made up? First, the AEC consented to alter the operation of the existing enrichment plants to lower the tails assay. With a lower ratio of natural uranium feed to LEU, more work could be accomplished (i.e., the number of SWUs increased) per period of operation. Thus, at the cost of inefficiency measured in natural uranium fuel required per unit of LEU produced, capacity could be somewhat expanded. The decision meant that the major reform (the LeGassie scheme) made a year earlier, according to a different preference scale, was now to be rescinded because of international considerations previously discounted. This reversal went against the grain of the commissioners, and annoyed the

JCAE as well. After all, it ran directly counter to the commercial philosophy that all agreed should govern AEC operations. That idea had been nurtured by the White House for four years, and favored by Congress for its own reasons. Unyielding opposition to the revision continued, especially from the Office of Management and Budget, which fought it to the bitter end – that is, until Nixon's political resignation and the collapse of his administration had cut the ground from under its feet.

A second provision gave the holders of conditional contracts first call on capacity freed by the withdrawal or scaling down of registered orders. By the end of July, there were not many still innocent about the unnatural boost given to orders by the introduction of fixed requirements contracts. The demand clearly was inflated and would be cut back as customers made firmer estimates of actual needs. Moreover, in the background were the European facilities that were expected to provide substantial additional capacity – before 1983, it was hoped – beyond that now available for contracting. Without suggesting specific arrangements (there could be none in the absence of consultation with the Europeans), the AEC communicated to buyers its expectations that some form of load sharing could be arranged. Washington would seek to work out these and other modalities of conditional contracts in individual private talks with buyers.

Among the details left unspecified was the target date for completion of new enrichment facilities (in addition to those provided by CIP–CUP for which contracts already had been let). Although even the most optimistic forecasts did not foresee their being in operation by 1982, the new U.S. plants conceivably could ease some of the burden at the end of the stipulated contract period. Because it had yet to be decided whether they would be government or privately owned, there was no way for customers even to know with whom they might be dealing. The commissioners wished to foster the expectation that privatization was established in principle, if not in fact. They insisted that official statements on conditional contracts contain the explanation that these contracts, made with the U.S. government, would be acknowledged only until industry was in a position to offer private enrichment services, at which time they would be transferred to the new corporate enterprise. On this point they won. But it was strictly a rhetorical victory. The question of ownership had not been settled: Opponents of privatization conceded nothing of substance; and subsequent presidential statements would place the full faith and credit of the U.S. government behind the conditional contracts.[40]

QUEUING UP

The agreed formula for squeezing more enrichment capacity out of the system left unanswered the question of the order in which conditional contracts would be fulfilled. Administratively, the simplest arrangement for determining access to freed-up capacity would be for parties to queue in chronological order by application date. This was the preference of the Production Division. The idea was vehemently opposed by Chairman Ray and Commissioner William A. Anders. The latter, who had taken his seat earlier in the year, quickly caught the spirit of enrichment debates. He and Ray demanded that U.S. utilities be given preference. On this, they received the active support of the JCAE, whose members were true to committee tradition and electoral need. Domestic political realities precluded adherence to a pure equity principle. Priority was in fact given to U.S. utilities according to a schedule determined by their date of application. (Further disturbance was caused by Ray's insistence that Puerto Rico be designated a nondomestic entity and placed in the alien category. It took no small amount of constitutional and political argumentation before she relented and grudgingly restored the commonwealth to U.S. suzerainty.)

The State Department had been unhappy about the discrimination against foreign customers. In exchange for a graceful bow to the inevitable, they succeeded in having the best possible face put on the conditional contracts. First, a statement was elicited that the United States recognized a tacit obligation to all customers and pledged strenuous efforts to meet all outstanding needs. A straightforward chronological ordering in the foreign category was not diplomatically advantageous. If that rule were followed slavishly, some countries (e.g., Japan) would have all their needs met before large utilities in the United Kingdom and France (not to speak of prospective buyers in Brazil) could receive shipments. State officials argued vociferously, and won acceptance for the idea of a "degree of redress"; that is, the equity principle would qualify a straight scheduling by the calendar.

Preparation of the final priority scale was complicated by the anomalies of presidentially sanctioned reactor sales (including requisite fuels and technical assistance) to Egypt and Israel, a commitment Nixon had made to these countries in the course of his Middle East trip in June. He issued a presidential directive that they be slotted toward the top of the list, in the national security interest. That demand threatened to dissolve whatever element of equity was incorporated in the conditional contract scheme. Preferential treatment for Israel and Egypt was especially awkward because neither country had as much as an agreement of cooperation with the United States, which is the normal legal–administrative vehicle for nuclear transfers. In the end, the matter of Israel's and Egypt's ranking was resolved through cancellation of the transfer agreement itself. Congressional and public opposition to the deal (along with the steady loss of presidential authority) saved the AEC from an embarrassing acquiescence to the president's dictate.

On August 3, the AEC broke its month-long silence. Appearing before the JCAE, Chairman Ray announced the proposed conditional contract plan with all its deletions and question marks.[41] The subsequent campaign to mollify foreign governments, and therby to restore a medium of credibility to the United States' image as nuclear exporter, was replete with ironies. White House policy makers who had disparaged the political repercussions of a contrived enrichment crisis as a small price to pay for the greater good of privatization now saw the administration searching for palliatives with which to assuage aggrieved foreigners. It was the Indian bomb, more than anything else, that had drastically changed the political terrain and shifted the weights of the players. For administration strategists it could have not come at a less opportune time. The crisis they had succeeded in provoking was not the relatively tame affair they had foreseen – a supply bottleneck painful enough to force support for private entry but not likely to upset any major U.S. international interest. Instead, the enrichment shortfall was being viewed as contributing mightily to a proliferation danger that threatened world stability. The new priority would be stopping the bomb from spreading; the question who owned new enrichment plants would have to take a back seat. Privatization was still alive; it had suffered no fatal damage from the crisis; and, despite corporate equivocation, it would come close to approval before losing narrowly more than two years later. But placed against the proliferation issue, which was generating a growing wave of anxiety in Washington, privatization was small beer. Although the free-enterprise ideologues still had the running on privatization, the bigger game of nuclear energy was being taken over by the political people who earlier had been kept on the sidelines so effectively. As for President Nixon, who set the plan in motion, he had other things on his mind in the summer of 1974. He could not resist the trend of events. Importuned by the NSC staff (David Elliott now fully supported by Kissinger), Nixon acknowledged the need for a diplomatic salvage operation – playing "catch-up," to use a favorite phrase of his administration. The campaign for the heart and mind of Richard Nixon on the nuclear issue culminated with a personal statement placing the president squarely behind the conditional contracts. It was issued the day he departed the White House for San Clemente.[42]

3

A new look at plutonium

RICHARD NIXON'S personal guarantee that the United States would satisfy all conditional contracts for enrichment services was extended the day he resigned the presidency. It was left for the lame-duck regime of his successor, Gerald Ford, to sort out the mess created by the mishandling of enrichment contracts and to soothe the ruffled feathers of distraught consumer governments. But that damage-limiting operation was soon caught in a wrenching reappraisal of Washington's entire policy for promoting the global development of civilian nuclear power. Beyond the immediate issue of reestablishing the United States' critical role in the market for reactor fuels loomed the growing menace of a spreading weapons capability. The year 1974 was the one in which proliferation became a *problem*.

In Washington problem status is accorded an issue when it ceases to be the exclusive preserve of the specialists in remote bureaucratic precincts and becomes the object of concern for the secretary of state, the national security advisor, and even the president of the United States – that is to say, the handful of people who command the power to shift the foundations of policy and to invest political capital in new undertakings. A "problem" gets attention elsewhere as well. Congressional committees hold well-publicized hearings. Senators pronounce the gravity of the situation, some issuing cries of alarm, while others call for a sober stocktaking. The press fills with stories of revelation, and the serious journals of commentary open their pages to articles of interpretation and sage prescription.

This new spate of interest in proliferation, or non-proliferation (the choice of label depending on whether one is emphasizing the threat or the goal), represented its second appearance on the nation's list of problems most wanting solution. It had enjoyed topical favor briefly in the late 1960s, at the time of the Non-Proliferation Treaty's negotiation, which was accompanied by lively debates over its signature and ratification by the then key nonweapons states, West Germany and Japan. Proliferation's subsequent relegation to the policy margins reflected less the treaty's actual success in neutralizing the dangers of spreading nuclear capabilities than the political judgment of the Nixon administration that the threat of weapons spread should be given a low priority. It was an assessment made all the easier by a more widespread misconception, in both branches of government, that the NPT was somehow self-executing and had placed an effective shield of safeguards around civilian nuclear power.

THE BACKDROP TO REFORM

During the Nixon years, non-proliferation simply did not figure as very important when staked against more pressing matters of state. The president and Dr. Kissinger were preoccupied with Vietnam and with their intricate games of great-power diplomacy, which were intended to clear the ground for a better-modulated and more manageable set of relations with Moscow and Peking. From their realpolitik perspective, proliferation was inevitable. The only question was which and how many states would take up the nuclear option. Any self-denying injunction on nuclear arms was seen as an unnatural political act that would soon give way to more conventional security-minded behavior. Therefore, it simply did not make sense for the United States to incur political costs in trying to avoid an eventuality that in all likelihood was beyond Washington's power to control. While acknowledging that the pledges of abstinence recorded in the NPT were a good thing, Kissinger viewed them as just that – "pledges" of states whose interests and commitments were constantly in flux. To move beyond the treaty to an elaborate program for removing the incentives and opportunities encouraging potential proliferators to build up their technical capabilities was deemed uncalled for, and in the end unavailing.

Whatever the implications of proliferating atomic weapons for the distant future (that "great beyond" which for politicians and most statesmen is anytime after the next national election), the short-term risks were downplayed.[1] The NPT, although a contrived and ultimately fragile arrangement, conveniently could be viewed as icing the immediate threat by binding the most obvious candidates to a restrictive covenant that encapsulated nuclear materials in a reasonably secure safeguards vessel. Unprepared to expend time and diplomatic effort on crafting an intricate regime of constraints and incentives for controlling nuclear power, the Nixon administration was too ready to accept the facile opinion held in many circles, and with special conviction in the AEC, that the treaty had put a cap on the proliferation problem for the time being.

In fact, as subsequent events were to reveal, it demanded constant and adroit diplomatic effort to assure the critical ratifications; to address the genuine security and energy considerations that figured in a government's decision whether to accept restrictions, of whatever character, on its nuclear program; and to monitor the growth of the civilian nuclear industry to prevent the introduction of new technologies (e.g., reprocessing), and new commercial distributors, that might breach the wall between civilian and military applications. Furthermore, anything less than universal adherence to the NPT left open the possibility that a nuclear explosion by one nation conceivably might undermine the credibility of the entire control system and tip the dominoes of proliferation.

The Indian detonation of May 1974 had exactly that effect. It was a stunning reminder of the NPT's only partial coverage, of the loopholes in safeguards and restrictions written into bilateral agreements, and of the close link between civilian power facilities and a weapons program. As much as the explosion itself, the manner of its preparation blew a psychological hole in the world's confident perception of how difficult it was for a marginally proficient state to build a bomb, and how hard it would be to evade safeguards against the surreptitious exploitation of a nominally civilian program.

THE NEW THREAT

India's demonstration of a weapons capability was one of a series of developments that drastically altered the climate on the proliferation front. The others were the oil supply crisis of 1973–4, the maturing of civilian nuclear power, and the moratorium on enrichment contracts. Together, they pointed to a situation in the not-too-distant future when the widespread *potential* for bomb making would become a fact of international life – *without any abrogation of existing agreements or violation of treaty obligations.*

Each of the events of 1974 affected the system differently. The oil crisis put into relief the overlapping relationship between domestic energy needs and state security. It introduced Secretary Kissinger to the political importance of economic interdependence, and raised a glimmering awareness of how seriously the Europeans in particular viewed the costs, financial and political, that dependence imposed on them.

The enrichment snafu, with its disagreeable diplomatic fallout, was instrumental in restoring the State Department's voice on nuclear exports. It also reminded official Washington that the United States' credibility as a supplier of nuclear fuels was crucial to the regulation of nuclear power, a goal at least as important as taking the righteous path of free enterprise on ownership of enrichment plants and earning a bigger handful of foreign exchange on the export market. So shattering was the disintegration of the

United States' reputation as a supplier that for a time the motto "Thou Shalt Not Undermine the Reliability of the United States" seemed to be carved in the marble archways that adorn senior offices in the AEC, the State Department, and other agencies of government relevant to nuclear policy. Restoration of credibility became the leitmotif for emerging policies.

The expansion of nuclear energy worldwide, with its growing demand for fuel sources, was being accelerated by the general desire to find at least a partial substitute for petroleum. The latter, the indispensable fuel for industrialized and developing countries alike, had undergone a drastic five-fold price hike. Its provision was dramatically shown to be vulnerable to disruption by the politically inspired action of a producer's cartel; and its long-term availability was put into question by pessimistic projections of supply-and-demand ratios. Continued dependence on petroleum jeopardized future growth, present prosperity, and political stability. Nuclear power seemed fortuitously to be waiting in the wings to fill the need. It promised an efficient, more attractively priced, and self-contained energy source. Its practicability was demonstrated by the steady increase in the number of plants on line in the industrialized West and by the sharp rise in contracts for new construction (the same upwelling of demand that contributed to the bottleneck on enrichment services). There were also the less tangible, but strong, appeals of nuclear energy as representing the crowning achievement of modern technology and, in some minds, the entry point to the ultimate military weapon.

Suppliers were ready and willing to meet the emerging demand. In the area of conventional reactors, several of the major industrialized countries – the United Kingdom, Germany, France, and Sweden – were commercializing and marketing plants of their own manufacture. Their search for foreign markets was motivated in part by a desire to recoup through exports the development costs of their expensive, high-priority domestic programs. The new suppliers were confronted with the formidable presence of the two U.S. firms that had dominated the market, Westinghouse and General Electric.[2] Now, though, the pervasive anxieties over supply reliability sparked by the oil embargo widened the opportunities to compete on grounds other than those of price and performance. The same sensitivity about dependence on external sources of conventional fuels that swelled nuclear demand was also weakening the inhibitions of nuclear-proficient governments about exploiting the worldwide appetite for more secure energy. Nuclear power's one shortcoming as a dependable fuel source had been the reliance of user countries on a foreign supplier for the low-enriched uranium fuel used by all light-water reactors. The U.S. monopoly on enrichment services had put the United States in a pivotal position and had given it exceptional leverage over the international market in nuclear reactors – hence the global repercussions of the foul-up over enrichment contracts. Hence, too, the opportunity for the exporters of reactors to sweeten their deals with the offer of fuel-producing facilities.

The transfer of fuel-producing plants and technology posed the most obvious proliferation danger. There were also good reasons to worry about the latent threat associated with the indiscriminate dissemination of engineering skills and know-how resulting from the widespread installation and operation of power-generating and research facilities. The Indians had made the point that a nation reasonably competent in nuclear skills and endowed with a diversified industrial infrastructure faced no insuperable technical or economic barriers to bomb manufacture. India had spent less than ten million dollars in building a clandestine reprocessing plant that separated the crucial plutonium, which was used as explosive material, from the spent fuel of a civilian reactor.[3] Given access to irradiated reactor fuel, a country could successfully implement a weapons program as long as it had the critical base of competent manpower. Experience acquired in operating civilian reactors (combined with the open transfer of unrestricted theoretical and engineering information, and training programs in plutonium separation and reprocessing such as those run by the AEC at its Hanford, Washington, facility) raised the standard of technical proficiency. By helping to satisfy an essential condition for an arms project, a large civilian program might well be a crucial factor tipping the scales of an internal policy debate on whether to take up the nuclear option.

RESPONSE TO THE INDIAN EXPLOSION

The end of U.S. dominance

As the U.S. government began, through fits and starts, to organize the rudiments of a non-proliferation policy, Washington found itself facing a situation far more troublesome, and less susceptible to U.S. control, than had been assumed scant months earlier by a preoccupied Nixon administration. Thanks to upheavals on the international energy markets and developments in technology that had simplified matters for an erstwhile bomb maker, the proliferation problem had undergone an important transformation. A prospective weapons state would have greater capability to build a bomb, would find it easier to do so – and to do so more quickly – than non-proliferation strategists had been accustomed to thinking. As one group of sober experts gloomily viewed the situation, "The question of whether a country has nuclear weapons will be answered not with a yes or no, but with a production schedule."[4]

The stunning nuclear developments of the first six months of 1974 put the world on notice that the metaphorical nuclear genie was at large, rambunctious, and appearing in new guises. But the display did not immediately galvanize the U.S. government into action. Consciousness raising is a slow process. Reordering foreign policy priorities and redirecting existing policy takes even longer. The process of intellectual change and political initiation is laborious and anything but smooth. Reviews are started; studies are made. Attacks on the custodians of established programs and ideas are launched and parried. Some players fight to bring the president and his most senior officials into the act. Others struggle to keep them out. Expertise is marshaled to explain what is wrong and how the situation might be righted. These judgments are contradicted on a variety of grounds by other experts and other specialists with different perspectives and different allegiances. Congress gets into the act with a succession of hearings and a barrage of proposed legislation and resolutions intended to rectify past mistakes and to set the nation on its true and proper course. In other words, the U.S. government is at work making national policy.

Conditions, too, proved less malleable and susceptible to U.S. direction than the AEC, and the White House, had believed in the early 1970s. At that time, the commission and administration officials could treat the Europeans with technological condescension in setting the terms of collaborative enrichment projects. They could hatch their schemes for reorganizing U.S. enrichment services with only the faintest regard for proliferation risks. But by mid-1974 the United States no longer ruled the nuclear roost, in part because it only belatedly realized that active political leadership was needed to hold its influential position. U.S. authority was not to be taken for granted. Nuclear technology and know-how were spreading rapidly, and into areas previously on the periphery of proliferation concern. There were powerful economic incentives for energy-anxious countries to look to nuclear power for their energy salvation. The international market had ceased to be amenable to regulation by unilateral U.S. actions, thanks to the appearance of active commercial rivals and avid buyers. It was all the less responsive to U.S. initiatives after the high-handed attitude toward enrichment services, which left a legacy of distrust and a general aspiration for self-sufficiency.

In seeking to reestablish its grip on the international nuclear market, Washington had to resolve a two-fold dilemma: (1) how to close the loopholes in export conditions and safeguards highlighted by the Indian explosion without losing further credibility as a supplier; and (2) how to achieve psychological denuclearization – that is, how to dissipate the growing sentiment that saw nuclear power as the salvation for resource-deprived countries – while moving to satisfy a justifiable need in a safe and politically acceptable manner. Any U.S. non-proliferation strategy would have to be many-faceted. It would have to deal simultaneously with the terms of availability of nuclear facilities and fuels supplied by the United States, the asymmetrical export standards set by commercial competitors, the pervasive quest for dependable and economical energy sources, the security worries that might motivate states to turn civilian capabilities into a military asset, and, not least, its own domestic program for deploying a reprocessing technology that carried an inherent proliferation risk.

The State Department reaction

India's entry into the nuclear club, however nominal, was the critical event. It catalyzed the process of change so that, in three years' time, official U.S. thinking about the dangers of nuclear proliferation, and the political resources that should be expended in an effort to prevent it, would be fundamentally transformed. Yet the external revolution in policy was in no way visible in Washington's initial reaction to the Indian explosion. The response was tardy and low-key and indicated neither profound concern nor sharp displeasure.

The best that the State Department could manage was a tepid expression of regret and a reminder that "the United States has always been against nuclear proliferation for the adverse impact it will have on world stability."[5] Secretary Kissinger's public statement, when it came, seemed more in the way of a wrist-slapping remonstrance than a stern rebuke. The delay, as well as the mildness of the reproach, reflected the quandary in which most officials, especially the secretary of state, found themselves. It was unclear what sort of response would have the desired effect of dissuading other governments from following New Delhi's example, and of discouraging the Indians from pushing ahead with their weapons program. To chastise India severely, perhaps going as far as to include punitive actions of one sort or another, would declare unequivocally the seriousness with which the United States viewed the spread of nuclear weapons. However, to spotlight the Indian action in this way, with all the publicity that attends a loud diplomatic confrontation, could have the undesired effect of inflating India's new status, even if only as an object of superpower opprobrium. The opposite tack, that of largely ignoring the explosion, had a superficial appeal. By pronouncing U.S. disapproval in words of studied understatement, avoiding histrionics and any precipitate action, by treating India on nonnuclear matters as if nothing had happened, the event's significance could be downplayed and the political benefits of demonstrating nuclear weapons capacity cast in doubt. The risk of taking this low-key approach was that it could convey the false impression of U.S. equanimity about proliferation. Moreover, the absence of sanctions might be seen as a sign that there were no diplomatic costs associated with achieving nuclear weapons, even where there had been a violation of the spirit (although not the letter) of nuclear exchange agreements.[6]

The dilemma was not discovered suddenly in the process of drafting a statement to the Indians.[7] It had been fully recognized and spelled out in a contingency paper dutifully prepared and filed by State Department officials some years earlier. There is no certainty, though, that the plans it contained ever saw the light of day or reached the secretary's desk. Kissinger was averse to reliance on the intellectual product of anyone not on his personal staff and especially wary of ideas generated by career State Department officials who had not received his stamp of approval. The stumbling that was witnessed as the United States searched for the appropriate reaction was due as much to senior policy makers' lack of anticipation, and to inadequate mechanisms for using staff, as to the inescapable difficulties of measuring the cost-effectiveness of the strategies being considered.

Kissinger's natural preference was for doing nothing. He ruled out any instant condemnation. Delay in making an official statement did not bother him. He instinctively opposed doing anything that could turn the episode into a cause célèbre. It was not because of any special sympathy he harbored for the Indians that the secretary instinctively inclined toward restraint: The administration's unqualified support for Pakistan in the Bengali War of 1972 revealed where New Delhi stood in the secretary's pecking order of foreign capitals. Instead, he resisted any action that would place the United States in the position of committing itself to taking severe retaliatory measures against all proliferators, present and prospective. In his judgment, the acquisition of a crude nuclear device should not be endowed with great instrinsic value. Nor should it be allowed to take precedence over all other interests that the United States might have with the country in question. It surprised no one in official Washington, therefore, that when presented with a range of options, the secretary explicitly opposed anything but a mild protest and rejected out of hand the idea of sanctions – whether an embargo on nuclear exports or retaliation by withholding U.S. support to the international aid consortium, composed of industrialized Western nations, to which the United States was the largest contributor.[8]

The blandness of the overall U.S. reaction to the Indian explosion was troubling to many, among them officials who appreciated the difficulty of finding the appropriate sanction and who were cognizant of the risk that a severe rebuke might harden New Delhi's determination to move down the nuclear path. For, as Washington gained a better understanding of what the Indians had done, it became evident that they had evaded, if not directly violated, restrictions on the use of U.S.-supplied heavy water. The heavy water had been employed as a moderating element in a Canadian-supplied research reactor, the CIRUS reactor. The Canadian–Indian bilateral agreement stipulated that the nuclear materials provided by Canada should be used only for peaceful nuclear explosives.[9] No Canadian uranium was used to produce the irradiated fuel from which plutonium was separated in the Indian-built reprocessing plant conveniently located close by. Instead, the Indians had inserted natural uranium of local origin, technically covering themselves against a possible Canadian complaint that they had surreptitiously diverted fissionable material received from Canadian sources. However, the United States' cooperative agreement with India banned the employment of heavy water for making peaceful nuclear explosives. The AEC admitted use of U.S. material in the Indian program only with reluctance. It had reason to be embarrassed – and not only because of the illicit use of U.S. heavy water.

India had made little effort to conceal her intentions. There was nothing clandestine about the unsafeguarded reprocessing plant, whose existence was known, and whose plutonium production was nominally earmarked to peaceful nuclear purposes. An internal AEC memorandum, prepared by its International Programs Division and drafted in September 1966, discussed the Indian reprocessing plant. Its authors, Abraham S. Friedman and Myron B. Kratzer, concluded that the United States should continue to provide "encouragement and assistance toward the recycle of plutonium produced in India's nuclear power plants," on economic grounds. By not putting the United States in direct opposition to Indian plans, the reasoning went, Washington would be in a better position to influence New Delhi's nuclear policy. So U.S. technical help to India's reprocessing was declared "of direct pertinence to encouragement of peaceful uses and deterrence of military uses."[10] The Freidman–Kratzer memorandum reflected a benign AEC attitude toward reprocessing's possible contribution to weapons spread, an attitude that was, in the eyes of the growing antiproliferation forces, a major impediment to gaining control over the international diffusion of nuclear materials.

The ingenious Indian circumvention of two bilateral agreements (not to mention the relative ease with which safeguards on the reactor had been eluded in spiriting away the required amounts of irradiated fuel) triggered an assault on the entrenched AEC position. It sparked moves in Congress, and in the Nuclear Regulatory Commission, to tighten conditions of export and to strengthen safeguards. It encouraged greater assertiveness from the State officials and NSC staffers, who had been brought into play gradually as the proliferation issue climbed the foreign policy priority scale. These officials saw the importance of readjusting the terms of nuclear cooperation to reduce the risk that the United States would unintentionally and unnecessarily contribute to the growth of nuclear weapons capabilities in recipient states. They also realized that the AEC stranglehold over nuclear export policy had to be broken in order to accomplish this goal.

But these were two imperatives that Secretary Kissinger was slow to acknowledge. He had other things on his mind, and no appetite for adding the still powerful nuclear establishment to his list of unfriendly executive branch powers. Only when forced to intercede by the undeniably damaging effects of the bumbling on enrichment contracts did he support State Department activism. Even then he held back from any serious personal engagement.

The principal influence pushing him toward a more proliferation-minded position was exercised by Joseph Sisco and NSC staffer David Elliott. They impressed their mark on policy during an incident in June, some weeks after the Indian test. It concerned a routinely scheduled shipment of LEU fuel for the Indians' Tarapur reactor. The export license received AEC approval as if nothing had occurred. When Elliott, now made aware of all policy questions pertaining to international nuclear energy, learned of the commission's casual business-as-usual attitude, he raised questions with the AEC's International Programs Division and the State desk officer whose review had led to favorable judgment. Sisco, when informed, jumped into the fray and blocked the shipment.

The ensuing jurisdictional wrangle was a forerunner to the bitter confrontation over enrichment contracts the following month. In this instance, it took much less bloodletting for a compromise to be worked out, one more in conformity with the AEC outlook. The shipment would be released, accompanied by a letter stating that, in the light of recent actions by the Indian government, no subsequent shipment licenses would be granted unless New Delhi accepted as a condition additional safeguards on its nuclear facilities (including the chemical reprocessing plant that produced the plutonium for the Indian bomb). The ambiguity surrounding the shipment left the broader issues of export policy up in the air. It also left unresolved the outstanding differences between the AEC and State over what conception of the proliferation danger should guide the redrafting of such a policy. For the time being, Secretary Kissinger was unwilling, and perhaps unable, to move the administration to the side of State and NSC proliferation officials.

Executive reorganization

However limited his enthusiasm about a reinvigorated antiproliferation campaign, Kissinger realized that the issue could not be swept under the rug. There was too much pressing business to attend to. Something obviously had to be done to straighten out the disarray on enrichment contracts that was poisoning relations with countries on three continents. In addition, the public and congressional outcry over the Indian test had created irresistible pressures to rewrite the rules governing nuclear exports.

The mood of congressional discontent and suspicion had been deepened by President Nixon's June announcement of his intention to sign agreements of nuclear cooperation with Egypt and Israel, a proposed move that left the impression of a too-casual approach toward the dissemination of nuclear technology. And, most disconcerting, it had become known that West Germany and France were negotiating deals with Brazil and Pakistan, respectively, for the sale of reprocessing plants – plants that would provide those latter states with ready means for obtaining the material, plutonium, from which India made its bomb. It was one thing to underplay the significance of a single new nuclear power, especially a country whose other political weaknesses were so apparent. It was quite different to accept with equanimity the advancement to the nuclear threshold of a clutch of countries, thanks to the opening of access to sensitive fuel-producing facilities, in a way that threatened to leave the IAEA–NPT safeguards system little more than a hollow facade.

The first step was to create a central unit that could give political direction to the administration's nuclear export and non-proliferation policies. In the past, the NSC had been uninterested in proliferation and the State Department had been either a nonparticipant or ignored. Both conditions reflected the low estimate of the national security advisor, now secretary of state, of the issue's importance. Involvement of council staff members had been limited to those with area responsibilities. They, like their counterparts at State Department country desks, had been in the habit of looking at nuclear export and proliferation through a filter colored by whatever political dealings the United States had with the country in question. Transfer of civilian nuclear materials was a currency of diplomatic exchange, a means to other ends. Only exceptionally, and for very few officials, was it a matter of major concern in itself. Too, the subject was in many respects an alien one. The NSC staff was deficient in the technical knowledge needed for making sense of recondite questions about nuclear engineering, safeguards systems, and the costing of enrichment. Without the expertise to understand these matters, staffers were hardly in a position to evaluate the risks attached to reprocessing facilities or the feasibility of a unilateral tightening of export controls – much less to confront AEC professionals in interagency meetings about them. The State Department, for its part, had found itself progressively cut out of the action in the nuclear export field under the reigns of Schlesinger and Ray at the AEC, until Sisco used the Eisenhower memo to lever the department back into the game during the May 1974 crisis on enrichment. Even then, only the Office of Science and Technology (SCI) had much experience or interest in proliferation issues. The political bureaus had paid proliferation only slightly more attention than had the NSC staff.

To fill the organizational gap, Kissinger assigned responsibility for overall policy development to the State Department's Policy Planning Staff (SP) and placed the Bureau of Political–Military Affairs (PM) in charge of diplomatic operations. They would work with the reconstituted Bureau of Oceans and International Environmental and Scientific Affairs (OES), which was the bureaucratic successor to SCI. OES continued in its AEC (soon to be ERDA – the Energy Research and Development Administration) liaison functions, collaborating with the commission in arranging for and overseeing the transfer of nuclear materials, and in dealings with the IAEA. Dominant in State as long as nobody else was paying attention to the international side of nuclear energy, OES officials now had to yield primacy to the political bureaus. PM's main task would be to take on the ticklish chore of approaching other nuclear suppliers, with a view to reaching accord on parallel export policies. Under its director, George Vest, the bureau became lead office for U.S. participation in the soon-to-be-launched London Suppliers Conference, joining major exporters of nuclear facilities in an effort to set common rules about the kinds of technology that should be made commercially available and the terms of their export. The bureau was also expected to make sure that proliferation policy did not cross circuits with other lines of U.S. foreign policy, a recurrent Washington problem. SP's job was seen as complementing PM operational responsibilities by shaping State's position on major proliferation issues, and assisting it to achieve a reasonable degree of coherence among them.

Over at the White House, the new national security advisor, General Brent Scowcroft (Kissinger's former subordinate and handpicked candidate for the job), designated David Elliott as the council's chief proliferation staffer. An engineer by training, Elliott originally had come into the government to serve as science advisor to the National Aeronautics and Space Council. As science staff member for scientific and technical affairs at NSC, he was by 1974 a respected council official. He was to act as a constant spur to the development of a more active non-proliferation strategy, and a watchdog over the chronically negligent AEC handling of sensitive export matters. As a State ally in the battle with AEC over enrichment, he was mainly responsible for eliciting the White House statement of reassurance to frustrated foreign customers. (Two and a half years later, as a Ford holdover in the Carter administration, he would play a surprisingly influential role in the presentation of that president's campaign against proliferation.) In the spring of 1974, he was assigned the oversight of the Kissinger-initiated review of the proliferation problem. National Security Study Memorandum (NSSM) 202, as it was known officially, had the specific objective of preparing U.S. positions for the NPT Review Conference scheduled for September 1975.[11] NSSM 202 was under way, with NSC supervision, when the Indians detonated their nuclear "device." The task immediately acquired new urgency, with stress placed on finding means by which the United States might avoid any further disagreeable surprises. Though administrative responsibility for the study lay with Elliott, the analysis was conducted primarily in the State Department. Day-to-day direction was the responsibility of Jerome Kahan, former ACDA and Department of Defense official (as well as Brookings scholar), who was a recent recruit to SP. He became a leading player in the proliferation politics of the Ford administration, and authored some of Kissinger's later antiproliferation initiatives.

A new Working Group (WG) of the NSC's Verification Panel (VP) was created expressly for the purpose of preparing NSSM 202. The VPWG would continue, after the study's completion, as the administration's formal body for coordinating proliferation policy. The interagency committee was chaired alternately by NSC staffers David Elliott and Ben Huberman, depending on whether the issue at hand was mainly political or technical in character. Members were representatives from SP, PM, and OES in State; ACDA; the AEC's (later ERDA's) Divisions of International Security and International Affairs; and, when appropriate, OMB and other executive agencies. The VPWG was supported by a backstopping committee under the chairmanship of ACDA's assistant director, Admiral Tom Davies; this committee was supposed to perform secretariat functions, such as clearing cables, drafting policy statements, and ensuring the transmittal of decisions to executing agencies. The presence of an ACDA official in the chair did not increase the agency's power or status: Hostilities between Kissinger and ACDA Director Fred Ikle effectively cut the agency out of the action on non-proliferation. Wherever ACDA had a formal position of leadership, it was a sure sign that informal channels would be established to bypass the agency.

The VPWG was further hampered from functioning as a mechanism for interagency coordination by the guerrilla war conducted against it by Dixy Lee Ray. First as chairman of the Atomic Energy Commission and then as assistant secretary of OES in State, after she was eased out of the commission slot during the AEC split into the NRC and ERDA at the end of 1974, she was uncooperative when not actually hostile. The personality clash between the overbearing Ray and the strong-willed Kissinger, rooted in the turbulent crisis management of the previous summer, culminated in the former's boycotting of all proceedings and committees installed by the latter. Ray's recalcitrance was an obstacle to winning the full participation of the old nuclear hands at the AEC, and even of some of those at the OES, in the new policy setup. Although there was an undeniable gain in harmony from the absence of Ray's prickly personality from the interagency forums, especially the VPWG, a price was paid in delay and policy disjointedness. NSSM 202 was an early victim of the festering personality feud and the generally poor relations between the AEC and State.

Kahan and his colleagues were prepared to address frontally the awkward questions of export conditions, reprocessing risks, and safeguardability made worrisome by the Indian explosion. They recognized early on that the widespread availability of separated plutonium could undercut the existing system of controls and inspection. The study did spotlight the danger. Against implacable AEC opposition, however, it could not declare flatly that the threat was so great or immediate as to demand an overhaul of U.S. policies. Nor could it, in offering a range of policy alternatives, fail to acknowledge the limits and constraints imposed by existing U.S. government commitments to the development of reprocessing technologies. An unambiguous call for reversal of official thinking and extant policy about plutonium would have to wait until the powerful AEC had been cut down to bureaucratic and political size. As of mid-1974 the commission was still so strong that its noncooperation could stall the completion of NSSM 202 for six months, and make certain that the final product would leave on the shelf the most crucial questions of technology transfer and the risks of new plutonium-based nuclear facilities.

By late 1974 non-proliferation had moved from the periphery of foreign policy closer to the center of things. A formal structure had been created for reconsidering proliferation issues, and new personnel had been assigned to the task. But Washington still lacked a comprehensive understanding of how the pieces fitted together. Still more important, the AEC (as it remained until it was legislatively bifurcated at the year's end) had not been brought into a cooperative working relationship with the new structure taking shape in State.

THE PLUTONIUM QUESTION

"Plutonium is the name of the game." So intoned NRC Commissioner Victor Gilinsky repeatedly as he made his case for a more restrictive U.S. export policy. This soon became the common belief of Washington nuclear officialdom. What to do about plutonium was the core issue, around which other policy questions revolved. Plutonium, the prime bomb-making material, is created in a nuclear reactor as a by-product of the production of steam for electric generation. Access to plutonium is tantamount to a weapons capability. The widespread availability of separated plutonium for use as a reactor fuel thus could be seen as constituting latent proliferation. That was the crux of the dilemma.

Plutonium has always been recognized as weapons-grade material: The atomic bomb dropped on Nagasaki was a plutonium bomb. What had changed to make people worry about plutonium was, first, that it had become technically easier and cheaper to separate plutonium from spent fuel and to refine it into a form suitable for weapons use than had been supposed, and, second, that the commercial reprocessing of plutonium to fuel light-water reactors, and ultimately breeder reactors, promised to introduce large amounts of plutonium into the nuclear energy market. As the picture was starkly drawn in a much-discussed report issued by the Council on Economic Development:

> If the plutonium economy becomes a reality, a country interested in acquiring at least a limited nuclear weapons capability could easily disguise that interest by stressing the economic case for investing in nuclear reactors to meet its energy needs. Inventories of plutonium or plutonium fuel assemblies would be common. World trade in plutonium will have to be carefully guarded in storage and shipment. Unlike gold, an amount of plutonium that a person can carry in one hand can be made into a bomb powerful enough to destroy a city. In a military sense, therefore, scores of countries, perhaps most countries, will have nuclear weapons. That is they have access to them. Upon a decision to proceed with assembly, test, demonstration, or military use, a growing inventory could be available on a predictable schedule with a brief lag of weeks or days rather than months. Whether or not they possess the material base and the technological base for producing nuclear weapons. In that sense . . . worldwide nuclear proliferation will occur in the early, if not immediate future.[12]

This was the nuclear Damoclean sword that Gilinsky, the active antiproliferation congressmen, and a growing number of executive branch officials saw casting an ominous shadow over civilian nuclear power; and this was what impelled the effort to get a better grip on the global spread of plutonium.

Safeguards alone did not seem the answer. The inspection system directed by the IAEA looked anything but airtight. It had been designed less to prevent the diversion of weapons-grade material than to ensure that any illicit diversion would be *discovered* and *reported*. The warning time thereby created could then be used to put pressure on the violater. But where the material being diverted was plutonium itself, the lead time for bomb manufacture would shrink to weeks or even days (depending on the diverter's skill in warhead design and engineering). Consequently, in the words of an ACDA report, "it is far less certain that safeguards can provide timely warning of diversion attempts when much shorter lead-times to weapons production are involved."[13] Using sanctioned facilities and materials, a proliferator conceivably might set about building plutonium bombs with reasonable confidence that the job would be completed before the IAEA and foreign suppliers knew for sure what was going on.

A related concern was equally worrisome. A state might build its own, unsafeguarded separation plant (as the Indians did at the less-than-onerous cost of about seven million dollars) and extract plutonium from spent fuel rods normally stored in cooling tanks that might be either unsafeguarded (if not of U.S. origin, and therefore free of U.S.-required controls) or inadequately safeguarded. With access to spent fuel, separated plutonium would be available for a prospective proliferator to use as it chose. The growing familiarity with reprocessing technology and techniques was opening this latter possibility for any country with a substantial scientific and industrial endowment.

From the vantage point provided in 1975, the perplexing question was how the U.S. government in good conscience could have permitted, indeed encouraged, general reprocessing, when to do so placed the material for bomb manufacture on the doorstep of any prospective proliferator, and gravely weakened the effectiveness of controls. The answer lies with the interests and outlook of the dominant AEC, which, until 1974, made U.S. nuclear policy with little interference from the White House or Congress.

A set of core beliefs welded thinking on every facet of civilian nuclear power, including reprocessing, into a rigid intellectual dogma. Two precepts guided thinking on reprocessing. First, for the AEC, *reprocessing was self-evidently the cheapest, the technically simplest, and the most logical way of closing the back-end of the nuclear fuel cycle*. In principle, the surest way to dispose of irradiated wastes produced by LWRs was to burn up the "hottest" element, plutonium, as recycled fuel. In principle, this approach would be more economical than providing for long-term storage of spent fuel. In principle, mixed oxide (MOX) fuels combining separated plutonium with residual uranium in new fuel assemblies were a necessary supplement to limited reserves of natural uranium. In time, MOX fuels would be less costly than LEU fuels, whose rising price would reflect the gradual depletion of limited natural uranium reserves and the inflated costs of constructing and operating new enrichment facilities. In practice, once the AEC had committed itself to reprocessing, none of these estimates was systematically and rigorously reviewed. Nor were estimates seriously reconsidered to take account of shifting costs or supply estimates.

The second precept declared that *commercial reprocessing of plutonium was the logical and desirable intermediary step toward development of the fast-breeder reactor*. The future of civilian nuclear power lies with the liquid-metal fast-breeder reactor (LMFBR), which has been clearly identified as the preferred technology for the next reactor generation. Good sense indicates that experience should be gained from reprocessing plutonium, and that plutonium stockpiles should be built up gradually, in readiness for use as start-up fuel in LMFBRs. Reprocessing on a commercial scale could begin when there were sufficient LWRs in operation, and large enough accumulations of spent fuel, to justify the investment in the large separation and fabrication plants needed for economical operation.

The advocacy of this position led the AEC to make a number of errors and omissions in its assessment of commercial reprocessing's potential. On the key question of the economic feasibility of operating reprocessing plants commercially, commission analyses were distorted by a failure to distinguish between the slightly irradiated fuel from which plutonium is extracted for military use and the highly irradiated fuels that would be the source of plutonium for civilian use. Commenting on the difficulties confronted by operators of commercial plants, one analyst explains: "One of the reasons that commercial plants have had so much unexpected trouble is that light water reactor fuel resides in the reactor five to ten times longer than fuel for military production reactors. The additional residence time boosts the radioactivity and decay heat of the spent fuel and places more demanding requirements on a reprocessing plant."[14] As a result, AEC estimates of reprocessing costs were found to be grossly underestimated, so much so that the DuPont Corporation, which designed and built the Savannah River plant for the AEC's military program, steered clear of civilian projects.

The technical and attendant economic miscalculations of commercial reprocessing gave unwarranted and premature credence to plutonium recycling as a viable means of closing the fuel cycle. It also led to a woeful neglect of the waste-disposal problem, a misfeasance that has haunted U.S. nuclear energy planners and non-proliferation policy makers ever since. The AEC, and its successor ERDA, based the case for reprocessing in part on its being a cheaper and easier way of handling the disposal problem. Yet, as of 1977, there had been "virtually no detailed studies in the United States to support such a conclusion." The NRC reported matter-of-factly in 1976: "It has been assumed in the past the uranium and plutonium in spent fuel would be recovered and recycled. Therefore, detailed analyses of the technology of spent fuel disposal are not to be found in the literature."[15] In its unblinking pursuit of commercial reprocessing, the AEC had promoted the idea that reprocessing was necessary to extend fuel life, was economical, and was an answer to the waste problem. It obviously was something that every country with a nuclear power program should have.

These articles of belief were imparted to the U.S. nuclear industry, whence they were in turn transmitted to foreign manufacturers, utilities, and atomic energy authorities. Misinformation and partial truths acquired sanctity through constant reiteration. As Irvin Bupp and Jean-Claude Derian argue in their cogent account of nuclear power's commercial history, "There has been the tendency to create a circular flow of mutually reinforcing prophecies insulated from outside criticism which hardened into doctrine that was everywhere accepted as revealed truth."[16] This closed intellectual system was most apparent in the underestimation of plutonium's weapons potential. Under any circumstances, agency officials found it difficult to make the connection between a civilian nuclear program and a weapons program. They assumed that a proliferator would follow the path taken by the United States and subsequent nuclear powers, who had used specially dedicated facilities to acquire weapons material. Any serious government would go about this process in the same way. One so unknowing or resource-limited as to take another route seemed hardly worth bothering about. Thus was achieved the pervasive attitude that there was no valid reason to block the flow of nuclear knowledge and materials, except for the explicitly proscribed enrichment technology.

The most crucial information that the United States had made available under Atoms for Peace was the basic technology of reprocessing. The PUREX chemical separation technique, which is the basis for both civilian and military plutonium reprocessing, became readily accessible in the open literature and widely diffused. A general authorization issued in 1958, interpreting the Atomic Energy Act, permitted the transfer of peaceful nuclear technology, much of which was declassified at that time. The engineering requirements for constructing and running a reprocessing plant soon were displayed in textbooks. The outflow of technology and know-how moved through scientific, commercial, and government channels. Viewed benignly by government nuclear authorities, it was speeded along by corporations active in building a market overseas, and by scientists overcompensating for past restraints once security restrictions were eased in conjunction with Atoms for Peace. The AEC, for its part, did its best both to enhance technical capabilities abroad and to create opportunities for foreign students, including instruction in reprocessing techniques at Hanford, Washington.[17] (The director of the Indian reprocessing program is remembered as "the sharpest trainee we had that year.") Express permission to reprocess was written into some agreements of cooperation; others required U.S. approval for the reprocessing of fuels supplied by the United States but said nothing of indigenous facilities.[18] Until 1972, Washington imposed no controls on the assistance provided by U.S. individuals and corporations to foreign development projects. Indeed, the Oak Ridge National Laboratory did the design review for the Eurochemic reprocessing plant at Mol, Belgium, that began operations in 1977.

It would be a slow process to convince the nuclear establishment that the commercial use of plutonium markedly lowered the barrier to weapons development, and thereby demanded the revision of basic thinking about plutonium recycling. Myron Kratzer correctly noted, a few years later: "Since 1974, U.S. policy has evolved, step-by-step, to one which views certain sensitive operations – those which involve direct access to plutonium and other weapons-usable material – as so inherently risky that they should not take place even under technically effective safeguards."[19] That critical milestone would be reached only under duress. Not until the accession of the Carter administration did U.S. policy set as its goal weaning the world away from the idea of eventual reliance on plutonium reprocessing. In the interim, Washington under President Ford tried to deal with the proliferation threat raised by plutonium through other, less drastic, means.

THE REGULATORY MISCONNECTION

The independence of the NRC

The effort to master the proliferation issue that got under way in the latter half of 1974 suffered from a number of liabilities. One was interagency dissonance. Even more vexing was the lack of executive branch control over the independent Nuclear Regulatory Commission (the old Regulatory Division of the AEC, which was given its own charter in the reorganization that took effect on January 1, 1975). The NRC was legally free to reach independent judgments on the licensing of nuclear exports, judgments that bound the U.S. government. The division of authority among governmental bodies made it that much more difficult to achieve a consistent and therefore credible U.S. policy aimed at establishing acceptable rules for the transfer and use of nuclear materials. Commitments made by the White House or State Department to foreign governments would have to be qualified with reference to the autonomous power of the NRC to say yes or no to any request for an export license laid before it. This was not a mere theoretical possibility.

Beginning in early 1975, the newly constituted regulatory agency gave every evidence of a readiness to use its independent powers. Even more disturbing to the orderly conduct of government, an articulate commissioner, Victor Gilinsky, was stepping forward as a persuasive critic of what he saw as an overly tolerant U.S. attitude toward recipient countries who did not adhere to the NPT, as well as a general slackness in the application of the export standards set down by the AEC. For the next three years, this "anomalous" role of the NRC, as it was popularly called, was to be a constant irritation to executive branch officials striving to restore order to U.S. export policy. It would be a sticking point in administration dealings with aggressively antiproliferationist elements in Congress; it would exacerbate the task of drafting an international code of conduct among nuclear suppliers; and it would serve to frustrate later efforts under the Carter administration to organize a system of fuel assurances for consumer states.

The story of this peculiar system's development is revealing of the odd ways in which major decisions can be made in Washington, and of absent-mindedness in high places. The NRC emerged on the administrative landscape on January 19, 1975, when the Energy Reorganization Act came into force. Among other things, this act divided the AEC's powers between two new agencies – NRC and ERDA. The move to break the old AEC into separate organizational parts was inspired by two laudable objectives: (1) the desire to consolidate in one agency, ERDA, all federal programs for research and development involving energy sources, nuclear and nonnuclear alike, and (2) the wish to place responsibility for the regulation of nuclear power in a new, independent body whose judgment would not be influenced by the promotional aspects of government's role in encouraging civilian nuclear energy. (This latter consideration mainly reflected concern over much-publicized shortcomings in the AEC's monitoring of nuclear health and safety standards, rather than the commission's slackness in regulating exports.) The reform legislation was less than consistent, however, in distributing the responsibilities between the two new agencies. For reasons having to do with the jurisdictional boundaries of the old AEC sections, the licensing authority was fragmented. Responsibility for the licensing of technology and know-how was retained by ERDA's Division of International Security. NRC was given export control over hardware, for example, reactors, reprocessing plants, and the special nuclear materials enriched uranium and heavy water.

The procedures and conditions for granting licenses were set down by the Atomic Energy Act and governed the procedures of both agencies until the Nuclear Non-Proliferation Act of 1978 went into effect. Simply put, any exported item had to conform to the terms of the agreement of cooperation between the United States and the importing country, and had to be, as stipulated in Section 810 of the Code of Federal Regulations, "not inimical to the security and interests of the U.S." In this sense, nothing was changed. In two vital respects, though, things were different. The AEC, however effectively it succeeded in protecting its operational autonomy, was susceptible to presidential direction. The NRC is a regulatory commission, independent of direct presidential control and acting in a quasi-judicial manner. Second, the NRC soon exhibited a growing inclination to conduct searching examinations of export licenses that raised questions about the sufficiency and appropriateness of the terms incorporated in agreements of cooperation.

Previously, license applications for nonsensitive hardware and materials (i.e., everything but enrichment and reprocessing plants) had been granted quite routinely under the umbrella agreements. As Herbert H. Brown, former director of international and state programs in the AEC Regulatory Division (and later a member of the NRC), testified before the Senate Government Operations Committee, "The regulatory function was purely ministerial," its actions being based upon an internal security review coordinated by the general manager's division.[20] That office was required to consult with SCI (later OES) in State, with the Department of Defense, and with the Department of Commerce. It had final responsibility for determining whether to grant an export license, a decision for which it was accountable to the commissioners and, through them, to the president. Reviews had tended to be merely perfunctory when the export of reactor equipment or contracted LEU was the issue and when a valid cooperative agreement was in force. Now, however, they would be subject to independent evaluation by an NRC that did not see itself as wholly bound either by past practice or – to Gilinsky's way of thinking – by the language of the bilateral agreements where it left doubt as to U.S. prerogatives.

The consequence was that, as an expert report explained, "if the NRC refuses a license, the export cannot go forward even if the executive branch favors it."[21] What bothered administration officials, and struck most observers as odd, was the commission's inheritance of a function that involved not just technical questions but matters of political judgment. The commission was generally acknowledged as competent to evaluate safeguards and physical security in the recipient country. But it also was being called upon to make political assessments of foreign governments' intentions, and evaluations of U.S. national security interests, for which it had questionable competence. Those unhappy with the arrangement were worried that the NRC was simply not equipped for the job, and had no place doing it. ERDA head Robert Seamans expressed the opinion of many in counseling that "it is not wise for a regulatory commission [to be] in a position to make its own judgment" on a matter of "foreign policy and a common defense." Whatever criteria commissioners might follow, however well or poorly those criteria might serve the end of non-proliferation, the very fact of the commission's independent authority was a wild card that made "it more difficult for the United States to give positive assurances to foreign governments about future fuel supply" (or about reactor exports, for that matter).[22]

How could an administration that had spent the greater part of 1974 trying to get its house in order on proliferation, and that was anxiously straining, after the enrichment contract fiasco, to restore confidence in the United States as a reliable supplier, support legislation that made its policies hostage to the independent judgment of the five Nuclear Regulatory Commissioners? To state it simply, neither the old nuclear policy offices nor the new coordinating bodies reviewed the Energy Reorganization Act to see how its grants of organizational authority might impinge on nuclear exports. The act was nominally a domestic piece of legislation. Its foreign policy aspects were secondary and not immediately evident – certainly not to the Domestic Council staffers who prepared it. Administration responsibility for clearing its passage through Congress lay with White House officials outside the NSC and with congressional liaison officers in departments other than State. Once again, a heavy price was being paid for fragmentation of authority in the executive branch and tolerance of administrative discord.

During the period 1969–74, proliferation worries had slipped into the shadowed recesses of U.S. foreign policy machinery. Even after the Indian explosion and the undertaking of NSSM 202, these concerns did not receive the sustained and searching scrutiny at the highest levels of government that they required. No report or analysis of the AEC had called attention to the alarming connections among commercialization of plutonium, technology and fuel transfers, and proliferation. No State Department task force had explored the problem. No National Security Council review had focused its finely honed intelligence on the issue, and cried havoc to the White House. Only the Arms Control Agency, with an institutional and intellectual commitment to the spirit of non-proliferation, as well as to the law of the Non-Proliferation Treaty, pursued the matter with diligence. Its efforts were made in what too often amounted to lonely splendor. (Testimony to the remoteness of the agency from the mainstream of policy was provided when ACDA's leading non-proliferation specialist, the able and indefatigable Charles van Doren, sought in late 1971 to organize an interagency colloquium to examine the plutonium dilemma. His invitation received so unenthusiastic a response that the gathering turned out to be an almost exclusively ACDA affair.) In this atmosphere, it is not surprising that in 1974 there was no mechanism or official deputized to track such matters as the bearing of AEC's reorganization on U.S. export-licensing policies and on the United States' credibility as a supplier.

There were a few perceptive and attentive minds. To their credit, two AEC officials, Nelson Sievering in the International Division and Angelo Giambusso, the office's deputy assistant administrator, had foreseen some of the implications of the NRC's proposed export-licensing powers. But their views seem never to have made their way through the bureaucratic underbrush. Certainly, there was no call for an assessment emanating from the secretary of state's office. After the die had been cast, and the potential for disruption generally recognized, Kissinger plaintively asked why somebody had not warned him. He *had* been forewarned, although late in the day. The NSC staff's main man on proliferation, David Elliott, picked up the issue of NRC licensing power when he got a look at the legislation in its final stages in December. He managed to corner his boss during the year-end rush long enough to point out the problem, and to ask what Kissinger thought should be done. The hurried response was, "I don't think it's a problem; take care of it." With instructions as precise as that, and with the bill sliding rapidly toward presidential signature, nothing was to be done but to let matters take their course. There would be ample time to deal with the consequences – three years, to be exact.

Statesmen who spend their long waking hours preoccupied with the diplomatic affairs of the moment have short attention spans and faulty memories. When they exercise enormous power, they are also inclined to believe that small procedural difficulties can be overcome by the exertion of their inherent authority. When his slowly awakened fear of what the Energy Reorganization Act had wrought was confirmed, Kissinger exclaimed that surely the commissioners were constitutionally constrained from using their statutory power to contravene presidential policy. He was chagrined to learn that they were not. The constitutional questions would be explicitly raised later in an informal exchange between David Elliott and Victor Gilinsky. Elliott disbelievingly queried whether the commissioner would really use the discretionary power to veto an export license sanctioned by the administration. Receiving an affirmative response, Elliott pondered and then thoughtfully asked, "How long is your term?" It was longer than President Ford's and Henry Kissinger's.

Awareness of the complications created by the NRC's autonomy dawned late. It did, however, produce an effort early in 1975, fostered by the AEC and backed by the White House, to negotiate a memorandum of understanding between the newly separated NRC and ERDA to the effect that the former would yield its export-licensing function to the latter. Commissioners and staff of the NRC, uncertain of their position under the new organizational scheme of things, sought to sidestep the proposal. They were saved from possible embarrassment or confrontation with the executive branch when the attempt at an informal transfer of powers was exposed by Paul Leventhal, chief non-proliferation staffer on Senator Symington's Government Operations Committee, a staunch advocate of tighter safeguards and a severe critic of the old AEC. With its cover blown, the administration backed away and disavowed any plan to detour around the law as set down in the Energy Reorganization Act. To make sure that the commission fully understood its legislated responsibility, and in the hope of stiffening the commissioners' resolve to use their authority, Senator Ribicoff pointedly asked each freshly appointed commissioner at his confirmation hearing whether he was prepared to use his power if, in his best judgment, such action was called for. Each indicated that he was indeed so prepared.

The NRC "slowdown"

The nervousness about an independent NRC was well founded. The commission's willingness to use its independent powers was soon in evidence. In a series of licensing cases, the commission made clear that it had no inclination to rubber-stamp applications, even when the export conformed with the enabling agreement of cooperation and when the State Department indicated that there was no threat to U.S. national security. Although there were no outright rejections of applications, the measured deliberateness with which the commission proceeded was witness to the seriousness with which the NRC disposed of its discretionary power.

The commission's demand that the State Department and other participating executive departments present detailed evaluations of whether the recipient country met standards of safety, safeguardability, and peaceful intent appreciably lengthened the time that elapsed between application and decision. So did the commission's internal examination, which not only critically examined executive branch views, but now also included a questioning of existing standards of evaluation. The resulting "slowdown" on applications, taken by itself, was enough to nourish doubts among consumers about doing business with the United States. The decisions, once set down, were themselves favorable, yet distressing to those in the administration who saw expeditious handling of license applications as crucial to reestablishing a favorable image of the United States as a dependable exporter. Not only was the protracted process itself a source of irritation; there also was reason to believe that sentiment was growing within the commission to impose tighter conditions in the future. The anxieties fed by delayed action on license applications in 1975 mounted in 1976 in the wake of a number of contested export cases.[23]

The most controversial episode, and the one with widest implications for licensing procedures, dealt with an application from the Edlow International Company (which brokers LEU contracts) to resupply enriched uranium fuel to the U.S.-funded Tarapur reactor in India. The administration sought approval on the grounds that the exported material would not contribute to any Indian weapons program. That judgment was based on the written assurance, elicited from the New Delhi government in June 1974, that "the special nuclear material that has been, or is hereafter made available for, or used, or produced in the Tarapur Atomic Energy Stations . . . will be devoted exclusively to the needs of the station unless our two governments hereafter specially agree that such material be used for other purposes."[24] This verbal assurance did not ring true to everyone in the United States.[25]

Vocal opposition to granting the request came from public-interest groups and congressional critics who opposed the continuing supply of nuclear materials to India as representing tacit acceptance of its action in building a nuclear weapons capability. One of the activist groups, the National Resources Defense Council, petitioned the NRC for the right to serve as an intervener and called for a public hearing. The commission denied the group's legal right to intervene.[26] The council nonetheless declared on its own volition that a public hearing with the participation of the petitioners was called for. A public hearing as part of the export-license proceeding was precedent setting. It guaranteed (1) that opponents of exports would have a forum for airing their proliferation concerns, (2) that the process would be protracted, and (3) that administration-supported export licenses would have to undergo a domestic political test. The action of the NRC understandably raised the hackles on the backs of officials at State and elsewhere, who were upset by the monkey wrench the commission had thrown in their plans for restoring the United States' reputation as a reliable supplier. Conversely, it was a source of gratification to those pushing for tighter conditions on exports.

The final NRC action on the Tarapur application was ambiguous. In a split decision, the commission approved the smaller of two proposed exports while postponing action on a larger shipment. The NRC's intent, as stated by Chairman Marcus A. Rowden, was to use the LEU export as leverage to persuade India to accept tighter controls on its stockpiles of plutonium reprocessed from waste generated from U.S.-supplied LEU. The dissent was from Victor Gilinsky, who pushed for an even more aggressive policy. He questioned whether adequate safeguarding of plutonium stockpiles was in fact possible. His opinion foreshadowed the growing debate over whether reprocessed plutonium was not so dangerous a substance from a proliferation point of view that its availability should be prevented by absolute prohibitions on its production.

Gilinsky pressed this thesis in another licensing case dealing with a Westinghouse application to export a power reactor to Spain, the ninth in a succession of exports to Spain under an agreement of cooperation. After a delay of nearly two and a half years (attributable in part to the restructuring of the AEC and in part to the more skeptical and contentious regulatory environment), the NRC majority ruled that the license did meet all relevant standards. Gilinsky filed a forceful dissent that added a dimension to the debate over nuclear exports. His criticism concentrated again on the inherent proliferation danger of stockpiled plutonium – a prospect raised in Spain's case by it plans for a separation plant that would extract plutonium from spent fuel and stockpile it in mixed oxide form pending its introduction into nuclear power reactors. He urged that the United States retain authority over the disposition of spent fuel, including a veto on its reprocessing, and, further, that acknowledgement of this authority by the consumer state become a condition of export. Until such time as IAEA safeguards were toughened to include airtight safeguards against diversion of fissile materials from reproducing facilities, he argued, the United States should withhold permission to use either U.S.-supplied fuels or fuels passed through U.S.-supplied reactors for reprocessing. In effect, Gilinsky was calling for a moratorium on plutonium reprocessing, and for its imposition as a condition for U.S. nuclear fuel exports. Equally daringly, he interpreted the NRC's legal mandate, as set down in the Atomic Energy Act, as *requiring* the commission to reject any license application when, in the commission's judgment, it might contribute to proliferation.

Gilinsky's dire view of the plutonium problem, his belief in stiffer export standards, and his interpretation of the commission's discretionary powers were not fully shared by his colleagues. The majority still felt that the question of plutonium reprocessing had best be left to the administration to work out with recipient states. They also felt that the proliferation threat it posed was largely muted by existing safeguards arrangements. On principle, they were also inclined "to give weight to Presidential views" in making their decisions.[27] Nonetheless, other commissioners, including Richard Kennedy and later Chairman Rowden, shared Gilinsky's dissatisfaction with the loose language of some agreements of cooperation. They harbored their own doubts about the effectiveness of IAEA safeguards and saw a need for a more systematic and critical review of applications by the executive branch. The last concern was partially answered by President Ford's issuance of Executive Order 11902 in February 1976 (see Appendix C). It stipulated that the State Department was to coordinate intragovernmental reviews of license applications and to make explicit the requirement that non-proliferation considerations prevail over commercial ones in evaluating the merits of any export request.[28]

Presidentially proclaimed review procedures notwithstanding, the awkward fact remained that the NRC had affirmed its legal right and obligation to make up its own mind whether the granting of an export license was inimical to the security of the United States. Chairman Rowden reiterated this position in hearings before the Senate Government Operations Committee, where he acknowledged to the sympathetic senators the commission's ultimate responsibility for passing on an application. The NRC's resolve to proclaim in principle the power of independent decision, and to act with greater initiative in individual cases, had been buttressed by requests from Congress that it stand firm as a bulwark against what some vocal critics saw as the executive branch's still excessively tolerant attitude toward nuclear exports.

The dilatoriness of successive administrations in taking in hand the nuclear proliferation issue had, as one effect, encouraged Congress, as well as the Nuclear Regulatory Commission, to fill the political void by taking its own initiatives to cut nuclear exports. The ensuing political tangles and jurisdictional disputes exacerbated the task of redesigning arrangements for regulating the transfer of nuclear materials and, by feeding foreign uncertainties about the constancy and direction of U.S. policy, reduced the chances of winning consumer acceptance of reasonable export standards, and of convincing other suppliers to join in a comparable international code.

THE CONGRESSIONAL MISCONNECTION

A new interest in proliferation

The period of executive branch consciousness raising on proliferation, 1974 to 1976, witnessed a similar phenomenon in Congress. Earlier, the subject had held interest for only a small band of arms-control–minded legislators; it was a familiar if not overly worrisome issue for the cognoscenti of the Joint Committee on Atomic Energy. Now it was becoming a prominent problem and a favored topic of proposed legislation. The Ninety-fourth Congress hurried to make up for past neglect by holding a brace of wide-ranging hearings on the spread of nuclear technology and the threat of weapons proliferation. They provided a field day for critics of an alleged AEC nonchalance about the risks of proliferation. The hearings also put the spotlight on practices and attitudes within the nuclear establishment that did not cast the AEC, or its successor, in a favorable light.

Consternation was the only possible reaction to revelations ranging from the custom of keeping accounts of transfers of certain nuclear materials in penciled ledgers to the evidence of official encouragement of Indian reprocessing. Congressional discovery that proliferation might be an imminent danger, and one encouraged by a less-than-vigilant U.S. government, prompted activists in both houses to make a lunge for the tail of the horse they visualized cantering out the open stable door. The action was frenetic, heroic in intention, and not always well aimed, and it often sent the rescuers tripping over one another's feet. A veritable flood of legislation spilled out of senators' and representatives' offices. It was directed at nearly every aspect of nuclear policy: the procedures for granting export licenses; the conditions of transfer, that is, the terms inscribed in agreements of cooperation; the encouragement of nuclear exports through Export–Import Bank loan concessions; the training of foreign nationals in sensitive skills at centers in the United States; and the dearth of U.S. leverage over states that sold fuel-fabrication technologies. Very little of the proposed legislation became law. But the extensive debates did serve to sharpen congressional appreciation of the dangers inherent in conducting nuclear business as usual, to draw attention to what had gone wrong with the United States' promotion of civilian nuclear power abroad, and above all, to keep the administration on tenterhooks.[29]

Members of Congress normally shy away from technically daunting subjects – especially those that do not directly affect their constituents' interests. It is in the nature of congressional life to defer on these recondite matters to colleagues who have chosen to make a specialty of them and who burrow into the committees with jurisdiction over them – hence the singular power of the Joint Committee on Atomic Energy. The delegation of legislative responsibility to a select body is an act of trust, and at the same time one of intellectual and political avoidance. The implied dereliction of individual responsibility also explains the strong reaction when things seem to have gone wrong. The righteousness of the criticism directed at existing policies and practices when they are seen to fail, the zeal to reform, is in part overcompensation for the earlier habit of evading personal accountability and for the failure to exercise oversight over those who wielded power. There was something of this sense of duty not done in the frantic congressional effort to get a grip on the nuclear energy problem.

The domestic political factor

The disquiet about the ways in which U.S. policies were contributing to the proliferation danger deepened along with growing worries about the safety and health effects of power-generating facilities in the United States. The domestic nuclear debate preceded that on proliferation through successive, partially overlapping phases. Drawing sustenance from the environmental movement, anti–nuclear power sentiment mounted simultaneously with the rising estimates of its place in the nation's energy future. The oil embargo had imparted enormous impetus to the nuclear industry; utilities hastened to line up plants to meet future needs. The prospect of scores of reactors mushrooming around the country also spurred the environmental critics. Questioning the assurances of industry and the AEC that the risk of accident was exceptionally low, and ecological damage less than that from alternative energy sources, the anti–nuclear power forces launched an attack on technical, economic, and environmental grounds.

The great debate over nuclear power's place in the nation's energy future remains unresolved to this day. The merits of the often highly technical arguments have been peculiarly resistant to determination; the differences of philosophy and social perspective unbridgeable. Irresolution has reflected both political stalemate and society's perplexity about the image and future of nuclear power. The success of the antinuclear movement has been greater in the courts (where protracted litigation has so extended the time frame for installation of new plants as to dissolve utility interest and to bring the industry to a near standstill) than in the political arena. Overall, it has had the crucial consequence of cultivating the deep-seated fears of nuclear power – civilian or military – that a large section of the populace has always felt.

The link between safety and environmental considerations, on the one hand, and the threat of weapons proliferation, on the other, was made overtly in unsettling analyses that pointed to the relative ease with which bomb-making materials could be diverted from civilian facilities and used to produce nuclear explosives. The alarm was sounded in a series of provocative writings in 1974 by Theodore Taylor, himself a skilled designer of nuclear warheads who worked in Livermore National Laboratory; Taylor underscored the problems of effectively sealing a power plant or storage site and noted that nuclear weapons manufacture, particularly of a crude device, is far less demanding than commonly assumed.[30] Though Taylor addressed himself mainly to the terrorist threat, and concerned himself largely with facilities on U.S. soil, his work had obvious implications for clandestine weapons development by foreign governments or even unofficial groupings and organizations acting outside any established political order. For it dealt a blow to the twin pillars of the system, erected since Atoms for Peace, for international regulation of civilian nuclear power: faith in the workability of safeguards, and belief in the demanding requirements in skills, resources, and fissile materials for bomb making. Taylor and his fellow critics had already succeeded in disturbing settled opinion on the security of domestic power facilities when the Indian explosion came along to lend credibility to doubts about existing controls systems, and to highlight the implications for containment of weapons spread.

Congress, therefore, had come to realize before the proliferation issue broke that all was not well with nuclear power. The safety of, and the overall desirability of, developing civilian facilities had become a domestic political issue, one that agitated enough people to win the attention of elected officeholders (and one that was likely to take on larger proportions as the demand for atomic power grew). The apprehension that surrounded all nuclear programs was a fact of congressional life. Feelings about domestic energy issues keyed a worried response to the emerging proliferation problem. At the emotional and political level, a connection had been made between the management of atomic power in the United States and the implications of its imperfectly regulated spread overseas. In more concrete terms, the link between domestic policies and international concerns became manifest in the foreign consequences, in June 1974, of a failure to resolve the disagreement over the expansion of enrichment facilities. This tie would become progressively tighter until the inseparability of domestic power programs and non-proliferation would be confirmed in presidential action, first by the Fri Review at the close of the Ford administration, and then in the decision of President Carter to curtail the U.S. reprocessing and breeder program.

However, these specific programmatic and policy connections were not immediately apparent to Congress. Although the legislature's uneasiness about nuclear power encouraged the initiatives of 1974–6 to put the brakes on transfers of facilities and materials with a weapons potential, Congress was not ready or able to couple domestic and nuclear foreign policies. Among the host of legislative proposals taking shape during this period, those that promised to have the most practical effect were concerned with the criteria and procedures governing U.S. exports. They shared three interlocking objectives: (1) to apply more stringent conditions than those currently prevailing; (2) to strengthen the congressional and/or independent regulatory voice on export decisions, relative to that of the executive branch; and (3) to specify penalties that would be imposed on those countries that violated agreements and gave indications of developing nuclear weapons.

The first piece of legislation of this nature that became law (and the only one until the Nuclear Non-Proliferation Act of 1978) was the Symington Amendment to the International Security Assistance Act and Arms Export Control Act of 1976. It restricted U.S. aid to any government providing or receiving materials or technology determined to be sensitive, except under certain exceptional circumstances. This bold action was sparked by the West German nuclear deal with Brazil and France's sale of a reprocessing plant to Pakistan. The amendment prohibited the granting of economic or military assistance unless all transferred materials were put under the custody of multilateral institutions and the recipient government accepted IAEA safeguards on all nuclear materials and facilities in the country, of whatever origin. An out was provided by the inclusion of a provision giving the president authority to waive the export requirements where he determined that withholding aid would damage U.S. national interests, and where he was prepared to certify that "the country in question will not develop nuclear weapons or assist another country to do so."[31]

The legislation revealed several aspects of the simmering debate about nuclear exports. First, it demonstrated the Congress's increasing readiness to restrict presidential prerogatives in foreign affairs by imposing specific obligations and prohibitions (although significantly qualified in this case by an escape clause). Second, among the export conditions incorporated was one, "full-scope safeguards," that figured prominently in legislative as well as regulatory debates over licensing standards; and also included was another congressional favorite, multilateral management, whose appeal would wax and wane in the executive branch as a possible way of neutralizing the danger inherent in nationally owned and operated waste-management and reprocessing facilities. The Symington Amendment also gave expression to deep unhappiness (anger was the emotion felt by some congressmen) at the Europeans' cavalier disregard for the proliferation threat in their unseemly rush to consummate sales of nuclear equipment.[32] German and French readiness to make fuel-producing plants available was the object of vehement verbal assault. Those feelings would lead to the insertion into the later Nuclear Non-Proliferation Act of clauses aimed at tightly restricting the retransfer of technology, which aggravated sensitive dealings with the European Community's nuclear agency, Euratom.

Pique at lenient European export policies was also an important motive behind the drafting of the Export Reorganization Bill introduced in April 1975 by Senators Percy, Ribicoff, and Glenn. This bill, which sought to rewrite the rules of U.S. nuclear exports, technical exchanges, and cooperation, would be the centerpiece of the antiproliferationist senators' campaign to restructure the U.S. export program and its procedures. After a tumultous legislative history, the bill evolved into the 1978 law. It went through so many revisions — with sections repeatedly deleted, recast, and reinserted, through two administrations and three Congresses — that no summary review can accurately recount all particulars or do justice to the views debated. The bill's importance lay in its attempt to legislate on the two crucial questions concerning export licensing: who would have authority to make determinations, following what procedures, and what standards and conditions should govern export decisions.

Wrangling over the shape of legislation needed to straighten out the confusion in existing regulations, and over the procedures for applying regulations, displayed chronic frictions between the legislative and executive branches. The inability of congressional sponsors and the Ford administration to compose their differences was due to a basic disagreement over executive prerogative. The dominant legislative viewpoint was that decisions as critical as the transfer of nuclear materal should not be hostage to the exigencies of foreign policy and to the variable judgments of officials overly responsive to circumstances of the moment. Proliferation, said Congress, was a matter of overriding national interest, beyond foreign policy as usual. It followed that the final authority should be vested in a body removed from the press of events. The administration, by contrast, saw as the paramount objective restoration of the United States' position as a reliable supplier in a market that had become highly competitive. This meant (1) removing the uncertainties that would unavoidably attach to any arrangement that forced a sharing of authority among the executive, Congress, and an independent regulatory body, and (2) avoiding strict and, above all, inflexible export criteria, such as those contained in an early legislative draft that followed closely the position advanced by Victor Gilinsky of the NRC.

The gap was too wide to be bridged during the life of the Ford administration. Undersecretary of State Charles Robinson led a strenuous effort late in 1976 to reach a compromise with Senators Percy and Ribicoff; it came close to success but in the end foundered. Further attempts to reconcile the White House's desire for flexibility in the interests of credibility and Congress's eagerness to nail a non-proliferation lid on U.S. exports would have to await a new president. For the time being, U.S. attempts to revamp the international nuclear market would proceed without a clear idea of what domestic rules and regulations would legally bind the United States.

THE LONDON SUPPLIERS' CLUB

If the administration had learned anything about the new realities of nuclear power internationally, it was that the United States could not unilaterally prevent the spread of facilities and fuels contributing to a weapons capability. Until the shocks of 1975 provided by the Brazilian and Pakistani deals, U.S. policies could rightly be accused of having failed "to anticipate the weakening of hegemonial control that has slowly been occurring."[33] The end of the United States' domination of civilian nuclear power, and its impending loss of a monopoly position on enriched uranium fuels, meant that any viable strategy for containing sensitive exports had to be predicated on close cooperation with other technically proficient states. As one analyst succinctly made the point: "It is no longer within the power of the United States, if indeed it ever was, to prevent the rest of the world from moving toward nuclear electric power."[34] The United Kingdom, Canada, West Germany, and France were marketing power reactors; the latter two were commercializing plutonium reprocessing plants independently, or as part of multinational consortia. The Europeans also were putting themselves in a position where they could sell enrichment services and facilities, as the Bonn government had done in the case of Brazil.

Some understanding had to be reached among supplier states on where to draw the line dividing safe civilian power from those facilities carrying an intolerable proliferation risk and on the safeguards or restrictions that jointly should be placed on recipients. Otherwise, as a commentator rightly predicted, the logic of a competitive market would "drive controls over nuclear technology exports down to the level of the lowest common denominator."[35] Already the United States claimed to see tangible evidence of how commercial pressures tended to degrade proliferation concerns. Revelation of the West German–Brazilian deal, and of France's negotiations to sell reprocessing facilities to South Korea and Pakistan, caused consternation in the National Security Council and State Department where Henry Kissinger was undergoing his belated awakening to proliferation problems. The previous year, in an address before the United Nations General Assembly, the secretary had voiced concern about unregulated nuclear exports: "Heretofore, the United States and a number of other countries have widely supplied nuclear fuels and other nuclear materials to promote the use of nuclear energy for peaceful purposes. This policy cannot continue if it leads to the proliferation of nuclear explosives. Sales of these materials can no longer be treated by anyone as a purely commercial competitive enterprise."[36] Spurred into diplomatic action by the unsettling disclosure from Bonn, Kissinger initiated a series of overtures to the states most advanced in civilian nuclear power: Britain, France, West Germany, the Soviet Union, Canada, and Japan. Acting in characteristic secrecy, he succeeded in bringing representatives of the seven governments together for unpublicized talks in London.

U.S. objectives were set out by Secretary Kissinger in July in an oblique allusion to the London talks:

> As peaceful nuclear programs grow in size and complexity it is crucial that suppliers and user nations agree on firm and clear export conditions and strengthened IAEA safeguards. An effective world safeguards system will minimize nuclear risks while fostering the development of peaceful nuclear energy. The priority now is to strengthen the safeguards on the export of nuclear materials for peaceful purposes. The oil crisis adds fresh urgency to this task because it has made the development of nuclear energy essential for an increasing number of nations.[37]

New safeguards could be imposed effectively only in conjunction with the United States' fellow exporters. Cooperation would not be easy to come by.

Reaching an agreement on an export code confronted three obstacles. First, as struggling competitors of the well-entrenched U.S. firms (albeit with considerable recent success to their credit), European rivals – heavily subsidized by their governments – had been inclined to view any proposal for restrictions on sales as masking a U.S. interest in protecting a privileged commercial position. Nations with a modest civilian nuclear industry had multiple reasons to seek customers internationally. Given heavy research and development costs and capitalization requirements, only an external market could make the investment economically feasible (for Western European manufacturers) or attractive and profitable (for U.S. firms). Domestic markets, apart from the American, had not been large enough to put reactor manufacturers in the black. And, ironically, as domestic opposition to nuclear power mounted in Western Europe, the financial pressures to recoup investments through foreign sales were accentuated. A complementary inducement to cultivate markets abroad was that the substantial value of nuclear technology made it a potentially big foreign exchange earner at a time when the hike in the oil bill had made industrial nations especially sensitive about their payments accounts. The anticipated nuclear deal between West Germany and Brazil, reported to be the largest external transaction ever by German industry, promised $8 billion of export revenue.

Second, advanced technology, as a high-prestige item, was a valuable currency of diplomatic exchange. The United States' allies were uneasy with their dependence on U.S. foreign policy for their energy security, just as they had been with their subordinate role in the nuclear energy field. Development of an extensive national and/or European nuclear program promised a greater degree of self-sufficiency *and* a political tool for forging bilateral relations with Third World governments, especially oil-producing countries and other suppliers of basic raw materials. (The element of political competition and the use of nuclear technology as a diplomatic instrument are, of course, even more prominent in the Soviet–U.S. rivalry.)

Third, the French and German governments were split internally over the export issue. The foreign ministry in each country was inclined toward the restrictive U.S. position, whereas those ministries reponsible for technological development and commerce pressed for a rejection of the U.S. overture. France's full participation in the talks – if not acquiescence to Washington's position – was assured by the intervention of President Giscard d'Estaing. The resignation of his Gaullist Premier Jacques Chirac shifted the internal balance in Paris away from the exported-minded Ministère des finances and toward the Quai d'Orsay, which was noticeably more attentive to the adverse proliferation effects of unhampered nuclear exports. Giscard created a special interministerial committee to coordinate all nuclear issues, the Conseil superieur de politique nucléaire, which became the vehicle for fashioning a more balanced French policy. The West German government was similarly divided. On the one hand, officials at the Foreign Ministry leaned toward cooperation with the United States. In opposition, the Science and Technology Ministry, which took pride in the development and promotion of civilian nuclear technologies, was allied with the Finance Ministry (where the foreign exchange potential of nuclear exports was smiled on) in support of an aggressive nuclear sales program. No less than in the United States, the domestic politics of nuclear power, and the intragovernmental conflicts they engender, have been a major hindrance to international agreement on non-proliferation policies.

Despite the formidable obstacles in the way, the suppliers' meetings eventually did bear fruit. It was not, though, as abundant a crop as Washington had hoped for, and it was one that matured slowly. The first round of discussions, convened in early 1975, concluded a year and a half later with the participants affirming four principles designed, in the words of the communiqué, "to inhibit the spread of nuclear weapons while permitting nuclear exports of equipment to meet the world's growing energy needs."[38] On January 27, 1976, the seven participants made public the uniform code they all endorsed. Nuclear importing states would be required:

1. To apply internationally accepted safeguards drawn up by the International Atomic Energy Agency (whether or not they formally belonged to the agency) to all *imports* (although not to indigenous materials and facilities).
2. To give assurances not to use the imports to make nuclear explosives for any purpose, military or peaceful.
3. To have adequate physical security to protect the imported equipment and materials against theft or sabotage.
4. To give assurances that they would impose the same conditions on any retransfer to other countries. (In order to prevent indirect utilization of transferred technology in support of a military program, the retransfer principle covered replication as well.)[39]

The agreement's value was as much symbolic as real. It proclaimed the danger of proliferation arising from the abuse of civilian facilities, affirmed a commitment to common rule setting, and recorded progress toward the writing of an export code. However, the areas of disagreement remained substantial. They touched on matters crucial to the creation of any solid system for international control of nuclear exports. The outstanding difference centered on the transfer of the most sensitive technologies, enrichment and reprocessing. The United States, with backing from Canada (and, more cautiously, the USSR), argued strenuously for outright prohibition, coupled with an undertaking to establish multinational facilities for reprocessing. The only concession the United States could win from its colleagues was a commitment to exercise restraint in the export of fuel-producing facilities. (In September of 1976, France would declare a unilateral policy of not seeking sales of reprocessing facilities. West Germany, at about the same time, gave indications that it, too, was leaning in that direction, but it made no announcement so stating and would not definitely come to this position until June 1977.) The other major issue of contention was whether the nuclear exports should be conditioned on the recipient's acceptance of full IAEA safeguards on all its nuclear facilities. This latter question was the international counterpart of the full-scope safeguards issue raised by the NRC in the debate over the Nuclear Non-Proliferation Act in the United States. The majority of the Suppliers' Club participants proved unwilling to impose so stringent a condition, even though it is accepted by signatories to the NPT.

Round one had been a partial success. Theoretically, the suppliers could attempt to deal with the dangers of weapons proliferation inherent in nuclear transfers by embargo or regulation. On balance they rejected absolute prohibitions and opted for controls and conditions. These latter were less stringent than the stauncher non-proliferationists – the United States above all others – thought were warranted and required. Round two got started in June, with the original seven joined by Belgium, the Netherlands, Sweden, Italy, East Germany, and Czechoslovakia, all of whom adopted the guidelines set down earlier. Switzerland and Poland were added to the group shortly thereafter, raising the membership to fifteen. These later sessions, whose discussions revolved around the plutonium issue, were part of the backdrop to the Ford administration's earnest attempt to rethink the United States' overall national nuclear energy policies in the light of the proliferation threat. That internal review, too, would be preoccupied with the plutonium question.

THREE APPROACHES

Denial

Three avenues of approach offered themselves to U.S. policy makers searching for ways to handle the plutonium problem, and forays were made along each. One was a strategy of denial. If countries could be persuaded not to seek separation technology, or prevented from obtaining it, access to plutonium ipso facto would be shut off. It was a captivatingly simple idea, but one with a number of all-too-apparent shortcomings. First, separation technology was already widely diffused, so that a moratorium on exports and technical assistance could not stop a technically proficient state from constructing a plant on its own, if its government so chose. Another class of countries was the group who were dependent on imported technology (and who might be tempted by the availability of plutonium to consider weapons development with a seriousness that would be lacking if they had to start from scratch). An embargo, in those cases, could be effective. However, its success would depend on agreement among all exporting countries to such restrictions. It could not be imposed by unilateral U.S. action. Therefore, premiums were placed on winning support from the London Suppliers' Club for a moratorium on sales of reprocessing facilities.

Finally, a ban on reprocessing, however achieved, ran the risk of alienating consumer countries who might see the action as reneging on the commitment, embodied in the NPT and bilateral exchange agreements, that promised them access to peaceful nuclear technologies in exchange for forgoing the weapons option. To draw a new line of discrimination between those technically advanced nations able to reprocess using independent means and those technically dependent countries prevented from reprocessing could badly undermine the existing international regime in nuclear energy. It might even end by creating new incentives and opportunities for proliferation by tearing apart the existing web of legal and political constraints. In theory, there were two possible answers to this last dilemma. Either *everyone* would have to agree on an indefinite postponement of reprocessing or arrangements would have to be devised for distributing the expected benefits to all states with an authentic economic interest in receiving them, arrangements contrived to deny them direct access to weapons-grade material. The former approach was not feasible. For one thing, the United States was as yet unready to sacrifice its own stake in plutonium fuels for the sake of the non-proliferation objective; this possibility was not officially considered until the Fri study in the summer of 1976. (The decision in favor of a self-imposed reprocessing moratorium would come only with the Carter administration.) For another thing, the Europeans and Japanese clearly would reject the idea out of hand.

Multinational fuel-cycle centers

The second possible means of developing reprocessing capabilities in a benign mode was more appealing and, perhaps, more practical. Few had enough faith in safeguards to consider national reprocessing susceptible to innoculation against the proliferation virus. Instead, the emphasis was placed on multinational fuel-cycle centers. A U.S. inspiration, and initiative, the notion of building and operating reprocessing facilities on some genuinely international basis was an item high on the agenda of non-proliferation strategists from the moment it was broached publicly by Secretary Kissinger. He launched the concept in the full limelight of the United Nations General Assembly. Instructing his audience that "the greatest single danger of unrestrained nuclear proliferation resides in the spread under national control of reprocessing facilities for the atomic materials in nuclear power plants," he proposed – "as a major step to reinforce all other measures – the establishment of multinational regional nuclear fuel cycle centers."[40]

The nebulousness of Kissinger's proposal (as well as the absence of even preliminary estimates of the multiple technical, institutional, and financial requirement for its realization) reflected the quick, decidedly informal preparation of the speech, as well as the idea's inescapable complexities. The promoter of the multinational idea was Jerry Kahan, the official in State's Planning Office who was heading the NSSM 202 review of U.S. non-proliferation policy. Taking up the idea that had been bouncing around AEC and IAEA (and that was a favorite of legal analysts sympathetic to world organization), he brought it directly to Kissinger. It was presented as the last hope for imposing a measure of control on what then seemed the inevitable spread of reprocessing technology. The secretary was ready to try panaceas. His past neglect of the proliferation issue and his disparagement of its dangers made him vulnerable to criticism and eager to find a way to put the brakes on the runaway market in sensitive nuclear technologies. A recent convert to the non-proliferation faith, he perhaps was too inclined to reach for quick fixes. Certainly a bold move to cut through the dense underbrush of NPT legalisms and intragovernmental wrangling appealed to his self-image as the "Lone Ranger" of international diplomacy. Before making his public overture at the United Nations, Kissinger did prudently lay the proposal for multinational centers before the London Suppliers' Club. It was received unenthusiastically. Polite noises were made about its virtues, and pledges to study it further were duly offered. (A few members, the United Kingdom in particular, were decidedly unhappy with the plan, viewing it as wholly unworkable – and perhaps a commercial threat to Britain's Windscale reprocessing plant.) The Suppliers were not ready to back multinational facilities and to make them the cornerstone of a joint approach to the plutonium issue.

In Washington, feelings toward the proposal were mixed. Because it had not been "staffed out," officials in ERDA and ACDA naturally were irked that they had not been given a chance to review and critique the scheme. On closer inspection, each agency saw some merits and numerous complications – not necessarily the same ones. ERDA came to view the idea in a sympathetic light because multinational arrangements held out the hope of salvaging reprocessing, whose fate had been put in doubt by the vigorous campaign of the ardent antiproliferationists. Indeed, an international arrangement would carry the seal of IAEA approval. On the debit side, such an arrangement threatened to remove ERDA's jurisdiction, or at least to attenuate its regulatory control, over the facility being built at Barnwell, South Carolina, and others planned elsewhere.[41] ACDA's initial reaction was to fix on the plan's provision for waste management. The accumulation of spent fuel was both a source of fissile materials and an encouragement to reprocessing. If an economical, safe way could be found to relieve states of their nuclear wastes, it would be a plus for non-proliferation. When the agency realized, though, that multinational centers could not be created without the presumption of reprocessing, it quickly cooled to the idea, as worried as ever over the growing availability of plutonium under whatever format.

Active interest in regional centers soon petered out. Responsibility for examining alternative arrangements, and for spelling out their requirements, was handed to the IAEA. The multinational idea would remain politically dormant until interest was rekindled five years later in the wake of the international review inspired by the Carter administration.

The incentive structure

The unrewarded search for a definite answer to the plutonium threat left non-proliferation policy makers in a quandary. Outright denial of reprocessing technology was ruled out by the unaccommodating stand of other suppliers. Besides, it would be politically costly to try forcing a reprocessing embargo down the throats of technology-dependent states while the nuclear-proficient states, the United States included, were going ahead with their own plans for commercial development. As for multinational approaches, they faced too many hurdles and were too ambiguous in overall effect to warrant full support and a diplomatic campaign in their behalf – at least for the time being. So if reprocessing technology could not be rendered benign through institutional innovation, and if an absolute denial of access was out of the question, attention had to concentrate on the existing incentive structure for acquiring and operating reprocessing plants.

Prevailing attitudes toward reprocessing were of U.S. origin. Unwittingly, the U.S. government had nurtured a view of the nuclear fuel cycle that provided other countries with reasonable grounds for entering into areas of civilian nuclear power that had unavoidable military implications. At the worst, those states harboring an ulterior interest in weapons acquisition could use civilian facilities as a screen for gaining access to plutonium on acceptable grounds. South Korea, Taiwan, and Pakistan were three countries who had been quick to see technical and economic virtues in the recycling of plutonium fuels. At the best, states debating whether to develop nuclear weapons might be influenced by having at their disposal the wherewithal for bomb manufacture. It followed that by changing its own attitude toward the commercialization of reprocessing (and perhaps, by example, changing that of other Western governments), the United States might reverse the process and undermine the credibility of reprocessing.

THE AGONIZING REAPPRAISAL

The possibilities inherent in reconsideration of commercial reprocessing were not recognized suddenly. The intellectual connection between domestic policies toward plutonium and the growing proliferation danger was itself made only slowly and grudgingly. Subordination of internal needs and programs to non-proliferation objectives was a turnabout that would take a year of wrenching self-examination and political changes at the top of the U.S. government. In early 1976 only a relatively few people clearly saw the link. Even fewer were prepared to follow the chain of analysis to its logical conclusion: a moratorium on domestic reprocessing.

Victor Gilinsky, who, backed by some NRC staffers, was using his position on the commission to try to move the government toward reconsidering its commitment to the Barnwell reprocessing facility (which would be the first commercial plant in the U.S.), was one who was prepared to deal with the consequences. Another was Albert Wohlstetter, the prominent and influential strategic analyst. As a special consultant to ACDA's director, Fred Ikle, Wohlstetter devoted his impressive energies and talents (in conjunction with those of colleagues at his Pan Heuristics consulting firm) to fashioning a powerful case against reprocessing, on grounds of economic impracticality as well as those of proliferation risk.[42] The ammunition he provided to the agency could do little to raise it from the bureaucratic limbo into which it had been cast by its own internal dissension and the hostility of Henry Kissinger. But his views circulated widely. Coming as they did from a certified hard-nosed hawk on national security matters, they could reinforce the steadily growing ranks of those who saw necessity and wisdom pointing the United States toward a drastic reevaluation of its commitment to plutonium as a critical element in its national energy strategy.

The Fri Review

The instrument for a root-and-branch reassessment of plutonium reprocessing was an interagency study led by ERDA Deputy Director Robert Fri. For a study that was destined to prepare the ground for a radical reversal of a generation's thinking on nuclear power and proliferation, the Fri Review had a humble beginning. It was initiated in the early spring of 1976 by a letter from Robert Seamans (director of ERDA) to the White House, drafted after consultation with Nelson Sievering, the agency's administrator for international affairs. The letter carried the message that the U.S. government had no coherent policy concerning the domestic and international sides of nuclear energy policy. Seamans voiced concern that people were driving to foreign objectives without due regard for getting the internal program in line with them. He recommended taking steps to get officials together to sort matters out.

The ERDA officials had more than good government on their minds, although Sievering undoubtedly was honestly worried about the penalties of policy disjuncture. The agency was growing anxious about the financially troubled Barnwell project. A salvage operation was in order. Calling attention to the project's mounting costs, the result in large part of shifting regulatory standards, the ERDA communication raised the idea of transforming the facility into an international demonstration plant, one that might usefully serve as a yardstick for examining costs and the performance questions that lingered about commercial reprocessing. Not only would the answers clarify prospects for plutonium recycling, it was suggested; they also might influence the design of any multinational facility. In this expediential way was the tie made between domestic energy and proliferation worries about reprocessing. Conceived as a device for mustering governmental backing for Barnwell, the study in the end would put in doubt the entire U.S. reprocessing program.

The immediate reaction was lukewarm. Secretary Kissinger responded taciturnly that he agreed that a higher measure of policy coordination was needed, and that the matter was being taken in hand. In fact, the reprocessing question was not getting the systematic review it deserved. And the parlous state of the Barnwell program, like the proliferation concerns, was demanding high-level attention. Barnwell's difficulties were substantial. Organized and financed by a consortium of private corporations, Allied General Nuclear Services, it was planned on a grand scale to fill the backend of the fuel cycle for domestic utilities. The principal partners – Gulf, Allied Chemical, and Westinghouse – divided responsibility for the four segments of the multistaged, multibillion dollar facility: chemical separation, the production of plutonium in oxide form, its fabrication into fuel assemblies mixing plutonium and uranium rods (for charging light-water reactors), and the building of waste facilities for handling the final waste stream. Completion of the plant suffered delays caused principally by problems with its ancillary waste technology. Although it was originally slated to begin operations in 1975, Barnwell's opening, as of spring 1976, had been pushed ahead to 1978. The slippage aggravated a spiraling increase in cost estimates; they rose by a factor of ten over the original estimates of seventy million dollars. Unforeseen technical problems and heavy cost overruns were in keeping with the experience of nearly every major civilian nuclear project. Barnwell's situation was exceptional in two respects: More aggressive NRC licensing caught up with the project, forcing further delay; and the growing economic, technical, and finally legal uncertainties besetting the project spurred ERDA to ask the White House for aid, inadvertently providing occasion for a hard second look at the country's commitment to reprocessing.

The Nuclear Regulatory Commission had begun its own review of Barnwell in early 1976, in accordance with its statutory responsibility for supervising the nuclear power industry to assure compliance with health standards and safety requirements. In the charged atmosphere that surrounded all licensing procedures, and given the landmark nature of the Barnwell action, the NRC review could not readily be insulated from the political debate. The commission conducted a comprehensive analysis, bearing the unfelicitous title *Final Generic Environmental Statement on the Use of Recycled Plutonium in Mixed Oxide Fuel in Light-Water Cooled Reactors* – GESMO for short.[43] The first segment of the compendious report was issued in August. It dealt mainly with technical matters of performance standards and reliability affecting safety and health, and was supplemented by an assessment of the comparative costs of plutonium recycling and low-enriched uranium fuels.

Although the staff analysts who prepared the report cautiously steered clear of the proliferation issue, supporters of Barnwell were genuinely concerned that the commissioners themselves would be less restrained. The experience of NRC activism on export licensing aroused suspicions that the commission might assume the discretionary power to incorporate evaluations of Barnwell's international impact into their nominally domestic licensing evaluation. Indeed, some activists were so inclined. (The outlook for Barnwell was further clouded in May when the federal Second Circuit Court, acting in response to a private suit, enjoined the NRC from licensing the use of mixed oxide fuels pending completion of the GESMO in all its aspects, now including a lengthy hearing process.) Seamans understandably found enough reason for worry to cause him to address his letter to the president. Appended to his recommendation for federal assistance to Barnwell as an international test project was the immodest suggestion that the White House consider protecting Barnwell against unwarranted NRC assault by shielding it behind a presidential claim of overriding national security interest.

By 1976 the NRC assessment of Barnwell was so heavily laden with proliferation implications that the eventual judgment could not fail to reverberate internationally, even were the decision to be limited strictly to questions of health and safety. Succinctly put by the Committee for Economic Development study group, "A 'go' decision by NRC would be a strong signal to the rest of the world that plutonium recycling was a part of the nuclear future. A negative decision would slow and discourage the development of the plutonium economy."[44] Yet the full consequences of Barnwell's fate were not immediately apparent at the time of the Seamans letter, either to its author or to those White House officials who read it. They readily passed it along to Secretary Kissinger for his predictably noncommittal response. The matter of a general review, focusing on the Barnwell question, was raised again at a luncheon meeting between Seamans and James Connor, now secretary to the cabinet, who had returned to the White House after his tour at AEC (ERDA), where he had served as custodian of the administration's privatization strategy. Their talk was held, not entirely by coincidence, in May, some days after Jimmy Carter had given a much-publicized address on the dangers of nuclear proliferation. An independent approach to the White House had been made through

Elliott Richardson, who headed the moribund Energy Resources Council in his capacity as secretary of commerce. Richardson used his good offices to bring the subject to the attention of the president's Domestic Council. Two persons there were unusually conversant with nuclear issues. One was Connor. Having personally experienced the enrichment-contracts crisis and the legislated restructuring of the now bifurcated Atomic Energy Commission, he was knowledgeable about nuclear policy and politics. Connor could appreciate the fact that only a centrally directed study could hope to get at the problem's several intersecting pieces. He could appreciate, too, the possible political consequences of leaving the political running to candidate Carter. The other experienced council staffer, who would become instrumental in organizing the review and who wound up riding herd over the final drafting, was Glenn Schleede. A former AEC official and a six-year veteran of the OMB, where he was one of the watchdogs over the funding of the government's nuclear program, Schleede too was at home in the special world of nuclear policy making. Connor and Schleede were themselves toying with the idea of a full-scale policy study of the reprocessing question.[45]

When the Seamans initiative converged on Connor and Schleede via two channels, it found fertile soil. In early 1976, the White House was besieged on all sides by nuclear energy issues. The administration simultaneously was fighting an uphill battle for its privatization bill; resisting the efforts of Senator Ribicoff and his brethren on the Hill to put exports in a licensing straitjacket (and to do even worse things to allies who did not go along with an U.S.-led embargo on fuel-producing facilities); being frustrated by an independent-minded NRC in its unavailing effort to restore the image of the United States as a credible supplier; and, now, facing the prickly question of what do do about Barnwell.

Connor and Schleede by this point had acquired enough wisdom to realize that everything they were doing in the nuclear field was related. It would be pointless, if not counterproductive, to treat the matter of Barnwell's viability separately from export and proliferation issues. Commercial reprocessing should be looked at as another piece of the puzzle. A comprehensive review was clearly called for. How should it be set up? The idea of reconstituting the State-led study group that prepared NSSM 202 was briefly raised and quickly dropped. Hamstrung by an uncooperative AEC, that body never had succeeded in establishing its authority. Wider support was needed. The planning group was broadened to bring in General Scowcroft, by then Kissinger's successor as national security advisor, and OMB head James P. Lynn. Together, Connor, Scowcroft, and Lynn drafted a memo to Ford urging him to establish a high-powered interagency body to review the nation's nuclear energy policy, with particular regard to proliferation. OMB would have been pleased to serve as lead agency, and proposed its associate director, James Mitchell, as chairman of the study group. Connor and Scowcroft were less than happy at having the group's deliberations dominated by what they saw as OMB's cost-accounting outlook. They successfully countered by supporting Robert Fri, ERDA deputy director; Fri was strongly recommended by James Schlesinger (who, by then serving as secretary of defense, played an informal role as adviser to former staffers on nuclear energy matters) and was highly regarded for his intellectual independence and capacity.

The Fri Review involved the entire alphabet of the nuclear bureaucracy: ERDA, NRC, ACDA, OES, SP, PM, the Undersecretary's Office in State, OMB, NSC, and even the Defense Department, newly awakened to its stake in weapons proliferation. By all accounts it was a wrenching experience. The study was one of the few on recent historical record that did not strain toward premature conclusions, exhibit an unbecoming willingness to accept prevailing beliefs as established facts, or accept flaccid consensus as evidence of mission accomplished. For the old nuclear hands at ERDA it was a thoroughly disagreeable affair. It could not be otherwise. For the creation of a powerful interagency study group that escaped their direction, whose terms of reference were set in the White House, meant they had lost control over nuclear policy. Two years earlier the AEC, without any political consultation whatsoever, could announce the termination of contracts for enrichment services with profoundly damaging effects on the United States' international position. The agency now was obliged to participate, among equals, in what amounted to critical examination of the principles and purposes on which the nuclear establishment's authority had been grounded, and according to which it had set national policy.

Although it was clear from the outset that the odds were against ERDA's nuclear offices preserving their bureaucratic territory intact, the hard-line defenders of the status quo on the two key issues under review, reprocessing and export regulations, did not give up without a fight. Basically, their strategy followed the time-honored practice of organizations on the defensive: retrenchment, or "stonewalling," as it had come to be known in more political circles. Asked what to do about the spread of sensitive technologies, or whether the domestic reprocessing program gave undue and premature credibility to the case for early introduction of plutonium, ERDA's unsmiling response was to deny that a problem existed: If there was no problem, there was hence no solution to be sought, no need to respond to calls for an overhaul of U.S. nuclear policies.

It was a strategy that could work only if launched from a position of overwhelming strength. The distribution of power in Fri's group, however, did not concede predominant authority to the agency. The White House made it clear that no predefinition of issues or preemptory vetoes were to be permitted. With Secretary Kissinger's backing, the State Department was now a far more formidable bureaucratic protagonist than it had been at the time of Ingersoll's and Sisco's frantic interventions in June 1974.

Moreover, Robert Fri as chairman was personally committed to a fair and incisive review of the issues at hand, unbiased by organizational interests. His position as deputy director of ERDA notwithstanding, Fri was not closely associated with the agency's old AEC operating divisions or inclined to run interference for them. By all accounts, he performed ably in directing his bureaucratically polyglot task force in a conscientious and intellectually disciplined exercise. The ERDA contingent participating in the review was itself indicative of the changing times. The most prominent role was played by the office of the administrator for international affairs, headed by Nelson Sievering. He was principally supported by Dr. Lawrence Scheinman, a highly regarded academic analyst of international nuclear policy who was serving on leave from Cornell University as head of the International Policy Planning group in Sievering's office. Sievering's office worked closely with Gerard Helfrich and Vance Hudgins in the Division of International Security Affairs, where there were personal and institutional commitments to a deliberate control of nuclear exports, and a sophisticated understanding of the proliferation danger. The active role played by officials in these two offices on the ERDA side did not prevent the more ardent backers of nuclear power elsewhere in ERDA from making a powerful voice heard on all matters affecting the commercial development of civilian nuclear energy at home and abroad. They still managed to make pro-nuclear pressure felt in the working group, favoring reprocessing and opposing tightened export conditions, albeit with less force than on previous occasions.

On State's side, responsibility for coordinating the department's position rested with a "nuclear group" set up by Undersecretary of State Charles Robinson. It brought together a team of antiproliferationist backstoppers: George Vest from Political–Military Affairs (along with Lou Nosenzo and Gerald Oplinger); Jerome Kahan and Jan Kalicki of the Policy Planning Office; and Myron Kratzer, director of OES (now relieved of the departed Dixy Lee Ray), with the support of Harold Bengelsdorf, formerly of the AEC, who played an important part in drafting the final report. OES was the formal link between State's nuclear group and the Fri working group. The whole operation was monitored for the secretary by Winston Lord, of the Policy Coordinating Staff, who reported directly to Kissinger. It was a large cast; proliferation had become an exciting issue.

State officials were not entirely of one mind. Myron Kratzer, the OES head and former director of AEC's office of International Programs, who had drafted many bilateral agreements in his days at the commission, was especially vocal in opposing the judgment that plutonium was an imminent proliferation danger, virtually unsafeguardable, and requiring a sharp tightening of export standards and a slowdown of the U.S. domestic program. His defense of plutonium recycling, reinforced by the pro-nuclear forces in ERDA, made it difficult for the issue of domestic reprocessing to be addressed frontally. It would be the last question decided. There was, though, strong agreement everywhere in State on the urgent need to restore the United States' position as a reliable supplier. This became the linchpin for the entire State contingent, and in the working group they constantly hammered away at credibility issues.

A number of attitudes followed from the preoccupation with credibility. First, stress was placed on the imperative need to resolve two legislative impasses: (1) that on the president's privatization bill, whose tortuous passage through Congress perpetuated the uncertainty about when the U.S. enrichment capacity would be expanded, the form it would take, and the terms under which it would be available; and (2) the languishing Nuclear Export Bill, whose clouded future left up in the air the issue of export-licensing procedures and terms. Second, the State contingent argued that the latent anxiety of consumers about LEU supply should be tackled head on. On this score, Robinson personally pushed the idea of creating fuel incentives for dependent consumer states who were being asked to forgo reprocessing. In order to make a moratorium on plutonium fuels palatable, he urged that the supplier states, with the United States in the lead, should offer an attractive package of proposals on low-enriched uranium fuels, including price and supply assurances. This package should be accompanied by a pledge of fixed arrangements for storage of burdensome spent fuel. Finally, he argued that the logic of the United States' argument about credibility led to the inescapable conclusion that restrictions on the domestic reprocessing program were absolutely essential to give substance to the U.S. call voiced in the Suppliers' Club, and repeated publicly, for a stop to the transfer of reprocessing technology. At this point, Kratzer parted company with his State Department colleagues. But he was in a decided minority. On the foundation laid down by Robinson, the State contingent made the case for a moratorium on domestic reprocessing.

Each of State's main contentions evoked a critical, often heated, response from the hard-liners in ERDA's nuclear operating divisions. They knew that Barnwell was the target, and fought tenaciously to protect the commitment to reprocessing that was its perimeter defense. Above all, Barnwell, as the symbol of commercial reprocessing, had to be protected. Curtailment of the program, ERDA stressed, would be a body blow to the future of civilian nuclear power in the United States. Moreover, in ERDA's view, it was tangential to the real proliferation threat. On other issues, the ERDA people were only slightly more accommodating. They were prepared to agree in principle on the importance of removing the uncertainty on exports through a streamlining of procedures and a clear stipulation of conditions. Their preferred method for reaching this goal, however, was new legislation that would both limit the NRC's licensing powers and keep out any language referring specifically to full-scope safeguards and a U.S. veto on reprocessing. As to the proposed fuel-assurance and waste-management program, it was deemed impossible to implement it in the light of unpredictable fuel prices, the uncertain future of enrichment plans, and the rudimentary state of storage and disposal facilities, a subject about which ERDA had firsthand knowledge. The ERDA position boiled down to one of tactical flexibility on the comparatively minor questions and unyielding resistance to any measures or policy declarations that might put in doubt the future of commercial reprocessing.

Two other bureaucratic participants weighed in when and where the ERDA–State standoff permitted. ACDA, predictably, supported State's call for a pause in domestic reprocessing (and phrased it with even greater conviction and urgency). The agency also urged acceleration of work on waste storage that might permit a program of repatriation and/or the establishment of multinational facilities. It placed greater stock, as well, in the improvement of IAEA safeguards, which it wished to be a main objective of a reinvigorated non-proliferation strategy.

The Office of Management and Budget's contribution was more narrowly focused. OMB's interventions consisted in reiterating one question, which it appended to each and every proposal under consideration: How much will it cost? Preoccupation with the budgetary impact led OMB to a number of obvious positions. First, the office argued that no commitment should be made on waste management and fuel assurances until the government had a far better idea of technical requirements and their financing than it did in the summer of 1976. Second, OMB emphasized the budgetary constraints on any support program for the exploration of nonnuclear energy sources that might be offered to foreign governments as compensation for temporary loss of the plutonium option. Third, as to Barnwell, OMB resisted the idea of a subvention by the federal government. If the administration felt compelled to offer financial support, for fear of jeopardizing the project's existence, than it was imperative that the Congress relieve the government of an offsetting fiscal burden – namely, public ownership of new enrichment plants – by passing the privatization bill.

Privatization and Barnwell reprocessing

The budgetary link between Barnwell and privatization was fully appreciated at the White House. Connor and Schleede at the Domestic Council were alternately riding herd on the backers of private enrichment in Congress, where they were girding for the final legislative push, and monitoring the progress of Fri's group. For the time being they concentrated their energies on winning the necessary votes to carry privatization. A year earlier, President Ford had made the connection between corporate development of new plant and the United States' position as fuel supplier. In his Uranium Enrichment Message, which introduced his administration's legislative proposals, Ford gave his pledge that the United States would "reopen its uranium enrichment book, reassert its supremacy as the world's major supplier of enriched uranium and develop a strong private enrichment industry." He added that "the government has a responsibility to help insure that these private ventures perform as expected, providing timely and reliable service to both domestic and foreign customers."[46] A year later privatization was still in trouble in Congress. One way to strengthen backing for the administration bill was to make another linkage, that between privatization and progress on the Barnwell reprocessing project, then threatened on financial as much as proliferation grounds.

Early in the fall of 1976, the White House called in the major corporations involved in the nuclear business. Administration officials had been irked by the lukewarm support extended by those elements in the industry that had no direct stake in the enrichment ventures. The point of the meeting was to give them a very simple message: Unless they all got behind privatization, the government could be faced with the burden of financing expansion of publicly owned enrichment facilities, and that development would limit the dollars available for propping up Barnwell and developing the Clinch River breeder demonstration project. The companies with direct stakes in the latter two enterprises (e.g., Gulf and Westinghouse – the latter involved in Barnwell, the Clinch River project, and the private enrichment consortia, to its growing discomfort) got the point. So did other manufacturers of reactor components (GE, Babcock–Wilcox, Garret) and the utilities, many of whom were convinced that the viability of civilian nuclear power, to which they had shackled themselves, depended on finally breaking through the enrichment bottleneck. For these utilities, the administration position looked like the best way to get things moving. But despite the redoubled lobbying efforts spurred by the White House pep talk, privatization would be denied congressional approval at the year's end.

Meanwhile, the Fri task force was making anguished progress in drafting a policy paper. The significance of the White House campaign on enrichment was not immediately apparent. On the surface it might appear that, by underscoring the trade-offs between public financing of Barnwell and the assumption of costs for new publicly owned enrichment plant, the administration was indicating a readiness, under financial constraint, to jettison the former. In fact, in early fall, the White House was still operating on the assumption that development of Barnwell would continue, and that Washington should be in a financial position to aid the project if aid became necessary. The administration certainly used the Barnwell issue expediently to sharpen its pitch to the nuclear industry for more active privatization lobbying. But there is no reason to doubt the conviction of White House officials that the Barnwell project would be kept going, even as a demonstration program, whatever the conclusion reached by the Fri study. Their thinking as of summer and early fall 1976 was that the review did not threaten the administration position on either privatization or Barnwell, and should be given a free rein. Only later did the crucial link between Barnwell and a viable case for non-proliferation become evident. It was then that the White House would be presented with blunt choices and Barnwell put in jeopardy.

The first phase of the struggle in the Fri task force concluded with the drafting of a compendious report forwarded to the White House in early September. The second, more dramatic scene would focus on President Ford's policy statement. The initial document drafted revealed that the major differences among the bureaucratic protagonists had not been resolved. That was not surprising. Oddly, though, they were not papered over in time-honored fashion and hidden behind facile compromises. Instead, the working group produced that most improbable Washington document – an authentic options paper. It was a comprehensive, well-organized report that neatly laid out the proliferation problem in its full dimensions.

Although objective in tone, and neutral on the issues it skillfully presented, the report did represent a victory of the antiproliferation critics of ERDA on two counts. Its cover sheet clearly stated that "our non-proliferation efforts must be viewed within a broader framework of foreign and domestic policy," thereby breaking down the arbitrary distinction between the domestic and international, civilian and military, facets of nuclear energy policy. Moreover, the report offered for consideration the daring proposition that the United States' domestic nuclear program should be guided by non-proliferation considerations.

The report was extensive, including nine annexes and totaling 150 pages. It identified four major international issues facing the president and organized its analysis around them:

1. How can we tighten international controls over the storage of sensitive nuclear material, safeguards or diversion of such material, and physical security to prevent its theft?
2. How firm should be the constraints we apply to our nuclear exports, and what sanctions should be invoked if our agreements are violated?
3. How aggressively should we apply these restraints to existing agreements, and how, if at all, should the nuclear export-licensing process, as contrasted to diplomatic techniques, be employed for this purpose?

4. What alternatives to national reprocessing should the United States offer?

Successive sections discussed each issue in turn and made tentative recommendations. First, with regard to the storage and safeguarding of sensitive materials, the report's principal recommendation was to place excess spent fuel and separated plutonium under IAEA control. At first glance, the report seemed to be calling for a revival of the multinational fuel center idea. In fact, there was no specification of what arrangement the group had in mind. Would storage treatment and reprocessing be conducted under international auspices, or would these activities merely be supervised in some manner by the IAEA? Would the facilities be located in regional centers or on the territory of technically proficient states? What would be the terms of transaction? The report was obscure on all these points. Other sections demonstrated a similar ambiguity. A principle would be enunciated, a direction indicated, but no plan or program detailed. This oblique approach made sense. The review group did not want to foist a fully developed strategy on the president. Rather, the report would express the group's thinking about how to proceed while leaving the design and orchestration of particulars to later decision. This approach also was a convenient way to keep the lid on still simmering disagreements.

In the "Restraints and Sanctions" section dealing with export policies, the report chose a cautious path that (a) cited the need for a clearer and firmer U.S. policy, which would set conditions tighter than those embodied in the Suppliers' Club declaration (the aim was NPT adherence, full-scope safeguards, and a veto over reprocessing), but also (b) recognized that conditions should not be so rigid as to obstruct further agreement with other suppliers and the hammering out of acceptable arrangements tailored to the individual national circumstances of consumers.

On the sticky issue of "Existing Agreements and Export Licensing," the review group faced the problem of retroactive application of the stricter export conditions. Appreciative of both the diplomatic niceties that must be observed and the continuing controversy surrounding the NRC's powers, procedures, and terms of reference, the group advised the president (a) to press for authority to override an NRC finding when it ran counter to his judgment of the U.S. national interest; (b) to prepare a "major diplomatic effort" aimed at upgrading existing agreements to make them accord with current NRC criteria; and (c) to strive at winning the adherence of suppliers and consumers to common standards.

The central question of "Alternatives to Reprocessing" also showed a discernible reluctance to make a clear choice. Here the report's authors were not even able to point a direction. After rejecting a number of approaches as unrealistic, for one reason or another, the paper reportedly drew two possible options for the president: "Contain the spread of reprocessing within acceptable limits, *or* strongly favor no further advances in

reprocessing while attempting to develop technology alternatives to reprocessing that would recover the value of the spent fuel without separating
plutonium." The cost–benefit analyses of each option, which the report
appended, were strictly limited to economic variables. The multiple political factors, domestic and international, were not sifted – a testimony to the
harsh crosswinds that buffeted the study group when the core issue of
plutonium was raised. To accept the second alternative would reverse a
generation of nuclear energy planning that took reprocessing for granted.
It would place the United States in a confrontation with other states, suppliers and consumers, who could not swallow an indefinite moratorium on
plutonium recycling while more benign technologies were studied. And it
would require substantial new research and development investments, not
to mention the cooperation of an aggrieved, and perhaps petulant, nuclear
establishment in government and in industry. Yet to opt for the minimalist
strategy would risk the slow but steady erosion of the technological *cordon
sanitaire* around the proliferation danger.

Clearly, a fuller and more precise estimation of the alternatives was in
order. The choices as outlined did not give the president, in the last weeks
of his administration, a strategy that was diplomatically viable and politically acceptable, even presuming that he was disposed to make a decision
before election day. He was. The Carter challenge on the proliferation issue
combined with the pressure of pending decisions on privatization and
Barnwell left him no choice. The task of shaping a presidential statement
fell to a small group drawn from the Fri participants under the supervision
of Connor and Schleede. Meeting in the middle of October with a preelec-
tion deadline, they soon found themselves in the familiar, but now wholly
uncomfortable, deadlock between ERDA and State.

The grey smoke that announced the unsuccessful conclusion of each
session was observed with increasing irritation at the White House. The
principals were gathered in the neutral territory of Scowcroft's office, where
Connor and Schleede set them to work on writing a presidential statement
on nuclear policy. It was literally a forced draft. The key participants were
Fri, Kahan, Mitchell of OMB, Bengelsdorf of OES, and Chairman Rowden of the NRC. Rowden's role was advisory. As head of an independent
regulatory agency, he had neither the authority nor the legal right to pronounce in the name of the commission or to commit it to any understandings. Rowden, properly restrained, would comment on proposed ideas
only to indicate how they would affect commission deliberations. Ironically, informal conversations during October between drafting group
members and Victor Gilinsky were more substantive. The latter did not
hesitate to tender his advice, albeit in a nonofficial capacity.

The sticking point was still plutonium. It was unstuck by the intervention of the Domestic Council staffers, particularly Schleede. His approach

was straightforward and wholly pragmatic. It became clear to him, as it had to others earlier, that there could be no credible strategy aimed at restricting the development of commerce in plutonium as long as the United States pushed ahead with its own reprocessing program. Weighting the proliferation factor more heavily than in earlier decisions, he asked if the energy value of proceeding with Barnwell were so great as to overwhelm the proliferation factor. If not, then his reaction was, "Let's hold on reprocessing." The conclusion of the Fri study clearly was ambiguous about the economic cost-effectiveness of Barnwell. If there were no irresistible case to be made on economic and technical grounds, Schleede believed that the president should be urged to slow the move to reprocessing, and thereby clear the stage for a deliberate review of alternatives.

The Ford statement

A proposed draft, incorporating the recommended postponement of Barnwell, was sent by courier to the president, who was on the campaign hustings in the Midwest. On October 28, the week before election day, Ford issued a seven-thousand-word statement that was the most extensive and detailed review of nuclear policy made by a U.S. president (see Appendix D).[47] The political setting could hardly be ignored. Yet the process of the statement's formulation was decidedly apolitical, involving mainly nonpartisan bureaucrats. Proliferation had been made an election issue by Jimmy Carter. Voicing his personal concern about nuclear power's proliferation risk, with the encouragement of academic advisors,[48] Carter had made his major policy speech on proliferation on May 13.[49] He pointed with alarm to the proliferation dangers inherent in the country's commercial approach to civilian nuclear power, especially reprocessing. In September, in a speech in San Diego, he staked out a position against reprocessing, promising that, as president, he would "seek to withhold authority for domestic reprocessing until the need for the economics, and the safety of this technology is clearly demonstrated."[50]

Cause and effect are not overly easy to establish, but the May address is widely interpreted as being the catalyst to the Fri Review, and the September speech as a prod to placing a moratorium on reprocessing. Undoubtedly, they were an encouragement to the actions taken. The Ford administration, however, did not need a political fire set under it to feel the need for a strategic rethinking of proliferation policy. It was being singed daily by the flames crackling inside the executive, not to mention the friction with Congress and the NRC. Carter's move to stake out the nuclear issue as his political territory may have fanned the flames, but cannot be accorded the honor of instigating the train of events we have just described or assuring its outcome.

The final drafting of the message had been overseen by policy people in Washington, the Domestic Council officials. The president's traveling staff and immediate political advisers were largely ignorant of its contents. It was the White House staffers who briefed Ford on the final version before its release. The candidate did want a statement. He wanted one that would deny his opponent the advantage of identification with non-proliferation. And it helped to be able to announce in Ohio that four thousand jobs would be saved by expansion of the Portsmouth enrichment facility alone (the Oak Ridge facility would also be preserved). Whatever the statement's political meaning, the Fri Review would have been an unusually cumbersome and politically undirected process for coming up with a campaign gesture, one that had as little potential to shift voter loyalties as did plutonium reprocessing in 1976.

The strongest and most overt political pressure was exerted by the nuclear industry. It came in support of Barnwell. On the eve of Ford's speech, officials of the Atomic Industrial Forum (AIF), and key corporations, got wind of the flavor that was being imparted to the president's message. Most probably, they had been tipped off by friends in the government who were themselves unsympathetic to the turn of events. The reaction was one of acute distress and outrage. Industry scented the development of an end-of-nuclear-power-as-we-know-it-now scenario. Under the leadership of the AIF's executive director, John Simpson, a former high executive at the Westinghouse Corporation, a barrage of calls and telegrams was directed at the White House. In the absence of its chief occupant, they were received by aides and Domestic Council staffers. The well-orchestrated campaign culminated in a call from Republican Governor James B. Edwards of South Carolina, who warned that Ford would lose the state if he came out against Barnwell, a project promising jobs and tax revenue. The sharpness and intensity of the attack led to a White House meeting on the morning of October 29 with a contingent of AIF and corporate people. Their unrestrained opposition to the thrust of the prepared presidential statement, with its substantive views on reprocessing, was duly registered. But it was too late in the day to change minds or to force changes in the speech. Ford did lose South Carolina, but also lost most other southern states – with or without unfinished reprocessing facilities on their soil.

Ford's statement was remarkable in two respects. It expressly recognized for the first time the international implications of a domestic action in the nuclear energy field; and it declared that commercial considerations would not dominate export policy. The danger of plutonium and the dilemma of reprocessing were the theme of the message. Rooting the problem in plutonium's dual nature as a key element in the fuel cycle and a material for making nuclear explosives, it affirmed that "the world community cannot afford to let potential nuclear weapons material or the technology to produce it proliferate uncontrolled over the globe." What should be done? The president saw as the only avenue of approach that could be successfully pursued in the long run "an international cooperative effort . . . including both nuclear suppliers and customers." In moving to create new cooperative arrangements, "we must recognize that some nations look to nuclear energy because they have no acceptable energy alternative." New initiatives were therefore in order. Above all, "reprocessing and recycling of plutonium should not proceed unless there is sound reason to conclude that the world community can effectively overcome the associated risks of proliferation." Accordingly, the "United States should no longer regard reprocessing of used nuclear fuel to produce plutonium as a necessary and inevitable step in the nuclear fuel cycle . . . We must ensure that our domestic policies and programs are compatible with our international position on reprocessing."

In support of this new policy, President Ford's statement called for a number of complementary actions:

1. A redoubled diplomatic effort to persuade other nations to join the United States "in exercising maximum restraint" in the transfer of sensitive technologies
2. Exploration with other nations of arrangements for coordinating fuel services in order to develop other means of ensuring that suppliers would be able to offer, and consumers would be able to receive, an uninterrupted and economical supply of low-enriched uranium fuel and fuel services
3. Steps to assure the existence of facilities for the long-term storage or disposal of nuclear wastes, with repurchase of spent fuel in exchange for LEU as one possible option
4. Initiation of discussions aimed at the "establishment of a new international regime to provide for storage of civil plutonium and spent reactor fuel"
5. Creation of a new program "to define a reprocessing and recycle evaluation program consistent with meeting our international objectives"[51]

The objectives were daunting in number and nature: the reinforcement of international export controls, an elaborate fuel-assurance program, an international regime to control nuclear waste and plutonium, and the origination of recycling techniques that would exorcise the proliferation genie. It was a formidable, even awe-inspiring, undertaking that the Ford administration had set itself. A week later, it was relieved of the responsibility by the U.S. electorate. The chore would now be passed to nuclear engineer Jimmy Carter.

4

Making the Carter nuclear policy

FOR each presidential administration, it is said, the world is born anew on Inauguration Day. This conceit usually is short-lived, abandoned under the weight of political inheritance and the pressures of an unaccommodating environment (although it does have a disconcerting tendency to reappear selectively in the self-congratulatory memories of public men who strain to stake a claim to innovation and imagination). Non-proliferation was celebrated as one of the Carter presidency's boldest and most venturesome foreign policy initiatives. Jimmy Carter's active efforts to stem the spread of nuclear materials with weapons potential have received due recognition as the first concerted attempt to give proliferation concerns their proper weight in the structuring of international civilian nuclear power. His campaign to keep plutonium out of commercial channels instigated an international debate, at times both acrimonious and agonized, that continues to engage the minds and consciences of political leaders and technical experts worldwide. Four years later, the outcome remains in doubt, and prospects for proliferation of nuclear weapons are unclear. One achievement of the Carter administration, though, is undeniable. No longer is it possible to ignore the intimate tie between the civilian and military applications of atomic power.

Still, the Ford administration had made a critical breakthrough, in attitude if not policies. Two crucial milestones were passed when Gerald Ford accepted the Fri Review's recommendations in October. The international implications of U.S. decisions on nominally domestic questions of nuclear power were frankly recognized; and commercial arrangements were subordinated to an overriding antiproliferation interest, and no longer permitted to be the controlling element in the global exchange of nuclear technologies and skills. Those judgments were the essential precondition to any reorientation of nuclear policy. Ford's October 28 statement spotlighted the choices to be made, and pointed the national interest in a new direction. It fell short, however, of actually making the critical decisions: about domestic reprocessing, about the stringency of export conditions, about nuclear fuel assurances, and about the strategies for winning international backing for a set of comprehensive new policies. That responsibility fell to the incoming Carter administration.

Three issues were of paramount importance. First, should the United States commit itself to an indefinite postponement of plans for commercial separation of plutonium, and its recycling through LWRs, in order to buttress a campaign for a worldwide moratorium on the fabrication and utilization of plutonium fuels? Second, what diplomatic priority should be accorded non-proliferation objectives, and how much political capital should the United States be prepared to invest in pursuit of that goal? Finally, what commitments should the United States undertake to satisfy the legitimate energy interests of fuel-dependent customers?

These were the questions with which the newfound proliferation community inside and outside government was wrestling during the election year of 1976. Candidate Carter had been introduced to the complexities and passions of the unfolding debate early on. Drawn to the subject of nuclear energy by his own experience as an officer, and studious engineer, in Admiral Rickover's nuclear navy, he had become conversant with the reemergent proliferation problem at the seminars of the Trilateral Commission. Deeper appreciation of its significance, and understanding of its several dimensions, was provided by academic supporters of his bid for the presidency with whom he established regular contact in late 1975 and early 1976. Among them were Richard N. Gardner, professor of international law at the Columbia University Law School, and Abraham Chayes, professor at Harvard Law School and counsel to the State Department in the Kennedy days. Both of them felt strongly about the needs for more strenuous non-proliferation policies. They introduced the concerned candidate to specialists actively involved in examining the technical and political aspects of the nuclear energy dilemma. Albert Carnesale, a nuclear engineer and arms control specialist who was associate director of the Program on Science and International Affairs at Harvard University, and John Palfrey, a colleague of Gardner's at Columbia and a former AEC commissioner who had participated in drafting the NPT, were the main tutors. They, along with Chayes, were the authors of Jimmy Carter's address on nuclear policy delivered at the United Nations in May 1976, which brought the proliferation issue into the presidential campaign. This address also foreshadowed the stress that President Carter would place on halting the spread of dangerous nuclear technologies.

The speech made four principal points:

1. The United States should face up to the risks and problems associated with the growth of civilian nuclear power.

Until outstanding problems were resolved, and anxieties eased, "U.S. dependence on nuclear power should be kept to the minimum necessary to meet our needs."

2.   There was a "fearsome prospect" that the spread of nuclear reactors would mean the spread of nuclear weapons, primarily because of the likelihood that plutonium would enter into commercial use.

3.   Collective international action should be undertaken to limit reliance on nuclear energy, to meet the undeniable energy needs of all countries, and to modify the characteristics of existing facilities for generating nuclear power and arrangements for its transfer – in order "to make the spread of peaceful nuclear power less dangerous."

4.   It was essential to halt the sale of reprocessing and enrichment plants. Supplier countries should join in "a voluntary moratorium" on the transfer of such facilities – one that should apply to the recently completed agreements with Brazil and Pakistan.[1]

The scope of the address, and its evident mastery of its subject, testified to the contributions of Carter's expert advisers, as well as his personal interest and conviction. His association with the concerned academics would grow closer, and his belief in the importance of a reinvigorated antiproliferation campaign fortified, over the course of the election year. The Ford/Mitre study was the tie that bound the advisers and the candidate intellectually. In the new administration it would bind them politically.

THE FORD/MITRE STUDY

The Ford/Mitre study entitled *Nuclear Power Issues and Choices* has often been cited as the administration's "Bible" on all matters nuclear.[2] If the scriptural metaphor is meant to connote a transcription of revealed truth and guide to correct behavior, it has some validity. But if there is a further suggestion of blind faith in observing the strictures of a sacred text, it fails to do justice either to the authors' intellectual discipline in avoiding oversimplification and pat formulas or to the conscientious deliberations of the Carter government (not to speak of its internal strains). There is no gainsaying, however, the marked influence exercised by the ideas and judgments contained in the report. It would be odd if its influence had not been pronounced. Numbered among members of the study group that prepared the report were several persons who would take up important posts in the administration: Joseph S. Nye, who, as special deputy to the undersecretary for security assistance, science, and technology, headed the office that had primary direction of the early attempt to design the U.S. strategy, and who represented this strategy diplomatically; Spurgeon M. Keeny, Jr., appointed as deputy director of ACDA; Harold Brown, secretary of defense; Albert Carnesale, U.S. representative to the Technical Coordinating Committee of the International Fuel Cycle Evaluation; and Philip J. Farley, chief deputy to Ambassador Gerald Smith (Smith, as the president's special representative for non-proliferation affairs, had overall responsibility for conducting the delicate diplomacy needed to gain foreign government support for the International Fuel Cycle Evaluation launched in late 1977, and later for the legislatively decreed revision of agreements of cooperation).

The report was a closely reasoned, comprehensive review that fulfilled its stated purpose of exposing to critical scrutiny the issues underlying the nuclear power debate. It set out to inquire into the current state of affairs, with a particular concern for determining how the subject's several segments were related and how nuclear power fit with broader national policy objectives, domestic and international. The group took as its point of departure the uncomfortable fact that imminent decisions were pending (on reprocessing at Barnwell, on breeder-reactor development), even though many controversial questions had been "treated complacently by the government."[3] In asking whether the pressures for immediate action generated by compelling energy needs permitted sober evaluation and reflection, the study concluded that there indeed was time "to assess carefully the potential risks as well as the benefits of nuclear power and to avoid hasty and uncritical decisions."[4] The most serious of those risks was opening access to weapons-grade materials. Widespread use of plutonium fuels posed the greatest danger. Their availability would dramatically shorten the lead time for developing a weapons capability. Equally worrisome, ready access to plutonium might tempt a security-anxious government to take up the nuclear option simply because of the ease and quickness with which rudimentary weapons could be manufactured. The study group stressed that plutonium separation was therefore "the basic point of connection between nuclear power and nuclear weapons capabilities"[5] (a judgment being reached independently and simultaneously by the Fri Review).

The critical position of plutonium in the proliferation equation meant that there was no way to avoid joining the issue between domestic energy programs and a policy aimed at preventing proliferation. For the separation of plutonium had been viewed as a key step in plans to extend the life of existing nuclear fuel resources, and as even more important to the development of breeder reactors.

On the surface, at least, non-proliferation and energy independence were contending policy goals in a zero-sum game. But the Ford/Mitre group made the argument that the prevailing assumptions about the time frame for expanding nuclear power, and the demand for developing new technologies, had not been carefully scrutinized. They pointed to large areas of uncertainty: the availability of nuclear fuels, the technical and financial costs and benefits of plutonium recycling, and the long-term projections of power demand. Even less attention had been paid to alternative fuel-cycle arrangements, whose technological and institutional characteristics might appear more or less attractive when viewed from a non-proliferation vantage point. The authors of the Ford/Mitre report stressed that it was not possible to make the value trade-offs that go into a policy decision, or even to state them fairly and accurately, without a far more rigorous examination of all relevant considerations than had as yet been performed – inside or outside government.

A major purpose of this review, then, was to estimate with greater precision than had been achieved previously the advantages, costs, and shortcomings of plutonium recycling – in the context of both the overall nuclear energy situation and larger security concerns. The authors of the study also took pains to indicate relevant time frames for performing the multiple assessments. The object of the exercise was to make some reasonable judgments about how economic and energy security values stacked up against the political and security value of non-proliferation. Some of the factors entering into an evaluation of the case for plutonium recycling were matters susceptible to objective calculation: the supply outlook for natural uranium (and enrichment capacity) for the LEU fuel needed to meet prospective increases in LWR demand; the projected economic cost of recycling compared to LEU fuel fabrication and spent-fuel storage; the technical feasibility, costs, and time horizon for commercialization of the light-metal fast-breeder reactor (LMFBR), and its requirements for plutonium as start-up fuel. Getting a sense of the answers to these questions was essential if the United States, preferably in cooperation with other principal suppliers, was to convince technology-dependent and fuel-dependent countries that "there are no significant economic penalties in deferring" reprocessing and breeder technologies.[6]

Drawing on its considerable collective expertise, the study group conducted just such a systematic cost–benefit review. Although indicating that many estimates were invariably soft, and that there were some unpredictable elements, the group could state unequivocally that "there is no compelling reason at this time to introduce plutonium or to anticipate its introduction in this century."[7] On the crucial matter of uranium reserves, it contradicted the commonly held view that reserves of low-priced uranium would be exhausted before the end of the century. The authors interpreted the evidence as indicating "that all predicted demand levels for LWRs could be accommodated with a reasonable expansion of present reserves at prices not exceeding $40/lb. (1975 dollars) for the balance of this century."[8] To appreciate how radical a departure from accepted belief this judgment was, one need go no further than the 1975 report of an Aspen conference on non-proliferation, attended by some of the Ford/Mitre group, which predicated that "without plutonium recycle, we may see the end of the sale of light water reactors within the next decade," for want of fuel.[9]

With regard to *the economics of plutonium recycling* in current LWR reactors, the Ford/Mitre panel estimated that recovery of plutonium and by-product uranium would "only reduce uranium fuel requirements by some 20%," and, at best, lower the cost of electricity in the latter part of the century by 1 or 2 percent.[10] As to the key question of *the future of breeder reactors*, the report's analysis determined that "the time when breeders may be economically competitive is sufficiently distant that present value of establishing plutonium is not economically justified for many years."[11] The implication for the U.S. breeder program was that early commercialization should be deemphasized, because not only was there no pressing need for its development but the "ultimate success of the breeder might even be compromised by telescoping development stages to meet an early deadline, freezing technology prematurely."[12] This last assessment suggested a postponement of the Clinch River project to build a breeder demonstration plant.

This set of calculations and assessments about nuclear power needs and opportunites made the case for a deliberate slowdown in reprocessing and breeder programs. They went even further in questioning whether the future shape of nuclear power should rest on the assumption that the uranium–plutonium cycle represented the most appropriate and only feasible technological base. By casting doubts on the practical gains from plutonium recycling, the report's authors were engaging in nuclear heresy. Their views ran straight against the grain of deeply held beliefs within the atomic energy establishments of government and private industry around the world. The U.S. industry, the pacesetter in the commercialization of nuclear energy, had acted in the conviction that reprocessing would begin when were sufficient light-water reactors to justify the large-scale facilities needed for economic operation, and that plutonium would be recycled in light-water reactors until fast-breeder reactors were introduced. The widespread expectation of and faith in plutonium recycling had been given concrete expression in the plans and programs of other countries (some of whom had far greater incentive than the United States to search out new energy sources). Those policies would not be readily modified, nor would the attitudes that underlay them bend easily to friendly persuasion from the United States.

Nonetheless, what the United States did about plutonium could be expected to have a bearing on decisions elsewhere, if not on the determining of them. As the Ford/Mitre people reasoned, were "the United States to proceed with plutonium reprocessing and recycle . . . (it) would probably ensure worldwide movement to incorporate plutonium in the fuel cycle."[13] Conversely, a U.S. government commitment to deferral would be essential to credit an official campaign to slow the trend toward reprocessing, even if there could be no assurance of emulation elsewhere. Lacking the power to set the course of international nuclear power unilaterally, the United States still retained an appreciable influence over visualizations of alternative nuclear futures. Subjective perceptions, images, and expectations count as much as hard logic. Pervasive beliefs about the inevitability of reprocessing were formed of largely uncritical economic and technical judgments. To brake the momentum driving toward plutonium recycling, these core ideas had to be changed. The strategy for doing so, advocated in the experts' report, and adopted later by the Carter administration, was two-pronged: (1) attack the old catechism with a forthright statement of contrary facts about the economic and technical realities of reprocessing, presented against the ominous background of a mounting proliferation danger, while (2) nurturing a new conception of civilian nuclear power's future that would permit modulated development of new technologies and fuel sources in a more stable, unthreatening setting.

Anything but political neophytes, the study group's members recognized that a U.S.-led and organized antiproliferation strategy would be singularly demanding – of political imagination, of technical ingenuity, and of Washington's diplomatic talent for blending into unison the several strains of a complex policy. They also saw the importance of achieving a higher level of internal governmental cohesion and collaboration with Congress than had been the norm under conditions of divided authority for energy matters and of strained legislative–executive relations.

The Carter administration's non-proliferation policy did follow closely the guideposts set down in the Ford/Mitre report. But it was less than entirely successful in meeting the postulated requirements for the policy's design and successful execution.

THE POLICY MAKERS

Like many of his administration's foreign policy initiatives, President Carter's approach to nuclear proliferation was earnest and ambitious while lacking in control and political subtlety (revealing, as critics would say with some justification, both the new president's inexperience and the executive branch's characteristic disorder). From the outset, the president accorded a high priority to his non-proliferation program. He prepared the rough design and took a direct hand in placing its stresses and accents. It figured near the head of his personal foreign policy agenda, alongside human rights, the SALT talks, arms-traffic limitation, and moderation of racial confrontation in Southern Africa. The appointment of avowed antiproliferationists to key positions followed naturally from his own strong feelings on the subject. Officials were chosen not to register the debate over what should be done, but rather to formulate the means for realizing ends that, as the president already had determined in his own mind, were essential to the U.S. national interest. Carter, in the early days of the administration, would personally act as a constant prod to getting non-proliferation policies in shape and the strategy launched. He protected the key elements of his policy, for example, unwavering opposition to commercial reprocessing, against erosion by bureaucratic compromise, and he guarded the presidential prerogative of deciding how the policy would be presented in both public statements and private diplomacy.

Jimmy Carter was then the primary actor, in fact as well as name, in fashioning his government's nuclear energy policies. While the president set the scene and roughed out the script, however, others in the administration had much to say about how the play was performed. As is habitually the case within the U.S. government, the number of players was legion – so numerous that at times even the most diligent observer had difficulty in keeping track of all the action, of distinguishing stagehands from stars, or even of making sense of the plot. For an understanding of the internal contention and of the way in which policies acquired the form they did, the main participants need to be identified. Placing them in three groups along a radical–conservative continuum (an ordering that I believe does not do excessive violence to the rich plurality of viewpoints and interests they expressed) will help to clarify their roles.

The administration's non-proliferation mainstream was represented by officials who accepted the thrust of the Ford/Mitre report and identified themselves with its line of analysis and broad conclusions. This school of thought embraced not just those members of the study group who had assumed official positions, as enumerated earlier. It also included the old non-proliferation hands at ACDA, such as Charles van Doren, who were restored to grace from the administrative purgatory into which they had been cast by Henry Kissinger, and members of that small group of officials who had pushed the Fri Review to a questioning of received wisdom on the reprocessing issue. In this last category were Lawrence Scheinman, who moved from a position in ERDA's International Division to become Joseph Nye's right-hand man in the small office set up at State to oversee non-proliferation, and Louis V. Nosenzo, from the office of Oceans and International Environmental and Scientific Affairs, who became deputy assistant secretary for nuclear energy and energy technology affairs and in that position took charge of many of the day-to-day operations associated with promulgating and winning acceptance for the administration's policies. This mainstream group was tied together by a commitment to reversing what its members believed was a generation-old mistake of letting commercial considerations dictate the development of civilian nuclear power.

They recognized that a turnabout could not be made overnight. Their political realism told them that the United States could not reach its objectives by fiat. But above all, they felt strongly that for the world to proceed with commercial reprocessing under existing modes would be to accept intolerable and avoidable proliferation risks. They thought that technical alternatives should be explored, although they did not believe in sure-fire technological fixes. The opportunities and costs of following different routes should be rigorously examined. Perhaps there were institutional innovations that could be devised (including the possibility of restricting sensitive facilities to the territory of weapon states), which, in conjunction with technical modifications, might permit the use of plutonium in the *next* generation of reactors (avoiding recycling into LWRs) at an acceptable proliferation risk.

To buy the time for examining these possibilities, Washington had to curb its own reprocessing plans and make an energetic effort to get other governments at least to slow their projects. The mainstream was prepared to invest considerable political capital in an attempt at getting other states to rethink their commitment to plutonium and to win them over to a similar line of reasoning. At the same time, these officials were sensitive to the limitations of U.S. power. They knew that the positive collaboration of foreign governments was a condition for building a proliferation-resistant international regime for nuclear energy. They were also aware that a new forum had to be established that would bring dependent consumer states into discussions with suppliers.

To the left of these pragmatic moderates on the spectrum of the Carter administration's antiproliferation thinking were a loose grouping of staunch environmentalists and passionate arms controllers. These "purists" tended to see the problem as an overly hasty and ill-considered commitment to nuclear power, of which commercial reprocessing was only the most egregious example. They drew much of their intellectual and emotional sustenance from the domestic campaign against atomic power facilities. The safety and health hazards they saw in power-generating reactors were linked with fears of military abuses in a highly skeptical view of atomic energy, and a blanket indictment of its management by the federal government. As to plutonium recycling, their opposition was absolute. To their mind, plutonium represented so obvious and present a peril that drastic measures should be taken to prevent it from circulating internationally. Those measures might have to include coercion of fellow supplier (and allied) states, as well as of the purchasers of reprocessing technology. If necessary, members of this group were ready to use the leverage provided by world dependence on the United States for LEU fuels against both suppliers and consumers. To the extent that they accorded a future role to a new generation of breeder reactors, the purists wanted it to be based on technology other than that incorporated in the uranium–plutonium fuel cycle. It followed that their interpretation of a pause in reprocessing appeared indistinguishable from a halt. They wanted to rethink the basic structure of nuclear power. That meant, at the very least, a vigorous comparison of existing and conjectured nuclear technologies unbiased by time pressures. Their own preference was for the weight of research and development to be shifted to exploration of wholly new processes: the thorium cycle, the tandem cycle, spectral shift, and so on.

The purists differed from the moderate mainstream in more than the unqualified negativism of the judgment they passed on the current setup for generating atomic power. They also were decidedly more parochial. Preoccupied for the most part with internal U.S. conditions, comparatively inexperienced in any foreign dealings (and in some cases ignorant of political and economic circumstances abroad), the purists were less atuned to the practical requirements of achieving a drastic overhaul of the world's nuclear energy infrastructure. They were also more inclined to incur the costs (to the degree that they understood them) of an attempt to impose a new U.S. scheme of values. They were unrelenting in pressing for the severest licensing terms on nuclear exports and in resisting any trimming of non-proliferation sails to political winds, and they were unyielding on concessions to technically proficient states desirous of undertaking commercial reprocessing. In short, they were novices in the field of international politics. If they recognized the trade-off that had to be made between, on the one hand, tougher restrictions on technology and, on the other, the loss of political influence that would result from foreign governments' taking an independent nuclear path (perhaps going so far as to withdraw from the NPT), they gave little indication of such awareness.

The purists were few in number and less prominently placed than the moderates. Yet they were able to place an unmistakable mark on Carter policies. Three persons were most influential. Dr. Jessica Tuchman was a National Security Council staffer whose brief included non-proliferation. As a member of the loosely structured Executive Office of the President, she acted with a fair measure of autonomy under White House authority. The chief issues person for Representative Morris Udall during the congressman's ill-starred run for the presidency, she had a broad mandate from National Security Adviser Zbigniew Brzezinski covering "global issues" – defined to include those functional areas of world affairs, such as food and energy, that shape the international environment yet are not evidently the responsibility of foreign policy offices defined by more conventional terms of reference. Dr. Gustave Speth was a member of the Council on Environmental Quality with principal responsibility for domestic nuclear energy programs. An arch foe of the civilian nuclear establishment, Speth was an antigovernment activist become official personage under the new regime. As director of the Natural Resources Defense Council in his previous political incarnation, Speth had achieved fame in nuclear power circles by bringing suit in the landmark *Erdlow* case that established the right of plaintiffs in NRC licensing decisions to public hearings. He lost none of his conscientious dedication to the environmentalist cause upon joining the government. The third member of the purist triumvirate was Katherine (Kitty) Schermer, a member of the White House Domestic Council. Her formal power, like that of many White House staffers, was unclear. In practice, proximity to the White House and access to its inner circles gave her undeniable influence. Her territory was energy, her special interest nuclear energy. Her attitude toward its development lay somewhere between deep skepticism and outright opposition.

The purists drew strength from three sources. One was the positions they held in the Executive Office of the President. Through the NSC and the Domestic Council funnel the papers and reports directed to the Oval Office. Staffers often have the power of the secretariat to determine what gets on the president's desk, in what form, with what commentaries, and when. The authority is dispersed, with a scope that varies widely according to individual and issue area. Supposedly, it is exercised with discretion under the watchful eye of staff directors. It is not meant to impede the line of communications between the chief executive and his operating officials. Yet in every administration a remarkable, and often dismaying, influence is exerted by junior staffers of uncertain status and often thin qualifications. Such is the advantage of proximity to the center of power. The opportunity to speak directly to the president, or at least to those who have his ear, can be easily translated into the currency of bureaucratic power. So too can the belief of other, less privileged, members of the government that propinquity confers authority.

Complementing the advantages of being placed in prestige locations at the antechamber of power was the purists' role as the conscience of the administration. Every president brings into office with him a coterie of supporters who are more strongly attached to the values and policy principles he is seen to embody than they are to him personally or to their official positions. They are inclined to take literally his pronouncements of commitment to noble causes, to brook no deviation from the true path, and to serve as custodians of his political virtue. They also are the surrogates for those earnest and industrious constituencies that are moved by moral or quasi-moral concerns, and that are peculiarly effective at marshaling support for or against a president on their chosen issue. They are there to counsel him against the sins of expediency. And, as a more practical matter, they help him to avoid succumbing to the constraints surrounding any public official. For President Jimmy Carter these people were more than an unavoidable, if occasionally awkward, fact of political life. They were the public manifestations of his superego. They cast a constant light on the path of righteous endeavor he had publicly marked out for himself, and they reminded him when he left it.

The purists gained further strength from close alliances with like-minded staffers on key congressional committees and in the NRC. As the earlier focal points of antiproliferation activism, these offices had attracted people dedicated to the goal of reforming the nuclear policies of the United States. The Committee on International Relations in the House and the Senate Committee on Government Relations were the critical locations on the congressional side. These two committees shared jurisdiction over the sensitive legislation covering nuclear exchange agreements, which would take final shape in the Nuclear Non-Proliferation Act of 1978. Both the committee staff and the offices of member congressmen harbored passionate advocates of a tough U.S. position on plutonium and export conditions. Under the Ford administration, they already had joined forces with NRC staffers to raise governmental consciousness about the proliferation peril and to work for the tightening of controls over nuclear transfer. The arrival of kindred spirits in the Executive Office of the President opened the way for creation of a powerful intragovernmental coalition that bridged two branches of government and an autonomous regulatory agency. Alliances built around cutting issues (often with emotional content), whose members act as internal lobbying groups, are a feature of contemporary Washington life. To a large extent they can and do supplant organizational loyalties. In this instance, the deep conviction of the participants left no inhibition about acting in a manner legitimized by the current political culture of the federal government.

If the purists personified President Carter's vow to strain mightily in a moral cause (one that also happened to be of great national importance), the old guard in ERDA represented the heavy clay that mires the body while the spirit soars. Officials in the operating divisions had fought a bitter war of attrition to prevent the Fri Review from undermining the foundations of U.S. nuclear energy policy as they had constructed it. Sorely pressed in their guerrilla war with the environmentalists on one front, under congressional guns in the export sector, and struggling to contain the breach in their position made by President Ford's slowdown on reprocessing, the veteran ERDA forces saw in the Carter people a threat to their institutional lives. There was good reason to worry. A dramatic reversal had occurred in the public's attitude toward nuclear power, and in the judgment of knowledgeable persons in and out of government about the wisdom and diligence of ERDA's (AEC's) past performance. Its well-polished image as one of the most astute and competent public bodies had been badly damaged by a series of embarrassing revelations – about casual bookkeeping (records of uranium export kept in penciled ledgers), about chronic acts of nonfeasance (the clear filure to prepare viable plans for waste storage and disposal), about political obtuseness (the 1974 enrichment snafu), and about an imprudent underestimation of proliferation dangers (the tolerant export regulations and the earlier uncritical approval of plutonium reprocessing). An image of the nuclear authorities as vigilant guardians of the nation's stake in nuclear power was being transformed into one of an overconfident and overbearing elite who were not half as good as they had been represented as being.

Now that the political tides had turned against ERDA, its nuclear divisions feared that they would become targets of bureaucratic retaliation by those segments of the executive branch over whom the nuclear knights had been accustomed to ride roughshod. The Fri Review had been an arena for bruising organizational battles, with U.S. policy on exports and commercial reprocessing the coin of contention. Once settled, so intense a struggle over matters so vital (whose outcome signaled a historic change in national policy) could not fail to produce some of the excesses of successful revolution. In late 1976 and early 1977 there were signs that members of the old regime were being stigmatized, and their credentials put in doubt, until they passed muster as adherents to the new way of looking at nuclear issues. In the end, no wholesale purge was made and the bloodletting was minimal. The real loss was a position of institutional dominance over nuclear energy policy. What remained was ERDA's formidable organizational apparatus – its skills, programs, and technical operations, on which any new strategy would have to rely, at the very least in order to implement its more technical parts. ERDA had another asset. It was at the center of an international network of communications among atomic energy agencies, industrial enterprises, and research laboratories. In many respects, ERDA was the United States abroad in the atomic power field. Its authority and influence with like-minded nuclear establishments could be overlooked only at the peril of the new powers in Washington. Those were the cards left to the nuclear old guard to play. They could use them to negotiate favorable terms of surrender and to reach accommodations with the victorious forces, or they could use them to hamstring the ambitious plans of Carter's staunch antiproliferationists.

The recalcitrant survivors of the old regime were on the sidelines for the transition and orientation period while the administration got its feet on the ground and set about hammering out its policies. They nourished the belief, however, that they had found a link to the new holders of power, and a source for restored legitimacy, in the person of James Schlesinger,

President Carter's designated head of the proposed Department of Energy and, for the time being, his chief adviser on energy affairs. Phoenixlike, Schlesinger had risen from the ashes of his precipitate dismissal by Jerry Ford from the top spot at the Pentagon to become an admired aide to the new chief executive. Originally interviewed as a candidate for a leading national security post, he had so impressed President-elect Carter in their talks at the latter's Georgia homestead that the energy job was proffered when political considerations foreclosed his return to the Defense Department. Personifying the game of musical chairs played at the upper echelons of the executive branch, James Schlesinger closed the circle by reappearing as director of the transmogrified energy agency he had left at the end of 1973 when it was still the AEC, before it had fallen on political hard times.

Under Carter, Schlesinger could not be expected to be the prominent defender of nuclear power he had been under Nixon. In fact, his main area of responsibility would lie outside the atomic energy field, and he kept a low profile on proliferation issues. At the president's behest, he would be preoccupied with putting together the administration's first comprehensive energy bill and shepherding it through a divided and rambunctious Congress. Framing a nuclear policy was left to others. (His chief deputy, Robert Fri, was even less suited to serve as point man for the nuclear diehards. Views shaped the previous year, while he was directing the review that bore his name, made him sympathetic to the new administration's mainstream and helpful in trying to establish a cooperative relationship with the nuclear energy people.) Schlesinger was unwilling and unable to lead the nuclear right. But as a trusted lieutenant of the president, with nuclear experience, he naturally would be asked for his advice and assistance when the inevitable bureaucratic tangles were laid on Carter's desk. The broader significance of Schlesinger's emergence as the administration's leading energy spokesman was to ensure that the nuclear establishment would retain a modicum of autonomy and freedom to exercise normal bureaucratic prerogatives under the new regime.

FORMULATING A STRATEGY

The administration that took office in January 1977 had pronounced views about the direction its nuclear energy policy should take. There were five agreed objectives:

1. To focus its non-proliferative efforts on the dangers of the fuel cycle, without disregarding safeguards (control and detection) or neglecting diplomatic attempts to remove political incentives
2. To use the time created by a moratorium on plutonium

to build a stable international nuclear regime based on rules and institutions that would make the fuel cycle more immune to proliferation abuse

3. To reestablish U.S. credibility as a nuclear supplier of non-sensitive materials
4. To stop, or at least slow, the move toward commercialization of reprocessing
5. To block those actions that would critically undermine the antireprocessing campaign, such as completion of the Barnwell facility, and the sales by France and West Germany of fuel-fabrication facilities

In pursuit of these goals two tasks had to be undertaken. Foremost was the drafting of a broad plan and operational strategy that would encompass all those elements of policy that had a bearing on the international nuclear fuel cycle. Second was a renewed attempt to dissuade the principals in the reprocessing and enrichment deals (France, Germany, and their buyers) from going ahead with their transactions. On the understanding that a strong effort would be made to enlist other governments in a review of existing technologies and rules of transfer, the administration intended to put off any diplomatic overtures until it was in a position to lay out its thinking and proposals in their entirety. A sense of urgency dictated that the Carter people act with dispatch, but they were equally attentive to the dangers of taking initiative in haste. They were committed to moving with deliberate speed in fashioning a coherent, yet flexible, policy that would have a reasonable chance of acceptance by other governments. The administration's sense of how to proceed was eminently sensible. However, fortune and the intractable processes of collective government decision making would come together to upset its well-laid plans.

Diplomatic dissonance

Bad luck took the form of a surprise visit of an envoy from German Chancellor Helmut Schmidt to Vice-President-elect Walter Mondale before the inauguration in January. The Bonn official, Peter Hermes, later ambassador to Washington, had been dispatched to carry the word of the Bonn government's impending approval of the export licenses for the sensitive reprocessing technology earmarked for Brazil. The gesture was meant as a courtesy, and not a declaration by the German government of its intention to confront the incoming Carter administration on nuclear issues. Bonn, however, chose the wrong man for the mission. Stiff in bearing and formal in diplomatic style, Hermes managed to deliver the message without communicating any sense of conciliation. Instead, he engaged in legal argument with Mondale (who was accompanied by David Aaron, his foreign affairs adviser and the man designated as the NSC deputy director) on the rights and obligations of parties to the NPT and Supplier Club members. Hermes's next stop was at the State Department, where he met with the administration's transition team on non-proliferation. Forewarned of the German hard line, they were ready to give measure for measure. The tense encounter left each side convinced of the other's recalcitrance. Hermes carried back to Bonn reports of the unreasonableness of the new people in Washington. Carter administration officials felt that they had been challenged by the Germans. A failure to respond swiftly would ensure that the German–Brazilian deal would go through as advertised; it would cut the ground from under them before Washington even had a chance to make its case for a worldwide rethinking of civilian nuclear power.

In direct response to the Hermes visit, the newly inaugurated Carter administration launched a round of personal diplomacy in what it saw as a last-ditch effort to prevent Bonn and Brasilia from going through with their precedent-setting exchange. Vice-President Mondale flew off to Germany for a series of high-level meetings that, in the charged atmosphere created by mutual perceptions of inflexibility, were doomed from the outset. Brazil, upon hearing of the Mondale mission, filed its own agitated protest. Brasilia government officials were upset as much by the failure of the United States to make its complaint directly to them as they were by intervention in what they saw as a strictly German–Brazilian matter. Accordingly, Undersecretary of State Christopher was dispatched to Brasilia to explain the U.S. position.

The frantic diplomacy triggered by the Hermes visit was singularly unsuccessful. Both Germany and Brazil responded stiffly in reaffirming their intention to go ahead with a transfer that was in conformity with international rules and that, in their view, did not violate principles of non-proliferation. The West German government was especially irked by what it saw as a righteous, uncompromising U.S. attitude that failed to pay due regard to the interests and concerns of allies. Bonn's irritation over the aggressive U.S. stance was aggravated by the importuning tone of administration approaches on other diplomatic fronts. In addition to the Brazilian matter, Washington was prodding Schmidt to accelerate expansion of the West German economy, and creating uneasiness by stressing a human rights policy that the Bonn government saw as a threat to its delicate ties to the East German regime. Schmidt was in no mood to accommodate the Americans. Carter's emissaries were rebuffed. The decision to go ahead with the exports to Brazil would be officially announced the same day that President Carter made his non-proliferation statement. Schmidt's action was applauded in West German political circles as "necessary to uphold the international credibility of the Federal Republic of Germany as well as to insure the future of German export technology."[14] A few weeks later the distance between the U.S. and German positions was underscored by Bonn's publication of a four-year, $2.7 billion energy research program, focusing on nuclear power, which gave a central place to plutonium recycling and the breeder reactor.[15] It anticipated a joint European breeder effort under European Economic Community (EEC) auspices outlined in an EEC communiqué a few months later.

The Brazilian response to the Carter administration's desperate attempt to block the deal with Germany was predictably more curt. Brazil's self-conscious quest for great-power status had made it increasingly sensitive to slights by its overweening North American neighbor. The atmosphere was still clouded by the unpleasantness over enrichment contracts three years earlier. Relations had been further darkened by strains with Washington over a State Department report criticizing the Brasilia regime's human rights record. Taking umbrage at what was deemed an improper and offensive interference in internal affairs, the Brasilia government anticipated congressionally inspired U.S. pressure by canceling Brazil's twenty-five-year-old military assistance pact with the United States. It should have come as no surprise to the U.S. envoys dispatched to Brasilia when they were told flatly that the nuclear sales were none of their business. The assertion by a high-ranking Brazilian military officer that the country's political emergence "will not be blocked by any difficulties, not even by the incomprehensions of our traditional allies," pretty well summed up the Brazilian attitude.[16]

The acrimonious relations engendered by the unfortuitous visit of Peter Hermes stacked the deck against the Carter administration's early non-proliferation diplomacy by creating the impression around the world that the United States was preparing for political warfare with other parties interested in nuclear energy. It also had the deleterious effect of distracting key officials, especially Joseph Nye, who accompanied Christopher to Brasilia, from the critical job of directing the interagency policy review. With his time divided between managing the review and conducting diplomacy, he found it that much harder to meet the late March deadline for official promulgation of the Carter program.

PRM-15

The task force constituted to fit together the pieces of a new and embracing non-proliferation policy was duly formed under the auspices of the NSC, with administrative direction given to Joseph Nye's small office. It was officially designated PRM-15 (Presidential Review Memorandum-No. 15) in the jargon coined by the incoming administration. The format conformed closely to plans developed in transition papers. A persuasive case had been made to center responsibility for proliferation affairs in one place, a specially designed office in the State Department. Nye's group was so designated. In keeping with its coordinating role, it was mandated to chair and to staff a high-level interagency committee. As conceived by the transition team, the group's members would be bound by collective decisions with a right of appeal through channels to the secretary of state and the president. In practice, cohesion and discipline would prove hard to maintain.

The Inter-agency Group on Non-Proliferation created to prepare PRM-15 drew its membership from across the executive bureaucracy. Participants, in addition to Joseph Nye, included Robert Fri, acting deputy administrator of ERDA; Nelson Sievering of ERDA's International Affairs Division; Jessica Tuchman from the NSC staff; Charles van Doren, ACDA; Colonel Bryce Harlow, representing the Department of Defense's office of International Security Affairs; alternating junior officials from OMB and CIA; and Ben Huberman, now on the staff of the Nuclear Regulatory Commission. (An innovation of the new setup gave the NRC representative observer status as part of a conscious effort to facilitate communication between the regulatory agency and the executive branch. The active part taken in the group's discussions by Victor Gilinsky, at a later date, would be a subject of controversy and a source of irritation to State officials.)

Their first meta-decision was whether to build on the Fri Review, using it as an intellectual foundation and incorporating portions of its options outline, or to do the job of assessing conditions and evaluating alternatives *de novo*. There was a persuasive case for making use of the previous administration's intellectual labors: The study was exhaustive and of uncommonly high intellectual caliber, and it had broken new ground in rejecting shibboleths and highlighting the issues of greatest concern to the new team. There was some overlap of personnel (Fri was working congenially with Joseph Nye), and incorporation of the Fri material into the current study would save a great deal of time when premiums were being placed on rapid action. On the other hand, each new administration has a visceral aversion to acknowledging an intellectual debt to its predecessor. This reluctance is particularly strong when it fancies itself as reformist, and is most apparent in those areas which it has staked out for priority attention. Some of the new Carter people, especially the purists, were inclined to see any product made before the changing of the guard as tainted through association, however strained, with the old-time nuclear establishment. The purists genuinely believed the Fri approach to be soft on plutonium, and they were worried lest the report's use bias the outcome of the expected clashes within the Carter administration. There also was the uncomfortable fact that in October, at the fag end of the electoral campaign, the Fri Review had been attacked as indecisive in its conclusions and equivocal on the critical question of commercial reprocessing. Above all, some of the new crowd simply wanted to do the job themselves. With the newcomer's usual hubris often goes a fondness for the process of policy deliberation and debate itself. Committee meetings, memos, plotting, stratagems, and ploys are among the odd attractions that many officials, newly appointed or holdovers, find in their jobs. It all too easily becomes more fulfilling and gratifying than producing a well-crafted policy and achieving its successful execution.

The PRM-15 study was duly launched in late January as an independent review, with a presidentially decreed deadline of March 21. The tight scheduling (by normal Washington standards) suggested the desirability of concentrating on the central issues requiring decision and conducting a closely managed exercise in preparing and evaluating options. Nye was committed to doing just that. He met regularly with Fri in the former's State Department office to get a firmer grasp of the work done by his functional predecessor, and to lay the basis for collaboration with the energy people. He made sure that certain of the main players in the Fri Review would have a central role in PRM-15 – Lou Nosenzo and Charles van Doren in particular. Above all, he was committed to providing the president with a set of concrete proposals that would enable the administration to move expeditiously toward realizing its proximate objectives on the non-proliferation front: making a declaration on U.S. reprocessing and engaging other governments in a collective examination of the nuclear fuel cycle. In this instance, the cause of good government fared better than usual. The Fri study would be quarried for the building blocks of the Carter policy.

It was no easy chore. The governmental traditions of excruciating deliberation and the self-centeredness of bureaucratic games players could not be completely denied. The dedicated efforts of Nye's group to keep the review focused and under tight intellectual rein did succeed in saving the study from being unraveled by the centrifugal force of the participants. PRM-15 nevertheless mushroomed into a more wide-ranging and diffuse exercise than was desired by State's head officer or was in the interest of incisive policy making. In the end, it went over much of the ground examined by the Ford/Mitre group and replicated, rather than simply borrowed, portions of the Fri Review's analyses and assessments.

The study was conducted in parts and at several levels. The various chapters were distributed among participating departments and agencies, who in turn broke them down by topic to be analyzed by their own staff. Paper proliferated. The sections were uneven and not always congruent. Nye's office persevered in its efforts to expedite the process and to prevent both the purists and the nuclear old guard from holding programs hostage to their own beliefs and interests. The problem, though, was classic: A formal policy review is undertaken to legitimize innovation action and to bring into working agreement the disparate parts of government. Yet when the bureaucratic minions are engaged, valuable time is lost in mapping the problem area and in fighting over old territorial claims; the product is less a statement of collective wisdom than a reflection of the bureaucratic battlefield at the moment when the deadline for filing a report imposes a cease-fire on the combatants. This was the condition of PRM-15 in mid-March.

Responsibility for producing a coherent document out of the welter of analyses and prescriptions was left to Lou Nosenzo. His draft laid down a policy direction, expatiated on the philosophy that underlay it, stated agreements where a consensus had been reached, and proposed a position where disagreements remained. Each of the agencies on the task force then voted on the PRM sections, in keeping with the principles of participatory democracy that governed policy procedure in the Carter administration. Those who took exemption to conclusions presented in the Nosenzo version were free to register their dissent. These outstanding differences were duly recorded in a reedited draft.

The document that emerged was not a clear blueprint for building the edifice of Carter non-proliferation policy. It was part problem assessment, part options paper, and part guide to prescriptive action. PRM-15 showed signs of its rough passage through the heavy seas of bureaucratic and intellectual confrontation. It was inconveniently long, and offered something less than an integrated package of succinct recommendations. These unfortunate effects of letting the review fall victim to an open-ended bureaucratic process were aggravated by severe time pressures. The president, firm in his commitment to the early deadline for making his non-proliferation statement, pressed for the report's completion. But Nye's overburdened office did not have the resources or authority to force the pace and to insist on reconciliation of divergent points of view.

Still, the study had its virtues, whatever it lacked in concision. PRM-15 was most decisive in squarely opposing continuation of the U.S. commercial reprocessing program. A moratorium on plutonium recycling would be the cornerstone of the administration's antiproliferation campaign. That act would convey to other governments the clear message that the use of plutonium in thermal (i.e., light-water) reactors posed a clear and present proliferation danger that overshadowed any economic or supply-assurance gains from recycling. All the participants in the review accepted this general proposition. Even ERDA, to the surprise of the people at State, acquiesced in the decision on Barnwell, while continuing to see tangible benefits in reprocessing under amended circumstances. The agency's accommodating attitude could be ascribed to three factors: a recognition that Barnwell, under the Carter administration, was a lost cause on which little of its remaining political capital should be expended; the growing evidence that, for financial and environmental reasons, the project was a dead issue anyway; and the influence of Robert Fri, who, with the tacit backing of Schlesinger, made the case against Barnwell within the agency, and who was prepared to use his position to put a damper on dissident offices.

Whereas agreement had been reached relatively painlessly on the key issue within U.S. jurisdiction, there was a clear split along purist–moderate lines on the policy toward foreign reprocessing. Facilities at La Hague, France, Windscale, England, and Mol, Belgium, were on the point of commercial operation, as was a demonstration plant at Tokai Mura, Japan. Several contracts for spent-fuel reprocessing were already pending. There could be no general call for a moratorium on plutonium recycling without specific reference to cases. On this crucial question, the divisions within the administration were least open to compromise.

Purists pushed for an absolutist position. They wanted the administration to come down hard on the West Europeans and Japanese, and they were prepared to take measures (including an embargo of LEU fuel) to coerce foreign governments into shelving their reprocessing plans. The moderate view, as represented by Nye's State Department team, foresaw the dangers of Washington's overreaching itself. They warned against threats of drastic U.S. action (a cutoff of enrichment services) to force other governments into line. Instead, they wanted an earnest diplomatic effort to push for agreement on stricter export ground rules and voluntary postponement on plutonium recycling. In the end, PRM-15 left open the question of how tough a line the United States should take on foreign reprocessing, and on what terms, if any, the administration would find reprocessing acceptable. That issue was slated to be at the top of the agenda for the meeting of the NSC Policy Review Committee that would decide the matter as part of its job in sanctioning official administration non-proliferation policy.

A flexible approach toward foreign reprocessing was seen by the State Department moderates and their allies as a condition for getting other governments to participate in a wide-ranging review of the international fuel cycle. They looked upon such a review as the diplomatic centerpiece of the long-term administration strategy. The unanimous recommendation for its inauguration was PRM-15's second major accomplishment. In conception, the international review would do on a governmental basis and global scale what Ford/Mitre had done unofficially in the United States. The brainchild of Joseph Nye and Robert Fri, the International Fuel Cycle Evaluation (INFCE), as it came to be known, had three purposes. First, it was viewed as the instrument for raising world consciousness about the linkages between the evolving civilian nuclear industry and the proliferation danger. Second, it carried promise of creating a keenly sought pause in plutonium recycling while the world debated its merits and demerits. Finally, it offered a diplomatic vehicle for engaging consumer as well as supplier states in a constructive dialogue. An INFCE-like exercise had to be gotten under way if the administration's overall non-proliferation program was to avoid being jerked around by events totally beyond its control, and, perhaps, being forced into a unwanted confrontation with friends and allies.

The hope of Nye and his associates was to use the INFCE to build a new consensus on what constituted a safe, as well as an economical and a technically sound, fuel cycle. A consensus would permit the sharing of responsibility for regime maintenance, which the United States, given its dwindling influence, no longer could shoulder alone. But the entire enterprise could be jeopardized by a showdown over reprocessing. Cast in this light, the stake in the contest between moderates and the purists over the administration's approach to foreign reprocessing was the survival of a viable non-proliferation strategy itself.

The Policy Review Committee

The forum for deciding the reprocessing question was the Policy Review Committee (PRC). It met on the third week of March to recommend a non-proliferation policy to the president. Its members included National Security Advisor Zbigniew Brzezinski, accompanied by staffers David Aaron and Jessica Tuchman; Secretary of Defense Harold Brown; CIA Director Stansfield Turner; ACDA Director Paul Warnke (and staffer Charles van Doren); Robert Fri and Nelson Sievering of ERDA; energy adviser James Schlesinger; J. Bowman Cutter of OMB; and NRC Chairman Marcus Rowden, accompanied by Ben Huberman. The State Department was represented by Undersecretary Warren Christopher and Joseph Nye.

Nye introduced the discussion, summarized the PRM conclusions, and noted the principle items on the agenda. Recommendations dealing with the INFCE, an addition to U.S. enrichment capacity, and export control legislation (firming up criteria and procedures) were accepted with little discussion. Reprocessing policy, as the great unresolved issue, was the focus of debate. Going into the meeting, Nye expected some sharp questioning of the decision to guillotine Barnwell. ERDA might well have been playing possum, waiting for the conclusive meeting to engage the enemies of reprocessing. Schlesinger, too, was an unknown quantity who could be a powerful ally of the nuclear establishment if he so chose. The "right" appeared, at least potentially, as a greater threat to the non-proliferation approach nutured by State than the purist "left." The protagonists on the left, after all, were mainly junior staffers outside the line departments whose principal support had come from a nonexecutive branch agency, the NRC.

Surprisingly, the more serious challenge came from the left while State was looking over its right shoulder. The recommendation to curb the U.S. reprocessing program passed the muster of the PRC with hardly a whimper of protest. Foreign reprocessing was another matter. Backing for a tough U.S. stance came from two unexpected quarters. Secretary Brown, drawing on his experience as a member of the Ford/Mitre group, declared his belief that because plutonium carried so large a proliferation risk, the United States had an obligation to do everything in its power to prevent its commercialization. James Schlesinger was an even less predictable recruit to the side of the purists. Identifying himself with the Brown position, he put his considerable influence behind a hard-line approach to the Europeans. Schlesinger's attitude seemed at variance with his generally sympathetic view of nuclear power and with a track record that revealed no special concern about the proliferation peril. We can only guess at his thinking. One interpretation of his action emphasized his personal relationship with the president, which made him exceptionally sensitive to Carter's own prejudices. In addition, the idea of getting tough with the Europeans was anything but alien to a man who had given short shrift to their enrichment plans, and other nuclear interests, a few years earlier when he was at the AEC. A less complimentary explanation, which cannot be substantiated, attributes Machiavellian motives to Schlesinger. This interpretation would have him supporting the more extreme version of a policy he opposed in the hope of improving the chances of its early demise. State officials, for their part, thought that he was simply expressing his independent opinion – one that was no less discomforting for its honesty.

In any event, the preponderant view expressed at the PRC meeting was closer to the purist position on foreign reprocessing than that recommended by Nye's team at State. However, no resolution was drafted or vote taken. The report to be sent to the president was supposed to reflect the discussion faithfully, and to offer options with the recommendations of the committee attached. It was an NSC staff responsibility to draft the document. In this instance, Jessica Tuchman was given the job of preparing a summary of the meeting and framing alternatives. She did this on a two-page paper that pronounced the group in favor of a staunch effort to block foreign reprocessing plans. It communicated little of the flavor of the debate on the issue or the widely felt concern about the diplomatic risks of so drastic an action. The PRC report, as written by Tuchman, was taken unedited to the president by National Security Advisor Brzezinski. It was a subject on which he professed no expertise. When, later, he was asked by State officials why he permitted the president to get so one-sided a view of the question, Brzezinski would point to Carter's own purported knowledge of nuclear issues, to which he readily deferred, and his policy of relying on the discretion and judgment of NSC staffers. In retrospect his confidence in both seems exaggerated.

Consultations abroad

When Nye and other interested officials at State learned of the message that had gone to the Oval Office, they were very upset. The president was preparing to make a public statement in a few days. It in all likelihood would put the United States on a collision course with the Europeans, and jeopardize the chances of the administration's broader non-proliferation policy ever getting a fair hearing. Entreaties to Secretary of State Vance and to Brzezinski led to their intercession with the president. Carter agreed, reluctantly, to put off his statement until the first week in April. In the interval he would get himself more fully briefed on the implications of a coercive approach to foreign reprocessing, and informed of differing views within his administration. The president did proceed to issue a Presidential Decision Memorandum (PD-8) intended to guide members of his government. It laid out the administration's deep concern about the proliferation danger and the need to tackle a critical set of fuel-cycle and nuclear export issues. It announced the negative action on Barnwell in emphasizing that firm decisions had been taken only on domestic matters. It also called for a number of follow-up studies by bureaucratic task forces, one of which would address itself to the question of reprocessing and plutonium recycling worldwide.

The postponement had the further effect of clearing some precious time for consultations abroad. They were badly needed to prepare foreign governments, especially France, for what it now appeared would be a U.S. attack on their reprocessing programs. A round of discussions had been undertaken by State Department officials in February, when the policy was still in its formative stages. These initial visits had been designed to ease fears of the new administration's reputed readiness to declare war on plutonium, and to open lines of communication. It was essential to do so, given fundamental differences in assessing the proliferation danger and a characteristic French unwillingness to subordinate France's national interests to a collective good defined for it by the United States. A month later, Joseph Nye (accompanied by Nelson Sievering of ERDA) set out for Paris bearing the bad tidings that Washington saw the French government's plans to recycle plutonium as an imminent proliferation threat, and that it might be constrained to take severe measures to block them. To the French, the news that their civilian nuclear activities were looked upon with anathema by at least some influential administration officials was bad enough. The reversal from what they had understood from the February talks was to be a more conciliatory tone only aggravated matters. The result was a singularly disagreeable meeting between the U.S. emissaries and French officials. Nye and Sievering were earnestly trying to fill a consultation gap. They could hardly make a success of the attempt when the drift of U.S. policy was toward confrontation, contrary to their own preferences, and when, to top things off, they were still unsure just how tough an antireprocessing stance the president would take.

Consultations in other capitals fared little better. There, too, only a general outline of the emerging policy could be presented. There was no opportunity for detailed talks. It appeared that the United States was simply declaring its intentions rather than soliciting foreign views for incorporation in a policy-making exercise still in progress. In truth, the intense intramural debate had not permitted external inputs. What was revealed of the debate's outcome left the clear impression that a hard-line approach was in the offing. Hostility toward Washington was increased in some quarters by the maladroit handling of some of the briefings given foreign leaders in late March and early April. The presentation made to German Chancellor Schmidt by an embassy official reportedly requested that any comments be communicated within twenty-four hours. Schmidt's tart response was to the effect that, as the White House apparently was hastening to an early deadline, any comments of his would have little impact, so he would refrain from offering them. Dr. Sigvard Ecklund, director general of IAEA, was notified of what the president planned to say just a few hours before his statement was issued, owing to a bureaucratic foul-up in the U.S. Embassy in Vienna. His pique at this cavalier treatment added a cutting edge to his later criticisms of actions he thought reneged on the solemn undertakings of the United States, embodied in the NPT, to assist in the development of civilian nuclear power. Other government heads were similarly annoyed by the administration's apparent disregard for their opinions.

PRESIDENT CARTER'S STATEMENT

With his administration's position on foreign reprocessing still unresolved, and his envoys engaged in preventive diplomacy abroad, President Carter committed himself to issuing his nuclear power policy statement on April 7. There were in fact two practical problems: Who should draft it, and what should be in it? Following a tradition honored by time, if not by success, the president answered the first by seeking the help of a confidant rather than relying on those who had been most active in preparing his policy studies. The trusted adviser's role in this case was filled by James Schlesinger. The guidelines were set down by the president and followed closely the recommendations that emanated from the PRC – with the outstanding issue of the United States' attitude toward the plutonium program of the West Europeans left in abeyance.

The statement would stress the symbolic unilateral action of deferring indefinitely the completion of Barnwell. It would speak in muted tones about what was expected of other governments, and what Washington might do to dissuade them from proceeding. Until a diplomatic plan of action had been worked out, it was prudent not to state intentions too boldly. The hostile reactions from foreign capitols to the last round of briefings strengthened the case for caution.[17]

These were the rough specifications for the president's speech given to James Schlesinger. In an irony not untypical of life at the high echelons of government, Carter's overture on non-proliferation was actually authored by a team of holdovers from the Ford administration. They were former associates assembled by Schlesinger from OMB, AEC, and ERDA. Appointed as coordinator was John Ahearne, lead energy man at DoD and then White House energy adviser under Schlesinger. Ahearne in turn gathered his collaborators. His list included names recognizable from previous proliferation policy dramas: Robert Fri, Roger LeGassie, Nelson Sievering, and David Elliott. The majority were nonplayers or marginal players in the current production. The primary responsibility for drafting a statement fell to Elliott. Previously Henry Kissinger's main man on proliferation at the NSC, Elliott was in the last days of an interregnum before departing Washington for a position at the Stanford Research Institute in California. For the time being, he was warming a chair at the reborn office of the science and technology adviser to the president, awaiting the arrival of the freshly appointed Dr. Frank Press from MIT. Elliott had been contacted by Ahearne on a Thursday. On Friday evening, following guidelines communicated by Schlesinger, he sketched out a draft statement in two versions.

Both conformed to the president's antiplutonium position. One predicated a U.S. reprocessing moratorium on parallel action by other countries. The alternative pointed to a unilateral action that would be an example to foreign governments, who were expected to follow the U.S. lead at some time removed, in some measure. This latter approach also called on the president to recognize the legitimate interest of the Europeans and Japanese in plutonium recycling while still urging them to slow the pace of their programs. Elliott's draft was laid before the group of five on Saturday morning. Melded to another draft prepared independently by Nelson Sievering, it was approved and passed along to James Schlesinger, who gave it to the president in a form that incorporated the second approach. Carter accepted the statement and read it with only slight modification – 80 percent of this version was Elliott's late March draft. Although the text did pass through the bureaucratic loop once again, time limitations and the president's apparent satisfaction with the version Elliott had produced left it largely unscathed.

On the whole, members of Joseph Nye's group at the State Department were satisfied with what they saw. The emphasis was on developing a cooperative, international approach. The references to foreign reprocessing were conciliatory rather than harshly critical. It appeared that the bias in the PRC discussions toward a hard line had been reversed.

April 7

President Carter's statement on Nuclear Power Policy, made April 7 as scheduled, was decidedly and unexpectedly low-key (see Appendix E). There was a striking contrast between the boldness of its declared objectives and the mildness of its tone. Also noteworthy was its failure to reconcile its profound implications for nuclear dealings between Washington and potential reprocessors with utterances offering a host of qualifications about the arrangements the United States would find acceptable.

In a brief, almost terse statement, the president made no bones about his conviction that "a serious risk accompanies worldwide use of nuclear power – the risk that components of the nuclear power process will be turned to providing atomic weapons" – and that "these risks would be vastly increased by the further spread of sensitive technologies which entail direct access to plutonium."[18] In support of this belief, Carter announced that the United States would "defer indefinitely the commercial reprocessing and recycling of the plutonium produced in the U.S. nuclear power programs." As part of the shift away from plutonium, it would also "defer dependence on the breeder reactor for commercial use," while continuing research and development programs "to give greater priority to alternative designs of the breeder other than plutonium." This forthright declaration of the U.S. position on the plutonium issue was *not* accompanied by any trumpet call for an international crusade against reprocessing wherever it might raise its spectral head. The president limited himself to the mild expression of hope that other governments "will join with us" – with an international fuel-cycle evaluation as the vehicle – "in trying to have some world-wide understanding of the extreme threat of the further proliferation of nuclear explosive capability." This tentative approach belied the signals that had been coming from Washington during the preceding month and that had alarmed so many governments, especially the Japanese and West European. There was no sign of an aggressive administration plan to bludgeon them into a shutdown of their own reprocessing and breeder reactor plans by threatening to cut off U.S.-supplied LEU.

His formal statement showed Carter as taking a remarkably accommodating attitude toward the allies' interests in plutonium. Indeed, his announcement was prefaced by remarks acknowledging that "many countries see nuclear power as the only real opportunity . . . to reduce the dependence of their economic well-being on foreign oil . . . [whereas] the U.S., by contrast, has a major domestic energy source – coal." (He added that "our plans also call for the use of nuclear power as a share in our energy production.") He made explicit that whatever decisions the United States took on its domestic nuclear program, it had "no authority over other countries." Washington was "not trying to impose its will on those nations like Japan, France, Britain and Germany, which already have reprocessing plants in operation. They have a special need that we don't have in that their supplies of petroleum products are not available."[19] Clearly, the president had come down on the side of the State Department doves, and had rejected the counsel of the hawks in his Executive Office. To some, he seemed dangerously close to tipping too far in the opposite direction. In the follow-up question-and-answer session with reporters, he did just that.

Asked what the unilateral U.S. action on Barnwell implied for reprocessing elsewhere in the world, Carter voiced his belief, in a tone of resignation, "that we would very likely see a continuation of reprocessing capabilities within those nations [Japan, France, Britain, and Germany] that I have named, and perhaps others." Moreover, that continuation would not be over the figurative "dead body" of the United States. Carter made plain that Washington's decision on Barnwell did not "imply that we prohibit them or criticize them severely because of their own need for reprocessing." In unequivocal terms, he declared that "they have a perfect right to go ahead and continue with their own reprocessing efforts."[20]

If this last statement was indeed U.S. policy, it represented a stunning turnaround in administration thinking. It ran counter to the general conviction that it was vitally important to avert the use of plutonium fuels, to Carter's own apparent belief in the imminence of the plutonium danger, and to all prior indications of what his message would contain. The purists in the administration were appalled to see how far Carter had moved from their (and presumably his) strong stand on foreign reprocessing. There also was consternation among the mainstreamers, who were troubled both by the president's excessive swing toward a position of tolerance of foreign reprocessing plans and by a growing ambiguity in U.S. policy, which could only breed confusion abroad. What had happened was that presidential improvisation, and overreaction to reports of the political fallout from his rumored hard line, had aggravated the effects of unresolved internal conflicts within his administration.

The deferential Carter remarks about the rights of other states to plot their own nuclear futures stifled any suggestion of a worldwide war on plutonium. This compromising attitude carried the president beyond the defensible soft sell of his policy to a veritable abandonment of a U.S. right to influence what foreign governments did with U.S.-supplied fuel. The president gave more ground than he had to, more than his own officials (moderates as well as purists) had wanted, and more than his own policy permitted. The inevitable and quick reversion to a tougher line had the predictable result of raising hackles again while discrediting the genuine concessions he was prepared to make. In the course of a few weeks, the administration would have changed its mind four times about its policy on foreign reprocessing.

The reversal came very quickly, immediately after the president's press conference. With the unfortunate consequences of what Carter had said obvious to all, senior officials huddled and decided that swift action to rectify his error was needed. Clarifications had to modify the impression of U.S. sympathy with nuclear aspirations abroad in the reprocessing field. The task of cleaning up Carter's remarks was left to Joseph Nye and Robert Fri. That afternoon they held a press conference of their own. Their message was simple: The only firm decisions already taken by the U.S. government dealt with domestic issues. All matters that affected the nuclear programs of the other states were still open, pending completion of consultation with all parties concerned. Because of these ongoing consultations, Nye explained to a Japanese journalist, the president's statement earlier in the day did not mean that a decision had been taken one way or another on the question of Japan's right to reprocess. The United States was not taking a hands-off position, but neither was it committed to stopping La Hague or any other facility. The two officials stressed that, on reprocessing, the overriding U.S. aim was to enlist other countries in a cool, deliberate review of the entire fuel cycle, in all its aspects, including proliferation risk. It obviously was taking some extraordinarily nimble footwork to preserve the credibility of the Carter administration's new non-proliferation policy, whatever it was.

Foreign reaction

If the administration itself had yet to make up its collective mind just where it stood on crucial parts of its policy, foreign governments were even less sure of what they were hearing. Washington's equivocation and the transmittal of rapidly changing signals created maximum irritation and minimal support for the U.S. position on plutonium. For three months, the Japanese and West Europeans had been kept in a state of suspended agitation. Their anxiety grew as every bit of information filtering out of Washington seemed to lend greater credibility to rumors of an impending assault against nuclear interests by the arch–non-proliferationists now enthroned in seats of power. The exceptionally violent reaction to the actual statement (or perhaps "statements" is more accurate), though the statement was quite bland compared to unofficial reports of its contents, was a release of pent-up steam. In three capitals, Bonn, Brasilia, and Paris, the temperature had been substantially raised in the preceding months by the strenuous diplomatic campaign to force cancellation, or at least deferral, of the

German–Brazilian deal and to push France to an outright withdrawal of its contracted offer to sell a reprocessing plant to Pakistan.

I have recounted the sharp exchanges with Bonn that left a residue of suspicion on both sides of the Atlantic. Nuclear relations with France were equally strained. Disagreements with the French, though, were kept private, and at less heated levels. The decorum owed much to the revision in French nuclear export policy forced by President Valery Giscard d'Estaing, which brought it within hailing distance of the U.S. position. Paris publicly proclaimed that, aside from the Pakistan sale, which it felt honorbound to complete (though Pakistan's agreement to a mutual recision would be welcome), it would discontinue any and all sales of sensitive technologies. It was an action that testified to growing sympathy for the United States' concern over the proliferation danger. However, France no more than Germany accepted the Carter administration's conclusion that commercial reprocessing was itself undesirable, and that the use of plutonium as a reactor fuel should be postponed indefinitely. French nuclear energy officials were as uneasy as anyone about the prospect that the United States might attempt to use its leverage as supplier of LEU fuel to coerce them into a temporary abandonment of reprocessing plans.[21] The conciliatory words President Carter uttered at his April 7 press conference were comforting, but U.S. intentions still were suspect.

Anxiety among the allies was compounded by their knowledge that drafts of the Nuclear Non-Proliferation Act lying before Congress contained provisions that would impose reprocessing controls as a condition for U.S. exports of enriched uranium. On this score, the administration seemed to be understanding of European sensitivities. Its public declarations, though, still left cause for worry. In a White House "Fact Sheet" released on April 27, accompanying the President's Energy Message addressed to a joint session of Congress that day, the administration stated its support for tighter export conditions (see Appendixes F and G). They would include a U.S. "right of approval on reprocessing extending to all special nuclear material produced through use of U.S. equipment."[22] The White House bill called for the "renegotiation of existing agreements to meet the same standards as those we will require for new agreements." The language employed, together with explanatory remarks for State Department officials, seemed to suggest that an exemption would be sought for Euratom – at least for reprocessing plants in operation before the law would come into effect.

However accommodating the United States might be, a U.S. request for renegotiation of the Euratom bilateral agreement itself promised to evoke a bitter reaction. Both the French and the Germans viewed any attempt at renegotiation as a unilateral abrogation of a binding treaty commitment and as unwarranted interference in their internal affairs. A U.S. veto (even a nominal one) implied an infringement of sovereign rights. The inclusion of a "grandfather clause" exempting existing facilities did not help matters. For it would draw a line of discrimination between those members of the supranational community (the United Kingdom and France) who beat the deadline and those (specifically, Germany) who would be compelled to gain U.S. sanction for the operation of their reprocessing facilities. The conflict over these issues that would erupt in 1978 with the passage of the Nuclear Non-Proliferation Act was the culmination of strains on the reprocessing issue that surfaced a year earlier, and that had been exacerbated by the maladroitness of the early Carter diplomacy. From the outset, the problem of reconciling genuine differences was compounded by confusion over administration intentions, as well as by the uncertainties associated with the unpredictable outcome of congressional deliberations on the nonproliferation bill.

Japan, too, found itself at loggerheads with Washington over the reprocessing question. The Tokyo government had made a major commitment to nuclear power as part of a program to attenuate its dependence on external energy sources. A key place in its strategy was accorded to a commercial reprocessing plant at Tokai Mura, slated to start up later in the year. Indeed, the Japanese had sought approval of the operation, and thought they had received it in December, from the lame-duck Ford government. (Unlike the Euratom treaty, the United States' agreement of cooperation with Japan retains for Washington a veto over the reprocessing of U.S.-supplied fuel.) President Carter's press conference comment citing Japan among those with "a perfect right to go ahead and continue with their own reprocessing efforts" met with satisfaction from Japanese officials. They quickly were disabused of their optimism. U.S. officials, following the line laid down at the Nye–Fri press conference, explained that the perfect right would apply only to spent fuel obtained from other sources and passed through non-U.S. reactors. Otherwise, Japanese freedom to reprocess was qualified by the bilateral agreement. This disingenuous explanation did not sit well with Tokyo officials. In follow-up discussions they were inclined to paint Nye as the "heavy" and to play off the State negotiators against what they claimed was a personal understanding between Carter and Prime Minister Fukuda.

The discrepancy between Carter's remarks and Nye's explanation of their meaning would be used in Tokyo as a debating point in the protracted exchanges on reprocessing rights and requirements. (The Japanese were also fond of reminding the United States that "our belief in the necessity of the plutonium cycle is based on American teaching.")[23] Japan could take some comfort from the generally more accommodating administration position that emerged from those early exchanges. It was expressed in a U.S. willingness to negotiate the terms of an experimental operation of Tokai

Mura, and an implicit acknowledgement that the United States accorded Japan the same status as Europe with regard to reprocessing. The equation of Japan with Germany, in particular, meant that any accord with Bonn on reprocessing could be no more generous than one reached with Tokyo. The pairing was perhaps even more important in that any agreement on the operation of Tokai Mura would be a precedent for the still-planned German facility.

The diplomatic political challenge created by the administration's uncertain position on plutonium was revealing itself as dauntingly complex and demanding of fine diplomatic skills. It was being made all the more difficult by the clumsiness of the initial presentation, which got the venture off on a discordant note, and by Carter's distressing habit of making policy off the cuff. The Carter non-proliferation strategy also bore the additional burden of strong domestic opposition, which would hurt the administration's diplomatic campaign both by putting in doubt the United States' avowed moratorium on plutonium fuels and by lending encouragement to unsympathetic governments to persevere in resisting the U.S. initiatives, in the hope that they would be undermined by that domestic opposition.

THE GREAT DOMESTIC DEBATE

The suspicion and hostility that greeted Carter's policy announcement overseas resonated among domestic critics in the nuclear industry and in Congress. At home, as abroad, the sharpest attack was leveled against the president's opposition to commercial reprocessing and development of the demonstration breeder reactor. The Barnwell facility and the Clinch River project had figured in the April 7 statements as projects that should be stopped (Barnwell) or slowed and redesigned (Clinch River), on the grounds that they represented a premature move to the recycling of plutonium. To go ahead with them would lead to plutonium's worldwide acceptance in the nuclear fuel cycle, with attendant proliferation dangers. Of the two, Barnwell was the more immediate concern. Reprocessing plants were already on the verge of commercial operation, and the technology was entering the international marketplace. Plans called for recycling the plutonium that was separated from spent fuel into light-water reactors (as opposed to breeder reactors) of the types in worldwide use. The appetite for reprocessed fuel, whether whetted by economic or by political considerations, might well outpace the hoped-for negotiation of organizational and technical means for making plutonium more difficult to divert.

Thinking about light-metal fast-breeder reactors (LMFBRs), and about the Clinch River project in particular, was somewhat different. The LMFBR was at least a decade away from commercial development. There was a period of grace in which to perfect designs and to devise arrangements for the tolerably safe use of the plutonium on which it depended for start-up fuel. To allow recycling into LWRs would clear the way for widespread and inadequately controlled distribution of plutonium. Recycling into breeder reactors seemed a less pernicious idea. It was acceptable in principle to administration moderates: They were prepared to concede this point in hope of winning from other governments an agreement to forgo recycling into LWRs, to proceed slowly in operationalizing their reprocessing plants, and to join in the review of safer modes for structuring nuclear fuel systems.

Mainstream administration thinking was anchored to this distinction between the recycling of plutonium in light-water reactors, which it opposed, and its use in breeder reactors, which it found conditionally acceptable. Maintaining this distinction would not be easy. For one thing, the two had become linked in many minds. Because the breeder, that most attractive of atomic power-generating systems, relied on separated plutonium, it was often argued that only through reprocessing would it be possible to acquire the technical skills needed for breeder operation. This linkage was inadvertently reinforced by the administration's mistake in speaking of the Barnwell reprocessing plant and the Clinch River breeder project as a package. The latter, although strongly backed by the nuclear establishment, was open to criticism on technical and economic grounds as well as for proliferation reasons. The negative judgment of the Carter administration followed the assessment of the Ford/Mitre study group, which emphasized the former. This group questioned whether the plant's design was outdated, using technologies already overtaken by subsequent advances and based on a dubious mode of operation. The administration's expert advisers on the fast breeder made a persuasive argument in support of their conviction that the project was cost-ineffective; that money, for the present, might better be spent on basic experimental and component design work; and that the outlook for energy demand and natural uranium supplies did not call for a crash LMFBR development program. The widespread perception of an intimate tie between reprocessing and the fast-breeder reactors, resulting in an accentuation of interest in acquiring reprocessing technology, capped the argument against Clinch River. But it was not absolutely essential to that argument: The fact that the technical case against Clinch River, implying no necessary devaluation of the LMFBR's ultimate desirability, could be kept separate from the proliferation case against it was obscured by President Carter's remarks, which referred the decision to postpone solely to his non-proliferation campaign.[24]

By lumping together the Barnwell and Clinch River actions, Carter offered a more inviting target to domestic opponents, who denounced these twin steps as a blow to the national quest for energy independence. Critics also claimed that they would cripple the U.S. nuclear industry in its competition with foreign firms, who now would have the field of second-generation reactors to themselves. The restrictive Carter policy came at a time when the atomic power business was already reeling from a series of setbacks. Domestic demand for power reactors was drying up, thanks to a combination of recession, environmental opposition, licensing delays, mounting worries about waste-management problems, and uncertainties over the availability of enrichment services and the spiraling price of natural uranium. Internationally, the U.S. atomic power business was already losing sales to the aggressive European reactor manufacturers, who benefited from the problems raised for U.S. suppliers by the unpredictability of export licensing and the blocking of enrichment contracts (as well as from the French and West German offers of fuel-producing facilities as sweeteners). Then along came the Carter administration, with a passionate commitment to non-proliferation that seemed ready to jeopardize future development by suppressing the two new technologies – waste management through the reprocessing of spent fuel – that had been expected to ease some current problems and to ensure the nuclear industry the paramount place in the nation's energy future. Within six months, the situation had been turned inside out. Barnwell would not demonstrate the commercial viability of reprocessing and establish U.S. leadership in the field. Clinch River would not narrow the French lead in fast breeders and lay the basis for a concerted development program. Moreover, the non-proliferation campaign (acknowledged to be genuine in its convictions, if misguided in its emphasis and priorities) was seen by many in the nuclear power industry as masking a more deep-seated opposition to nuclear energy, personified by arch-environmentalists ensconced in positions of power in the administration.

Feelings of desperation, hardened by anger at the collapse of a generation-old alliance with government, lay behind the vehement, at times vituperative, assault on the Carter policies. Industry fears had been aroused, and anger stoked, at a mid-March conference sponsored by the Atomic Industrial Forum (an umbrella association covering all segments of the industry) on international commerce and safeguards for civil nuclear power. The conference chewed anxiously on the reports then circulating about the impending administration initiatives. The failure of the White House or State Department to send a representative only added to the sense of grievance and aggravated feelings of abandonment. The government's decision not to attend the meeting was not meant, however, to imply opposition to the industry. The simple truth was that the administration, in the throes of its own internal debate, was not in a position to make any statement of its policy. Silence was the only course. The price of reticence imposed by bureaucratic dissonance and delay was to encourage the deepest fears of commercial interests, and to remove whatever inhibitions they felt about fighting the administration's policies.

From every corner of the industry came a barrage of criticism, in public pronouncements, newspaper advertisements, petitions, and congressional testimony. Carl Walske, president of the Atomic Industrial Forum, expressed the dominant mood in declaring:

> The President is, in effect, asking Americans to forgo an essential element in their nuclear future in order to create a bargaining chip for the U.S. in our efforts to influence other countries. At the same time, he has stated that certain other countries will continue with their programs to utilize plutonium, whatever course the U.S. follows. Our domestic sacrifice appears to be for naught.[25]

AIF Chairman Clyde A. Lilly, Jr., chimed in with a telegram to the president warning of the high risk being run by the United States in an indefinite reprocessing interregnum. He complained, "We are already on the verge of seeing one nuclear power supply capability disintegrated in the face of a near vacuum of new orders, now approaching three years." In the climate of uncertainty about the disposal of spent fuel (accentuated by the indefinite postponement of Barnwell), Lilly continued, "utility executives could hardly be expected to order new plants."[26]

A blunter appeal was made by those with a direct stake in the survival of the Barnwell and Clinch River projects. Allied-General Nuclear Services, the industrial consortium directing the Barnwell operation, took out full-page ads in the *New York Times* addressed to the White House. They declared:

> We can't turn back the clock . . . plutonium is here and now. The real question is: what do we do with it? Reprocessing has a big advantage . . . We believe the only practical way to reduce the proliferation threat from nuclear power programs is to have spent fuel returned to the supplier nations in exchange for low-enriched uranium. Completion of Barnwell would provide the facility for receiving and processing that material.[27]

The Clinch River interests were no more reticent. An open letter to President Carter written by technical personnel involved with the project expressed their astonishment that, "when energy conservation is vital, . . . the economic conservation potential of the Liquid Metal Fast Breeder Reactor (LMFBR) is apparently ignored . . . that is an energy resource worth $20 trillion."[28]

Distress over what critics saw as the gratuitous rejection of a vital energy resource was echoed in Congress as well. Although the joint session that heard his nuclear message had applauded Carter's statement that "there is no need to enter the plutonium age by licensing or building a fast breeder reactor such as the proposed demonstration plant at Clinch River," influential representatives on both sides of the House were disturbed by the decision to postpone.[29] Some represented districts that benefited economically from the location of nuclear facilities; some enjoyed the support of nuclear industries and were susceptible to their formidable lobbying efforts; and many simply believed that a policy of self-denial was unwarranted and did not make sense in the context of the nation's overall energy needs. Congressman Mike McCormack, chairman of the House Science and Technology subcommittee on energy, which had legislative jurisdiction over the research and development budget, was one skeptic uninhibited about expressing his disappointment with the president. In a *Washington Post* feature article, he offered the judgment that "President Carter's recent proposals . . . would probably deny our country its only chance to produce the energy we will need for economic stability," and added his doubt whether a unilateral U.S. action curbing plutonium-based technologies would reduce the risk of proliferation.[30] McCormack was joined by Senator Frank Church of Idaho, who used the occasion of an address at MIT to subject the president's program to scathing criticism. "I am convinced," he said,

> that the Administration's nuclear energy policy is a formula for nuclear isolationism . . . The breeder program is the only technology now on the horizon that holds out the promise of relieving Europe and Japan of an unremitting dependence upon foreign-held fuel policies . . . Neither the governments in Western Europe nor Japan are going to remain bound in the energy straightjacket if they have a chance to achieve, through the breeder program, eventual energy independence.[31]

Church concluded that a self-imposed U.S. moratorium would be to no avail. It would wind up hampering the United States' ability to control the fuel cycle internationally (and delaying the acquisition of a new energy resource) while offering no dividend in restricting the availability of worrisome technologies.

The ensuing congressional debate over the president's recommendation to kill Clinch River demonstrated how deep the disagreement was. There was strong sentiment, among what turned out to be a majority in both Houses, that it did not make sense to forgo the potential benefits of breeder development for the sake of intangible proliferation advantages (advantages that looked all the more elusive, given the reaffirmed intention of other countries to push ahead with their own breeder programs). The promised loss of technological leadership to foreign industry did not make the pill more palatable. As for the administration argument that Clinch

River was unsatisfactory on technical and engineering grounds, that analysis was taken by many as a rationalization for a decision really determined by its purported proliferation significance. The president was out of step with congressional thinking on Clinch River.

But Congress's favorable attitude toward the breeder did *not* imply a diminution of concern about the proliferation danger or a weakening of the forces pressing for tough export conditions. As Congress moved to a legislative resolution of both Clinch River appropriations and a nonproliferation bill, it became apparent that while there was overwhelming support for a highly restrictive approach to export licensing, a smaller majority rejected the view that stopping work on the breeder was a crucial element in a strategy of denial. On Barnwell, Congress recognized a closer link between the U.S. program and the country's external objectives. The approach receiving greatest favor on that score was multilateralization of the international fuel cycle, in which a U.S. reprocessing facility could play a key role. Strongly backed by Senator Glenn and others, the idea of an international fuel authority was urged on the president in the Non-Proliferation Act of 1978 that came into law a year later. Its popularity owed much to its appeal as a politically painless way of neutralizing the plutonium problem, as well to as its promise of meeting the U.S. interest in exploiting the energy potential of nuclear power fully without inadvertently encouraging activities that carried with them a severe risk of proliferation.

The evidence that the administration was not in tune with congressional opinion was soon forthcoming on Clinch River. On June 14, the House Science and Technology Committee voted nineteen to eleven to disregard the president's objections and authorize $150 million to begin construction. A month later, the Senate, too, turned a deaf ear to Carter's plea to limit new funds to the smaller amount needed for phasing out the project. Instead, the upper house accepted a compromise offered by Senator Church to earmark $75 million in the ERDA budget in order to allow the project to retain its current status. Presented with an eventual authorization of $80 million for the project, Carter used the first veto of his administration to reject the approach, which he claimed would "imperil the Administration's policy to curb proliferation of nuclear weapons technology."[32] A compromise reached after months of strenuous negotiation involved earmarking an augmented $160 million for construction of a larger facility using other technology in a wholly new undertaking. The sum would bring to over half a billion dollars the money that the Department of Energy already planned to spend on breeder projects. That compromise was modified somewhat and then abandoned the following summer when the House, acting on the Energy Department authorization bill, voted large sums for operating expenses at Clinch River. After a turbulent summer of executive congressional politicking, with another presidential veto threatened, Congress and the president reached an understanding (linked to the outcome of the conference report on the pending natural gas price-deregulation bill) that committed the administration to a three-year development program for the LMFBR. Clinch River itself was allowed to die on the vine. The engineering teams remained in place, although there was no expectation of getting down to bricks and mortar; design work and component development would go on elsewhere. It was an imperfect compromise that left doubts about the U.S. government's true policy on breeder reactors and about its capacity to act consistently and predictably. Those doubts would never be removed, because Carter and the Congress continued to duel over Clinch River for most of his administration. In the end, the project survived.[33]

One of its supporters' most potent weapons was the marshaling of comments favorable to the breeder from foreign sources and the insertion of them into the domestic debate as evidence that other countries were not following the U.S. lead, in order to draw the conclusion that Carter was demanding a sacrifice that promised no reward. Indeed, it would only make the United States dependent on European breeder technology. Playing both sides against the middle in classic fashion, these advocates conveyed to the Europeans the message that an unsympathetic chorus of off-stage voices would assist the U.S. advocates of nuclear power to blunt the Carter attack on plutonium, which was seen as a threat to civilian nuclear power worldwide. As an exasperated administration official complained, "Here in the U.S. breeder-interests are saying you can't kill the breeder because foreign countries are going ahead anyway, and overseas they're telling the foreigners that if they hold tight we can turn it around at home."[34]

Carter's stance on the fast breeder and the controversy surrounding it in Congress were vulnerable points in his non-proliferation campaign, which naturally came to bear the brunt of the assault on it. For by making the link between a proliferation-motivated strategy of plutonium self-denial and the breeder, he opened the way for critics to argue that the administration's policy would mortgage the energy future of the United States (with no reasonable expectation that other nations would follow the U.S. lead), in the illusory hope that sensitive nuclear materials thereby could be kept out of the hands of potential proliferators. The argument for a strategy stressing denials rather than safeguards was in its own right difficult enough to sell to countries with a stake in reprocessing. The implication that the price was also the one technology with the golden promise of energy independence made the proposal unpalatable.

DIPLOMACY: OPEN AND CLOSED

Two international conferences

The administration had gotten a taste of the foreign antipathy toward its nuclear initiatives in the original diplomatic reaction to Carter's April statement. A full appreciation of how high feelings ran came at two international conferences, unfortuitously scheduled a few weeks later. One was a gathering of five hundred industry and government officials at Shiraz, Iran, in the Conference on Nuclear Technology Transfer. The Persepolis Conference, as it was called, was jointly sponsored by the American Nuclear Society and its counterparts in Europe and Japan. This commercially minded group indulged in an orgy of abuse against the Carter policy, unrestrained by diplomatic niceties.[35] The conference's concluding statement, the "Persepolis Declaration," was a resounding attack on the new U.S. policy and a metaphoric call to arms in defense of nuclear power. It was in fact drafted by the U.S. nuclear industry.

A more equitable atmosphere was expected at the IAEA-sponsored International Conference on Nuclear Power and Its Fuel Cycle held at the end of April in Salzburg. Planned long before Carter's accession to the presidency, it brought together national delegates from the four corners of the worldwide nuclear establishment to discuss the global outlook for civilian nuclear power, focusing on the question of what policies for closing the fuel cycle would avoid the increased danger of weapons proliferation. Washington had foreseen the meeting as an excellent opportunity for some quiet diplomacy. In the corridors, and at informal gatherings, administration representatives would add subtle shadings to the president's rather stark sketch of the new U.S. policy. They also would expand upon his brief references to a fuel-assurance program and an internationally conducted review of alternative nuclear futures. The point man in this exercise, and head of the U.S. delegation, was Joseph Nye.

Nye's life had not been made any easier by happenings in Washington, where the internecine battle over the administration's reprocessing policy continued unabated. In the aftermath of the embarrassing April 7 statements, misstatements, and restatements, he had moved to get an unequivocal commitment to the flexible, yet not totally indulgent, approach State had promoted from the onset. As part of the follow-up exercise laid down in PD-8, Nye's office had been given the responsibility of forming a clean set of options from which the president would choose. Through an assiduous lobbying effort, this office was able to align the entire bureaucracy behind a paper designed to win presidential backing for its preferred position. The paper presented the classic three choices. The two extremes offered either a laissez-faire attitude toward foreign government plans to recycle plutonium or implacable opposition that would entail at least the threat of an LEU embargo. Sandwiched between them was the comparatively reasonable option of opening a campaign of education and persuasion to slow the move toward reprocessing, restructuring its location and operating mode. This strategy would make U.S. approval of any request to reprocess spent fuel of U.S. origin contingent on the party's readiness to cooperate with Washington in serious efforts to reduce proliferation danger. Carter, being a reasonable man, was expected to opt for the middle course. Nye, however, reckoned without Jessica Tuchman at the NSC. As the funnel to the White House, the council staff monitors policy papers going to the Oval Office. A protagonist in the proliferation debate, Tuchman used the prerogatives of her office to add a fourth option. It declared the United States in opposition to foreign reprocessing of U.S.-supplied fuel except in extreme circumstances, when the president would entertain petitions requesting special permission. To the joy of the purists and the anguish of State officials, Carter chose this last option. Official U.S. policy had now taken another sudden turn, its third, this time strongly in the direction of a hard-line, absolutist antiplutonium position. It fell to Joseph Nye to announce this policy in Salzburg, where he had hoped to devote his energies to publicizing the reasonableness and flexibility of the administration's position.

Instead of participating in low-key discussions, Nye found himself in a cauldron at Salzburg. He became the target of denunciation and recrimination. For those bitter about what they saw as a high-handed U.S. effort to impose anti–nuclear power beliefs on the world, he was a convenient object of attack – being physically present and identified as a leader of the Ford/Mitre gang at work in the new administration. The most pointed criticism was aimed at several features of the Carter initiative and had more than one motive. Some saw the move against plutonium as a cover to protect U.S. commercial interests by drawing the rug from under the Europeans, who had stolen a march on the United States in the breeder and reprocessing fields. The French were especially prone to this opinion, which conformed at once to their own avaricious view of human nature and to their pronounced belief that most of the United States' behavior toward its allies was inspired by a consuming desire to strengthen its own nuclear hegemony. One French delegate suggested that the Carter policy was a commercial ruse dressed up in ideology, declaring it "politically, economically and ecologically absurd."[36] Others, less preoccupied with export markets, condemned Washington for arrogant self-centeredness in assuming that foreign governments could afford an indefinite delay in their nuclear power programs as readily as could an energy-rich, technologically well-endowed United States. Heavy investment requirements, the political importance of maintaining program momentum in the face of domestic opposition, and the balance-of-payments strains created by the outflow of petro-dollars – all dictated making firm plans for the expansion of civilian nuclear power. To accept the Carter approach would mean compounding uncertainty, perpetuating the uncomfortable situation of energy dependence, and encouraging antinuclear forces ready to take advantage of every opportunity to undermine the credibility of nuclear energy. These feelings were pervasive among the European and Japanese nuclear officials present at Salzburg.

As for the technically less-proficient consumers, they were doubly annoyed by a U.S. policy reversal that, in their eyes, overturned the bargain incorporated in the NPT. In that treaty they had traded the weapons option, and a chunk of their sovereignty in permitting the regulation of civilian facilities, for a pledge of full support and assistance in exploiting the peaceful potential of the atom. Washington now appeared to be unilaterally declaring which forms of civilian power, using which technologies, would be permitted, thereby threatening to draw a new line of discrimination between those states with access to fuel-producing technologies and those without such access. IAEA Secretary-General Sigvard Ecklund lent his voice to this criticism, suggesting that the United States was abrogating an international agreement by failing to live up to the terms of Article 4. "The U.S. statement," he complained, "disregards [NPT] requirements for the exchange of information on nuclear know-how." In any case, Ecklund declared that he did "not believe it is possible to put a lid on technological development."[37] He further argued that the United States, by weakening the confidence of consumers in its promises of nuclear fuel supplies, weakened the commitments of nonweapons states to accept the restrictions imposed by the NPT and bilateral agreements, and created incentives for them to seek national sources of supply.

The administration's attackers shared the irritation over what they considered an overbearing U.S. attitude and a predilection for making international policy by fiat. Primed to dislike Carter's approach by reason of its rumored lack of sympathy for nuclear power generally, and nervous about the threat the untamed U.S. president posed to their highly vulnerable nuclear programs, they saw a generation's work at building atomic power jeopardized without the courtesy of consultation or a serious effort to reach a common understanding. Those officials in attendance at Salzburg were particularly inclined to be upset by the Carter administration. Representation was drawn almost exclusively from governments' technical ministries, research laboratories, utility enterprises, and commercial organizations – that is to say, the nuclear establishment. For the most part, foreign ministries and politically minded officials were absent. It was the latter who had to concern themselves about proliferation dangers, and who had the responsibility for assuirng that their colleagues' enthusiasm for nuclear power did not carry the day without due regard for the constraints under which nuclear programs and policies for international transfers had to operate. Salzburg therefore was very much a conclave of the true believers in civilian nuclear power. They were men with a professional and intellectual stake in exploiting nuclear technology to the utmost. They were out for blood, and the tactless Carter style gave them a good excuse to bare their teeth.

The depth of feeling, as well as the vehemence with which it was expressed, was genuine – but not entirely spontaneous. There was a measure of calculation and some orchestration in the greeting that was accorded Joseph Nye and his associates. Over the years, a network of closely knit ties had formed among scientists, engineers, bureaucrats, and businessmen active in the nuclear power field. These associations crossed national boundaries and resulted in an international interest group promoting the cause of peaceful atomic energy and lobbying in its behalf. Early on, the dominant influence had been American. In the fifties and early sixties, AEC officials, along with representatives of the emerging nuclear industry, exercised substantial influence in shaping the nascent program of Euratom and in instilling a vision of the nuclear fuel cycle that closely approximated the thinking prevailing in the United States.[38] Joint industrial ventures, entailing the transfer of much U.S. know-how and technology to European associates (who, ironically, became the major competitors of their U.S. mentors), and extensive exchanges among specialists, added other dimensions to these affiliations. One outgrowth of this fraternization was the development of a community of like-minded people and institutions with effective communication channels at their disposal.

The network was activated to marshall opposition to the Carter campaign against plutonium. Actually, there were two interlocking networks, one corporate, the other governmental. The industrial channel consisted of the corporations with an economic stake in the growth of nuclear power and in closure of the fuel cycle via reprocessing. A leading role in encouraging a coordinated response was played by Carl Walske, president of the AIF. Immediately after the president's April 7 statement, he traveled to Europe with the message that a unilateral reprocessing and breeder moratorium was part and parcel of a non-proliferation strategy that would involve coercing the Europeans not to proceed with plutonium recycling. The common interest the Europeans shared with U.S. industry, he argued, was in discrediting the administration's position, rather than seeking to take advantage of U.S. industry's uncomfortable position. One discrediting tactic, as noted before, was assembly of a barrage of statements of confidence in commercial reprocessing to be used in the domestic U.S. debate.

The other was presentation of a solid political front of opposition to Washington, which would accentuate the international costs of the administration's pushing ahead with its strategy.

Complementing this corporate lobbying was a more subtle signaling between some of the staunchly pro-nuclear people at ERDA and their counterparts in other capitals. (The distinction between an industrial and a governmental network is somewhat arbitrary. Not only are ties within each country close, but in much of Europe the leading nuclear firms are publicly owned, publicly financed, or dependent on government-controlled technology.) Although these U.S. officials could not risk outright opposition to the administration policy, they did not feel especially inhibited from undercutting it in other ways. They provided encouragement and support by passing information embarrassing to the official U.S. position (for example, technical studies questioning administration assessments of the costs and benefits of reprocessing, of uranium reserves, and so on); by making known the schisms and frictions within the administration that could be played upon to reduce its inner cohesion and public unity; by voicing cautious doubts and qualifications about elements of the policy at the Salzburg sessions themselves; and, later, by delaying in the formulation of the specific spent-fuel storage and fuel-assurance proposals that were meant to be key elements in the president's policy. (On this last count, the ERDA old guard had little difficulty in performing according to expectations, as all that was required was business as usual.)

In a story replete with ironies, Joseph Nye's fate as the target for the nuclear establishment's counterattack is among the most poignant. As a political scientist and international relations theorist, he was best known for formulating a theory of transnational politics that called attention to the influence exerted on world affairs by nongovernmental actors. Among the more interesting aspects of this theory was the "transgovernmental connection" among department officials with analogous responsibilities and convergent interests. Nye, in collaboration with his coauthor Robert Keohane, spoke of "sets of direct interactions among sub-units of different governments." In some instances, where they are "not controlled or closely guided by the policies of the cabinets or chief executive of those governments," officials might be in a position to take advantage of the ambiguities of central policies to influence the course of action significantly. Basically, Keohane and Nye postulated two kinds of transgovernmental behavior: "Transgovernmental policy coordination refers to activity designed to facilitate smooth implementation or adjustment of policy, in the absence of detailed higher policy directives. Another process, transgovernmental coalition-building, takes place when sub-units build coalitions with like-minded agencies from other governments against elements of their own administrative structure."[39] In his official capacity, Joseph Nye, deputy to the undersecretary of state for security assistance, science, and technology, became a victim of machinations by a transgovernmental (and a transindustrial) concert like those he had portrayed in his scholarly writings. As he would remark ruefully, and not without humor, it can be distressing for an academic to learn that the real world can actually work as depicted in academic theory.

Surprised by the tumultuous reception he received at Salzburg, Nye persevered in the assigned mission of fleshing out the Carter policy, making it more comprehensible, and eliciting a greater appreciation of – if not sympathetic support for – what the administration was doing. His speech to the conference sought to take some of the sting out of the president's call for a reprocessing moratorium by underlining the United States' continuing support for civilian nuclear power and by stressing that it proposed to meet the world's legitimate interest in securing energy resources. He emphasized first that "the United States remains committed to the use of nuclear power at home and to peaceful nuclear power abroad"; President Carter, he reminded the delegates, backed expansion of the United States' nuclear generating capacity and recognized publicly the stake of other countries in nuclear power's increasing use. Defining the key issue as "how we can reconcile the *next stage* of nuclear power development with the increased threat of nuclear weapons proliferation," Nye declared that the solution had to be an international one. It could not "be achieved by one country or even a number of countries." The United States was therefore asking all interested governments "to join it in a major program to examine fuel cycle alternatives" – an International Fuel Cycle Evaluation review (INFCE) – and to devise means for dealing with "urgent problems associated with the current operation of the fuel cycle, such as reliable fuel supply and means of storing spent-fuel." The goal of INFCE would not be a "single agreed product," but rather "mutual education and voluntary harmonization of policies." In instigating the review, the United States recognized that "it has a special responsibility to share with others the benefits of nuclear energy, and does not prejudge the question of reprocessing in some form." At the same time, Washington saw a matching responsibility "to search for alternatives that will meet our energy needs while reducing security risks," and to avoid "premature entry into a plutonium economy."[40]

The complementary theme of his address emphasized incentives. It recognized the need for a wide-ranging program "to provide assured supply of non-sensitive nuclear fuels on a timely, adequate, reliable and economic basis." Here he could point to a concrete U.S. action: a commitment to expanding its enrichment capacity (the administration energy budget included funds for an addition at the Portsmouth, Ohio, plant, using the diffusion technology, and for design work on a new centrifuge facility) and a reopening of the order books on enrichment services. In addition, Nye spoke in very general terms of "multilateral arrangements designed to substantiate guarantees," and "international arrangements such as stockpiles that might serve as [a] contingency reserve." He also made passing reference to measures to deal with the problem at the back-end of the fuel cycle that would "alleviate the pressure for acquisition of reprocessing capabilities." Without offering detailed proposals, he conveyed the impression of a genuine U.S. concern for the energy needs and problems of dependent nuclear countries. On the whole, the speech read as an earnest, reasonably persuasive exposition of the overall situation associated with managing the international fuel cycle. It also ably presented Washington's sober view of how the issue of reconciling the non-proliferation and economic aspects of plutonium recycling might be approached. Although this exposition of administration policy did not still the vocal criticism (nothing short of total recantation could have quieted the Salzburg crowd), it did provide a basis on which to launch a diplomatic effort to win sympathy and support.

Reprise

The Carter administration attempt to divert or at least to slow the trend toward plutonium recycling was radical because it entailed a basic restructuring of the world's institutional framework for civilian nuclear power and also a fundamental rethinking about what technologies and processes might safely be incorporated into the international fuel cycle. By putting in doubt the assumed right of states (even those which adhere to safeguards) to market, purchase, and operate reprocessing and fast-breeder facilities – technologies with the promise of energy self-sufficiency – the United States was instigating a general debate, one that already gave signs of being both acrimonious and agonized, over what constitutes a nation's energy and security interests when nuclear arms capabilities become the global rule rather than the exception.

Having itself reached the first conclusion that plutonium recycling, as presently conceived, carried on intolerable proliferation risk, the administration faced the more daunting challenge of convincing governments elsewhere to reverse their thinking about plutonium. The guillotining of the Barnwell facility and the dropping of plans for the Clinch River breeder were intended as strong talking points in a lively campaign to dissuade other countries from going down the plutonium road. Yet to accept the U.S. judgment that commercial spread of reprocessing was tantamount to latent proliferation would credit a case for restricting (or significantly modifying) the development of an entire class of nuclear technologies – ones that many governments were inclined to see as crucial to their energy future and economic well-being. This was the crux of Washington's non-proliferation dilemma.

Carter administration officials confronted four awkward issues: (1) how to persuade those governments in Western Europe and Japan who were programmatically and financially committed to reprocessing that it was in their interest to hold in abeyance their plans for plutonium, in order not to lend commercial credibility to civilian reprocessing in its present form; (2) failing a complete moratorium on plutonium recycling, at least into LWRs, how to avoid drawing a new line of discrimination on the civil side of nuclear power between those nonweapons states (e.g., West Germany) who might reprocess and those (e.g., South Korea) who might be coerced into not doing so; (3) how to shape an incentive program comprising fuel assurances and spent-fuel disposal arrangements sufficiently attractive (to both classes of countries) to remove any legitimate economic–energy-security interests in reprocessing; and (4) how to establish an optimal mix of coercion and inducement in U.S. policies directed both at industrially advanced countries competent in reprocessing technologies (who also were potential suppliers of sensitive technologies) and at consumer countries dependent on external supply or reactors and fuels, whose access to pluto-nium fuels would also arouse acute proliferation worries.[41] The goal was to fashion a set of agreements, or understandings, that were sensitive to the specific interests, opportunities, and vulnerabilities created by particular national circumstances, and yet sufficiently uniform and consistent to con-stitute a viable institutional framework for international nuclear transac-tions.

The diplomatic agenda

The diplomatic agenda was a long one, and the list of U.S. objectives formidable. To accomplish them, Washington somehow would have to manage to realign diverse national programs with reformed international fuel-cycle arrangemnts, and to make both broadly congruent with U.S. non-proliferation objectives.

U.S. diplomacy would be employed on several fronts at once. In its dealings with each set of interlocutors, it had a range of minimum and maximum achievements that, if realized, should add up to a stable and effective whole. The goals can be summarized as follows:

From the Suppliers' Club
1. An unequivocal commitment to withhold all sensitive facili-ties, including reprocessing, from the world market
2. A joint requirement for strict full-scope safeguards as a con-dition for reactor and fuel exports to consumer countries
3. Participation in a fuel-assurance program that would guar-antee a reliable supply of LEU fuels for those consumers that accepted restrictions on sensitive fuel-fabrication facilities and met safeguards conditions
4. Earnest participation in the International Fuel Cycle Evalua-

tion program (INFCE) for reviewing and evaluating short-
and long-term alternative techniques and technologies, with
a view to identifying those which would be advantageous
from a non-proliferation standpoint and which would be
economically viable

*From the Japanese and West Europeans having plans for commerical
reprocessing*

1. The deferral of commercial separation and recycling of plutonium in mixed oxide form in LWRs, pending the outcome
of the INFCE review
2. Slowing of breeder development
3. As a second-best, fall-back position (failing deferral of reprocessing and the LMFBR), acceptance of technical modifications that would be preferable models from a proliferation
standpoint, and/or consideration embedding any reprocessing facilities in multinational arrangements, thereby avoiding the precedent of a purely national closure of the fuel
cycle

*From the suppliers of natural uraniums (principally Australia,
Canada, and South Africa)*

1. Broad agreement on export conditions in line with the U.S.
goal of consumer acceptance of complete system safeguards
and a veto over national reprocessing (but not rigid, inflexible rules that could not be adapted to individual national
circumstances)
2. An undertaking to earmark some portion of their supply for
a strategic reserve, which would stand as a physical guarantee to assured natural uranium, protected against politically
motivated interruption (i.e., for reasons other than those
specified by the NPT and bilateral agreements of cooperation)

From consumers not having proficiency in sensitive technologies

1. Agreement not to purchase or develop reprocessing facilities
or to use plutonium fuels, pending the outcome of the
INFCE
2. Participation in a multilateral program to provide an assured
supply of LEU fuels on a reliable, economical basis (along
with safe disposal of spent-fuel loads)
3. Acceptance of complete fuel-cycle safeguards and a U.S. veto
over the reprocessing of U.S.-supplied LEU fuels as a condition for sale of power plants and fuels

These objectives would be pursued in several diplomatic forums, with the United States serving as host or promoter of all of them. At the Suppliers' Club, Washington would continue in a quiet communion with the technically proficient exporting countries. In an even lower key, the administration would initiate informal talks with those countries who provided the greater part of the world's natural uranium. A third area would be the battery of bilateral discussions between the United States and those governments with whom it had outstanding nuclear business; given the United States' commitment to renegotiating agreements of cooperation (as well as its other initiatives), they were numerous. Finally, there was the proposed International Fuel Cycle Evaluation, which would be the global forum in which all parties might consider together the framework for peaceful development of civilian nuclear power.

INFCE was viewed as by far the most important. Administration officials realized that they could not get their assessment of the proliferation situation accepted by exhortation alone. An institutionalized format was needed in which the United States could develop its case, deal with the views of others, and make an effort at reaching a satisfactory synthesis. The International Fuel Cycle Evaluation was the mechanism Washington had in mind. INFCE was visualized as a set of cooperative research and study programs addressing the several technical, institutional, and economic facets of the nuclear fuel cycle internationally. In Nye's words, INFCE would provide a "two-year period in which nations can re-examine assumptions and find ways to reconcile their somewhat different assessments of the risks involved in and the time scale for commercialization of the various aspects of the nuclear fuel cycle." INFCE would serve the basic U.S. objective of developing "an international framework that will minimize the incentives and opportunities for nuclear proliferation."[42] The administration fear that weapons acquisition through misuse of the fuel cycle was a real danger meant placing premiums on reducing "the vulnerability of sensitive points in the fuel cycle," thereby removing temptation from a would-be proliferator.[43] One of the INFCE's hoped-for fruits would be agreement on proliferation-resistant technology and institutional arrangements for using it.

The May summit

The first test of the willingness of the United States' friends and allies to cooperate with Washington in shaping a new approach to managing civilian nuclear power internationally came at the May summit of Western leaders (plus Japan). It had been scheduled as an occasion for the heads of government to get to know the new U.S. president. The main item of business was to be the world economic situation, and differences in national approaches to the problem of lingering unemployment and high inflation. Carter's early activism made other governments especially anxious to test the mettle of the titular leader of the free world. The furor aroused by his antiproliferation campaign ensured that the nuclear issue would figure high on the agenda. Responsibility for briefing the president lay primarily with the State Department. The State officials took pains to draw his attention to the hostile reactions that had met the proclamation of U.S. policy and to urge the wisdom of not pressing the reprocessing issue or making a last, personal try at sinking the German–Brazilian nuclear trade pact. They saw their job as counteracting the influence of the purists – who were calling on Carter to stick to an unbending opposition to reprocessing – by reminding him of the practical political realities in the governments with whom he would be dealing. Whereas the purists appealed to Carter the man of strong moral convictions, the State Department moderates addressed Carter the pragmatic politician. The more knowledgeable and politically experienced mainstream people know that there was no hope that the Germans, French, British, and Japanese could be induced to forgo reprocessing. The goal was to get them to accept terms and conditions that slowed the timetable and encouraged technical modifications. That would buy time for instituting new international arrangements and for perfecting alternative technologies. As one State official commented, the department people held up the mirror to the president so that he could see the virtue of this more modest position and not let the "bee in his bonnet about reprocessing" distort his political vision.

In the event, the president conducted himself very much as Carter the pragmatist. The pitch he made followed closely the line taken at Salzburg. As the soul of moderation and understanding, Carter repeated his appreciation of the keen interest other countries took in getting on with the process of turning nuclear power into a prime energy source. He explained why his administration thought that reprocessing gave a wholly new coloration to the proliferation problem, and stressed the United States' firm intention to join in programs to minimize any sacrifice entailed in slowing the move toward a plutonium economy. Above all, he sought to win the participation of other governments in the cooperative International Fuel Cycle Review. The reaction at London was more positive than expected, and a refreshing change from the strident polemics of Salzburg. There were a number of reasons for the change of mood. Tempers had had a chance to cool and minds a chance to distinguish between what Washington had actually said and fears of what it might have said. Political leadership was not emotionally involved with nuclear power (as were the technical people from the atomic energy agencies), and it was more prepared to take seriously the proliferation problem. Approaches made by the State Department to sympathetic counterparts in foreign ministries, especially at the Quai d'Orsay, succeeded in fostering a better understanding of the flexibility in the U.S. position. And, by no means least important, heads of allied governments could not afford to engage in confrontations with U.S. presidents where vital national interests were not at stake. Moreover, there was little reason to do so when the United States was showing signs of a more accommodating tack.

It was particularly reassuring to his fellow heads of government to learn that Carter was not the simpleminded country preacher that he had appeared in the more jaundiced of European eyes. Although his counterparts were still inclined to view him as an accident-prone amateur, untutored in world affairs and unskilled in the diplomatic arts, they drew comfort from seeing that he listened to his more experienced advisers and obviously had the intelligence to appreciate their position and to make discriminating judgments. The productive outcome of the London conclave was an agreement in principle to the wide-ranging international review of nuclear issues represented by INFCE. After discussion of several possible formats for the review, the parties eventually came around to the U.S. conception, which the State people had sketched for their foreign colleagues in the confidence that it would be accepted as the most reasonable way to proceed. It was seen as a set of coordinated research and study programs organized around task forces, each headed by a team of lead countries. At London, a small intragovernmental group was set up to do a quick "mega-study" of the review's terms of reference as a prelude to soliciting the participation of interested parties.

Overall, the encounter between Carter and the allies was a success. The way was clear for getting down to the hard business at hand without rhetorical flourish. Shortly after the president's return, the administration made a conciliatory gesture in announcing the release of the HEU uranium deliveries that had been held up since January. Delay in granting export licenses had been one action that gave allies the impression of nuclear extremism in the new administration. In fact, the officials involved never had the Euratom countries or Japan in mind when they imposed the moratorium pending a review of regulations, and of NRC licensing procecures, controlling HEU exports for use in experimental facilities. As on so many other matters of detail, political insensitivity extracted an unnecessarily high price for an uncertain gain. In the end, it was decided that the president would personally approve all shipments greater than fifteen kilograms. Washington had made its point about the seriousness with which it viewed the plutonium problem, and could now assume that other governments would think twice before plunging ahead with commercial reprocessing using current techniques. The technical bureaucracies would be engaged in a reexamination of alternative designs and processes, as well as of alternatives for handling nuclear waste. The political bureaucracies had been induced to confront the challenge of devising politically acceptable arrangements that would effectively safeguard the new generation of nuclear facilities against military abuse. It would now be up to the Carter administration to demonstrate dexterity and judgment in drawing the pieces into a viable whole.

REORGANIZATION AT HOME

Gerard Smith

Having partly repaired the damage caused by its fumbling start, the administration needed to get its own house in order. President Carter's deep personal involvement in nuclear policy, and his dislike for tidy organization at the White House (whatever his feelings about governmental efficiency at lower levels) meant that policy making would still be something less than a fully integrated machine. One recognized need was to relieve Joseph Nye's shop of part of its multiple responsibilities. In theory at least, his five-man staff was expected to direct the entire intragovernmental apparatus engaged in the formulation of non-proliferation policy, to consult and negotiate with a demanding Congress, to conduct the most sensitive diplomacy with foreign governments, and, in the midst of all this, to do some serious thinking about the aims and requirements of the overall strategy. Each of these tasks was arduous enough to test a small office with limited past experience in government. To do them all was simply impossible. (The burden of travel was itself enormous, keeping Nye out of Washington one week out of four.)

In June, Gerard Smith, the former chief negotiator of SALT I, was given the joint appointment of ambassador to the IAEA and U.S. special representative for non-proliferation matters, with the understanding that he would assume the principle responsibilities for nuclear diplomacy. Though his brief appeared to duplicate Nye's in several respects, the two had no difficulty in working out a division of labor. They agreed on all the essentials of a non-proliferation strategy and shared a common view of the approach to be taken in meeting the administration's long diplomatic agenda, and, perhaps more important than intellectual compatibility, they were not rivals for power. Smith, an upright and self-effacing man, had no ulterior ambitions. Nye, prepared to return to Harvard after a two-year stint, was eager to use the time at his disposal to tackle some of the other issues that fell into his domain, which preoccupation with the nuclear question had prevented him from approaching. Besides, to be point man for the Carter administration on non-proliferation was no bed of roses. The assistance of an experienced hand like Smith (seconded by Philip Farley, his chief deputy, who was a Ford/Mitre coauthor and former associate director of ACDA) increased the chances of salvaging something that approximated a success from the enterprise.

Smith's priority tasks would be overseeing Washington's participation in the INFCE and renegotiating the United States' bilateral agreements with foreign governments to bring them into conformity with the new export criteria emerging from administration and congressional deliberations. This renegotiation would be an especially ticklish undertaking, demanding the patient skills of a conciliator – a role for which Smith was well suited. In effect, the United States would be calling into question certain provisions of the old treaties pertaining to reprocessing. Whatever the precise conditions set down in the pending legislation, it certainly would withhold approval for reprocessing activities where U.S. sanction was acquired, and would seek to extend the right of approval through a renegotiation of bilateral nuclear exchange agreements. Renegotiation, whatever its exact conditions, could not be accomplished without friction. The administration was neither inclined nor able to start immediately on a massive series of treaty revisions. The political climate made stormy by Carter's early maladroitness was not propitious for bold U.S. requests. Moreover, the administration was not in a position to make firm recommitments until Congress passed a nuclear export bill that would determine the legal constraints under which the executive branch would operate. Throughout 1977, the administration would be conducting its diplomacy on two fronts, foreign and congressional, with developments in one bearing heavily on the other.

Central management: theory and practice

The technical complexity and multifaceted nature of the problems under examination made central management and coordination exceptionally difficult. The mechanism for pulling the pieces together was still the NSC ad hoc committee on proliferation chaired by Joseph Nye. It was the body that had conducted the PRM-15 study. Its coordinating role was more nominal than real, though, and it never served effectively as a directing body. The committee was too big, bringing into its orbit just about every office or bureau involved, however marginally, in some segment of nuclear energy policy. The lead office, Nye's, still lacked an unambiguous mandate of authority that would enable Nye to force the pace and to force resolution of differences.

The committee's several subcommittees tended to become self-contained little bureaucratic entities. The body's membership was too diverse – in seniority (some agencies sent high-ranking officers, others junior staffers), in organizational status (involved were White House staffers, officials of executive branch departments, and the still welcome NRC commissioners, who appeared on an irregular basis), and in viewpoint. Under the circumstances, the non-proliferation committee's greatest value was not as a forum for thrashing out policy differences and fashioning a common strategy. Rather, it was as a clearinghouse for information that kept all parties advised where things stood in the several areas of proliferation policy. Within the committee, the bureaucratic baronies confronted each other like friendly rivals rather than collaborators. Positions were stated, and then there were brief and stilted exchanges of view. This formalism made it easier to protect organizational preserves and to conceal their workings from the inquisitive eyes of outsiders.

The serious effort at coordination and orchestration was made along informal channels by Nye's office. The people there were the ones who held the whole picture in their heads. But their power to deal with it was not commensurate with the scope of their responsibilities as members of the lead agency. Although Nye enjoyed the full backing of Secretary Vance and had been mandated by the president, he was in fact outranked by many of the people he had to deal with elsewhere in the bureaucracy. Washington is very sensitive to rank. It is also ready to interpret any hesitation as a sign of weakness. Nye's early decision not to consolidate power within his office by creating a corps of deputies, but to rely instead on administrative resources located elsewhere in the State Department, could be seen as reducing his direct control over operations. In fact, daily staff meetings in Nye's office with eight of State's bureaus were a very effective vehicle for briefing the department's personnel and concerting activities. More important, and damaging, the organizational modesty involved in not building up a big staff encouraged doubts elsewhere about whether Nye truly would or could take charge. The combined uncertainties of rank, authority, and prerogative of the directing office had the effect of prolonging debates, and leaving disagreements unresolved. Most major actors were unwilling to accept a matter as closed, or the specification of an assignment as definitive, unless it was known to come from the White House – that is, from the president directly. Because Carter did not limit himself to a single chain of command, and was in the habit of talking personally to a number of officials about proliferation and nuclear energy issues, there was reason for a recalcitrant official to ask whether Nye carried the president's word on a given subject when State tried to bring the bureaucracy into line with what it claimed was the administration's overarching policy.

James Schlesinger was one of those consulted personally by Carter. He was not the only official with privileged access, however. Just about all members of the NSC's Review Committee had the opportunity to talk with the president about the administration's non-proliferation efforts and to receive personal guidance or instruction from him. Even staffers – although this occurred rarely – were in direct communication with the president.

The weakness of the Carter style of governance was twofold. It failed to make a clear designation of responsibility with an appropriate grant of authority, and it created constant uncertainty over the precise policies to which the administration had committed itself. As one practical consequence in the non-proliferation sphere, the interagency Non-Proliferation Committee was rendered utterly ineffectual. Without an acknowledged leader backed by the White House, and without the discipline of definitive policy guidelines, it became a disruptive force in which purists maneuvered to insert themselves between the president and Nye's office in State. The presence of Victor Gilinsky did not help to compose differences. Being politically and institutionally outside the administration, he felt no compunction about acting to undermine unity, where it was tenuously established, and to push the purists toward confrontation on the sensitive issues of reprocessing rights and export conditions. In frustration, Nye in effect abandoned the committee as an instrument of policy integration. After the disagreeable experiences of April, especially Jessica Tuchman's sabatoging of the critical options paper on foreign reprocessing, he decided that he had to do something to keep from being jerked around by the White House staffers.

Accordingly, Nye instituted a lunch group of executive branch officials, cohosted by Robert Fri, which met every two weeks. Its initial membership included Gerard Smith, van Doren and Keeny from ACDA, Nelson Sievering, Robert Thorne, John Deutch and later Dale Myers (undersecretary of energy) from ERDA (later the Department of Energy), and Albert Carnesale (who would be appointed the United States' technical representative to INFCE). Jessica Tuchman was intentionally excluded. This lunch group became the administration's de facto policy-making body on non-proliferation, where the real work of shaping policy and making strategy was done. Although it was the key coordinating device, it could not cut the staffers in White House offices completely out of the action or entirely neutralize their influence. Their location at the central information transfer points next to the Oval Office assured that they would continue to leave a mark on administration policies. The lunch group alleviated but did not remove the problem of bureaucratic guerilla war with the purists.

Organizational weaknesses in the Carter administration's setup for conducting its non-proliferation policy were noteworthy for reasons more consequential than their indication of untidiness in high places. The president and his lieutenants had embarked on a risky strategy to retrieve an important national stake from a deteriorating situation. They were gambling that they could reverse the trend toward plutonium recycling, or at least direct it into less dangerous channels, from a position of considerable but no longer overwhelming influence. This task would have to be accomplished without gravely damaging foreign relations in other areas that were equally important and equally sensitive. Success depended on sagacity and political craft as much as on correctness of vision and audacity. It would come only through artful manipulation of incentives, leverage points, and reasoned argumentation. Clarity of policy design and dexterous execution were crucial to the effective application of the available instruments of persuasion. The proliferation problem's intricacy; the intertwining of political, technical, and economic elements; the delicacy of diplomatic dealings with a multitude of foreign governments and the U.S. Congress – all placed premiums on the executive's powers of orchestration and skill in playing the several themes of its composition. The administration's goals and the circumstances in which they were pursued left little margin for error. It could not afford the luxury of discord, delay, and disjointedness, which often were the hallmarks of its operation.

MIDCOURSE

By the end of 1977, the Carter non-proliferation strategy had survived despite its inauspicious launching. The amateurism that produced the early series of gaffes and fumbles gradually gave way to a more controlled and knowledgeable approach. The arrival on the scene of experienced hands like Gerard Smith helped to smooth some of the rough edges, as did the growing bureaucratic skills of Joseph Nye and his assistants. A greater measure of internal cohesion emerged as the purists gradually learned some of the facts of governmental and diplomatic life. And Jimmy Carter was devoting more of his time to other affairs of state. Organizational problems did remain, however. A firm consensus had yet to be reached among the three forces at play in the arena of non-proliferation policy both on what constituted acceptable proximate goals (and satisfactory measures of success) and on tactics. An effective interagency mechanism for policy coordination was not yet visible. And significant pieces of the policy – that is, fuel assurances and waste management – were still missing. These deficiencies would harm the administration as it moved on the several fronts where it was engaged simultaneously.

Diplomatically, INFCE was now the main sphere of activity. Carter had succeeded in the important objective of creating a forum, in which all interests were represented, to take a good look at nuclear events and outcomes. Having overcome their initial pique at the unilateral and irksome steps taken by the new administration (though they still harbored a healthy dose of skepticism), the major suppliers and consumers were committed, at the very least, to examining the serious issues raised by Washington. INFCE had created the much-sought "pause" – "slowdown" is perhaps more accurate – in the push to reprocessing. There was no assurance, though, that this rethinking would result in conclusions satisfactory to the

Carter administration. There were many questions to be answered and disagreements to be resolved:

1. Could new technologies be identified, and their feasibility established, that would make reprocessing and the operation of breeder reactors more proliferation-resistant? Would the time lag between identification and commercialization be unduly long?

2. Could a credible fuel-incentive program be put together that would dull the appetite for sensitive facilities, and fuels, available on a national basis?

3. Could a credible waste-disposal program be designed that would remove the presence of large waste-fuel inventories?

4. Looking further into the future, what institutional arrangements might be conceived that could permit the technically proficent "needy" countries to reprocess a portion of their spent fuel, without imposing intolerable discrimination on less-proficient countries?

The attempts to work out answers to these problems in INFCE would be influenced by developments elsewhere. The open questions fell into two groups. First, what strictures on reprocessing and what safeguards would be contained in the Nuclear Non-Proliferation Act? How much diplomatic flexibility would the new act leave the administration? Would it limit the kinds of undertakings the United States might make in the areas under review? Second, what degree of agreement would be reached in new deliberations of the Suppliers' Club? Would its members exhibit a united front on full-scope safeguards as an export condition, thereby relieving the pressure on Washington? How rigid would restrictions on the transfer of sensitive technologies be? The array of unresolved issues and the pitfalls to be encountered by an attempt to settle them were impressive. The U.S. government's readiness to deal with them was somewhat less impressive.

5

The Carter strategy: phase two

PROGRESS in realizing the Carter administration's non-proliferation objectives had three immediate requirements: (1) a sustained dialogue with all those interested parties whom the United States was trying to convince of the virtues of its position; (2) a concerted effort at putting in place the pieces of a restructured international fuel cycle; and (3) constructive bilateral dealings with those countries whose nuclear programs posed the most immediate threat to the principles of a safe global order for nuclear power as conceived in Washington. This last was, for the moment, hostage to the uncertain outcome of the congressional effort to legislate the Nuclear Non-Proliferation Act. The International Fuel Cycle Evaluation provided the opportunity to pursue the other two, complementary, ends. At the time of its inauguration in October 1977, INFCE had assumed the central place in Washington's thinking.

INFCE

As it emerged from the organizing conference, the fuel-cycle review had the shape hoped for by its U.S. sponsors. Participation would be extensive and broad-based; the review would be loosely organized as a series of floating seminars on the disparate issues raised by global transactions in nuclear technologies and fuels; and there was evident, widespread interest in opening these issues to a searching examination. The administration had reason to believe that it had gained the dearly sought pause in which to rethink the recycling of plutonium and related fuel-cycle questions. There was a tacit understanding that, for the duration of the two-year review, the major parties in the nuclear debate would refrain from any action that might provoke a confrontation. That meant European restraint on the sale of sensitive fuel facilities and a slowdown on reprocessing. On the other

172

side, it meant deferring the question of a U.S. right of consent on the reprocessing of fuel supplied by the United States. The official U.S. view of INFCE – as "a cooperative effort to evaluate the role of nuclear energy technology and institutions in an international context and help develop an objective appreciation of the non-proliferation, economic, and other implications of different fuel cycle approaches"[1] – may have been idealized. There certainly was more involved than a detached, "objective" assessment of fuel-cycle forms and formats. The exercise was political in meaning and purpose even if the subject matter was technical. It could not be otherwise. Potentially, the stakes were very high: availability and access to a critical energy source at the time of tightening oil supply.

Nonetheless, some comfort could be taken from evidence that the participants would seriously engage themselves in the work of the specialized committees, and that they had made an implicit commitment to consider the results conscientiously, and sympathetically. Washington's openness in making available its store of technical knowledge gave incentive to other governments to move beyond pro forma involvement. The meaty technical diet served at once to attract their nuclear establishments and to suggest to more political offices that alternatives to existing, proliferation-risky technologies might just be found. Political leadership in key states, however nettled by the Carter style, was inclined to hesitate before irrevocably committing itself to plutonium fuels. INFCE provided a fair opportunity for sober reexamination, bound the countries involved to nothing, and enabled them to keep on the right side of the new administration in Washington.

Whatever the mix of motives, Carter's people were pleased by signs of agnosticism on the plutonium question, and by slowing of the momentum toward reprocessing. INFCE would force governments to think hard about the implications of widespread plutonium recycling, some of which were undeniably disagreeable. In some optimistic breasts, there was the further hope that, in the two-year life of the review, foreign political opposition to plutonium would mount to the point where it could act as a serious brake on national nuclear programs. More realistically, the breathing space created by INFCE would give the United States a chance to make a case for alternative, more proliferation-resistant technologies and to pursue its multifaceted diplomatic strategy aimed at creating a more restrictive international regime for nuclear transfers and use of sensitive fuels.

The inaugural conference

The organizing conference that opened on October 18 to set the evaluation in motion was a decidedly low-key affair. The posturing and shouting of the spring had given way to quiet deliberations. The parties still did not agree, but they finally had learned where one another stood. In the process, they had acquired a sharper awareness of their own interests. U.S. administration officials now recognized that their objectives could not be achieved by proclamations. Their partners realized that the U.S. campaign could not be shut off by cries of outrage. The more politically sensitive officials on both sides were ready to admit that their opposite numbers were not wholly devoid of goodwill or good sense. In the new atmosphere of sweet reasonableness, it was possible to institutionalize a dialogue on what Ambassador-at-Large Gerard Smith called "the nuclear decisions that nations [would take] on civilian nuclear power in the coming years."[2]

The tone was set by President Carter's keynote address, which was remarkable for its modesty and circumspection. Long on goodwill and short on specifics, the speech noted,

> The challenge [that] presents itself to this group and to me, as one of the world leaders, [is] to find a means by which the consuming nations who need atomic power to produce electricity and to serve peaceful purposes [can obtain that power], [and] to draw a distinction between that need which is legitimate and the threat of the development of atomic explosives themselves.[3]

No definitive response to that challenge was presumed. Rather, the president expressed his hope "to learn from you." He continued, "I will welcome your caution, and on occasion your criticism, about American policies." Carter's remarks accurately conveyed the shift away from his administration's earlier righteous attitude, which had implied, even if it did not directly threaten, coercive action, and toward a position that would favor providing technological and economic inducements to other states in order to cool their interest in reprocessing and breeders. The effort would now center on "educating governments," rather than on imposing U.S. views on the nuclear plans of foreign governments. The change could only be applauded by delegates at INFCE. The United States simply asked for their full cooperation in the working groups organized by the conference, and requested that they listen attentively to what the United States had to say about alternative technologies, fuel assurances, and waste management.

There was still no guarantee, however, that the change in emphasis (if not direction) of administration policy would prove successful in winning support for the U.S. position. Nor was it self-evident that this new policy had achieved the mix of incentives, logical argument, and veiled threats of sanctions that was most likely to produce positive results. The shift in stresses and accents did not reflect the administration's mastery in arranging contrapuntal themes; it represented an expedient adjustment to uncongenial circumstances. Having been badly burned by the storm of protest that met its ill-defined and clumsily launched campaign against plutonium in April, the administration's non-proliferation mainstream was now taking pains to display the positive inducements that, it claimed, had been integral elements of its strategy from the beginning, and to declare its open-mindedness about the shape and character of future fuel-cycle arrangements. This more accommodating approach helped to get INFCE afloat on an even keel.

However welcome the reorientation, though, the inconstancy of the U.S. administration ran the danger of being interpreted as evidence of Washington's indecisiveness, and the lack of a clear vision of where it wanted to go. The stumbling performance of April already had fostered the belief that the government was in the hands of amateurs headed by a president unable to keep his ranks in order (or, worse, unconcerned about their disarray). Foreign governments were by no means sure in October what priority Washington still attached to a moratorium on plutonium recycling; whether it was total or allowed for qualification; what costs the United States was prepared to incur in the interests of a moratorium; and what exactly it was prepared to offer in the way of incentives for other governments to postpone plans for the recycling of plutonium. INFCE would be one place to find out – and, for the time being, a cost-free device for alleviating some of the U.S. diplomatic pressure. So the United States and its interlocutors moved together into a bloodless series of seminars, each somewhat unsure of its own intentions, as well as of those of its partners.

The document drafted at the conference's conclusion made it clear that no commitments were being made by anyone. As the accompanying communiqué stated:

> The participants agreed that INFCE was to be a technical and analytical study and not a negotiation. The results will be transmitted to governments for their consideration in developing their nuclear energy policies and in international discussions concerning nuclear energy cooperation and related controls and safeguards. *Participants will not be committed to INFCE's results.* The evaluation will be carried out in a spirit of objectivity with mutual respect for each country's choices and decisions in this field, without jeopardizing their respective fuel cycle policies or international cooperation, agreements, and contracts for the peaceful use of nuclear energy, provided that agreed safeguards measures are applied [italics added].[4]

INFCE was organized around eight working groups, headed by designated cochairmen and open to all states "desiring to make a contribution to their work." (See Appendix H for the list of chairmen.) The subject areas were: (1) Fuel and Heavy Water Availability (assessing the future market characteristics for nuclear fuels); (2) Enrichment Availability ("enrichment needs and availability according to various fuel cycle strategies"); (3) Assurances of Long-term Supply of Technology, Fuel and Heavy Water and Services in the Interest of National Needs Consistent with Non-Proliferation (a stilted euphemism for the sensitive issue of security of supply); (4) Reprocessing, Plutonium Handling, Recycle; (5) Fast Breeders; (6) Spent Fuel Management; (7) Waste Management and Disposal; and (8) Advanced Fuel Cycle and Reactor Concepts.

It might have been expected that the conference would deal directly with the crucial question of plutonium and alternative fuel cycles. That was not the case. The conference was an organizing meeting, not a negotiation. There was a common interest in agreeing to hold in abeyance any major national decisions on those sensitive, and contentious, issues until the technical review groups had had a chance to do their work. In addition, there was the still uncertain status of U.S. legislation on export terms. It was expected to require renegotiation of the agreements of cooperation, including provisions governing the reprocessing of U.S.-supplied fuels. Conflict over that prickly issue might become unavoidable, and no one wished to anticipate it.

Alternative fuel cycles and alternative technologies

INFCE deliberations on Reprocessing (group 4), Breeders (group 5), and Advanced Fuel Cycle and Reactor Concepts (group 8) were viewed as most crucial in determining the future shape of the international fuel cycle and the place that plutonium would have in it. They were the key to the entire exercise. Because INFCE itself was the pivot of Washington's nuclear diplomacy, the review's conclusions in those areas could decide the fate of the Carter antiproliferation campaign.

Continuing efforts to strengthen Suppliers' Club agreements, and to tighten U.S. export conditions, were aimed at containing the spread of fuel-producing technologies and raising the odds against clandestine programs. But in the wider perspective, they constituted only a holding operation. Reprocessing of spent fuel and the introduction of regenerative reactor types (breeders) would occur in some form, on some appreciable scale. The overriding objective was therefore to find operating modes for those technologies, and ways of organizing arrangements for their product utilization and distribution, that did not have the effect of markedly lowering the technical barrier to weapons manufacture. The proximate goal was to put off as long as possible the commitment to a particular system.

Plutonium was still the crux of the problem. As the report of an Atlantic Council study group succinctly stated the issue: "Once countries engage in reprocessing and plutonium recycle, for light water reactors or for fast breeder reactors, or both, the line between nuclear power and nuclear weapons is no longer the presence of separated plutonium but the use of separated plutonium for a fuel element in a reactor or the explosive material of a bomb."[5] The trick would be to devise technical and/or organizational arrangements, in a modified version of the fuel cycle, that would deny easy access to plutonium, and thereby create neither opportunity and temptation to a would-be weapons state. The dilemma was simple to state and profoundly difficult to resolve, for the critical liability of a system based on plutonium recycling, as conventionally conceived, was that "separated, irradiated plutonium is present in the system in some form from the product discharge point of a reprocessing plant, to the time of its insertion in a reactor."[6] The ubiquity of diversion risk associated with plutonium was the reason critics of recycling viewed the emergence of reprocessing and the push toward the LMFBR with alarm. As Harold Feiveson and Theodore Taylor wrote in their plea for a review of alternatives: "By involving countries in the separation, fabrication, transport, and stockpiling of weapons-grade material, the plutonium economy would obfuscate irretrievably much of the existing distinction between activities intrinsic to civilian nuclear power production and those required to produce nuclear weapons."[7]

Three approaches

What could be done to ameliorate the proliferation danger inherent in the widespread commercial use of separated plutonium for reactor use? In theory, three approaches presented themselves: (1) Alterations of reprocessing and breeder processes might be found that would strictly limit access to plutonium and make its extraction and use inordinately difficult; (2) entirely new reactor designs based on a different fuel cycle (e.g., the much-discussed thorium–uranium-233 cycle) could be explored seriously, in the hope that they might not involve access to inventories of weapons-grade materials at any point in the process; and (3) for want of adequate or acceptable "technical fixes," institutional formats might be created that would place all sensitive materials in international custody under strict safeguards (this meant some version of the multinational fuel-center concept). A flurry of innovative ideas, along all three lines of inquiry, already had begun to appear when INFCE got under way.

The ferment of concerned reexamination first stirred by the Indian detonation, and given official impetus by the iconoclasm of the Carter administration, was bringing to the surface numerous proposals that seemed to warrant serious attention. Though none had yet met the hard tests of technical flexibility and efficacy, this upwelling of ideas (some old, some new) with at least a hint of promise underscored the narrowness of the thinking according to which the AEC establishment, a generation earlier, had committed itself to a particular mode of design and operation for the uranium–plutonium fuel cycle. Reprocessing and plutonium recycling had been presented to the world as the only reasonable – that is, technically and economically feasible – way to construct an atomic power system capable of capturing the full energy value of its fuel. Once the underlying premises were scrutinized and the neglected proliferation factor was given its due weight, a variety of modifications and some less compelling basic alternatives presented themselves. They were not panaceas. They did, however, point to avenues of approach that had been neglected previously.

The technical approach. The area that seemed to offer the best opportunity for practical innovation was the design and operating modes of reprocessing plans. "Coprocessing" received the greatest attention and was most widely discussed. Even before the INFCE task force got underway, and the backstopping technical study groups unlimbered themselves in Washington, coprocessing was being publicized as an alternative to conventional reprocessing and was winning some official acceptance. (Coprocessing techniques were to be tried on an experimental basis at Japan's Tokai Mura plant; this was the basis for the U.S.–Japanese agreement of September 1977 that permitted the plant's opening.)

Coprocessing was an old idea whose time seemed to have come.[8] It differs from normal reprocessing basically in that the plutonium and uranium drawn from the spent fuel, which appear in the form of nitrate solutions, are not separated. They are intermingled in one stream, while the residual waste is diverted into another. After some of the uranium nitrate is stripped out in order to get an economical fuel mix, the two elements are converted into oxide form. The oxides of plutonium and uranium are blended into pellets (coconversion), and then fabricated into fuel assemblies (in which small amounts of highly enriched uranium may be added to improve the fuel efficiency further). Coprocessing's attraction is that pure plutonium, in either nitrate or oxide form, is not directly available at any point in the process. Although coprocessing could not be regarded as by any means a fail-safe method,[9] it would impose on a would-be proliferator the need for the facility that could chemically separate the plutonium from the uranium oxide.[10]

Any estimate of the non-proliferation dividend of coprocessing, and of other fuel-cycle innovations as well, depended on both technical judgments about the difficulties of performing chemical separation and the proliferation scenario in mind. Were the process technologically challenging and costly, coprocessing would be a real hindrance to clandestine exploitation of reprocessed fuels. Were it judged possible for separation work to be done in laboratory facilities of modest size, and easily concealed by properly qualified individuals, then the benefit would be relatively small.[11] In the latter case, however, the proliferator would have to make substantially greater preparations before diverting the material containing plutonium. A government could make military use of its mixed-oxide fuel assemblies only if it had a premeditated strategy that committed it to construction of a facility that would take some time to build and would be more readily detectable (to what extent is debatable) than the comparatively simple covert preparations needed for conversion of unblended plutonium into an explosive device.

Some argued that a more deliberate approach, whether aimed at exploiting conventional civilian fuel sources or focusing on clandestine facilities built expressly for military purposes, was in fact the more plausible route for a potential proliferator to take. If so, success would not depend critically on the character of open civilian facilities on its territory; that is, it would not matter greatly whether a separation plant operated in a reprocessing or a coprocessing mode.

But the threat that served as the anxious reference point for Carter administration officials (and many nonofficial critics of plutonium commercialization) was a different one. It was the danger that a hard-pressed government, confronted by an external security threat and/or under the control of reckless leadership, might take a gamble on diverting relatively small amounts of fissile material readily available from a legitimate facility and fitting this material to elementary ordnance before anyone had an inkling of what was happening. Such a rudimentary arsenal could be built in four to six weeks. The "seizure" scenario, as it was dubbed, would be exceptionally hard to safeguard against or to detect. Even if it were discovered, there would still be little time for asserting diplomatic pressure. Against this backdrop, coprocessing looked like a promising option.

Another, related variant of conventional PUREX reprocessing that received the attention of the INFCE working group involved the "spiking" of plutonium (whether blended or not) with highly radioactive nonfissile isotopes such as cobalt-60. Spiking renders nuclear materials exceptionally difficult to handle. If nuclear fuels can be kept in this "denatured" state through all stages of the fuel cycle (without exacting too severe a penalty in cost or normal utilization), then they are rendered nearly immune to seizure, as in the most fully developed spiking method, CIVEX. Although the separation of plutonium is possible, the process is technically more demanding than is the chemical separation of plutonium from uranium oxides.[12]

As a technical answer to the plutonium problem, spiking had two shortcomings. One was its potential economic drawback: By all estimates, it would place a substantial financial penalty on the use of plutonium fuels. The other was its technical inappropriateness to the current generation of reactors. For CIVEX was "a design for a diversion-proof plutonium fast-breeder reactor system, and not a technique readily applicable to the operation of reprocessing plants." CIVEX did not provide an answer to the question of what to do with "the stocks of spent fuel from the present generation of power reactors."[13] Its promise was a decade into the future; the need was more immediate.

Although there apparently was no foolproof technical answer to the plutonium problem, administration officials did see some fairly promising opportunities for lessening the dangers inherent in the recycling of plutonium. They began to think in terms of marginal antiproliferation gain from pragmatic modification of existing technology. To achieve the maximum feasible protection against proliferation risk in a fuel cycle that still entailed the recycling of plutonium, a package of measures was envisaged. They included blending plutonium and uranium in mixed oxide (MOX) fuels where the proportion was 1:4 in a preponderantly uranium mixture (a variation of the coprocessing method); inserting "hot" isotopes into the blend so as to complicate the task of plutonium separation for a potential diverter, that is, a limited spiking; and devising procedures so that at no point between separation and insertion of an MOX fuel assembly into a reactor would plutonium be available in (militarily useful) metallic form.

A new fuel cycle.   Purists in the administration had a more radical idea of how to remove the proliferation danger latent in civilian nuclear power. They looked beyond modifications of a system built around the uranium–plutonium linkage to a wholly different fuel cycle. They wanted to hold all reprocessing and breeder development in abeyance while intensively studying drastic alternatives: the thorium cycle, the tandem cycle, spectral shift. None was new in conception; all had received some attention in the late 1950s and 1960s. But now, their advocates argued, a sharper appreciation of the proliferation factor dictated that they be given another, more sympathetic look.

Administration moderates, though, never took the idea seriously. They were skeptical of the belief that these alternatives were indeed more proliferation resistant. Moreover, they judged it utterly unrealistic to expect the rest of the world (not to speak of the U.S. Congress) to march in place for the fifteen or twenty years it would take to research, develop, demonstrate, and commercialize a new breeder type. As the moderates viewed the situation, the plutonium breeder had too bountiful a potential, and the thirst for energy was too sharp, to postpone its promised gratifications for a generation. The West Europeans and Japanese, who considered the Carter request for a moratorium on the LMFBR lasting the two-year life of INFCE an unwarranted imposition on their national energy programs, could hardly have been expected to set aside their existing technology in exchange for the glimmer of a more proliferation-resistant fuel cycle sometime in the future. To their credit, the more technically knowledgeable of the Carter administration's non-proliferation policy makers were fully cognizant of how unrealistic the idea of introducing a substitute to the uranium–plutonium fuel cycle was. Officials responsible for overseeing U.S. participation in INFCE were quite prepared to have alternative fuel cycles treated as an academic subject in Working Group 8 on Advanced Fuel Cycle and Reactor Concepts.

The institutional approach. There might well be meaningful non-proliferation dividends from a series of technical adaptations along the lines just indicated. In and of themselves, though, they would not be sufficient to meet the goal of minimizing national access to sensitive materials and sensitive facilities. It was necessary to think of organizational constraints as well as of technical ones. An institutional approach would go beyond making it more difficult to extract weapons-grade fissile material from the commercial fuel cycle. It would render the material inaccessible to a prospective proliferator. This might be done in a number of ways: by creating multinational bodies to perform the most critical fuel-cycle operations, plutonium separation and fuel fabrication; by empowering the IAEA to exercise custodial control over plutonium products and to extend it through all stages of the fuel cycle; and/or by institutionalizing fuel exchanges between nonweapons states and the current weapons states on whose territory the sensitive facilities would be located.

Nonweapons states would ship their fuel for reprocessing in the "safe" countries and would receive in return either prefabricated MOX fuels or an equivalent fuel value of enriched uranium. These devices for placing plutonium under some form of closely safeguarded, jointly managed facilities had two obvious attractions: They would shift nuclear operations to centers where there would be minimal threat of seizure and only marginal spin-off of technical capabilities to national nuclear establishments; and they also would provide an opportunity for technically dependent countries to benefit from the converted recycling of plutonium fuels. Any combination of these arrangements would represent a major structural innovation in the international regime for civilian nuclear power. The myriad obstacles to multinationalization could not be tackled directly in INFCE – they were decidedly political questions, and INFCE was nominally a technical review. Pieces of the issue were to be discussed, though, in the working groups dealing with fuel assurances, spent-fuel management, and reprocessing.

The U.S. strategy in INFCE, as drawn by State officials in collaboration with senior officials at the Department of Energy (including the U.S. representative to INFCE's Technical Coordinating Committee, Dr. Albert Carnesale of Harvard, who had the related responsibility of seeing that the Non-Proliferation Alternative Systems Assessment Program pointed in a direction appropriate to the review), sought to keep open the option of institutionalizing the international fuel cycle. However, Washington was far from ready to commit itself to multinational arrangements in any form. It was too early in the review process to anticipate major exercises in institution building. A move in that direction would have to await the emergence of a broad political consensus from the narrowly focused INFCE process. Furthermore, an administration still internally divided on the prior question, whether there should be commercial recycling of plutonium at all, was not in a position to pronounce its views on possible multinational setups. Thinking among moderates, though, was beginning to gravitate toward the view that some kind of institutional arrangement for segregating plutonium would have to be part of an eventual accommodation to reprocessing.

A combination of technical and organizational reforms could reduce the risk that civilian facilities would be exploited for military purposes. But though they would lessen the proliferation danger associated with surreptitious diversion (the "seizure" scenario), they would have little effect on possible clandestine programs – the other, and perhaps more probable, route to weapons acquisition. The principal way to deal with the latter situation would be to impose full-scope safeguards, that is, to open a country's entire nuclear program to international inspection and thereby make it that much harder to keep surreptitious activities secret. The critical role assigned to full-scope safeguards by the administration underscored the importance of continuing Suppliers' Club deliberations, because the United States was pushing for inclusion of such safeguards in a common export code. In addition, legislation taking shape in Congress would set comprehensive safeguards as a condition for U.S. licensing of exports to all foreign governments. The proliferation threat took many forms. The view of it that each government took helped to color attitudes toward the issues of reprocessing and export politics that were the core agenda of INFCE, the Suppliers' Club, and bilateral negotiations.

THE SUPPLIERS' CLUB, AGAIN

The administration's efforts at the Suppliers' Club, and in INFCE as well, aimed at overcoming one basic obstacle. Other views of the proliferation problem were basically different from Washington's. They conformed more closely to the position expressed by the administration's domestic critics. Officials in foreign capitals did not see the danger as so imminent, or as so inexorably bound up with the commercial use of plutonium, as did official Washington. For one thing, foreign governments were far less anxious about the "seizure" scenario. As for a deliberate policy of weapons acquisition, they felt that it should be dealt with politically rather than by the imposition of strict conditions (i.e., full-scope safeguards) on nuclear exports. Their viewpoint can be summarized in several propositions.

1. Civilian power facilities were the least likely basis for building atomic weapons. Diversion from civilian facilities would be inefficient, politically costly, and uncertain. Therefore, a policy that sought to deny states access to plutonium separated for commercial purposes would be unavailing, and would extract an excessively high price in lost energy resources.

2. A highly restrictive nuclear transfer policy would encourage self-sufficient, uncontrolled national programs. Technically dependent states would accept no plan that compounded the existing discrimination between weapons and nonweapons states by leaving to the technically proficient countries decisions about which civilian technologies would be permitted in the hands of the dependent states, and which would be proscribed. The wounded pride of the dependent nations, heightened by a keen sense of energy vulnerability, would offer them a powerful motivation to develop independent programs, which they would strain to keep outside the irksome control and safeguards system.

3. The existing system of regulation and safeguards, somewhat strengthened, provided adequate guarantees against the abuse of civilian facilities. Any attempt to extend them by providing for a supplier veto on reprocessing, or by requiring full-scope safeguards, would be unpalatable to major consumer states and would represent an abrogation of obligations assumed under the NPT and bilateral agreements.

This was, in very condensed form, the dominant view among the United States' partners in the Suppliers' Club. There were many variations of theme and emphasis, the manner of expression differed from one capital to another; the interests involved and the political attitudes were not uniform. Nonetheless, this summary does capture the essential thinking of those governments who took exception to the U.S. push for stringent transfer conditions and who successfully resisted the Carter administration's campaign for a tough export code.

The existing agreement (discussed in Chapter 3), which had been reached in late 1975 and announced the next year, set six conditions for the transfer of nuclear materials, equipment, or technology. Its main provisions stipulated acceptance of safeguards on the facilities in question and adequate physical security (an antiterrorist measure), and referred to "restraint" on the possible export of "sensitive" items. During the ensuing two years the United States fought for a more restrictive approach. It acted against the backdrop first of the Ford administration's gradual shift away from the traditionally liberal export policies, and later of the Carter administration's adamant opposition to reprocessing and plutonium recycling. U.S. diplomacy had two main goals: to win agreement to a moratorium on export of reprocessing plants and to obtain an accord on common export criteria that would include two critical provisions (which were also central to the debate over U.S. national legislation). These were the imposition of international safeguards on all facilities in recipient countries, whether of foreign or domestic origin, and a requirement that supplier permission be received before foreign fuel could be reprocessed.

Washington had only partial success. In their public declaration of January 1978, (see Appendix I), the Suppliers' Club members addressed obliquely the touchy question of sales of enrichment and reprocessing equipment. They urged "restraint in the transfer of sensitive facilities, technology and weapons usable material," and in Article 7 asked suppliers to "encourage recipients to accept, as an alternative to national plants, supplier involvement and/or other appropriate multinational participation in resulting facilities." [14] On this last issue, the official statement only hinted at what was a diplomatic compromise reached between the United States and its German and French allies: Washington abandoned efforts to block the Brazilian and Pakistan deals, and, in turn, Bonn and Paris gave tacit undertakings that they would not enter into other such agreements in the foreseeable future. The United States had succeeded in bringing its fellow suppliers around to its way of thinking on this most critical matter. It had gained acceptance of a de facto moratorium on the transfer of reprocessing plants.

In the area of export criteria, U.S. efforts were not as availing. Its partners refused to require that recipient countries agree to full-scope safeguards. The export guidelines were silent on this score. Nor would the suppliers demand a right of prior consent on the reprocessing of fuel passed through facilities they supplied. Their sole concession on the supply of nuclear materials or of facilities that produced weapons-usable material was to "recognize the importance of provisions . . . calling for mutual agreement between the supplier and recipient on arrangements for reprocessing, storage, alteration, use, transfer or retransfer of any weapons-usable material." The declaration called on suppliers to "endeavor to include such provisions whenever appropriate and practical." [15]

Among provisions that were included in the "fundamental principles for safeguards and export controls on nuclear transfers to non-nuclear weapons states" were the following: (1) Suppliers were obligated not to transfer fuels or materials without a pledge from the recipient state to refrain from setting off any nuclear explosions, even for so-called peaceful purposes; (2) governments of recipient countries were required to give assurances that exports would not be used in weapons production; (3) inspection by the IAEA of the facility in question was to be a condition of export; (4) physical protection against theft or sabotage would have to be demonstrated by the recipient; (5) any retransfers to third parties had to conform to these guidelines; and (6) suppliers were prohibited from inserting themselves into a commercial situation when another supplier and a prospective consumer were in disagreement over the terms of a transaction.[16] An export trigger list of proscribed items was appended.

These guidelines added little to the export code first laid down two years earlier. They did convey greater concern about the proliferation danger latent in plutonium reprocessing. When it came to practical expression of this shared sentiment, the remaining points of contention appeared in sharper relief. Within a few years, a series of controversial export deals revealed how much distance remained between the United States and its partners. West German and Swiss sales to Argentina of a heavy-water reactor and a plant for producing heavy water, respectively, aroused acute concern in Washington. For they placed Argentina (which was well endowed with natural uranium and which was a nonsignatory of the NPT) in the position India had been in when the latter detonated its nuclear bomb. Italy's decision to transfer to Iraq two "hot-cells" – laboratories that can be used to obtain weapons-grade plutonium – was also a source of consternation. In Washington's view, the two deals indicated that some suppliers were construing the export guidelines too literally. The U.S. call for a stricter definition of controlled technologies, which was coupled with a renewed plea for full-scope safeguards, met with a cool reaction. Although France and Britain had moved close to the U.S. position, West Germany (followed by Switzerland) remained unsympathetic. The international mechanism for regulating nuclear exports was only as strong as its weakest link. The depressing truth was, as one commentator observed, that "unless the United States was successful in obtaining a general agreement by all major supplier countries, it was unlikely that any would accept it for fear of giving other exporting nations an advantage in the competitive market."[17]

With the publication of its second agreement, the Suppliers' Club ceased to serve as the central forum for constructing a new international regime in civilian nuclear power. It was being superseded by INFCE. (The Suppliers' Club did stay in being to serve as a consultative body and to monitor compliance with its agreed-upon rules.) The Europeans had never been entirely comfortable with a restricted grouping that left itself open to consumer charges of acting as a cartel and a (civilian) nuclear power condominium. Less anxious than the United States about the proliferation danger (the United Kingdom excepted), and more worried about amicable trade relations with the developing world, they favored enlarging the discussions to encompass both suppliers and consumers. A broader negotiating forum also would have greater legitimacy as a rule-setting body. On this score, the attitude of the Carter administration came to coincide with that of the United States' partners. It was evident to Washington that the

Suppliers' Club had reached the end of its useful life. INFCE had become the preferred instrument for the effort to fashion a consensus on the shape of the nuclear future, one that Washington hoped would bear a reasonable resemblance to its own model.

But the divergent outlooks that surfaced in the Suppliers' Club could not be reconciled by a change of venue. They reflected deep-seated differences of interest in civilian nuclear power and disagreements over the nature and urgency of the proliferation threat. Moreover, most governments were skeptical of the U.S. belief that a global consensus on the form of a new regime in civilian nuclear energy – and specifically, one that matched administration expectations – could be reached. They saw a pragmatic, country-specific approach as the only reasonable approach. Many of the moderates in Washington shared the view that the attempt to build comprehensive institutions would not be entirely successful, and that it must be supplemented by down-to-earth diplomacy.

A flexible case-by-case approach could not easily be reconciled with a principled search for total solutions, however. For it to have a reasonable chance of success, two basic conditions would have to be met. First, the executive badly needed the administrative leeway to make selective decisions – on exports, for instance – according to what a given situation dictated. Restrictions imposed by statute would deny the executive that latitude, as did the autonomous authority of the NRC over the issuance of export licenses. Second, the United States needed to implement an adroit diplomacy responding to the particular interests and sensitivities of nuclear consumers. The ticklish chore of renegotiating nuclear exchange agreements, to which the administration was already committed, had been exacerbated by the clumsiness of its early approaches to major foreign governments. Some of these faults had been corrected, their effects mitigated, and sounder approaches taken under the joint stewardship of Ambassador-at-Large Gerard Smith and Joseph Nye. However, lingering skepticism about U.S. intentions and distress at Washington's inconstancy remained.

THE NUCLEAR NON-PROLIFERATION ACT

Lobbying

The U.S. non-proliferation campaign was not about to become a process of calm diplomacy and deliberate technical assessment. The crucial issue of U.S. licensing conditions and procedures had yet to be resolved between Congress and the executive (and between moderates and purists within the administration). Legislation still pending in Congress would determine the distribution of powers among the NRC, the executive branch, and

Congress. It also would set export terms, ones that in all likelihood would restrict administration flexibility and threaten confrontations with both fellow suppliers and consumers. The uncomfortable fact was that Washington's political moves to restrict reprocessing depended not merely on the reflective judgment of administration officials, made against the emerging diplomatic and technical background. They would be influenced, constrained, and in some respects dictated by what the law would say.

The administration, on its own volition, had committed itself to the renegotiation of its bilateral nuclear agreements of cooperation. This was the difficult task that had been assigned Gerard Smith when he was brought into the government as ambassador-at-large with a non-proliferation brief. His approaches to foreign governments were necessarily tentative until Congress had acted on the outstanding legislation. Without a stipulation of terms and procedures, the administration was not in a position to devise a strategy, or even to know what bargaining leeway it had. The legal obligations and conditions written into the act would fix the boundaries for U.S. negotiators and color the political environment. A tentativeness in diplomatic approaches was also indicated by the concern that any suggestion of U.S. "softness" in the negotiations might provoke Congress into stiffening the bill's provisions.

State Department officials, led by Smith and Nye, were eager not to be stampeded by a Congress that still had the proliferation bit between its teeth. In testimony before Senator Glenn's Non-Proliferation Subcommittee of the Senate Foreign Relations Committee, they made the case for a flexible, adaptive approach. Stating the administration's position on the attitude it would take toward states that balked at accepting U.S. conditions (full-scope safeguards and a veto on reprocessing), Nye explained, "We will have to judge whether our non-proliferation objectives are best served . . . by continuing cooperation with countries that have not agreed to all the new conditions we will be seeking."[18] He went on to argue that these judgments could not be made in the abstract and applied across the board. Each case could and should be evaluated on its merits. Two questions would be asked: (1) What was the best deal the United States could expect to obtain under a given set of circumstances, including the relevant country's state of nuclear technology, energy needs, and waste-storage situation, and what was the proliferation threat the deal was seen to pose? and (2) on balance, would the best feasible arrangement serve to advance U.S. non-proliferation objectives?

Nye was seconded by Spurgeon Keeny, deputy director of ACDA, who made the point that "the most effective non-proliferation policy is not necessarily the one that appears to impose the most stringent conditions on export."[19] Administration officials took especial pains to voice their concern that clauses in the pending legislation imposing tight restrictions on retransfers would cause a crisis in relations with Euratom. The United States' agreement with the European Community explicitly granted permission for materials to move freely among member countries. It also allowed for reprocessing. As Lou Nosenzo of OES told the subcommittee, at present "we have no voice in the transfer within the Community or alteration or reprocessing of that material within the Community."[20] If the legislation forced a reconsideration of those provisions, Washington would open itself to charges that it was guilty of a "material breach of an agreement."[21]

The State Department people were of one mind about the kind of export legislation they wanted. But their strenuous efforts to ensure that the bill left room for bilateral diplomacy were hampered by the internal lobbying of the administration's purists against any concessions on reprocessing and safeguards. Intramural politics was still alive and well as 1977 turned into 1978. The purists were disturbed by evidence of State's "backsliding" on reprocessing. They were fearful that officials there would carry the day with a president who was exhibiting signs of being less single-minded and unyielding in his commitment to the war on plutonium than they would have liked. They believed that any discretionary power conceded to the executive by the Non-Proliferation Act would be used to strike deals that tolerated some measure of reprocessing. They also worried that State might well be lax about full-scope safeguards if a lenient policy permitted the department to retain a measure of influence over the national programs of other governments. On this count they were correct. Prevailing thinking among the State people foresaw, as the outcome of their multiple discussions, a situation in which the United States (1) acceded to agreements with the Europeans and Japanese that permitted the reprocessing of indigenously generated fuel, incorporating, they hoped, some of the new technologies; (2) permitted a modicum of reprocessing of transferred fuel, to be retained for recycling into LMFBRs, but not LWRs; (3) tightened restraints on retransfer of sensitive technologies to the nonproficient states; and (4) looked ahead to multilateral management of collective facilities and reinforced safeguards. Overall, this was not a prospect to gladden the hearts of the purists. They were prepared to resist its realization.

In August 1977 the administration had moved to break the deadlock over the non-proliferation bill by agreeing to accept a softened version offered by Senators Glenn and Percy as a substitute for its own. The two parties had not been especially far apart in philosophy. They differed, however, on the important principles of who should have the final say over export licensing and who would make the ultimate determination whether a recipient country had conformed to legislated requirements. The administration strove to maintain its executive prerogatives, whereas Congress was adamant about having a check on executive actions. The non-proliferation bill was yet another instance of the conflict over legislative veto that has become a fixture of relations between the branches of government. Congress, in this instance, was encouraged in its obduracy by what it saw as irresponsible leniency in the past, and by the clumsiness of the Carter administration's dealings with the legislature. Over the course of the year, the non-proliferation officials in State had learned something about congressional sensitivities and how to cater to them. They entered into the August compromise with the confident expectation that the administration would come away with the discretionary power it needed. They did not fully reckon, though, with Congress's new mood of righteous independence, with the machinations of the purists, or with their chief executive's chronic ambivalence.

The months between August and eventual passage in March were ones of constant hauling and pulling between executive and Congress as each struggled to keep the locus of export authority closer to its side of the line. (Actually, the contest focused on a third party, the Nuclear Regulatory Commission. At stake was its degree of independence from the White House, and Congress's right to disapprove a decision that might be worked out between the commission and the administration.) An equally lively tussle was going on between factions of the executive unable or unwilling to compose their differences, and not forced into an armistice by the president. Their field of combat was not just the White House. It included the congressional offices and committee rooms to which they sent different, at times conflicting, signals.

Three incidents reveal how confusing the situation had become. In late October, Senator Frank Church offered to assist the administration in getting into the bill some language more favorable to its view on the conditions that would satisfy the requirement for "timely warning" of possible diversion. Having been burned in previous dealings with White House operatives, he volunteered to introduce the amendment only upon receipt of a letter of support from the administration. An endorsement was favored by Gerard Smith – well and good. To the senator's chagrin, however, he soon discovered that a letter emanating from State's OES supported Glenn's contrary position. Apparently, Lou Nosenzo in OES, in ignorance of the Church initiative, had inquired from the White House what the president's attitude was. Being told by Jessica Tuchman that it pointed away from the Church position, he dutifully passed the word along. Senator Church abstained from any further alliances with the administration.

In January 1978 there apparently occurred an even more egregious instance of State Department and White House officials acting at cross-purposes. At issue was a letter from NRC Chairman Joseph Hendrie to the Senate Government Operations Committee stating that, as the legislation was then written, the procedures were so convoluted and the licensing conditions so rigid that the commission would find itself unable to meet its obligations. The administration was asked to comment. Joseph Nye drafted a response stating agreement with Hendrie's view. Nye's letter, sent to the White House for transmission, passed through Jessica Tuchman's office, from which it reportedly left unaltered except for a change of the word "agree" to "disagree." No consultation with State had taken place. Later that month, a similar conflict arose over the McClure–Dominici Amendment, which aimed at giving the administration greater latitude in exempting Euratom from some of the bill's more stringent requirements. In this case, Nosenzo prepared a letter (to be forwarded over the signature of Undersecretary of State Lucy Benson) that approved the amendment and urged McClure and Dominici to go even further. It was blocked en route by Jessica Tuchman and Kitty Schermer of the Domestic Council. Again, the matter did not receive the benefit of internal review and discussion. In the end, the law's discouraging complexities, constraints, and anomalies survived in the face of the State Department's forceful effort to convince Congress of the need for simple procedures and straightforward standards. Characteristically, the administration's good intentions fell victim to its internal disunity and uncertain tactics, as opposition from its own hard-liners on export licensing helped undercut the lobbying campaign.

The disarray within the administration exposed by these episodes was by no means uncommon, as my account of PRM-15 and the preparation of the president's April statements pointed up. The consequences for the nuclear export legislation were not as dire. The administration got less than it wanted or hoped for in the way of flexible export conditions, and less room for the exercise of political judgment in renegotiating agreements of cooperation. Its fumbling approach in bargaining with Congress over specific clauses aside, it probably would not have fared very much better if it had been more adept at lobbying. The powers that be on Capitol Hill were stubbornly unwilling to give the executive its cherished discretionary authority. As an issue that lacked saliency for the large majority of legislators, the nuclear export bill was controlled with relative ease by those ardent non-proliferationists who shared deep convictions about severely tightening the screws on licenses. In effect, they were granted by their colleagues the power to promote a universally acceptable "motherhood" cause – and to do it in a way that extended congressional oversight over the executive.

Terms and conditions

The Non-Proliferation Act of 1978 is an extraordinary document. It may represent the apogee of congressional activism, with its penchant for detailing the "dos" and "don'ts" of executive implementation. After three years of debate, Congress legislated an export licensing system that set firm, strict conditions and installed a cumbersome process for acting on export applications. Most striking is the sheer complexity of the procedures it institutionalized. They were not designed to instill confidence in the hearts of importers reliant on the United States for nuclear materials. (Some countries might even lack the legal staff to interpret so dense a document.)

As Frederick Williams has explained in his exegesis and interpretation of the law, it defined "four major mechanisms for the control of nuclear exports" and established "two nearly identical sets of substantive criteria" applied to agreements of cooperation and to export licenses.[22] The four control mechanisms were (1) codifying and tightening conditions to be incorporated in new agreements of cooperation; (2) requiring that existing agreements of cooperation be renegotiated to comply with the statutory criteria; (3) establishing an elaborate procedure for acting on applications for export licenses; and (4) setting down procedures by which recipient countries were to obtain U.S. approval for a series of actions related to enriching, reprocessing, and retransferring U.S.-supplied fuel.[23] The Non-Proliferation Act revealed the Congress at its most pedantic.

Most disturbing to technically dependent consumer states were the laborious licensing procedures that required detailed reviews for each export license (and were not limited, as the administration wished, to major transactions). Foreign governments, and State Department officials too, were faced with a madcap system that distributed decisional authority among the executive, the legislature, and the NRC. The stipulated review process covered several steps. First, the secretary of state would have to determine that "the proposed export . . . will not be inimical to the common defense and security."[24] That determination was to be grounded on an interagency study, with evaluation to be completed within sixty days. Upon receipt of the recommendation, the Nuclear Regulatory Commission would inaugurate its own review, which might entail public participation. The NRC decision would be forwarded to the president. The chief executive would be bound by the commission judgment, *unless* he made the exceptional determination that failure to approve an export would be seriously prejudicial to the achievement of U.S. non-proliferation objectives or would otherwise jeopardize the common defense and security. Were the president to take such action, he would have to submit to Congress his decision, "together with a detailed assessment of the reasons underlying [his] determination." This would lie before Congress "for a period of sixty days of continuous session." Congress could block the export by adopting "a concurrent resolution stating in substance that the Congress does not favor the proposed export."[25]

Hence the White House was granted a veto right over NRC's decision, but was itself open to congressional override. The president in effect would have to petition Congress for an exemption. In this way, the legislation built in a political cost for a chief executive who wished to exercise his discretionary power. Political resources being in short supply, congressional activists expected that he would husband them strictly. The administration, for its part, hoped that the deadlines and cutoffs would be little more than rubber guillotines. Indeed, Congress showed itself accommodating to waiver requests in the cases of Euratom and, later, Pakistan. In the eyes of many foreign governments, though, the possibility of such a presidential waiver might appear a thin reed to lean on. In any case, uncertainty would seem to be the hallmark of the procedure. As Williams concluded, "Despite the law's explicit mandate in those sections for expeditious procedures, the opportunity for bureaucratic obstruction and delay in the handling of license applications is enormous." [26]

The guidelines for negotiation of export controls with recipient countries were as disturbing as the procedures. The bill stipulated nine requirements, the two most crucial and controversial being "that IAEA safeguards be maintained with respect to all nuclear materials in all peaceful nuclear activities within the territory of [a consumer] state," and that consumers give "a guarantee . . . that no material used in or produced through the use of any material, production facility, or utilization facility transferred pursuant to the agreement for cooperation will be reprocessed, enriched or . . . otherwise altered in form or content without the prior approval of the United States." [27] A presidential exemption from any of these conditions had to be submitted to the Congress for approval, following the same procedures laid down for departures from NRC licensing decisions. The executive was granted eighteen months in which to renegotiate agreements of cooperation to bring them into conformity with the new export requirements. Clearly, the administration had its work cut out for it.

RENEGOTIATION

With passage of the non-proliferation legislation, the State Department could shift its diplomatic drive out of neutral. The probings and exploratory discussions of the preceding nine months all had a tentative quality. The United States was now in a position to make known its intentions and to make such commitments as the law's provisions permitted. It had eighteen months in which to consummate its nuclear relationship with consumers if there were not to be a rupture of ties, and with it a dissolution of hopes that the international regime in civilian nuclear energy could be reconstituted on more satisfactory foundations.

The ensuing diplomatic campaign to shape agreements in conformity with the U.S. legislation would revolve around three key issues: winning acceptance of the stringent provisions on full-scope safeguards and a reprocessing veto as preconditions for U.S. exports, in the renegotiation of bilateral agreements in cases in which no previous agreement existed or the agreement in force did not include those provisions; applying the reprocessing and third-party retransfer provisions to those countries with reprocessing capability who had entered into contracts for reprocessing services with other governments; applying those provisions to transactions among members of Euratom, whose existing agreement of cooperation with the United States explicitly permitted both reprocessing and the transfer of fuels within the community.

Euratom

Dealing with Euratom carried the greatest potential for creating political havoc, and it swiftly succeeded in doing just that. For the issue was not just divergent attitudes toward plutonium. It was the threat of a U.S. attempt to impose its views on the Europeans and, moreover, to do so in the face of existing treaties. The administration was fully aware of the danger that the Nuclear Non-Proliferation Act could set off a round of recriminations that would upset the whole gamut of delicate nuclear dealings. It was especially concerned about possible NRC actions during the interim eighteen-month period between the legislation's enactment and the deadline for renegotiation of agreements. There was reason to believe that the NRC, in its review of export licenses, could not help having its judgment influenced by the requirements that would come into force once the period of grace was over. Prudently, the administration undertook to consult with commission members about its renegotiation efforts, in an attempt to avoid having political initiatives undercut by NRC rulings. Though it was guarding the autonomy of its administrative process, the commission was prepared to keep open lines of communication with the administration. A fruitful outcome of this consultation was the expeditious approval in mid-April of high-enriched uranium shipments to three European countries (Denmark, France, and West Germany).[28] The export licenses were sped through in twenty-four hours. The licenses, the ones that had been pending for up to a year and had been a source of irritation and suspicion a year earlier, had been personally approved by the president. Speed was essential because Congress had also set a preliminary deadline of April 8, by which date the governments of recipient states were to state in principle their willingness to enter into renegotiation talks, at the risk of a ban on exports if they failed to do so.

The solicitous Carter action was a calculated attempt to mollify the Europeans. It was fully expected that they would balk at the U.S. demand for revision of the existing agreement of cooperation. The community had pointedly let the April 8 deadline go by without responding to the U.S. call for talks. Europe was particularly disturbed by those provisions of the legislation that mandated a U.S. right of approval over their plans for reprocessing, threatened the free transfer of materials among Euratom members, and implicitly discriminated against West German nuclear programs (an escape clause permitting presidential waiver applied only to reprocessing plants already in existence, whereas Bonn's was slated to open some years later). European anger was not abated by the administration's apparent interest in tempering the effects of an action for which the Congress, and not the executive, was responsible.

Even the United States' closest allies never quite seem to understand that the separation of powers is a political fact, and not an arcane subject of interest only to tidy constitutional lawyers. Helmut Schmidt was reported in *Der Spiegel* as considering the Non-Proliferation Act an "unfriendly act" and "a breach of law."[29] He gave vent to spleen accumulated from other dealings with the new administration in referring to Carter as "an unfathomable amateur who tries to stamp his private morals on world politics but in reality is incapable of fulfilling his role as leader of the West."[30] The law, and administration efforts to implement it, were also vehemently attacked by French Foreign Minister Louis de Guiringaud and by the community's commissioner for energy, Guido Brunner, who suggested that "waving an embargo on uranium supplies in the face of close allies was not very smart."[31] The inevitable moves to compromise differences were most strongly resisted by the French government, which contended that the Carter administration had committed itself the previous year not to change existing export requirements while the two-year international fuel-cycle review was underway. The promise, if in fact made, should not have been, given the constraints imposed on the administration by the then-unresolved congressional action.[32]

As with other interallied clashes, the common stakes dictated that the parties reach some *modus vivendi*. At the end of June, a fragile settlement was finally reached with the EEC. Preliminary talks were agreed to, but they were to be confined to uncontroversial subjects. By mutual understanding the crucial matters were postponed until completion of INCFE, two years from October 20; the date fell eight days after the eighteen-month grace period for renegotiation – a close fit. Whatever the calendar might permit, or preclude, the dispute had further clouded the United States' nuclear relations with her closest allies and weighed against the composing of differences. Those relations were further worsened by the touchy questions of reprocessing contracts with third parties and the re-transfer of nuclear fuels, which surfaced later in the year.

Two provisions of the Nuclear Non-Proliferation Act had a bearing on ties with Euratom. The first was the legislation's criterion, applicable to Agreements of Cooperation, that prohibited "storage of separated plutonium derived from U.S. supplied material in any facility not approved in advance by the U.S."[33] The other was the criterion, applicable to both agreements of cooperation and export licenses, that prohibited the reprocessing of U.S.-supplied fuels, or fuel passed through U.S.-supplied reactors, without U.S. approval. The effect of the latter was attenuated by an exemption for existing facilities in cases in which approval of reprocessing had been extended prior to the law's enactment. Included in this category were the facilities at Marcoule and La Hague in France; Windscale in the United Kingdom; Mol (Eurochemic) in Belgium; and Tokai Mura in Japan. The sticking points concerned the U.S. claim of a veto right on reprocessing of third-party fuel at those plants and the disposition of the plutonium once it had been separated. If the United States were to insist on the prerogative to decide when and if a reprocessing agreement between two governments met a U.S. non-proliferation standard (a determination involving the executive, the NRC, and Congress), then Washington in effect would be in the position of controlling reprocessing contracts for the European facilities.

The retransfer question

The matter of transfer arrangements took on a concrete form for the administration with the receipt of two requests from Japanese utilities, the Tokyo Electric Power Company (TEPCO) and Kansai Electric Power, for permission to ship spent fuel for reprocessing in the United Kingdom and France. The pending contracts called for the reprocessing of up to two thousand pounds of fuel annually, with the total contract amounting to over one billion dollars. The initial request awaiting administration action concerned a transfer of twenty-four tons of spent reactor fuel to Great Britain. Consideration of the request forced Washington non-proliferation officials to interpret the new legislation and to produce a decision that conformed at once to diplomatic interests, congressional intent, and the administration's views about what constituted an acceptable outcome.

The TEPCO request was approved. The 1978 law provides that the "foremost consideration" be whether the transfer would take place "under conditions that will ensure timely warning to the United States of any diversion well in advance of the time" needed to transform the diverted material into bombs.[34] On this count, the administration concluded that the proposed transfer met the antidiversion standard. In testimony before the House Committee on Foreign Relations, Joseph Nye noted that "both Japan and the United Kingdom have also been cooperative in non-proliferation areas. Both are parties to the NPT, both are active participants in the IAEA, in the Nuclear Suppliers' Group and more recently in INFCE, and both have a strong political commitment to preventing the further spread of nuclear weapons."[35] As further evidence of Japan's peaceful intent and constructive attitude, Nye cited the 1977 agreement on operation of the Tokai-Mura plant. Tokyo, he said,

> shares the view that plutonium poses a serious proliferation danger, that its recycle in light water reactors is not ready at present for commercial use, and that its premature commercialization should be avoided. Japan also agreed to undertake experimental coprocessing work at its operational test laboratory and, if such coprocessing is found to be technically feasible and effective in light of this work and INFCE, to convert the Tokai reprocessing facility to coprocessing at the end of the initial period of operation. In addition, Japan has agreed to defer the construction of its planned plutonium conversion facility at Tokai-Mura for two years and is now studying possible alterations for a combined uranium/plutonium product. Japan is also working with the IAEA at the Tokai reprocessing facility to test the application of advanced safeguards instrumentation.[36]

In approving the TEPCO transfer, the United States made clear that it was not enunciating a general policy. It emphasized that requests to reprocess would be treated on a case-by-case basis. Two conditions would have to be met (once the "timely warning" criterion had been applied). One was "a clear showing of need." This was interpreted quite specifically to mean spent-fuel congestion on such a scale as to create a severe economic and/or environmental risk. The congestion standard would serve as a rough litmus test of whether reprocessing would satisfy a genuine fuel-cycle need or might be masking other objectives.

The other condition was the existence of contracts to reprocess predating the new U.S. policy. A subsequent request from the Kansai utility added this significant consideration to the evaluation of fuel transfers. That request, to send spent fuel to France for reprocessing in its UP-2 Cogema facility, was not based on a spent-fuel storage congestion problem. The full-scale interagency review called for by the legislation reached the conclusion that "our non-proliferation objectives would be best served by approval."[37] The key to this favorable recommendation was a recognition that "the contract was concluded in 1975, before the current U.S. policy had been enunciated. Although the utility was aware that U.S. approval for the retransfer would be required to fulfill the contract, it could not have foreseen that U.S. policy would change from a permissive policy on retransfers to a policy where approval would be granted only as a 'last resort.' "[38] So "preexisting contracts" were added to the factors to be considered in approving reprocessing requests. (This criterion applied to the four countries – Japan, Switzerland, Sweden, and Spain – that had reprocessing contracts predating current U.S. policies.)

The export licenses for TEPCO and Kansai were dutifully laid before Congress, along with their justification, for the stipulated period. They came into force without any interference by either house. The administration's case was persuasive and reasonable. The number of contracts involved were few, and an important qualification had been added to the approval of spent-fuel transfers: This was that subsequent transfer of the separated plutonium, including return to the country with title to the material, would require later U.S. approval. This ingenious formulation served the dual end of meeting the most stringent interpretations of the law and leaving the door open for administrative leverage over the shape of international reprocessing arrangements (i.e., the technical mode, the way in which plutonium fuels would be packaged and shipped, and the uses to which the fuel would be put).

Officials were especially keen to maintain the distinction between recycling into breeders and recycling into LWRs. Japanese authorities had defended the reprocessing contracts as a necessary step in building an inventory of plutonium for recycling into experimental breeder reactors. The Tokai Mura agreement of September 1978 had included this clear distinction. Washington was most concerned about recycling into LWRs because it promised to put plutonium into circulation sooner rather than later, and it would confirm the economics of prompt reprocessing. Plutonium separation done for research and development on advanced reactors, it was understood, should be at a rate not exceeding actual plutonium needs for such purposes. It was by no means obvious, though, what that rate was. Two thousand tons annually seemed a lot of separation work for research and development purposes, but there was an innocent explanation. The Japanese government, like the West German government, had reason to be ambiguous about the LWR–LMFBR distinction. In order to maintain the political credibility of their nuclear programs at home, both felt it essential to avoid any break in momentum that would allow doubts about nuclear power's viability to take root. Both wished to project an image that all was going as planned, and approximately on schedule. Hence they preferred to proceed with the reprocessing of spent fuel without clarifying the end goal of the separated plutonium.

Washington had few instruments for directly influencing internal Japanese and German politics – with the possible exception of help in relieving the problem of spent-fuel management. It had yet to dissuade either government from belief in the inevitability of reprocessing, but it would use its leverage to prevent an early commitment to commercial recycling into

LWRs. Moreover, the United States could influence their attitudes and programs regarding the imminence of reprocessing. The open question remained whether the policy of selectively approving reprocessing contracts, while retaining a veto over eventual retransfer, would further the goal of establishing an international fuel cycle that was effective and acceptable from a non-proliferation standpoint. Some saw the administration's formulation as too clever by half. It irritated those countries operating reprocessing facilities and those seeking their services, raised questions of how firm Washington's opposition to plutonium recycling was, and threatened to introduce major new elements of discrimination into the existing global regime for civilian nuclear power. Appropriately, it was Victor Gilinsky who stated Washington's dilemma most succinctly:

> Strict consistency with its stated policy against premature reprocessing meant withholding assent to the transfer of spent fuel (arising from U.S. supplied fuel and reactors) to the European plants, thereby pulling the rug from under close allies and friends. But total acquiescence in the fulfillment of the contracts implied acceptance of defeat in the effort to control reprocessing and the widespread use of plutonium before adequate protection is in place . . . The implementation of U.S. nonproliferation policy thus becomes an extremely delicate balancing act. How many exceptions will need to be made? And how strict will be the conditions on plutonium return? The most interesting question in nuclear energy policy today is how the United States will thread its way through this minefield.[39]

In the absence of common international agreement on the rules governing reprocessing and plutonium recycling, the United States' only course of action was to try establishing implicit guidelines acceptable to the parties concerned. It was hoped that they would cover the awkward transition between passage of the Nuclear Non-Proliferation Act and a satisfactory conclusion of INFCE, and perhaps carry beyond that point. Viewed optimistically, the body of "case law" they were building would set precedents and be codified in principles emanating from INFCE. There was reason, though, to be dubious about such an optimistic forecast.

The criteria set down by the administration were based on notions of what was "reasonable." It was reasonable to make "need" a primary consideration. It was reasonable to pay attention to a state's overall nuclear policies and its willingness to accept various measures intended to reduce the opportunities for bomb manufacture. It was reasonable to insert a grandfather clause applicable to contracts antedating the new legislation. It was reasonable to do all of this while engaging in the multilateral diplomacy of INFCE, and seeking a longer-term solution. Unfortunately for the administration, governments are not always, or even normally, reasonable when matters affecting their national interests are at stake. For the parties involved in the transfer agreements immediately at issue, there were sound practical reasons to receive in silence the favorable U.S. decisions, with all their qualifications and explanatory footnotes. But a readiness to go through the procedural maze did not self-evidently imply acceptance of U.S. veto rights and of the U.S. standard of need, or great sympathy with Washington's views about the values that should underlie fuel-cycle arrangements beyond the reach of the United States' legal statutes. Other parties, with no such pending requests, had even less incentive to legitimize U.S. case law.

Specifically, a de facto arrangement that restricted reprocessing to proliferation-secure states (i.e., those already in possession of the bomb) and controlled access to reprocessing services ran counter to both the widespread concern about energy dependence and the principle of nondiscrimination in civilian nuclear power embodied in IAEA statutes and the NPT. Unpalatable to many, if not most, governments in theory, this conception also raised some very sticky practical questions. Above all, who would decide such issues as what states had a need and right to reprocess, whether conditions met a given safeguard standard, and when a state's actions called for imposition of an embargo on the separated plutonium to which it held title. None, in the end, could be left to U.S. discretion *or* to negotiation between the United States and the other parties concerned. An international agreement had to be grounded on fixed arrangements, and given some institutional form. The broader subject of an international fuel authority was being discussed by INFCE. It embraced many issues other than selective fuel transfer. Given the lack of clear indications about what would emerge from the conclave, Washington had no assurance that its approach to reprocessing and transfer contracts would be confirmed. Nor could administration policy makers be sure that the INFCE consensus would not, in Gilinsky's phrase, "vindicate plutonium" by supporting larger-scale reprocessing under technical and institutional conditions that did not meet the United States' non-proliferation standard.[40]

India

The inescapable difficulties of maintaining credibility while trying to deal realistically with an array of individual cases were visible in the administration's handling of other bilateral relations. The attempt to renegotiate the agreement with India epitomized the problem of winning acceptance of the new, more stringent export conditions. Predictably, it also proved to be the most irksome case. The Indian affair not only tried the skill and patience of the administration's diligent officials. It also aggravated the controversy with the Europeans and opened a breach in the administration's relations with the NRC. Later, the issue would be caught up in the intricate regional politics of the Indian subcontinent, as Washington struggled to recast its priorities in the wake of the Afghan crisis.

The immediate issue was whether to grant an initial exemption of the law to permit a single shipment of nuclear materials for which the Indians had contracted. On April 20, 1978, the commission, on a tie vote, had rejected a license application for the export of seventeen thousand pounds of enriched uranium, an application that had been pending for a year and a half. The fuel was earmarked for the Tarapur power plant that supplies the city of Bombay with most of its electricity. Commissioners Victor Gilinsky and Peter Bradford voted to deny the license because India "has refused to accept comprehensive safeguards," and had made known her intention to reprocess spent fuel. In so doing, they rejected the recommendation of the State Department that the license be approved on a one-time basis, so as not to disrupt its delicate diplomatic attempts to nudge New Delhi away from a recalcitrant position opposing the new U.S. terms of export.[41]

Gilinsky's position was that, because India clearly never would accept the U.S. conditions, there was no point in dragging out the agony. The United States, he argued, should state unequivocally its readiness to act in keeping with its antiplutonium convictions, and let the chips fall where they might. Deferring to the administration, two commissioners supported the granting of the license. Chairman Joseph Hendrie and Commissioner Richard Kennedy rebuked Gilinsky and Bradford for usurping the role of the White House in conducting foreign policy. Kennedy argued, "The law did not intend this Commission to rule on foreign policy . . . This license rejection is not only incorrect, it may even be illegal."[42] The license rejection might well have been impolitic, and certainly it was a nuisance to the administration. By most readings, though, the commissioners' action was within their powers as defined by the Nuclear Non-Proliferation Act.

Availing himself of the discretionary authority accorded him by the act, Carter overturned the decision in an executive order transmitted to the Congress. He then defended his action as necessary to avoid jeopardizing U.S. efforts to get India committed to safeguards by the March 1980 deadline.[43] He cited the assurances given by then Prime Minister Morajai Desai that India would refrain from making or exploding nuclear explosives, and expressed his administration's hopes that the New Delhi government would accept full-scope safeguards. The embargoed shipment to Tarapur and the safeguards issue had been the subject of talks in New Delhi during the president's whirlwind global trip of December 1977.[44] The positive impression Carter's entourage received on that occasion encouraged the administration to believe that the Indians could be brought around to its way of thinking. Those hopes were dampened during Desai's return visit to Washington in June. The venerable Indian prime minister showed himself unbending in his refusal to accept nuclear facility inspections, which he termed "against our national respect."[45] Ironically, his remarks were made the same day that the House International Relations Committee voted to uphold the president's approval of uranium shipments to India.

The Indian attitude placed the administration in an awkward and delicate position. It believed that Desai's nonweapons pledge was made in earnest. It feared that a cutoff of U.S. fuel supplies would lead India to use its two unsafeguarded reprocessing plants to reprocess the spent fuel stored at Tarapur, in order to recover the plutonium as a partial substitute for the loss of uranium fuel. Yet Washington was bound by law to stop all deliveries of nuclear materials unless India agreed to full-scope safeguards and a U.S. right of approval over reprocessing by the March 1980 deadline. While the administration sought to buy time by sanctioning two more routine shipments of fuel to Tarapur (a decision eased by the appointment of a more amenable fifth member to the vacant NRC slot), it could not resolve its basic dilemma. The problem was political as well as legal. Even if it had a free hand, the administration would find compromise with the Indians difficult. First, any understanding that exempted India from the safeguards criterion would undermine its position elsewhere, including that in INFCE. That position was based on the oft-stated belief that an extension of safeguards over facilities and fuels was crucial to a proliferation-resistant fuel cycle. As with exemptions on reprocessing, such departures from the general objective threatened to dissolve the already fragile credibility of the U.S. policy.

Even greater complications grew out of other diplomatic dealings with India and its neighbor Pakistan. The non-proliferation campaign never was completely sealed off from the currents of international politics, nor could it be unless Washington was prepared to accord it unchallenged priority. One of the administration's incentives (beyond the requirements of the law) for pushing New Delhi hard on safeguards and reprocessing controls was the desire to deny Pakistan reason to pursue its own nuclear ambitions. The latter had done little to conceal its keen interest in evening things up on the subcontinent by matching its old rival's nuclear device. The revelation in the winter of 1979 that the Islamabad government had been secretly acquiring the means of producing weapons-grade uranium sharpened the issue. It also heightened administration efforts to put a cap on both countries' weapons capabilities. For to make concessions to one dictated concessions to the other, with the risk of a rapid nuclearization of the subcontinent.

The initial Washington response was to take a tough stance with Pakistan and India. When the former rejected a U.S. demand that the uranium enrichment facility be placed under international safeguards, the administration announced the cutoff of all assistance except food aid. The 1977 Symington Amendment to the Foreign Assistance Act forced the president to take such action for want of "reliable assurances" that Pakistan had renounced the nuclear system. The administration remained equally adamant in demanding that the Indians accept full-scope safeguards and a U.S. right of consent on reprocessing (even though it risked the removal of existing safeguards on facilities of U.S. and Canadian origin if there were a halt to all fuel supplies). With the legislatively decreed deadline of March 1980 approaching, the picture was dramatically changed by the Soviet Union's invasion of Afghanistan.

Military aid to Pakistan to bolster rebel defense became a priority administration objective. President Carter urgently sounded out congressional leaders about removing the prohibition on assistance, and received a favorable response. Though it continued to stress its strong opposition to the development of a nuclear fuels program, the administration's actions had the unavoidable effect of arousing endemic Indian anxieties about Pakistan's augmented military capabilities. The tacit alliance of China, the United States, and Pakistan – one that might even be directed against the Soviet Union – could not fail to color New Delhi's view of Moscow. In order to prevent a Soviet–Indian entente, Washington felt the need to lend a sympathetic ear to India's concerns, this time voiced in the unfriendly tones of Indira Gandhi, newly returned to power as prime minister. In the geo-political interest of keeping some distance between the USSR and India, the Carter administration was prepared to make concessions on the nuclear export issue. In February, a few weeks before the legal deadline for revision of the agreement of cooperation, it appeared that the administration would request a waiver permitting it to release the final shipments to Tarapur. Washington's commitment to maintaining political equity on the subcontinent dictated an even-handed nuclear policy toward Pakistan and India. The bending of the rules for one necessitated that the same be done for the other. Diplomatic pressures clearly pointed to such an accommodating approach.

The administration's dilemma seemed to be eased when Pakistan spurned the U.S. aid offer (for reasons having more to do with doubts about the wisdom of realigning itself with the United States than with unhappiness about pressure from Washington to renounce its interest in nuclear weapons). Freed of the need to seek an exemption for removing the cutoff on aid to Pakistan, the administration could treat the question of Indian exports on their own, by no means uncomplicated, terms.

In June 1980, Carter decided to go ahead with the Tarapur shipment. The White House's executive order authorizing the shipment overrode an NRC determination, made in May, that the sale was not permissible under the Nuclear Non-Proliferation Act. The president's statement supporting his action argued that a U.S. fuel cutoff, in the long run, would be more likely to help than hinder the spread of nuclear weapons capabilities.[46] At present, Tarapur and other facilities are subject to IAEA inspection. The termination of U.S. fuel supplies would provoke an Indian abrogation of its safeguards agreement, with the consequence that, in the words of Deputy Secretary of State Christopher, "we could close the door on any opportunity for influencing India's future nuclear activities."[47] There was another consideration. Because of the turmoil in Iran and the Soviet intervention in Afghanistan, it was deemed vital for the United States to bolster relations with India. Critics in Congress disagreed with these assessments and quickly moved to introduce coincident resolutions in the House of Representatives and the Senate opposing the sale.

The House acted first. In early September it rejected the administration's argument and voted to revoke the export license by an embarrassingly large margin. Sentiment in the Senate also seemed to be leaning in favor of recision. Administration officials were facing what they saw as a direct threat not only to U.S. diplomatic interests in India, but to a policy of applying the provisions of the Nuclear Non-Proliferation Act in a realistic (i.e., flexible and adaptive) fashion. They were not about to allow themselves to be locked into the rigid position the law insisted on, and from which the exemption clause provided the only release.

On White House direction, a powerful lobbying campaign was launched, spearheaded by former Senator, later Secretary of State, Edmund Muskie. The administration pulled out all the stops. National interest was invoked, as was the authority of a Democratic president at the height of an election campaign. Less exalted forms of persuasion were also employed. The Senate debate over the shipment of nuclear fuel to India took on some of the dramatic quality of the confrontations over the Panama Canal Treaty and SALT (although the alignment of forces was far more diverse and less partisan). Opponents of the sale used the ardent rhetoric and arguments of the early Carter administration. Defenders of the president's action, making their case on grounds of practicality and drawing attention to the unavoidable trade-offs among foreign policy objectives, came to sound more and more like their critics in overseas capitals. Whether by weight of argument or force of office, the administration prevailed in the end by the narrowest of margins. The Senate voted forty-eight to forty-six to uphold the executive order releasing the Tarapur fuel.

The immediate question of nuclear relations was resolved. The larger issue of the credibility and consistency of the United States' non-proliferation policy was still open.

The Euratom and Indian episodes were ample evidence, if any were needed, that the reconciliation of non-proliferation concerns with other

foreign policy interests was no easy matter; and the failure of such a reconciliation was a constant threat to Washington's campaign against the
spread of nuclear weapons. It was also evident that legal constraints and
cumbersome legal procedures heightened the dilemma.

The rigid requirements of the Nuclear Non-Proliferation Act were a
handicap to U.S. diplomacy engaged in an uphill struggle to build support
behind a more proliferation-resistant version of the international fuel cycle.
It locked the United States into an inflexible position on a host of issues
about which other governments were highly sensitive. It also made U.S.
non-proliferation diplomacy vulnerable to the vagaries of politics on matters that ranged from the disputed prerogatives of the European Community to the geo-political intricacies of the Indian subcontinent. Despite
ingenious adaptations and applications, the administration could not avoid
the resulting strains and frictions. The inevitable compromises made on
individual cases fed skepticism about the United States' true commitments
and intentions. The rigid moralism of the initial U.S. position was unpalatable. But a series of more accommodating actions taken a year and a half
later, against a backdrop of reiterated commitment to non-proliferation,
could not fail to raise questions of consistency of purpose.

The non-proliferation legislation also generated acute time pressures
through its series of eighteen-month and two-year deadlines in negotiation. They added tension to bilateral negotiations, while placing unnecessary pressure on the INFCE discussions as well. INFCE participants had
the uncomfortable feeling that they were deliberating with a shotgun
pointed at them, which was timed to go off automatically.

THE INFCE REPORT

The Carter administration had staked much on a positive outcome of the
International Fuel Cycle Evaluation. Whatever measure of success it had in
bilateral negotiations, the durability of the agreements reached depended
on a new globally accepted framework for developing civilian nuclear
power. Without it, the nuclear future would be hostage to the vicissitudes
of a highly unstable and unpredictable international environment. The
INFCE report would indicate, if not decide, whether such a consensus was
in the offing.

The report of INFCE's Technical Coordinating Committee (TCC) was
presented to a plenary session in February 1980 and unanimously accepted.[48] It conveyed both the mood of compromise that had come to
pervade the review's deliberations and inconclusiveness about how the international fuel cycle should be shaped to conform to participants' needs,
to technical and fuel-supply conditions, and to non-proliferation objec-

tives. Prolix, massive, and cast in a language of studied neutrality, the TCC report left parties free to interpret its assessments and tentatively worded recommendations as each saw fit. In so doing, it was true to INFCE's purpose. It was not to draft a blueprint for developing civilian nuclear power, but rather to create a better climate in which to work out future nuclear relations. It hoped to do so by establishing a commonly accepted foundation of facts, by offering a range of reasonable projections of nuclear futures over the long term, and by estimating the relevant costs and benefits of different fuel-cycle arrangements.

The report's introduction emphasized that the review was not a negotiation, and that the participating governments were not committed to its results. With that disclaimer on the record, it proceeded to comment, in the stilted prose reserved for such documents, on the myriad issues that the review had studied. Its major conclusions can be summarized as follows.

On *resource demand* and *availability*, it projected a significant increase in the role of nuclear energy over the next half century. Both its low and its high estimates exceeded those calculated in Washington. Nonetheless, it was judged that uranium requirements up to the year 2000 could be met with little difficulty, provided that there were adaptations in reactor operation that would make the most efficient use of uranium. Improved technology could produce a 10 to 15 percent dividend in fuel utilization. Sometime after 2000, however, deployment of fast-breeder reactors would be needed to meet electricity demand.

One estimate with implications for *reprocessing* was that plutonium recycling would contribute considerably to a stretching out of available fuel. Working back from its estimates of LWR capacity, the report calculated that the recycling of plutonium into LWRs would produce savings in fuel assurance in the range of 35 to 40 percent. The cost advantage from reprocessing would be small, if there were any at all.

Benefits from reprocessing were expected in energy independence as well. The report stressed that the evaluation of benefits and drawbacks was, in the final analysis, a function of a country's overall energy strategy and the major considerations that governed it. No one fuel cycle was seen as having advantages across the board.

Reprocessing was also examined in relation to breeder reactors and the waste-disposal problem. The report noted that reprocessing in itself was important because it was an essential preliminary step to many of the possible fuel cycles.[49] That statement was qualified by the declaration that there would be no compelling need for breeders in this century, and that *economic* justification for their deployment would be found only in those countries with large nuclear power programs. If the pull from new reactor types was not overwhelming (at least not economically speaking), the push exerted by accumulation of spent fuel might be stronger. It was expected that spent-fuel storage could be a problem for some reactor operators, in several countries, over the next few years.[50] One answer was the construction of large Away-from-Reactor (AFR) storage facilities organized nationally or on an international basis. Another partial solution could be reprocessing, which might be part of a plan for fuel-cycle self-sufficiency, or which might be done through multinational or regional centers. In the latter case, the plutonium fuel produced could be either returned to the country from whose waste it was separated or recycled through reactors in the host country. The final waste product most likely would be stored in AFRs on the latter's territory.

Prospects for reprocessing and plutonium recycling were considered without regard for *proliferation risk*. The report perhaps spoke loudest in what it did not say. It declined to call the dangers of proliferation inherent in reprocessing so grave that they should be given exceptional weight compared to other considerations. Without gainsaying the threat that civilian facilities might be used for military ends, the report declared its neutrality on the central issue in affirming the difficulty of judging the dangers of misuse in one fuel cycle as opposed to another.[51] INFCE's sanction of reprocessing was implicit and conditional. Considerable attention, though, was given to ways in which the risk could be reduced. Among technical measures, it saw practical benefits in coconversion (which would keep pure plutonium oxide from appearing at any point in the fuel cycle); in co-location of reprocessing plants and fuel-fabrication plants that would improve the effectiveness of safeguards; and, further down the list, in co-processing. It expressed less enthusiasm about spiking techniques.

On the institutional side, the report devoted considerable space to *multinational facilities* and exchange arrangements. It broached the idea that reprocessing, in the first phase at least, should be restricted to countries with the need and economic incentive to undertake it. They, in turn, would offer reprocessing services "to countries which are at an earlier stage of nuclear development."[52] (Left unstated was that countries in the first category were either weapons states already or signatories to the NPT, and not candidate proliferators). These institutional arrangements were seen as evolving toward authentic multinational and regional fuel-cycle centers at some time in the future. No practical steps to reach that end were outlined.

The report was only somewhat less vague in its extensive recommendations on enhancing energy security for fuel-dependent countries (while stressing the importance of such security in reducing the incentives for an early, i.e., premature, move toward fuel-cycle self-sufficiency). It attached greatest weight to the modest goal of strengthening and stabilizing commercial contracts. In passing, it took note of the disruptive effects produced by the decision of supplier states to apply new conditions to existing contracts – an oblique slap at the United States and the Nuclear Non-

Proliferation Act. Also proposed was consumer participation (principally via capital) in joint development of production and service facilities.

Beyond these steps to assure access to supply, the report sketched two more far-reaching plans. One, a Uranium Emergency Safety Network, would give institutional form to current ad hoc arrangements for fuel swapping among utilities. The commitment of a portion of existing stockpiles to a common pool would protect a consumer against short-term supply fluctuations. An alternative would be a full-fledged International Nuclear Fuel Bank of the sort that had been debated within the administration in Washington. There was a basic difference, though, between the United States and most other INFCE participants in conceptions of how this bank would operate. The report underscored the point that the material to be transferred would be exempt from the requirement of approval. In the case of supply interruption, where no breach of non-proliferation undertakings had occurred, it was deemed essential that the transfer be prompt and automatic.[53] The United States had pressed for more elaborate "release criteria" that could qualify the right of a consumer to obtain fuel. U.S. law dictated this position: The Non-Proliferation Act establishes a U.S. right of prior consent over retransfer to third parties and over reprocessing as a condition of export for all nuclear materials. The INFCE report condemned these regulations as having "a negative impact upon assurance of fuel supply and a consequent adverse effect upon . . . nuclear programs."[54]

THE OUTLOOK

The issuance of the INFCE report in one sense lowered the curtain on the drama instigated by Jimmy Carter's ambitious antiproliferation campaign. It signaled the close of just the first act, though, for the action still had a long way to go. Nothing final had been decided. Nonetheless, the review did provide a vantage point from which the future course of nuclear events could be plotted. Indeed, there seemed two routes that the world might follow – one that pointed optimistically toward a reasonably safe and conflict-free future, the other headed in a decidedly more somber direction.

The optimists

For those inclined to look on the brighter side of things (among whom were numbered most officials of the Carter administration), INFCE confirmed a newfound prudence about the use of plutonium fuels. It reflected a keen awareness of the proliferation threat that lurked within expanding nuclear power programs. Concern over weapons spread had prompted the emphasis on containing sensitive technologies and fuels within a system of institutional safeguards and technical controls. A second positive development, in keeping with the cautious tone of the INFCE report, was an undeniable slowdown of the move toward reprocessing. Admittedly, it owed more to changes in the energy environment than to a dramatic re-estimation of the political costs and benefits of bringing plutonium into commercial use. The effects were no less welcome.

From an economic perspective, recycling had become less and less appealing. It promised no great cost savings; uranium fuels would be abundant for the foreseeable future; and reprocessing programs had encountered a number of troubling problems. With the lowering of estimates for future nuclear capacity, the demand for recycled fuels was weakening. One could make a fair estimate that there would be few or no additions to the existing reprocessing plants – all located on the soil of weapon states and/or of NPT signatories, who gave every sign of treating the issue of plutonium transfer with great circumspection (consider, for example, France's reluctance to ship separated plutonium to her ally and partner, West Germany).

Skeptics might ask: Could not a would-be proliferator hide behind INFCE's sanction of reprocessing? The answer would be yes, but not as easily as before. For the report set a more exacting standard for economic justification of reprocessing. Were a country with a limited atomic power program to acquire a reprocessing capability, its ulterior motive would be transparently obvious. And it was hoped that sufficient pressures would be exerted by a mobilized international community to dissuade that country from proceeding to completion of its plans. The optimists took encouragement from what they saw as both a generally more concerned and cautious attitude toward reprocessing and a greater disposition to resist the spread of sensitive technologies.

The pessimists

Others tended toward a more pessimistic assessment of emerging trends. They focused on a different set of background conditions, and they viewed the reprocessing situation as less benign. Prominent among the developments that could disturb a pattern of modulated nuclear growth was the tightening of the international oil market. The Iranian revolution, with the attendant cutback in the production of crude, demonstrated once again how vulnerable resource-poor states were to supply interruptions. The subsequent round of price rises reinforced the belief that continued energy dependence made economic welfare, and social stability, hostage to forces beyond the control of national governments. At least some countries were drawing the conclusion that efforts at achieving a greater measure of energy self-sufficiency should be redoubled. Nuclear power's attractiveness could only be enhanced thereby, and public concern about its safety and adverse environmental impact partially muted. Moreover, anxiety over supply was rekindling interest in the fuel savings from plutonium recycling, while burnishing the already shiny image of breeder reactors.

Disturbances on the oil market gave the impression of being only one manifestation of a more general unraveling. Stable arrangements of international order at both the economic and the security plane seemed in danger. Multiple crises associated with the collapse of detente, conflicts in the Islamic world, and unsettled financial conditions worldwide (not to mention regional tensions in the Middle East and the Indian subcontinent) gave governments reason to concentrate on their own immediate problems. There was evidence of a growing sensitivity to any perceived derogation of sovereignty and a battening down of the hatches in anticipation of storms ahead. Some observers (including a number of Washington officials) interpreted the growth of anxious nationalism as a clear threat to a sober international regime in nuclear power, such as was sketched in the INFCE report. That report's hallmark was reasonableness, combined with a fairly large measure of mutual trust. In a world wracked by crises, both domestic and international, and characterized by free-floating anxiety, the outlook for non-proliferation would be much bleaker than the bland outline of the world according to INFCE would suggest.

The status of reprocessing in particular would not look the same in the pessimists' gloomy vision of things as in the optimists' views. Whereas the objective economics seemed to point away from an early, large-scale resort to reprocessing, political developments were creating new motives for states to gain access to plutonium fuels. Worries over supply established one rationale, while security concerns strengthened the military interest. Both temptation and the opportunity would be there. For one thing, the capability for building reprocessing plants, overtly or clandestinely, was spreading even with the tacit sales embargo. Second, plutonium separation would be occurring on a fairly large scale in countries where facilities already existed. Some would be done on an exchange basis. Indeed, there was the prospect of excess reprocessing capacity, which could lead the operators to seek out new customers. Large accumulations of plutonium would result, whether stored under national or under international auspices. Their presence, in turn, could create pressures for recycling into LWRs, an action that would both set a precedent for other interested parties and perhaps weaken inhibitions about the release of plutonium fuels under uncontrolled conditions. The outcome of this scenario, as depicted by Dr. George Rathjens (then serving as Gerard Smith's deputy), would be the worst of all worlds, "a waste of scarce resources on facilities that will be largely irrelevant to the solution of energy problems for many years, but which will be worrisome from a proliferation perspective."[55]

This skeptical view of the post-INFCE world holds that the firebreak Washington sought to build between recycling into breeders and recycling into LWRs would be crossed as soon as sufficient demand for reprocessed fuels developed. Under conditions of tenuous energy supply, it would be sooner rather than later. Once that distinction had broken down, the line drawn between states with justifiable economic needs for reprocessing (who also happened to be considered proliferation-safe) and those with none (who were proliferation threats) would also prove untenable.

To prevent a distressing rush to reprocessing, it would be helpful to have in place a framework of multinational facilities.[56] They, at least, would assure that plutonium fuels were kept reasonably safeguarded, and in relatively inaccesible form. An International Plutonium Storage System (IPS), as was being discussed by the IAEA,[57] received only mixed reviews from the United States. Whatever merits the scheme might have, Washington was unready to drop its bilateral controls and conditions on reprocessing (which, in any event, were legally imposed) in exchange for an international custody arrangement. Uneasiness over the old, and basic, question of release criteria provided an additional reason for the United States to keep its distance. Paradoxically, the only way for the United States to get a setup more to its liking was to become so deeply involved in the talks as to commit itself implicitly to a plan that could put the final stamp of approval on the recycling of plutonium. Fear of recycling, and fear of Congress, kept the Carter administration from taking that risk. In the process, it was running another risk – letting its remaining influence over the international nuclear fuel cycle slip from its grasp.

THE PROSPECTS

Skepticism about the long-term prospects of a stable regime for civilian nuclear power, based on self-restraint and a set of tacit understandings, was strengthened by the decline of U.S. influence. Washington's leverage over other countries had been diminishing. As alternative sources of enrichment services opened up, and states gained greater confidence in their technological capabilities, it would drop even further.

During the Carter period, the United States found itself in an anomalous position. It retained a disproportionate share of the international market in nuclear power; yet it labored under a set of self-imposed and external constraints that severely limited its effectiveness. Neither suppliers nor consumers were inclined to follow its lead on crucial aspects of the fuel cycle. Coercive policies entailed unacceptably high costs, both for a collective non-proliferation strategy and for other issue areas. The weakening of U.S. influence, as other countries continued to expand their own nuclear resources and extend their competence into new fields, meant that the United States had to walk an even thinner tightrope. It had to avoid being too timid to gain its objectives, yet not so aggressive as to alienate other governments and push them toward more independent nuclear policies. The only conceivable way out of this dilemma was to pursue collective diplomacy, as it did in INFCE, and to seek to strengthen the international "constitution" for governing international dealings in nuclear energy. Success seemed elusive.

The cooperative attitude of the INFCE participants owed something (if by no means everything) to their perception that time was on their side. They could accommodate the United States on paper, and exercise restraint in practice, without forgoing any rights to conduct their nuclear affairs as they saw fit. In a few years things would change. They would be less vulnerable to a U.S. fuel cutoff, and therefore would be free to act just when the demand for nuclear energy might dictate a more rapid move to plutonium fuels. There was also the possibility of a change in presidents that would bring to power an administration sharing their viewpoint. Whoever governed the United States, the overall decline in U.S. prestige, credibility, and power in the world was likely to weaken the incentives to accept U.S. tutelage in the nuclear field.

The Carter administration had believed that it could force governments to make trade-offs between energy interests and security interests as viewed through the lens of proliferation risk. It would do so by holding up to them the frightening vision of a world where nuclear arms have become common military currency. Then, as John Palfrey has put it, "They left it to the outraged but uncomfortable consciences of supplier and consumer countries to make their own decisions in response to a respectful but relentless series of United States questions."[58] The supposition was that those with clean hearts would come through the ordeal with a clear vision of nuclear realities very similar to the U.S. one. But, in the end, foreign governments flinched only slightly, if at all. It was not because they harbored a secret desire for the bomb, or callously disregarded the dangers of proliferation. Rather, despite external pressure and instruction, they found it convenient to compartmentalize policy issues, and simpler to look much more intently in a narrow line of vision, fixed on the near rather than far future. In the end, the fate of the administration's non-proliferation strategy depended on the readiness of states to confront harsh realities head on, and to make tough decisions on an enlightened, reasonably long-term view of their national interests. The evidence suggests that, on the whole, governments in the pivotal states (proficient suppliers and nonproficient consumers) are only exceptionally able to do so.

By mid-1980, with the INFCE report having emerged from over two years of deep discussion, and with the course of bilateral negotiations clearly defined, a tentative assessment of the Carter campaign became possible. The final outcome was still unclear. Two conclusions, though, could be stated with some confidence. First, the global nuclear regime would have a noticeably different look from what would have been likely if the trends under way in 1976 had been extrapolated into the future. International transfers of sensitive reprocessing and enrichment technologies were now out of the question. Attention had been focused on the proliferation risk inherent in the civilian regime for atomic power generation. As part and parcel of this sharpened awareness, the foreign offices of other governments, especially in supplier states, had been brought into the act. Their more active voice in nuclear energy matters was having a pronounced effect on export and transfer policies, France being the outstanding case in point. Generally speaking, the outlook was that plutonium would be introduced far more cautiously, and slowly, then planned or predicted a few years earlier.

The other salient fact was that the recycling of separated plutonium remained, in the minds of most national nuclear establishments, the principal means for closing the fuel cycle. There also was a general conviction that recycling would occur. In doubt were answers to the key questions where, to what degree, when, and under what technical and institutional conditions. One thing had become evident: The push toward a second generation of regenerative (i.e., breeder) reactors, using plutonium as a start-up fuel, could not be kept in suspended animation. Moreover, the pull of the breeder would continue to sustain interest in reprocessing (whatever the latter's economic outlook – cloudly – or contribution to the waste problem – mixed but promising). The momentum in advanced industrial countries was too strong, the craving for energy security too compelling, and the skepticism about U.S-supported schemes for providing functional substitutes too pronounced, for other governments to accept the Carter administration's brief on behalf of a protracted moratorium.

The achievement of the Carter antiproliferation campaign was, then, only partial, but nontheless real. One of its architects estimated that the fuel-cycle issues on which it concentrated, as opposed to those of political motivation, were half the problem, and that the administration's dealings with those issues were half successful. That seems a fair judgment. Reducing the threat by a quarter seems a fair accomplishment.

6

Conclusion: an assessment of performance

I INTRODUCED this study by raising the question of the U.S. government's competence in fulfilling one of its most challenging policy responsibilities. The development and spread of nuclear technologies with a weapons potential is a problem that sets an unusually high performance standard. It is well suited for revealing government's abilities and limitations. In addition to the issue's great intrinsic importance, the handling of nuclear power questions gives us a look at the system under stress. Washington has been asked to do things that it normally finds uncongenial – planning carefully synchronized programs, projecting their results well into the future, and subtly phasing them into a diplomatic strategy. The sense of urgency felt after 1974, with the collapse of earlier policies, made the task that much harder. Even under less strained circumstances, the kinds of dilemmas posed by spreading nuclear capabilities test policy-making institutions, as well as intellect and diplomatic skill. They are exceptional in several respects. They cut across the conventional axes – running from the domestic to the international, from economic to security spheres – that normally arrange the position of subject areas in the universe of governmental affairs. They starkly draw the challenge of developing and applying new, sophisticated technologies so that they will accord with divergent social needs and political purposes. And they demand the reconciliation of an issue's long life cycle with the limited attention span of political leadership.

PERFORMANCE FUNCTIONS

Each of these features of the proliferation problem focused our attention on a particularly difficult policy function. In combination, they created the severest of tests for public institutions and the officials who work the system. The first of these functions, *coordination*, asks of government that it overcome the usual compartmentalized treatment of issues, pulling into unison the diverse strands of policy and integrating programs. The second, *technology assessment*, requires that technical expertise and specialized knowledge be brought into the service of wider public objectives so that technological innovation is consonant with political judgments of the opportunities, benefits, and risks of a technology's commercialization and deployment. Finally, there is *planning*, the requirement that the confined political space and organizational constraints that have come to typify the U.S. political system be loosened enough to permit policies with a scope and reach to match the long-maturing, multifaceted problems that have to be dealt with. What measure of success has Washington scored on the challenge presented by nuclear energy and proliferation?

The narrative and analysis presented in this study do not permit a facile answer. It is too early to pass a final verdict. Any evaluation, negative or positive, unavoidably has a touch of tentativeness, because we will not know conclusively for several years what the results will be – that is, how many countries will join the nuclear club, with what consequences. Even then, we still may not be able to estimate with complete confidence the degree to which U.S. policies influenced the actions of other governments.

Grading the policies of individual administrations is even more difficult. Each was heir to the accumulated effects of its predecessor's policies and world developments. Each confronted the proliferation problem in a different phase of its reemergence as a threat to global stability. Assessing the actions of the Nixon and Ford administrations must, in some important respects, be qualified by reference to the subsequent efforts of their successors, which altered the direction and velocity of policies in midcourse. The Carter administration, which made the most sustained and forceful attempt at rectifying a situation seen as highly dangerous, can be most fairly judged. Yet criticism of it cannot fail to pay due account to the heavy legacy of misguided programs and absentminded policies left by past presidents.

These caveats duly recorded, there remain sufficient grounds for commenting on the performance and apparent effectiveness of the United States' handling of the nuclear export and proliferation issues. Some general traits that appear across administrations stand out and deserve examination. Equally, there are peculiar features of each, and individual episodes, that say something important about the conduct of government affairs. They, too, will be noted and discussed. Any judgment presumes a standard of achievement and performance criteria. Definitive conclusions of success or failure are not in order. What an analyst reasonably and fairly can do is to assess policy according to outcomes on proximate objectives that government leaders themselves viewed as being of importance to the overall goal of non-proliferation, and that can be confirmed by a reasonably detached observer. This observer can look for internal consistency, for a logical relationship of ends and means. He can seek to discern rigor and intellectual honesty in the decision process, and he can examine a policy maker's assumptions and premises in the light of subsequent events. Inevitably, there is a subjective element in concluding what measure of success there has been in meeting objectives. Personal interpretation plays an even greater role in determining that certain approaches were ill considered, procedures defective, and individuals inept, unperceptive, or mistaken in their judgment. But that is in the nature of a policy study. Its judgments, when clearly stated, are then open to rebuttal by others making different interpretations or with access to fresh information.

Overall, my evaluation of U.S non-proliferation policy is skeptically critical; and my assessment of policy-making processes is largely negative. A scanning of Washington's generation-long experience in grappling with the perhaps not-so-peaceful atom provides few grounds for congratulations.

The general failings of U.S. policy have been ones of inadequacy and mistiming – lack of foresight, one-dimensional planning, poor coordination, maladroit diplomatic initiatives – rather than outright mistakes of judgment (although the latter are not entirely absent). They can be seen as highlighting characteristic weaknesses of the United States' manner of managing its governmental affairs, ones also evident in areas that do not exhibit the singular traits associated with nuclear energy.

The most grievous errors occurred *before* the watershed year of 1974. They have yet to be fully overcome. Above all, the United States government displayed *a failure to provide clear and continuous political guidance to its international program for supporting the civilian use of nuclear power*. Official policy oscillated from the highly restrictive approach taken by the Atomic Energy Act of 1946, to the generous and tolerant attitude inaugurated by the Atoms for Peace program (and embodied in the revised Atomic Energy Act of 1954), back to the current position, which aims at strict controls over the use of all U.S.-supplied hardware, know-how, and fuels. For the most part, these shifts did not record fundamental changes in conviction about the potential danger of weapons spread, or even deliberate choices of the best means for avoiding it. They were pragmatic responses to events and were, at times, incidental to the pursuit of other ends.

The turn toward active promotion of atomic energy was inspired by an upsurge of exaggerated enthusiasm (partly activated by the AEC) for the benevolent promise of nuclear technology, which intentionally downplayed the risks of disseminating nuclear knowledge, skills, and materials. Return to a more restrictive policy came in reaction to the imminent danger of widespread plutonium use, underscored by the Indian explosion which had been overlooked in the years of export promotion. It was a danger exacerbated by the absorption of the government (executive, legislature, and AEC) with the domestic question how the enrichment industry would be organized. Meanwhile, large and perhaps irreversible changes had occurred in the global distribution of nuclear resources and interests without evident appreciation in Washington that this transformation was undercutting existing arrangements intended to prevent proliferation.

The opening of widespread access of PUREX reprocessing technology, the appearance of the West Europeans as suppliers of sensitive fuel-producing facilities, sharpened export competition, growing international demand for nuclear power – these developments should have been seen as eroding the foundation of the U.S.-designed non-proliferation regime by emptying the safeguards system of much of its practical meaning. Yet Washington did not recognize that something was amiss until so late in the day that the eventual attempts to reverse the situation incurred a high penalty in political costs, while yielding an uncertain dividend of restored control. Only in 1972 did the United States move to restrict the outflow of technical assistance on reprocessing and to rescind what amounted to a blanket sanction for recipient states to develop their reprocessing capabilities. It took the Indian detonation to focus attention on the link that reprocessed plutonium made between civilian programs and weapons development. Not until the public revelation of the blockbuster German–Brazilian deal, and the disturbing announcement of French reprocessing sales to Pakistan and South Korea, was there a full recognition that the growing size and sophistication of the European nuclear industries meant not merely the emergence of commercial rivals to the U.S. manufacturers of power reactors, but an alternative avenue of access to critical technologies.

The most egregious failure to pay proper attention to the proliferation consequences of nominally internal policy matters was the self-created crisis over enrichment contracts. The seemingly endless delay and confusion (extraordinary even by current Washington standards) that surrounded the six-year debate and political struggle over expansion of U.S. enrichment capacity is also striking evidence of a second, chronic failing of nuclear policy: *government's repeated inability to synchronize domestic programs with international policies*. They all too often lived independent existences, the one marching blithely along its own path, seemingly oblivious, or avoiding knowledge, of where the other was headed. The Nixon administration's single-minded commitment to putting the AEC's international dealings on a "sound business footing," coupled with its campaign for privatization, left little room for contemplation of secondary effects, even ones that increased the threat of nuclear weapons spread. When those considerations received attention, as in the estimates allegedly made by James Connor's group as a prelude to implementing the White House strategy for creating a crisis on the order books, there was a pronounced tendency both to underplay the adverse results and to conclude that current trends were so well established that any U.S. action was likely to be unavailing. Therefore, no good reason existed for the United States to deny itself the presumed benefits of privatization. A more perceptive analysis, one more attuned to world energy developments (and one that did not view the enrichment question through thick ideological lenses), probably would have reached other conclusions. Good policy making and well-conceived policy mechanisms are so disciplined as to discount bias. They prevent the analysis of a complex issue from being dominated by just one of its facets and the conclusion skewed by that preoccupation. Governments pay a price for permitting themselves the indulgence of cherished political and economic philosophies, and the relentless pursuit of narrow goals. In the enrichment case, the price was the precipitous loss of control over the world market for nuclear fuels. Neither members of the Nixon administration nor any other of the principal actors demonstrated foresight about that eventuality or let self-interested actions be much affected by whatever awareness they did have.

Storage and disposal of spent nuclear fuel is another, only somewhat less striking, case in which international concerns could not break into a process geared to domestic conditions. The twenty-year failure to establish a sound, acceptable program for handling the irradiated, toxic waste product of light-water reactors is a stunning case of bureaucratic nonfeasance. The AEC consistently looked upon waste management as unsavory and unrewarding – not a task to be done unenthusiastically, but one to be done negligently if at all. The agency disregarded the long-term disposal problem and hastened to shift the burden of storage for civilian waste onto a private industry that was unprepared to assume it, and before the means had been proven. It compounded the error by pushing reprocessing as the necessary solution to a situation it was not ready to face. Among the unfortunate effects of this protracted exercise in avoidance were the gilding of reprocessing as the answer to waste management, as well as a step toward the second generation of bountiful breeder reactors, and the foreclosing of a U.S. option to relieve other states of their legally and politically cumbersome spent fuel.

By the time the Carter administration moved (at its own excruciating pace) to put in place a credible system, new complications had arisen to force even further delays. Popular opposition to nuclear power, political sensitivities about the location and form of disposal facilities, and the regulatory maze of the NRC and EPA emerged to frustrate the recent commitment to resolve, finally, the problem of waste management. In such instances, long periods of neglect tend to be followed by frenetic efforts to recoup lost time and lost opportunities. Too often, these efforts create their own problems of timing by declaring objectives and setting unrealistic timetables that do not take full account of what is required to unknot the tangles left by years of inadequate planning. The financial costs of accomplishing these ends also become inordinately high, thanks not only to dollar inflation but also to a political inflation that in the present governmental environment imposes on any programmatic venture the heavy burden of regulatory procedure, legislative delay, and public skepticism. Playing catch-up under those circumstances is that much more difficult, and costly.

Another aspect of the disjointed management of nuclear energy policy that overlooked proliferation dangers was *the imperfect coordination of private industry's commercialization of civilian nuclear power and the government's actions in designing the fuel cycle as a whole.* The U.S. government was the parent and custodian of the peaceful atom. However great the AEC's pride in its offspring, the parental agency did not always provide the discipline and guidance it deserved; nor was it always sufficiently careful to create the conditions under which the peaceful atom might live a safe and socially productive adult life. In a precocious industry, filled with all the self-confidence of its progenitor, reactor manufacturers accomplished the remarkable feat of laying the technical and organizational foundations for a worldwide system of using nuclear technology to generate electric power. They succeeded in spite of the unusually large cost uncertainties, and stubborn design and operational problems. Their success is a compliment to corporate enterprise, as well as to AEC encouragement and the unique attraction of things nuclear.

However, from today's perspective, when the security issues raised by spreading technical capabilities preoccupy government, the speed and range of nuclear power's implantation around the world seems premature cause for worry as much as celebration. The loose ends that should be neatly tied together to make nuclear power safe and credible are still dangling. The institutional and technological conditions for closing the nuclear fuel cycle in ways that are technically, economically, and administratively viable – and that do not markedly increase the risk of proliferation – have not been met. The U.S. government, rather than private industry, is accountable for this failing. Its agencies have had the mandate to ensure that nuclear power be developed in the public interest. The charge implies responsibility for defining that interest with regard to all legitimate concerns, taking steps to make sure that commercial activities conform to it, and monitoring the growth and expansion of the civilian nuclear power system internationally.

The indictment of the AEC for slackness in overseeing the building of an institutional and technical infrastructure for civilian nuclear power is based on the legal and programmatic dependency of private industry on government. The commission, which clearly had the regulatory authority and the political responsibility for superintending and channeling commercial applications of the peaceful atom, properly can be taken to task. It is culpable both for using selective criteria in gauging whether the broad standard of viability was being met and for not being rigorous enough in observing those guidelines it did set for performing its promotional and regulatory functions. Non-proliferation and environmental criteria were loosely drawn and only intermittently applied. Stable commercial development of atomic power, and acceptance of a system that placed reliance for fuels on a select number of stable suppliers, was put in jeopardy by avoidable disruption of LEU supply and inconstant prices at the front-end, and by the lack of waste disposal and safeguardable reprocessing at the back-end. The AEC's uncritical commitment to the promotion of nuclear energy and its organizational hubris have been correctly cited in explanation of a record marked by zealous encouragement of atomic power development and negligence in putting in place the necessary foundations.

A casual acceptance of the way U.S. business was operating overseas aggravated the adverse consequences. The normal corporate behavior of U.S. industry magnified the consequences of the government's sins of omission and nonfeasance. The companies did a more thorough job of disseminating the technology and know-how for atomic power generation than even the AEC expected – more thorough, in the end, than the U.S. government might have liked. In keeping with the postwar internationalism of U.S. business, the corporations entered into an array of collaborative dealings with foreign firms whose form was dictated by corporate convenience and promised profitability, not by a concern for control over proprietary technology – so long as relinquishing it entailed only political costs, for which they were not responsible, as opposed to commercial costs. The affiliations established by the main U.S. reactor manufacturers, Westinghouse and General Electric, were the vehicles for transferring much U.S. know-how to their European affiliates, who became the core of proficient French and German industries. Westinghouse's licensing arrangements with Creusot-Loire in France (later taken over by Framatome) and with Siemens in Germany, and General Electric's partnership with AEG in the latter country (Siemens and AEG ultimately consolidating into Kraftwerk Union), made sense for the companies who were seeking commercially feasible routes for entering those national markets. Eventually the ties were loosened, when governments sought greater control over national nuclear programs and (as in France) demanded fuller access to sensitive technologies, which even a tolerant AEC could not permit U.S. firms to release. On balance, the risks of losing corporate control and the nurturing of a commercial rival might have made corporate sense. They did not make sense, though, for the U.S. government, which cast a benign eye on those affiliations. The transfers from Westinghouse and GE to their counterparts helped to build sophisticated, autonomous European industries that themselves became exporters of both power reactors and fuel-fabricating technologies.

This commercial pattern was reinforced by the coincidental development of a European enrichment capability. The latter has gradually weakened U.S. influence over both technically proficient suppliers and consumers *and* has created financial incentives for the sale of enrichment technology. In the case of enrichment, it was overly protective AEC and White House attitudes toward the existing monopoly that spurred European plans for independent development. With regard to commercial partnerships in power reactors, it was lack of foresight about the long-term repercussions of a tolerant policy toward corporate technology transfers that facilitated the growth of new national centers of nuclear technology. Here, the error was a failure to anticipate how transnational corporate systems have greatly accelerated the pace at which technology is diffused, and in ways often beyond the power of governments to control. Both examples illustrate the U.S. government's subordination of proliferation considerations to commercial and institutional interests, and its unperceptiveness about the shifting contours of a world system for developing and organizing civilian nuclear power.

The relatively casual way in which nuclear authorities fostered reprocessing, based on the PUREX method, and facilitated its acceptance abroad is witness to another shortcoming of nuclear policy making: *the apparent inability to do an effective job of technology assessment*. Devising procedures and techniques for anticipating and analyzing the social impacts of innovative technologies has become a favorite pastime of policy analysts. The faddism that surrounds the subject should not be held against it. Charting routes of social effect, estimating outcomes, and projecting the costs and benefits of introducing a given technology, at a certain time and in certain ways, have essentially prophylactic ends. They are precautions against the damage that can result from the unconsidered, or too cursorily considered, exploitation of mechanical invention and operating technique. Commercial development of the technology for generating civilian nuclear power, especially the commitment to the reprocessing of plutonium to close the back-end of the fuel cycle, provides a classic example of what happens when the parameters that bound the area of review are too narrowly drawn.

The conception of the fuel cycle that guided atomic energy officials was one based on engineering standards of efficiency and elementary notions of marginal economic cost. Both the central role assigned to the recycling of separated plutonium and the commitment to the early commercialization of reprocessing technology were based on an analysis whose dominant considerations were technical congruence and fuel savings. By technical congruence I mean the convenient way in which reprocessing technologies linked the LWR and the fast-breeder reactor. Reprocessing facilities would neatly join the two generations of reactors. Even with the question defined in those nonpolitical terms, the evaluation was inadequate. To do a fair and credible assessment of the alleged need for plutonium recycling one should calculate uranium reserves and price levels, waste-management costs for handling spent fuel from LWRs, and the disposal costs for the radioactive residue of reprocessing plants; in addition, one should estimate what it would take to build and run reprocessing plants. Calculations on all these points are necessary to compare the cost-effectiveness of "once-through" and "regenerative" fuel cycles. *This kind of comprehensive study was never done*; the rough cost projections for reprocessing owed as much to the hopeful expectations of technology's supporters as to whatever hard figures actually were available.

Whereas the assessment of technical feasibility was made from a narrow engineering perspective, and the financial assessment done with a looseness that typifies most planning for nuclear facilities, *the broader assessment of social and political impact was hardly made at all.* The critical questions of whether commercial reprocessing would increase the likelihood of civilian facilities' being used in support of military purposes, and whether plants could be effectively monitored within the existing safeguards system, were not taken seriously as central to the assessment of commercial reprocessing. The most convincing evidence in support of this judgment is the early rejection of coprocessing and related techniques as alternative modes to PUREX. There is nothing recondite about those other processes. As atomic energy officials in government and industry persistently reminded all who would listen, they were old hat, talked about and rejected in the 1950s. The principal reason they were not given serious testing is that they were technically less elegant and marginally more costly. To coprocess is to use a less refined procedure, one that does not take full advantage of technical capabilities, and one that slightly reduces fuel values. Against the engineering sweetness of PUREX reprocessing and its economic efficiency could be placed its formidable political liabilities: It lowered the threshold for the making of atomic explosives and tore a hole in the fabric of international safeguards. If a proper weight were accorded the debit side of the balance sheet, a comparison of reprocessing and its more proliferation-resistant variants might well have pointed to acceptance of the latter. But in fact the two sets of factors never were juxtaposed; no systematic comparison was made.

It fell to the Carter administration at the very end of the game to force attention to those trade-offs and to instigate a conscientious review of alternative technologies. Joseph Nye was correct in prefacing one of his public calls for a moratorium on reprocessing with the claim that

> particular technologies always reflect certain social assumptions prevalent at the time of their origin: the objective of embarking on

the PUREX process some thirty years ago was to derive plutonium in as pure a state as possible . . . Today, our societies are more concerned about non-proliferation, and we must look again at alternative technologies that may have been rejected in the past as suboptimal.[1]

There was an understandable tone of plaintiveness to these comments. For, in effect, the Carter administration was trying to institute a full-scope technology assessment, of the kind that should *precede* major technological choices, at the point where the technology had already passed through the research, development, and prototype stages to commercial deployment.

THE ORGANIZATIONAL FACTOR

Political leadership and the AEC

My broad-stroke evaluation of where things went wrong in the U.S. strategy to foster the international development of atomic energy inescapably concentrated on the shortcomings of the Atomic Energy Commission. It was the cynosure of prevailing beliefs about the innocuous nature of the peaceful atom; it was the agency with direct responsibility for developing the atom's potential and for regulating its spread abroad; it had the authority and power to structure programs to close the fuel cycle and to satisfy fuel needs. The AEC, as an organization, rightly bears a heavy portion of the criticism for the neglect of non-proliferation dangers. Equally important for understanding the weaknesses of U.S. policy is the inadequate provision for political oversight and direction by elected officials.

The AEC – like its successor, ERDA, – was a quintessential example of a bureaucracy grown imperial in proportions, with the conceit that accompanies power acquired in what society has proclaimed a virtuous cause. The companions to bureaucratic empire are organizational rigidity and the sanctifying of an orthodox code of beliefs and doctrines that provides its members with a common vision of the universe in which they operate. Serving successively as instigator, catalyst, backer, and protector of civilian power development, the agency acquired an exceptional self-esteem that was matched by public reputation, if not by quality of performance. Imbued with the mission to fulfill the atom's promise of beneficence, and steeped in the traditions of what had become an insular service, commission officials fell victim to their own stylized way of approaching nuclear power development and to an exaggerated organizational conceit that deprived the agency of internal correctives. Idealization of goals replaced the thoughtful formulation and reconciliation of what were at times divergent objectives. The liturgical incantation of shibboleths (about the technical attractiveness of reprocessing, about readily manageable waste, about "safeguard envelopes") substituted for skeptical scrutiny of the premises that underlay policies and programs. As Irvin Bupp and Jean-Claude Derian have aptly stated in their account of nuclear power's commercial history, there has been "the tendency to create a circular flow of mutually reinforcing prophecies insulated from outside criticism," which "hardened into doctrine that was everywhere accepted as recorded truth."[2]

The AEC's tendency to treat civilian nuclear energy as a mundane technology (not remarkably different from technologies with less horrific potential) moved the world to the brink of a "plutonium economy" without critical scrutiny of its full implications for the international regime in atomic power. The logic of organizational routine joined with the impulse toward bureaucratic empire building, and with an engineer's approach to technology, to build the momentum behind reprocessing (à la PUREX), and then led to an unduly optimistic view of the safeguards network it helped to create. Moreover, in following its intellectual inclinations and organizational dispositions, the commission carried out its tasks over the years in ways that qualitatively changed the nature of the problem they were charged to deal with. The shape the AEC gave civilian power made proliferation control all the more difficult. Nothing that was done violated the commission's legislated mandate or departed from the rough guidelines set down, at long intervals, by political leadership. But in practical effect, the agency's actions heavily favored the achievement of one national objective – the promotion of civilian nuclear power worldwide – at the expense of another stated objective – preventing the spread of nuclear weapons. Moreover, internal decisions, especially those having to do with alternative technologies, limited the choices available to central policy makers when the White House, along with political departments, began to recognize the mounting proliferation danger attendant upon the widespread recycling of plutonium.

The AEC is certainly culpable, in the many respects I have cited. But an indictment of the commission, however well founded, is the starting point for an explanation of governmental failings in the international nuclear energy field, not the conclusion. Bureaucracies behave according to their nature, however nice it might be if they did otherwise. Left to their own devices, it is no surprise that they will do the things that conform to their own inner workings and gratify institutional needs. They trim issues to fit prevailing interests and ideas; protect organizational domains; see external events through the filter of orthodox belief; declare as relevant and important only those matters that can be managed through existing policies and programs; and fashion compromises among divergent factions and ideas with internal solidarity, not coherent policy, as the principal goal.

The nub of the issue is that *political leadership neglected to perform its proper oversight function*. The president and his appointed officials on the AEC and in the State Department did not take the necessary steps to assure themselves, first, that the implementation of programs was continually reviewed in order to determine whether they conformed to all national objectives in the nuclear field, taking due account of political considerations, and second, that technical choices were informed by an understanding of the larger purposes the peaceful uses of atomic energy were intended to serve. These responsibilities are simply stated; but they are anything but elementary to execute. They are not beyond the capacity of a government properly organized and led, yet they can hardly be expected to be done well, if at all, unless leadership recognizes the importance of doing them – as successive administrations have not.

At no time between 1954, the inauguration of Atoms for Peace, and the 1976 Fri Review, were the nuclear energy policies of the United States submitted to critical scrutiny and comprehensive examination by an executive body reporting to the White House and accountable for its conclusions. Political debates over pieces of the program – privatization, for example – abounded. There were major diplomatic undertakings, such as the building of the IAEA and the negotiation of the NPT. Innovative programs of technology development, like the breeder program, were begun. Yet none of these activities prompted a critical analysis of how the various elements fit together or provided a framework that encouraged an administration to base decisions taken on any one matter on a reasonably complete appreciation of how it was related to the country's overall nuclear energy interests. Hence the U.S. government could spend years in hammering out a non-proliferation treaty, and engage in a protracted, animated debate over enrichment formats, without confronting the plutonium question head on.

The most striking case of political nonfeasance was the Nixon administration's campaign to commercialize the enrichment program. My chronicle of that singular episode revealed it as being the outstanding miscalculation, from a non-proliferation perspective, that has been made in the nuclear energy field since the United States started down the road marked by Atoms for Peace. The chain of events set in motion by that initiative altered the United States' position in the world energy market profoundly and weakened its leverage with supplier and consumer states alike.

Can the decision to push privatization be explained as mere organizational behavior and bureaucratic machination? By no means. The process was started by the determination of the president, encouraged and assisted by White House advisers, to cut back the government's role in civilian nuclear power. In most important respects, the policy went against the grain of the AEC. It threatened to curtail the commission's control over a critical portion of the fuel cycle, enrichment; it imposed new practices for running its commercial operations; and it ran counter to the spirit, although not the letter, of the bilateral agreements of cooperation it had fostered with foreign countries. James Schlesinger was appointed as AEC chairman for the express purpose of making the new policy stick in a notoriously hidebound organization. So was his successor, Dixy Lee Ray. The selection of commissioners was guided by similar considerations. And the agency bureaucracy was put under the thumb of loyalists like James Connor. To be sure, there were points of convergent interest; and there were ways in which commission behavior compounded the problem. Those in the AEC protective of the United States' technological advantage were only too pleased to have their opposition to joint enrichment enterprises with the Europeans supported by a White House made unaccommodating by its desire to carve out a privileged position for U.S. industry. The AEC's staunch resistance to losing its hold over enrichment, and its behind-the-scenes lobbying against privatization, helped to drag out the debate and to slow congressional action. There is also evidence of silent complicity with the strategy to confect a crisis of capacity in the hope that it would redound to commission advantage. Certainly the AEC contributed to the confusion and aggrieved feelings that resulted from the closing of the order books, first by failing to make more realistic estimates of actual supply and demand ratios, and then by dealing with outraged applicants with its habitual hauteur and officiousness. The essential point, though, is that the agency's responsibility for the snafu itself was secondary. AEC officialdom was an accessory to policy failure, not a principal cause or fomenter.

If the policies that triggered the progressive weakening of the United States' position as a nuclear supplier were shortsighted, it was the president, the commission chairmen, and their deputies whose ideological single-mindedness about privatization distorted their vision. If the concern with revising the arrangement between government and industry in the United States came at the expense of international relationships, it was political leaders who were so absorbed with domestic affairs that they slighted the consequences for foreign relations. If the non-proliferation factor appears to have been given insufficient weight, the decision to downplay it was made by the White House and the NSC. The AEC officials may be faulted for their own failure to anticipate the eventual repercussions and to make the case against administration policies on these grounds. Disagreement was selective, variable, and keyed to other, largely domestic considerations. But, most important, it was not permanent officials who set the direction – that was done by political leadership.

Political leadership and "bureaucratic politics"

To judge political leadership as blameworthy is not to denigrate the problem of mastering a huge, highly specialized organization. It is a formidable chore. The Nixon administration's relative success in breaking the AEC's independence (if not in bending the agency to its will) was a considerable achievement, albeit for dubious ends. The Ford and Carter administrations (especially the latter) had the even more difficult task of bringing the nuclear establishment's activities into line with non-proliferation policies moving in a wholly uncongenial direction. Their problem was twofold: (1) to subordinate the AEC (later ERDA, and later still the Department of Energy) to central policy makers and central policy; and (2) to coordinate the several executive branch departments and bureaus that had a role to play in fashioning and executing a set of interconnected policies. Steady progress was made in reducing the exceptional organizational prerogatives of nuclear energy officals, although the process was painful and never entirely successful: These officials *were* gradually cut down to size. ERDA (and the subsequent Energy Department) came to be seen and to be treated as one among other self-willed agencies whose recalcitrance was a major obstacle to expediting decisions and achieving coherent policies. Over time, the problem of the AEC was submerged within the wider problems of controlling the propensity for bureaucratic games playing and overcoming the defects associated with fragmented government. Success on this score was less than complete, as is evident from my account of nuclear policy making in the Carter administration. Internal dissonance and lack of synchronization were the administration's Achilles' heel in its ambitious attempt to revamp U.S. policy. More than other administrations, it suffered heavily from the disorder and debilitation produced by unbridled internecine conflicts.

The organizationally, and often individually, self-interested behavior of officials is an undeniable fact of life. Yet for all that can be said about the weaknesses of bureaucracies, and the centrifugal forces they generate, there is abundant evidence that the defects of government owed at least as much to the frailties, shortsightedness, and indecisiveness of senior officials – that is, the president and his appointees. There is a persuasive case to be made that it is within the power of a president and central policy-making units to achieve a higher degree of coordination and control than in fact has been achieved. Our narrative of the Carter administration policies provides ample basis for this assertion.

THE CARTER REFORMATION: IDEAS, ORGANIZATION, AND TACTICS

Jimmy Carter's great achievement was making an unequivocal break from the beliefs and philosophies that had permitted almost casual acceptance of a situation pregnant with proliferation risk. Directly confronting the issues that had been drawn in the last weeks of the Ford government, the Carter people boldly and honestly committed themselves to a basically new and different conception of nuclear power development. There is no denying the president's intellectual courage on this count. However, practical performance was not always as praiseworthy. Criticism focuses on the lack of coherence and finesse that marked administration strategy at its troubled inception in early 1977. The string of errors and omissions that accompanied the policy's formulation and presentation bedeviled the more impressive subsequent effort at winning wide international acceptance.

The tribulations experienced by Carter's non-proliferation warriors can be ascribed in part to the problem's intractability. But they also can be seen as the costs of Carter's failure to bring expectations and capabilities into reasonable alignment. Fine-line strategic plans, deftly manipulated execution, and well-prepared diplomatic campaigns have never been U.S. trademarks. For all its dedication and ingenuity, the administration's conduct on non-proliferation policy does not suggest a drastic change of government personality. A political enterprise undertaken in highly adverse circumstances was made all the more unlikely of ultimate success by poor organization and maladroit diplomacy. In January 1977, the proverbial horse was nearly out of the stable when the Carter administration made a grab for its tail. Any improvement in its tenuous grip was hindered by the way in which a flock of attendants fumbled among themselves over tail, gate, and the moral question of keeping horses at all.

The Carter government took a loose, undisciplined approach to policy making. The president and his associates referred to it as decentralized. But the decentralization of administration practice was synonymous with disorder in too many respects and in too many instances. Outstanding disagreements about proximate goals, priorities, and acceptable outcomes often were not composed, nor was a conscientious attempt at resolution always made. Unresolved differences over ends led to uncoordinated, even contradictory, tactics. This was especially apparent during the first, critical year of the administration's antiproliferation campaign. Organizationally, there was no effective mechanism for channeling divergent advice into clear options, for forcing decisions, or for overseeing implementation. Diplomatically, the administration sowed confusion by speaking with several, often discordant, voices and weakened its already fragile position through a striking disregard for the sensitivities of other governments and a failure to relate non-proliferation initiatives to other items on very full diplomatic agendas. Relations with Congress, already strained, suffered from the lack of political subtlety, a disregard for procedural niceties, and, above all, frictions within the administration that made Congress uncertain just what the executive branch's commitments were, and what outcomes would be acceptable to it. The result was to magnify the appearance of divided government created by the righteous independence of the legislative branch, and to open gaps in the credibility of the radical new U.S. policy.

For want of clarity and constancy, the Carter administration paid heavy penalties on all fronts. Its shortcomings were ones of leadership and organization, the latter defect being attributable directly to the president's style of governing. It should be underscored that the internal troubles encountered by the Carter administration owed more to the president's own notions of what constituted orderly government, his distribution of tasks and responsibilities, than it did to any unavoidable, bureaucratically induced ailments of government. Carter was averse to formal organization and neat, logical procedures for making decisions – despite his purported engineering bent and much-publicized yen for government reorganization. This aversion showed in the way he set up his administration and in the style of his relationship with subordinates.

As one expression of the disregard for clear structure and proper procedure, Carter shied away from clear assignments of responsibility for specific policy questions, and did not draw clear jurisdictional boundaries. The most striking case in point was the drafting of the non-proliferation policy itself. Although Joseph Nye's team in State was declared the lead office for drafting PRM-15, the president permitted other agency officials participating in the review to procrastinate, to insist on organizational prerogatives, and to resist Nye's authority to define issues or to move the exercise from an analysis of conditions to a statement of policy alternatives. Carter refrained from communicating to the heads of other departments his determination that Nye's group have not only nominal leadership but substantive, presidentially sanctioned authority to ride herd on the exercise and to get the PRM completed on schedule.

The upshot was that on the eve of Carter's keenly awaited policy announcement, his principal non-proliferation strategists had yet to agree on key elements of the policy. The unpredictable, and ultimately unsatisfactory, product of an eleventh-hour meeting of the Policy Review Committee created further delay and confusion. Having prevented his administration from doing its job properly, the president then fell victim to his own attempts at improvisation.

Presidential staff

An indictment of the chief executive for not assuring that an interagency task force perform expeditiously and efficiently may be seen as too severe, imposing an unrealistic standard of executive performance. It may be said that a president cannot exercise personal supervision over every one of the numerous projects undertaken by his administration. True, he cannot. For that reason he should take pains to organize the Executive Office of the President so that his support staff on the National Security Council (and Domestic Council) does the job in his behalf. Carter's failure to do so is a second major weakness in his conduct of policy. For example, it should have been the NSC adviser, Zbigniew Brzezinski, who checked progress on PRM-15 and made certain that it was proceeding in keeping with the president's wishes (and, equally important, in a shape that conformed with the president's needs).

The NSC staff exists to assist and to protect the president by acting as custodian of the policy process. Whatever the specific format, whether the staff itself plays a more or less active role in directing policy reviews and supervising the implementation of policy, it functions uniquely as the music director for the president acting as orchestra leader. It is intended to serve the interest of the president in a number of ways: by following-up on his instructions, contained in presidential decision memoranda or conveyed orally, and seeing to it that department officials understand *what* he wants done *by whom*; by keeping an eye on deadlines; by watching out for discrepancies and divergences in the formulation of policy; by getting to the president a fair range of cogently stated policy choices; by encouraging him to consider as many aspects of an issue as he reasonably can manage; by confronting him with the full implications – as they are best understood – of his choice; and by monitoring the execution of policy so as to pinpoint practical difficulties of execution or uncover conflicting interpretations from different parts of the administration and to assess progress made and the reactions of pertinent constituencies.

This type of high-powered secretariat function is demanding. Complete success is rarely, if ever, achieved. In its heyday under Henry Kissinger, the National Security Council staff had considerable success in disciplining the policy process. It created pressures on the bureaucratic units to focus on problems as formulated by the president and his NSC adviser and to conduct analyses with the requirements for decision clearly in mind. The system's weaknesses were equally manifest. The tasks of policy planning and review were gradually squeezed out by a deepening involvement in operational matters; and failure to devise a strategy for making the agencies of government willing participants in the overall process caused important issues to suffer from neglect (as was the case with regard to proliferation matters). The decentralized Carter system, by contrast, left responsibility obscure and lines of communication tangled. It achieved flexibility and openness while losing coherence. Most important, it shared with its predecessor the fault of having staffers act as advocates of particular policies rather than as neutral assessors and monitors.

That inherent tendency of the NSC system is most apparent when staffers have been selected without regard to their professional and intellectual aptitude for the self-effacing job of policy management. When the president himself does not demonstrably appreciate that his performance is handicapped by the lack of a disciplined custodial staff, the liabilities are increased. If the NSC staff, or the Domestic Council staff, is to serve primarily as a high-powered secretariat, it must be stocked with people of maturity, experience, and a measure of intellectual detachment, if not neutrality, on the issues they handle. Instead, under Carter, the NSC staff was composed disproportionately of young, ambitious recruits who had strong convictions about policies in the areas for which they were responsible. Many of them had never before been in government positions, where their personal beliefs had to bend to accommodate larger purposes and a resistant external environment. Nor had some of them ever learned what it meant to deal with foreign governments, especially the importance of tact and an understanding of how others perceive reality. These persons bring a welcome freshness of thought and sense of principle to government. But these virtues can best be displayed in the line agencies where policy ideas are generated and debated. They are least suited for the Executive Office of the President, where the imperative need is for proportion, perspective, and commitment to procedure. The presence there of passionate devotees to causes is disruptive and an obstacle to any substantial accomplishment.

The role of the *national security adviser* is crucial to shaping staff functions. Carter looked upon Zbigniew Brzezinski primarily as an advisor on substantive policy issues. Brzezinski served as an all-purpose guide to assist him in navigating the tricky, largely unfamiliar waters of international politics. Management of the foreign policy process and coordination of the foreign policy bureaucracies were viewed as secondary functions that the president was disposed to perform himself. Brzezinski was temperamentally ready to conform to Carter's wishes. He thought of himself, and was, principally a man of ideas, not a manager.

With the Kissinger experience as a negative reference point, Brzezinski and the president determined to avoid concentrating in one pair of hands the responsibilities for making policy and for implementing it. The stress on a sharing of influence with Secretaries Vance and Brown (among others) in an "open administration" reflected this conviction. So did Brzezinski's decision to avoid interposing himself between the president and NSC staff specialists. Jessica Tuchman briefed Carter personally, on behalf of the NSC, on proliferation questions, in keeping with the custom reintroduced under Brzezinski. This arrangement was meant to provide the president with multiple viewpoints and varied advice, while giving him a sense of attitudes and operations within his government. The costs, though, were striking. Lines of communication got confused, and enormous energies were wasted in intramural wrangles over what the president ought to do and what he should think. The staff's essential duty – that of protecting the president against himself – was not done. Staff members failed to protect him against his own exuberances and excesses of zeal by pointing up constraints and possible costs, to cover him when the government took risky and controversial actions by maintaining a prudent distance between the person and the policy, and to keep him honestly apprised of how his policies (including favored projects and notions) were faring.

They were custodians not of the process, but of Carter's principled opposition to plutonium and his anti–nuclear arms idealism. They thereby denied the president the detached judgment and deliberate skepticism made essential by his impulsiveness and tendency to fix on only one part of a problem, his habit of grabbing onto some detail of policy and worrying it like a bulldog while basic questions remained unsettled.[3] On one matter after another – the question whether the West Europeans and Japanese should be threatened with a uranium embargo to keep them from recycling plutonium, the exemption of Euratom from certain export conditions, an offer to repatriate spent-fuel rods from U.S.-supplied fuel and reactors, the terms of bilateral agreements with Iran and India, the stress to be placed on wholly new fuel cycles to substitute for the uranium–plutonium cycle – the principal NSC staffer was a protagonist, not an objective analyst, compromiser, or fair guide to presidential decision. In other instances, junior members of the NSC and Domestic Council staffs took it upon themselves to superimpose their views on the positions reached by responsible office heads, and to substitute their judgment in communications to Congress. This was done without consulting the officials concerned, and often without any opportunity for the contending parties to lay their arguments before the president. Simply stated, this type of behavior is a perversion of the NSC system and an abuse of the power it embodies.

The costs of fragmentation

A formless system for making policy produces equivocation and ambiguous decisions. In the absence of clear and agreed purposes, execution also suffers. Not only are actions themselves uncoordinated, but, with each player supplying his own criteria, it is exceedingly difficult, if not impossible, to evaluate results and to determing why success is or is not being achieved – and all the more difficult to make the necessary corrections. Without clear reference points against which to measure reactions of other governments, there is no way of estimating which among the several signals sent were received and listened to, and which underlying policy assumptions were proven accurate.

For example, should the snappish response of the West Europeans and Japanese to Carter's April 7 statements be ascribed to a fundamental disagreement over objectives? Or was the unusual bite of their reactions evidence that they were antagonized by reports of an extremely hard-line position emerging in the White House, including coercive measures (which never materialized), and/or by the inconsiderate way in which their views were solicited only at the last moment? To what extent was their feeling that Washington had not offered a viable program strengthened by Carter's failure to say anything concrete about the fuel-assurance and waste-management incentive packages?

To take another case, did the United States' tough line on reprocessing make it more or less likely that India would accept U.S. conditions for the receipt of LEU fuel?

Or consider another example: Should the criterion of success in INFCE have been a universal moratorium on plutonium recycling and a common commitment to another, more proliferation-resistant fuel cycle? Or should it have been an agreement that limited recycling to breeders and accepted modifications in the techniques for reprocessing and breeder operation? What tactics should have been pursued accordingly?

The administration was in no position to answer these questions because it had not spoken with one voice. It had overloaded the diplomatic circuits with verbal stimuli that had either proved mutually destructive, like MIRV warheads, or evoked equally confused responses. Officials could not tell what prompted a given reaction, nor could they weigh its significance for a policy only partly formed and still under debate. Nor, therefore, could they take the compensatory or supplementary measures that might be called for. A discordant policy and an uncertain strategy do not generate responses that can be read for clues about the attitudes and interests of other parties or the impact of one's initiatives, knowledge of all of which is essential to an informed assessment of one's objective and approach. More-over, even the most unambiguous evidence cannot be put to productive use when continuing internal conflicts do not allow for sober evaluation and interpretation of performance according to common standards.

U.S. officials abroad, already reduced to acting as sometime messenger boys, are pushed farther into the background when policy is hostage to the outcome of Washington power struggles and governed by improvised actions. The costs are substantial. Diplomats lose credibility and effectiveness. The resource of knowledge and experience they represent is squandered. Approaches to foreign governments become episodic and intermittent rather than part of a sustained effort. The thinking and reactions of those governments are imperfectly understood. The lack of consistency, combined with fluid measures of success, reduces the ability of diplomatic representatives to monitor feedback and to make deliberate tactical adjustments. Not least, the energies of senior Washington officials are drained in frantic efforts at personal diplomacy to do the job that is properly that of representatives on the spot, and to undo the damage of inconsistency in Washington.

The sins of tolerance

There are, of course, situations in which a president may find it politic not to force a confrontation between rival factions and differing opinions within his administration. Sensitivity to the electoral constituencies they may represent (and ties to influential congressional power centers); an unreadiness to expend the time and political capital when other, higher-priority matters are at hand; or a belief that events will generate some more conclusive evidence on which way to move – all provide cause for tolerating internal friction and the bureaucratic jousting that goes along with it. But such tolerance can make sense only so long as no decisive public actions have been taken, no national goals proclaimed, and no specific plans for achieving them laid out. Subsequently, the penalties extracted by internal discord will far outweigh any benefits from leaving multiple advocacy unrestrained.

The deleterious effects are registered in congressional relations and in the wider forum of public debate, as well as in dealings with foreign governments. The Carter administration paid an especially high price for its intramural conflicts. Its ambitious goals, and the exceptional requirements they created for finely tuned execution, made its policy peculiarly vulnerable to lapses in planning and diplomacy. Tolerance for disjuncture and irresolution extracted a less obvious but no less real price in earlier administrations. Under President Ford, sharp differences among bureaucratic interests at first obscured the central issue of plutonium recycling. Later, they forced delays in getting the problem to the president and in laying the hard but unavoidable choices before him. The Ford administration's slowness in making the connections between important aspects of the domestic nuclear program and the proliferation question owed much to the partitioning of government responsibilities and the inadequately developed mechanisms for imposing a political frame on nominally technical and economic policy decisions. Two unfortunate consequences were (1) the building of momentum behind commercial reprocessing, which hardened opposition to U.S. initiatives when they did come, and (2) the legislative reconfirmation of an anomolously independent NRC licensing authority, with resulting confusion over U.S. export conditions. As for the Nixon administration, it suffered little from equivocation, but much from its war of attrition with the AEC and with Congress. Internally unified in its thinking on enrichment and proliferation matters, it was spared the costs of intramural conflicts over policy ends. Its failing was to miss vital connections between its campaign to reform the organization of nuclear energy programs and the growing danger that civilian facilities might be exploited for military ends. The damaging consequences were aggravated by the inattentiveness to those wider considerations of all the governmental parties concerned, as they fought for ideological principle and organizational interest.

THE CONSTRAINTS ON PLANNING

Choosing not to plan

Common to all three administrations we have looked at is the segmentation of government policy making and a chronic inability or unwillingness to bring the pieces together into a reasonably coherent whole. The central question of this study is why government so rarely plans, or, more precisely, why its actions are taken on a scale and in a time frame inappropriate to the problems it is addressing. The study opens two further questions: whether governments *can* "plan," and *whether it is a good thing* for them to try to do so. My review of Washington's performance on non-proliferation uncovered ample evidence of its failure to conduct its affairs in an orderly fashion, of the costs of unplanned policy, and of a multitude of factors (familiar to political scientists and practitioners) that militate against a more systematic approach – the personalities of presidents and senior officials high among them.

One striking conclusion to draw from this welter of constraints and inadequacies is that government officials – high and low – most often *do not want to plan*, even when they are temperamentally and intellectually capable of doing so and can see virtues in the procedure. For one thing, planning involves *commitment*. The unequivocal statement of goals and a priority ordering of objectives are preconditions for consistent, well-integrated policy. But they also are seen by a chief executive as denying him the highly valued margin for maneuver to respond to shifting or reevaluated circumstances. It becomes more difficult for him to redefine purposes or to scale down expectations without explicit admission that he has changed his policy.

An administration may discover, as it moves to execute a policy, that conditions are far less propitious for achieving its goal than had been assumed. Cost–benefit ratios must then be reevaluated, opportunities reexamined, and, perhaps, the value accorded a given objective reduced. Under those conditions, a taking in of sails is called for. Yet a formal retraction of an officially promulgated, well-publicized policy is to be avoided, for any of several reasons: Perhaps an improvement in conditions at a later time is foreseen, and a public retreat would result in a loss of credibility; perhaps diplomatic tact dictates that other governments not be forced to retract equally public commitments that the United States extracted from them; perhaps a multifaceted diplomacy might originally have involved plans to approach different governments with nuanced variations of the same policy (a reason for keeping the initial statement general and imprecise); or perhaps the administration does not wish to present a sitting target to domestic opponents, ready to pounce on any evidence of failure, by inflating expectations. Concern about all or any of these possible consequences creates incentives encouraging a government leader to shy away from the comprehensive, finely drawn policy design – even at the cost of some incoherence and dissonance.

Second, the *conviction* may be lacking. High officials are as often as not unsure of what they want to do about a problem. They are constantly asking themselves (and not giving answers to) questions like: Exactly how troublesome is the problem? What is it costing me in goals thwarted, status diminished, political capital lost? How confident can I, or my advisers, be that a course of action will succeed, and at what price? Do we fully fathom the forces at work? Are our estimates of alternatives based on an accurate cause-and-effect model of the reality we are dealing with? Procrastination in coming to grips with the issues posed by plutonium can be understood in these terms.

Another set of questions concerns an administration's perceived *capacities and commitments*. What are the opportunity costs encountered in developing a full-blown policy, staking out a firm position, and marshaling the administrative and political resources to advance it – time, political support, and administrative capacity, all of which are finite if not wholly inelastic? Is the necessary technical expertise available? What would have to be done to secure it? What sort of positive results and dividends might be expected were the policy to be reasonably successful? Would they be realized during the present occupant's tenure in office? These are all questions that point to delay, prevarication, and a perpetuation of internal debate and politicking.

Yet another major consideration is the strong aversion to the *discipline of planning* at the working levels of government. The readiness of officials to pursue narrow, self-interested ends is at once cause and effect of the typically fragmented approach to policy noted herein. Staffers and agency officials alike find gratification in pressing their own version of the truth and seek to defend the prerogatives that an unstructured system gives them. Liberties that too often have become license are not readily yielded in response to demands (much less requests) made in the name of procedural order and policy coherence, when the policy itself remains inchoate.

The "organizational culture" factor

My account of Carter administration policy making paid particular attention to the abuse of authority by staffers. This abuse was only the most insidious and damaging expression of a more widespread tendency for officials to lose sight of overall policy goals and needs as they become enmeshed in the high-pressure and highly politicized workings of government. Indeed, the incentives and preferences for playing the policy game can make the idea of orderly government itself alien.

Whereas a political leader often finds it inconvenient to plan, the attitude at lower echelons in the executive departments is closer to antipathy. For the centralization of decision-making authority, and formal mechanisms for disciplining the policy process, threaten to shift power out of the hands of agency officials and to restrict the ways in which they do things (if not necessarily their right to do them). The type of concentrated control represented by Henry Kissinger's early NSC system (when it was still restrained and did more planning than operations) drastically alters the policy environment, to the discomfort of bureaucratic officialdom. By defining problems for analysis, it opens agency orthodoxies and pet solutions to skeptical attack. By stipulating set procedures for reaching decisions, it curbs bureaucratic games playing and imposes what may be an uncongenial intellectual discipline. By stating policy decisions with clarity and precision, it sets a standard of accomplishment that puts agency performance under strict scrutiny. By allocating responsibilities in accordance with need rather than organizational jurisdiction, it can disturb a comfortable sense of bureaucratic territory and prerogative.

Moreover, systematic policy making is at variance with the norms and attitudes that thrive in the peculiar cultural ethos of bureaucratic government. Nothing is more alien to the prevailing culture and its codes of behavior (and nothing is more perishable in that atmosphere) than the kind of approach that emphasizes (or worse, requires) deliberate, systematic analysis, a carefully drawn policy design, and a well-coordinated strategy for executing it – that is, the approach to which we have given the shorthand label "planning." A little-recognized truth of current governmental life is that it attracts a peculiar type of intellectual temperament and personality. The hard-nosed, ultra-pragmatic, unceasingly competitive style makes exceptional demands on those who share in it. A whole lifestyle has developed around the "hard-ball" ethic that predominates in policy-level offices of the executive branch. It has its own proscriptive and prescriptive behavior norms, hierarchy of values, reward structure, and imagery. Anyone familiar with the high-pressure environment of executive government is aware that problem solving is not the sole, or even main, criterion of success. A superior record in the endless struggles to maintain access to decision centers, to exercise leverage on decisive actors, and to win acceptance among constituencies – congressional, electoral, media – is taken as the surest indicator of achievement.

These things are by no means separable from, or necessarily contrary to, programmatic ends. But neither are they equivalent to the realization of policy goals. When a reconciliation – by no means inevitable – is made between the demands of good policy, on the one han, and the inclinations and interests of middle-echelon officials, on the other, it usually involves the redefinition or scaling down of objectives. They are accommodated to an institutional environment in which "working the system" is as important as the outcome (and where one's view of the outcome is strongly colored by one's role and influence in the process). This judgment is not meant to question the dedication and conviction of officials, or their ability. Indeed, the manifest talent visible in key executive branch offices prompts querying how we have managed to devise a system that uncannily contrives to generate a product distinctly inferior to that which any small group of the participants could have managed on its own vastly more limited resources.

The point of this commentary is, rather, to call attention to those aspects of our political culture, within government, that nurture an aversion to planned policy, as we have conceived it. The prolix organizational style of policy making immerses officials in a dense, highly incestuous environment where immediate, narrow, and institutionally construed problems squeeze out or transform the concern for policy substance. By so doing, it both enormously complicates the task of making coherent, coordinated policy and disparages more orderly approaches.

Where officials spend their working lives struggling to maintain control over the paper flow and embroiled in endless bureaucratic tussles, it is not surprising that coping behavior supplants goal-oriented behavior. At the end of the obligatory ten-, eleven-, or twelve-hour day, a warm feeling of gratification comes just from knowing that one has not been excluded from communications traffic; that one has finally gotten one's memo in the strategic place on the task force agenda; that one has caught the technical people in Department X trying to slip through plans for the new review without getting the prescribed input from the interagency working group; that one has blocked the publication of a press story inspired by opponents (in or outside of government) that misrepresented the administration's policy (i.e., the version of it upheld by one's own office); that one has satisfied the combative, self-righteous staff of a congressional committee that no sub rosa commitments presuming positive legislative action were made at last week's international meeting. Days and weeks consumed by survival efforts like these leave little time for a deliberate review of how a particular policy is working; time to be spent evaluating responses from relevant constituencies, ensuring that the various programmatic support elements are coming together as projected, scheduling the phasing of the policy's various components to achieve maximum effect, or encouraging superiors to resolve outstanding, disruptive disagreements within the executive branch on the interpretation of stated administration policy.

Many of the same pressures are also felt by senior officials, who then, by failing to impose design and discipline on their subordinates, suffer doubly from its corrosive influence on deliberate policy making. Enormous demands are placed on the time, energy, and forbearance of even the most senior officials, just to keep the oversized and underdesigned machine of government ticking. Without central direction and ordering mechanisms, they come to expect that they must surrender to the system as encountered in order to make any progress at all. They all too quickly learn to live with its inconveniences and idiosyncracies, to maneuver within it, and to adjust expectations to the constraints it imposes. In other words, high officials undergo a socialization process. None, individually, feels himself in a position to do more than modify selective aspects of prevailing arrangements and codes of conduct, within his own domain. Collectively, this acquiescence by central policy makers confirms the rightness, that is, the inevitability, of the existing state of affairs.

Moreover, these officials' habituation to a system of fragmented authority and ad hoc cooperation creates strong disincentives to doing the three things critical to a better-planned, more comprehensive approach to policy: stating objectives with clarity, drafting a clear strategy for reaching them, and making a concerted effort to harmonize the strands of a multifaceted policy. To achieve a working consensus in a governmental setting featuring elaborate consultations among a congeries of self-centered subunits, two generally unsatisfactory choices present themselves: settling for the least common denominator of agreement, or restricting the field of action, and thereby the number of actors. The former option is much discussed, and its implications are fully assessed in the policy-making literature. The latter phenomenon, however, has not received the attention it deserves.

Given the apparent impossibility of achieving a unity of views among a host of policy actors (in the absence of the all-too-rare assertion of presidential authority), officials see a narrowing of the problem area and a scaling down of objectives as conditions for making any headway at all. They show a disposition to exclude secondary aspects from consideration, to reduce the number of elements on which to focus remedial attention, and to shorten the time frame. In these ways, they trim policy to more manageable proportions.

The total number of actors is not shrunk; rather, they are clustered and compartmentalized by specific areas of responsibility. The practice is to break the policy problem into its several more-or-less discrete constituent parts and to parcel them out to different agencies or interdepartmental clusters. Unfortunately, this fragmentation tends to be a unidirectional process, and not a prelude to resynthesis. (This is the strategy Carter pursued after his April 1977 statement, in assigning follow-up tasks to six interagency task forces. The central coordinating body, the NSC ad hoc group on non-proliferation, which was supposed to monitor their progress and to assess their product in reference to the administration's overarching strategy, never functioned as a true coordinating unit. No one expected it to, or was surprised — much less displeased — by its performing short of specifications.)[4] This kind of organizational division of labor has its attractions. The frustrations of trying to hammer out a common policy and to design supporting programs are soon felt by a president or his officials, who may lack a clear vision of policy outcomes, the talent for commanding their fractious and undisciplined bureaucratic army, and a bent for orchestrating grand strategies. Compartmentalization promises a way out of the morass of inconclusive meetings, sterile communications, and interminable disputes. However, it also promises a high degree of disjuncture, and it offers no formula in the end for bringing the pieces together, except through rather crude splicing. The process is made tractable at the cost of comprehensiveness and reach.

These more modest and tentative approaches make good sense under certain circumstances. But they should be a matter of choice and judgment about what conditions allow, and what the requirements for problem solving are, and should *not* be dictated by the deficiencies of government institutions or the inadequacies of leadership. The sensitivity to political and institutional constraints is well founded. The desire to retain a large measure of flexibility is reasonable. Yet political leaders have an overriding obligation of public office to meet the conditions for effective policy. The issue is whether it can be established that, on balance, the forces against "planned" policy must be accommodated in order for government to act with *any* degree of effectiveness. For if they are not so compelling as to outweigh their costly defects, then an easy tolerance of disordered or segmented government amounts to dereliction of responsibility. On the subject of nuclear energy and non-proliferation, the evidence we have adduced suggests that the latter is the case.

SOME RECOMMENDATIONS

This unsparing criticism of government performance carries an obligation to suggest how things could be done better. That is less intimidating a challenge than the dense literature on the policy process would lead one to believe. The chronicle of derelictions and inadequacies (only partially offset by recognized accomplishments) presented here bears the message that the causes of failure are not concealed deep within the warp and woof of the political system. Improving government performance does not demand intricate strategies, ingeniously contrived and applied, to outfox the bureaucratic games players or to manipulate the cognitive processes of officialdom. For the most part, the shortcomings of government leaders we have noted are attributable to quite basic failings.

Too much policy analysis is pitched at the level of advanced algebra when the errors are in basic arithmetic. To use two glaring examples from the Carter administration, consider a setup that permits an NSC staffer to intercept and edit a sensitive official letter from the lead agency to a congressional leader without any consulation, or one that winds up having its decisive policy statement written hurriedly by a holdover from a previous administration with little knowledge of the interagency review on which it was supposed to be based. These are exceptional cases. Yet, by a reasonable estimate, most of the non-proliferation policy failings we cited in the Carter administration and its predecessors can be ascribed to a weakness in the fundamentals of governance and diplomacy. So, if my recommendations strike the reader as simple and uncomplicated, I urge that they be viewed in light of the account I have written, and not interpreted as evidence of a lack of sophistication about the complexities of government or ignorance of the theoretical literature.

Two essential elements

Above all, the president as chief executive must take a direct hand in protecting the integrity of his administration's policies. This means, first, making appointments appropriate to the functions and requirements of logical policy making and assuming that officials with overlapping or complementary responsibilities should be chosen with regard to some minimal compatibility of outlook. A president appreciative of his needs for a staff that acts like a high-level secretariat would not, as Jimmy Carter did, appoint a man of Zbigniew Brzezinski's temperament as the head of NSC, permit him to stock it with uninhibited young advocates, and encourage their independence. He would not leave uncomposed the basic differences among purists, moderates, and the nuclear establishment old guard.

Presidential leadership also means mandating authority commensurate with formal responsibility. The cause of effective government would be well served by clear distribution of functions and the designation of accountable parties. The common confusion about who has charge of what, and who the president supports or listens to, is a boon to bureaucratic games players and an encouragement to personality feuds. Multiple advocacy and broad consulation contribute to the prudent formulation of intelligent policy – *when* they are part of a process with built-in decision points, one that is being managed with the need to choose and to resolve clearly in mind. Unless there is someone to direct the process, it too easily becomes a quagmire that can neither offer firm policy guidance nor expedite the making of decisions. Though neat arrangements for assigning lead offices and officials are not a panacea for internal dissonance, more attention to how tasks are allocated, and whether the power for accomplishing them is available, could reduce substantially the costs imposed by free-form government.

White House leadership might well take even more concrete form. It is not unreasonable for a president to convene periodic meetings of those senior officials who share responsibility on a major issue. Together, they could review the progress of major policy initiatives, consider questions of phasing and synchronization, and make tactical adaptations or strategic adjustments as developments dictate. There seems no doubt that had Jimmy Carter called together his feuding nuclear energy and non-proliferation officials to sort out differences and bang heads, when necessary, his administration would have been spared much hardship (surrogates for President Ford did this in hammering out the October 1976 policy statement). Presidential involvement to this extent may appear at first glance to be overly time-consuming and too demanding intellectually. But recent experience belies these doubts. The fault with President Carter's active role in overseeing nuclear energy policy was his excessive concern for detail at the expense of a coherent overall framework. He clearly knew more than enough about the issue to provide the kind of guidance outlined above. He devoted large chunks of time to it, often delving into the most minute questions. More careful preparation and oversight in the end would have been a time-saver. Once the contours of the policy are established, and a common frame of reference is agreed on, the time requirements are minimal. Certainly they are far less than those needed to untangle recurrent bureaucratic backlashes and to rectify diplomatic misunderstandings – without even considering the time and energies of key officials squandered in fighting over old ground in unresolved intramural debates about principles and premises.

The second essential ingredient of a sounder policy approach is a concise statement of just what policy *is*, and the communication of that policy to all parts of the government. A clear enunciation of objectives, and a reasonably detailed exposition of the strategy for achieving them, can go far in avoiding much of the wasted motion that typifies executive branch work patterns. Such a specification cuts down on the merry-go-round of circular memos interpreting, reinterpreting, and debating the vague, often divergently worded declarations of a president and his senior deputies. It encourages agencies to pull together, and makes it less likely that implementation will fall hostage to the vagaries of interdepartmental working groups and higher-level duels among rival agency heads. Policy making as an interminable shuffling, where ends as well as means are in a constant state of negotiation among bureaucratic baronies, is as inefficient in execution as it is unavailing of intelligent policy.

Greater clarity in the formulation of policy also makes more feasible the practice of designating lead offices. A grant of authority from the White House can be most effectively used when there is a sure understanding of the policy direction to be taken. In such cases, this authority cannot easily be eroded by using debate over policy substance to mask power games. Then a lead office (ideally, in association with tempered executive office staffs) can do its job: ensuring that pieces of the policy are smoothly melded; seeing to it that public pronouncements and statements before congressional committees (and in international forums) are compatible, if not uniform; checking that basic policy is not evaded or distorted in the development of supporting programs and in diplomatic execution; and, by no means least, periodically reviewing the situation to see how its underlying premises are holding up. With a lead office benefiting from the direction provided by clear and fixed reference points, individual agencies will find it harder to latch onto those themes and extract those elements that most interest them, pursuing these goals oblivious to all else.

The chief executive who strives to give his policies readily identifiable shape also will have an administration in a good position to manage technology intelligently. The more succinctly the reasoning behind broad policies can be laid out, and the general strategy explicated, the greater the chance that its basic purposes will guide technical judgments. If successive presidents and chairmen of the AEC had made clear that the United States' interest in non-proliferation could not tolerate facilities that offered ready access to bomb-making materials, then it is less likely that a series of incremental decisions would have given the civilian reprocessing program the shape that it eventually took. At the very least, the value trade-offs incorporated in the commercialization of reprocessing would have stood a better chance of being revealed, and the opportunities for taking compensatory action increased. The raising of consciousness about the many aspects of a policy area, and heightened awareness of their intersections, helps to reduce technological determinism. That in itself could be a major asset for U.S. nuclear policy.

The congressional factor

The intrinsic problems of organizing and orchestrating the executive branch are formidable, if not insoluble. The undertaking is revealed as all the more difficult when we consider that important pieces of the policy puzzle elude even the most tenuous control of administrations. The credibility and effectiveness of U.S. non-proliferation policies have depended on the actions of the Congress and semiindependent regulatory bodies. For an administration's efforts to have a reasonable chance of success, the legal and political pieces at home must be in order. In the past, they rarely have been so ordered.

Most troublesome has been Congress. Jealously guarding its prerogatives against an uncompromising Nixon administration, the legislature helped drag out the dispute over expanding enrichment capacity that ended in a crisis of the United States' international nuclear relations. A stubborn and outspoken Congress also put a crimp in the Carter administration's efforts to get its non-proliferation campaign off the ground. It kept the Clinch River breeder project firmly fastened around the administration's neck, to the latter's embarrassment, chagrin, and damaged credibility. At the height of tense negotiations with the Japanese over the future of the Tokai Mura reprocessing facility, it undercut strenuous efforts to assuage Tokyo's energy anxieties by prohibiting a proposed oil exchange that would have diverted North Slope Alaskan crude to the Japanese market. And its protracted exercise in drafting the Nuclear Non-Proliferation Act produced legislation so extraordinarily intricate as to add appreciably to the administration's difficulties in renegotiating agreements of cooperation. Additional problems were the administration's unavailing attempts to get both approval of financial support for a fuel-assurance program and agreement on the siting of storage facilities to handle nuclear waste.

Many of the Carter administration's headaches with Congress were of its own making. Others were rooted in the underlying friction between the branches that is characteristic of this period in U.S. political history. In the post-Vietnam, post-Watergate era, Congress has been righteous, highly protective of its independence, and unamenable to direction by its own leadership. There were special reasons why nuclear energy programs should face particularly rough sailing. Non-proliferation as such has no natural domestic constituency, nor does it evoke whatever lingering deference to presidential judgment on national security issues still remains. Moreover, it straddles two spheres of discourse and program jurisdiction: the domestic and international. In keeping with the majority view of national energy interests, the Congress has guarded Clinch River against the administration's meat-ax. In keeping with the majority view of the national interest in stopping weapons proliferation, Congress has imposed rigid and stringent export conditions. The legislature reconciles its policies no better than the executive does. Even its organization has come to mirror the overspecialization of executive offices. Nuclear power as an issue area is divided into its component parts – domestic energy production, environmental and safety regulation, non-proliferation – with each assigned to a separate committee. The committees in turn tend to be dominated by self-interested specialists who act as custodians of that piece of the issue placed in their charge, and who are watchful of any trespass. They are, as often as not, even less susceptible to outside influence than the most hidebound fief holders of the executive branch.

Two things can be said about White House approaches to Congress on matters affecting non-proliferation. First, when shortsightedness and narrow-mindedness occur in the executive they are reflected in, and magnified by, parallel tendencies in Congress. One-dimensional planning and compartmentalized policy making (as with the Nixon administration's push for privatization) encourage the legislature to focus on selected issues without reference to the broader context or regard for secondary effects. Had the crosscutting nature of the nuclear energy policy been noted earlier, and efforts made to shape the domestic program so that it could be fitted to the rough specifications of a broad nonproliferation strategy, Congress would have been more likely to pay attention to the compatability of its own actions. Similarly, the longer a policy's time horizon, the greater the opportunity to prepare the intellectual and the political ground. The full dimensions of the problem, as seen by an administration, can be laid before Congress and interested constituencies, the proposed course of action and the thinking behind it explained, and its practical requirements in the way of legislative action fully assessed. Before bureaucratic or industrial interests have congealed, before reputations have been put on the line and intellectual positions staked out, before international pressures are acute – then is the time when legislators are most susceptible to friendly education. Effective executive leadership, in today's unaccommodating congressional atmosphere, depends in large measure on nurturing a sympathetic understanding of the premises and purposes of presidential policy. Favorable predisposition toward administration requests, built on that understanding, is a vital asset. It raises the odds that specific analyses will be credited, that information will be taken at something like its face value, and that the executive will receive the benefit of the doubt, if not supine acquiescence.

Furthermore, a longer time perspective makes it that much more practical to involve Congress in the formulation of policy, which in turn prepares it for anticipating what trade-offs are going to have to be made down the line, and for making them more knowingly. This is not to suggest that Congress can be transformed into a paragon among rational legislatures. There are a myriad of institutional and political reasons why its workings always will be characterized by an ad hoc process in which the fluctuations of popular mood, individual idiosyncracies, and the internal dynamics of the two chambers (not to mention the machinations of lobbying groups) are important influences on what is done in committee and on the floor. The more reasonable, and by no means insignificant, expectation is (1) that with a better articulation of policy deliberately formulated, the normal inertia of the legislative process, intellectual and institutional, will be working in favor of a broadly cast administration approach to a cluster of interlocking nuclear energy issues, and (2) that the amount of unnecessary friction between the two branches will be reduced when the executive does not need to make sudden demands whose rationale is imperfectly understood, and whose substance might conflict with existing legislative preferences – and constituency interests. Finally, the time and understanding gained by better planning will remove the temptation for an administration to press Congress in a tactless and ultimately counterproductive way.

Diplomacy

U.S. non-proliferation diplomacy in the 1970s had a checkered record. Under Richard Nixon it was almost nonexistent. The administration of Gerald Ford saw a stuttering start at catching up with events that always seemed to keep a step ahead of it. The Carter government exhibited its typically odd mix of frenetic amateurism and ultra-pragmatism, leavened, in this area, by a larger-than-normal dose of professional competence (mainly in the handling of INFCE and the renegotiation of bilateral agreements). Nixon's hard-nosed attitude toward nuclear commerce served to antagonize foreign governments, to hasten the reduction of U.S. influence, and to damage irreparably the United States' credibility as a supplier. Efforts made between 1974 and 1976 to repair the damage demonstrated a growing awareness and had some small success. But they never confronted head on the central issue posed by the spread of civilian nuclear technologies, especially reprocessing. The sounder, more ambitious Carter strategy was badly hurt by an early series of distressing malapropisms, contradictions, and delays, from which it never fully recovered. There is no need to harp on the early failings and foibles of foreign policy making in the Carter administration; they are discussed in Chapter 4. But some lessons for the pursuit of non-proliferation aims under current international circumstances do deserve mention.

One, the United States would benefit by making up its mind precisely what it wants from other governments, what it is prepared to accept in the way of nuclear programs accommodated to U.S. desires, and what it will give in exchange. An unambiguous public statement of objectives and conditions has the apparent drawback of reducing U.S. negotiating flexibility as the United States conducts multifaceted diplomacy with different classes of consumers and suppliers. But that loss is more illusory than real. The U.S. government has never demonstrated a national genius for devising elaborate, carefully crafted diplomatic strategies, or a talent for their subtly phased implementation. For all its ingenuity and dedication, the conduct of the Carter non-proliferation policy did not often suggest a drastic change of governmental personality. Coordination was poor, approaches to foreign governments lacked sensitivity to national conditions, and supporting programs were not properly synchronized with the overall strategy. And Jimmy Carter himself gave the idea of an active presidency a bad name by demonstrating an unfortunate tendency to misspeak himself and to meddle fitfully in policy details.

The evidence is strong that the United States government is not well equipped to carry out a sophisticated, highly differentiated foreign policy campaign. Even were government's undeniable resources better used, this account suggests that a subtle diplomacy with a deft tactical sense is probably impossible in an area where the congressional role is so prominent, and external dealings are inseparable from domestic programs and policies. The simpler and more straightforward the U.S. position, the easier it will be to reach consensus internally, and so to make commitments to other governments.

An added dividend would be an expanded opportunity to use diplomatic representatives abroad. Knowing what U.S. policy was, and confident that its lifespan would be longer than the interval between presidential statements, would enable them to serve as effective spokesmen and informed analysts. Major policy initiatives would benefit immeasurably from having officials in foreign capitals able to explain them, to relate them to other diplomatic business, and to exercise their discretion in making tactical adjustments. The restoration of U.S. diplomats to a significant policy role would also have the desired effect of freeing administration officials to do their policy-making job in Washington without the distractions of flying diplomacy.

A second word of counsel concerns the dangers of procrastination for an innovative policy. When asking to do things counter to their inclinations and to what they have come to perceive as their interests, one must hasten to exploit the moment of doubt and irresolution. The Carter pronouncements in April of 1977 were intended to, and did, shake governments out of their habitual ways of looking at civilian nuclear power. The time to recast ideas and programs is when old attitudes are loosened, before the previous tendencies and programs are reasserted, and the established interests have recrystallized. A new U.S. president in particular always has unique leverage. Everyone listens carefully. Many wish to win his favor. He has the power to set the agenda for allies and the terms of debate on global issues generally. That advantage was lost by the indecisive and equivocal presentation of the Carter administration's policy.

It should be borne in mind that *U.S. political capital is scarce in the world.* Doubts about U.S. credibility are pronounced, cynicism about its intentions is rife, and there is a general skepticism about its ability to understand other peoples' interests. The situation has been aggravated by a loosening of political security ties with some countries, and by sharp clashes over other issues. In this atmosphere of suspicion, it is exceptionally difficult to catalyze a presumed collective interest. That is why serial approaches that table one proposal after another in the order of a U.S. priority list tempt failure. So does the inability to synchronize the policy's mutually support-ing elements. Failure to elicit a positive response to Carter's initial round of proposals (and thereby to lay the foundations for a new international regime in nuclear energy) diminished the chances of success on subsequent proposals and diplomatic initiatives, whatever their intrinsic merits.

The political space is also confined. Non-proliferation diplomacy cannot avoid being influenced by other dimensions of foreign policy. At a time of sensitive dealings with many suppliers and consumers, there is an ever-present danger of disadvantageous spillover from economics, security, or human rights. The flare-up of major conflicts in any of these fields could so poison the diplomatic atmosphere as to make any effort at construction of a regime – a chancy venture under any circumstances – well nigh impos-sible. The United States does retain considerable power for positive politi-cal construction, but its use is very much hostage to the vicissitudes of an uncongenial environment. Washington's plans are susceptible to contin-gent factors the United States is less and less able to control.

Political space is confined in the domestic sense as well. Governments today in the United States and elsewhere operate under unprecedented pressure from organized interests. The ability of governments to protect their pre-rogatives from the demands of aggressive claimants (and, in the United States, from Congress) has been further impaired by the pervasive flight from authority (not to mention governments' own derelictions). The up-shot is the imposition of severe temporal and latitudinal constraints. This is reason for making foreign policy in full awareness of domestic circum-stances elsewhere. It is also an argument for supporting well-publicized collective arrangements that can spotlight common interests, take the sting out of verbal exchanges, and promise effective policing of international behavior (and, in exceptional cases, even confer special privileges where such treatment would facilitate the achievement of a larger end). Political leadership that must balance particular interests against the general inter-est, national and international, should welcome external support to assure that it is not submerged beneath an avalanche of particularisms. Interna-tional cooperation can be an assist to internal discipline.

Finally, the attention of political leadership is fleeting. Enlightened policy is more likely to come from heads of government than from bureaucrats. But the former are rarely able to give any issue their attention long enough to elaborate a policy and to oversee its execution. Thus, at critical stages, policy comes to be dominated by the compartmentalized views of the bu-reaucratic games players. (Or, equally damaging to coherent policy, it falls prey to the intrusive contribution of Congress.) Policy making by bureaucracy is not only prone to narrow-mindedness. It also is enslaved by a consensus-building process that leaves little place for the views and concerns of foreign governments. At some point, the elaborate process of deliberation and debate must be brought to a halt. Only when the chief executive has declared himself on matters of internal dispute is there a hope that White House staffers and agency officials can be brought into line and kept there. A government that has mastered itself and knows its own mind will have met the key conditions for pushing back the time horizon in which it operates. An administration will have won for itself a margin for diplomatic maneuver with domestic as well as foreign protagonists. It will be in a position to combine leverage and persuasion in more artful and effective packages. It thus will have gained partial protection against unforeseen, neglected, or unsettling developments of the sorts that have mortgaged so much of U.S. non-proliferation policy to chancy improvisation.

So, as always, we return in the end to political leadership. Political will is crucial, yet too often mercurial. At the best of times, it is not constant but intermittent, of varying intensity and duration. That said, it is imperative that when hard decisions impend, the heads of government should be actively engaged and encouraged to act with directness and dispatch, at least to set the process in motion.

Glossary

ACDA: Arms Control and Disarmament Agency.

AEC: Atomic Energy Commission.

AIF: Atomic Industrial Forum.

BARNWELL: The site in South Carolina of a large unfinished plutonium reprocessing plant owned by Allied General Nuclear Services.

BREEDER REACTOR: A nuclear reactor that produces more fissile material than it consumes.

CANDU: A nuclear reactor of Canadian design, which uses natural uranium as a fuel and heavy water as a moderator and coolant.

CENTRIFUGE ISOTOPE SEPARATION: A new isotope enrichment process that separates lighter molecules containing uranium-235 from heavier molecules containing uranium-238 by means of ultra-high-speed centrifuges. The process is now being successfully exploited by the URENCO consortium in Western Europe.

CIP: Cascade Improvement Program.

CLINCH RIVER BREEDER REACTOR (CRBR): A proposed demonstration of the liquid-metal fast-breeder reactor. The CRBR, which would operate on a plutonium fuel cycle and be cooled by molten sodium, would have an electrical output of about 350 megawatts.

CUP: Cascade Upgrading Program.

ENRICHMENT: The process by which the percentage of the fissionable isotope uranium-235 is increased above that contained in natural uranium.

ERDA: Energy Research and Development Administration.

EURATOM: European Atomic Energy Community.

EURODIF: A joint venture, involving France (52%), Italy, Belgium,

249

Spain, and Iran, which is building a gaseous diffusion plant in France.

FISSILE MATERIAL: Atoms such as uranium-233, uranium-235, or plutonium-239 that fission upon the absorption of a low-energy neutron.

FUEL CYCLE: The set of chemical and physical operations needed to prepare nuclear material for use in reactors and to dispose of or recycle the material after its removal from the reactor. Existing fuel cycles begin with uranium as the natural resource and create plutonium as a by-product. Some future fuel cycles may rely on thorium and produce the fissile isotope uranium-233.

GASEOUS DIFFUSION: A process used to enrich uranium in the isotope uranium-235. Uranium in the form of a gas (UF_6) is forced through a thin, porous barrier. Because the lighter gas molecules, containing uranium-235, move at a higher velocity than the heavy molecules, containing uranium-238, the lighter molecules pass through the barrier more frequently than do the heavy ones, producing a slight enrichment in the lighter isotope. Many stages are required to produce material sufficiently enriched for use in a light-water reactor.

GESMO: *Final Generic Environmental Statement on the Use of Recycled Plutonium in Mixed Oxide Fuel in Light-Water Cooled Reactors* (Nuclear Regulatory Commission Report, August 1976).

HIGH-ENRICHED URANIUM (HEU): High-enriched uranium used for nuclear weapons and for certain types of nuclear research.

IAEA: International Atomic Energy Agency.

INFCE: International Fuel Cycle Evaluation.

IRRADIATED FUEL: Nuclear fuel that has been used in a nuclear reactor.

ISOTOPE: One of perhaps several different species of a given chemical element, distinguished by variations in the number of neutrons in the atomic nucleus but indistinguishable by chemical means.

JCAE: Joint Committee on Atomic Energy.

LIGHT-WATER REACTOR (LWR): A nuclear reactor that uses ordinary water as a coolant to transfer heat from the fissioning uranium to a steam turbine and employs slightly enriched uranium-235 as fuel.

LIQUID-METAL FAST-BREEDER REACTOR (LMFBR): Liquid-metal fast-breeder reactor. A nuclear reactor that produces greater fissile material than it consumes, of the type that uses no moderator. It uses a mixture of natural uranium and plutonium as start-up fuel, producing new plutonium in the process.

LOW-ENRICHED URANIUM (LEU): Low-enriched uranium fuel used

for conventional power reactors.

MIXED OXIDE FUEL (MOX): Nuclear reactor fuel composed of plutonium and uranium in oxide form. The plutonium replaces some of the fissile uranium, thus reducing the need for uranium ore and enrichment. This is the form of the fuel that would be used in plutonium recycling.

NPT: Non-Proliferation Treaty.

NRC: Nuclear Regulatory Commission.

NSC: National Security Council.

NUCLEAR WASTE: The radioactive products formed by fission and other nuclear processes in a reactor. Most nuclear waste is initially in the form of spent fuel. If this material is reprocessed, new categories of waste result, including high-level, transuranic, low-level, and others.

OES: Bureau of Oceans and International Environmental and Scientific Affairs.

OMB: Office of Management and Budget.

OSTP: Office of the Science and Technology Adviser to the President.

RECYCLING: The reuse of unburned uranium and plutonium in fresh fuel after separation from fission products in spent fuel at a reprocessing plant.

REPROCESSING: The chemical and mechanical processes by which plutonium-239 and the unused uranium-235 are recovered from spent reactor fuel.

SCI: Office of Science and Technology.

SEPARATIVE WORK UNITS (SWUS): A measure of the work required to separate uranium isotopes in the enrichment process. It is used to measure the capacity of an enrichment plant independent of a particular product and tails. To put this unit of measurement in perspective, consider that it takes about 100,000 SWUs per year to keep a 1,000-megawatt LWR operating and 2,500 SWUs to make a nuclear weapon.

SPENT FUEL: The fuel elements removed from a reactor after several years of generating power. Spent fuel contains radioactive waste materials, unburned uranium, and plutonium.

SPIKING: A technique to deter theft of nuclear fuel by the addition of radioactive substances.

TAILS ASSAY: The percentage of uranium-235 in tails. Natural uranium contains 0.71% uranium-235; the tails assay may be 0.3% or lower.

UEA: United Energy Associates.

URENCO: A joint British, Dutch, and West German organization that operates centrifuge isotope separation plants.

APPENDIX A

President Dwight D. Eisenhower's "Atoms for Peace" address to the United Nations General Assembly, December 8, 1953

WHEN Secretary-General Hammarskjold's invitation to address this General Assembly reached me in Bermuda, I was just beginning a series of conferences with the Prime Ministers and Foreign Ministers of Great Britain and of France. Our subject was some of the problems that beset our world.

During the remainder of the Bermuda Conference, I had constantly in mind that ahead of me lay a great honor. That honor is mine today as I stand here, privileged to address the General Assembly of the United Nations.

At the same time that I appreciate the distinction of addressing you, I have a sense of exhilaration as I look upon this Assembly.

Never before in history has so much hope for so many people been gathered together in a single organization. Your deliberations and decisions during these somber years have already realized part of those hopes.

But the great tests and the great accomplishments still lie ahead. And in the confident expectation of those accomplishments, I would use the office which, for the time being, I hold, to assure you that the Government of the United States will remain steadfast in its support of this body. This we shall do in the conviction that you will provide a great share of the wisdom, the courage, and the faith which can bring to this world lasting peace for all nations, and happiness and well-being for all men.

Clearly, it would not be fitting for me to take this occasion to present to you a unilateral American report on Bermuda. Nevertheless, I assure you that in our deliberations on that lovely island we sought to invoke those same great concepts of universal peace and human dignity which are so cleanly etched in your charter.

Neither would it be a measure of this great opportunity merely to recite, however hopefully, pious platitudes.

SOURCE: *Congressional Record*, vol. 100, Jan. 7, 1954, pp. 61–3.

A danger shared by all

I therefore decided that this occasion warranted my saying to you some of the things that have been on the minds and hearts of my legislative and executive associates and on mine for a great many months – thoughts I had originally planned to say primarily to the American people.

I know that the American people share my deep belief that if a danger exists in the world it is a danger shared by all, and, equally, that if hope exists in the mind of one nation that hope should be shared by all.

No idle words or shallow visions

So my country's purpose is to help us move out of the dark chamber of horrors into the light – to find a way by which the minds of men, the hopes of men, the souls of men everywhere, can move forward toward peace and happiness and well-being.

In this quest I know that we must not lack patience.

I know that in a world divided such as ours today salvation cannot be attained by one dramatic act.

I know that many steps will have to be taken over many months before the world can look at itself one day and truly realize that a new climate of mutually peaceful confidence is abroad in the world.

But I know, above all else, that we must start to take these steps – now.

The United States and its allies, Great Britain and France, have over the past months tried to take some of these steps. Let no one say that we shun the conference table.

On the record has long stood the request of the United States, Great Britain, and France to negotiate with the Soviet Union the problems of a divided Germany.

On that record has long stood the request of the same three nations to negotiate an Austrian State Treaty.

On the same record still stands the request of the United Nations to negotiate the problems of Korea.

Most recently, we have received from the Soviet Union what is in effect an expression of willingness to hold a Four Powers meeting. Along with our allies, Great Britain and France, we were pleased to see that this note did not contain the unacceptable preconditions previously put forward.

As you already know from our joint Bermuda communique, the United States, Great Britain, and France have agreed promptly to meet with the Soviet Union.

The Government of the United States approaches this conference with hopeful sincerity. We will bend every effort of our minds to the single purpose of emerging from that conference with tangible results toward peace – the only true way of lessening international tension.

We never have, we never will, propose or suggest that the Soviet Union surrender what is rightfully theirs.

We will never say that the peoples of Russia are an enemy with whom we have no desire ever to deal or mingle in friendly and fruitful relationship.

On the contrary, we hope that this conference may initiate a relationship with the Soviet Union which will eventually bring about a free intermingling of the peoples of the East and of the West – the one sure, human way of developing the understanding required for confident and peaceful relations.

Instead of the discontent which is now settling upon Eastern Germany, occupied Austria, and the countries of Eastern Europe, we seek a harmonious family of free European nations, with none a threat to the other, and least of all a threat to the peoples of Russia.

Beyond the turmoil and strife and misery of Asia, we seek peaceful opportunity for these peoples to develop their natural resources and to elevate their lives.

These are not idle words or shallow visions. Behind them lies a story of nations lately come to independence, not as a result of war, but through free grant or peaceful negotiation. There is a record, already written, of assistance gladly given by nations of the West to needy peoples, and to those suffering the temporary effects of famine, drought, and natural disaster.

These are deeds of peace. They speak more loudly than promises or protestations for peaceful intent.

For the benefit of mankind

But I do not wish to rest either upon the reiteration of past proposals or the restatement of past deeds. The gravity of the time is such that every avenue of peace, no matter how dimly discernible, should be explored.

There is at least one new avenue of peace which has not yet been well explored – an avenue now laid out by the General Assembly of the United Nations.

In its resolution of November 28, 1953, this General Assembly suggested – and I quote – "that the Disarmament Commission study the desirability of establishing a subcommittee consisting of representatives of the Powers principally involved, which should seek in private an acceptable solution . . . and report on such a solution to the General Assembly and to the Security Council not later than September 1, 1954."

The United States, heeding the suggestion of the General Assembly of the United Nations, is instantly prepared to meet privately with such other countries as may be principally involved, to seek an acceptable solution to the atomic armaments race which overshadows not only the peace, but the very life, of the world.

We shall carry into these private or diplomatic talks a new conception.

The United States would seek more than the mere reduction or elimination of atomic materials for military purposes.

It is not enough to take this weapon out of the hands of the soldiers. It must be put into the hands of those who will know how to strip its military casing and adapt it to the arts of peace.

The United States knows that if the fearful trend of atomic military buildup can be reversed, this greatest of destructive forces can be developed into a great boon, for the benefit of all mankind.

The United States knows that peaceful power from atomic energy is no dream of the future. That capability, already proved, is here – now – today. Who can doubt, if the entire body of the world's scientists and engineers had adequate amounts of fissionable material with which to test and develop their ideas, that this capability would rapidly be transformed into universal, efficient, and economic usage.

To hasten the day when fear of the atom will begin to disappear from the minds of people, and the governments of the East and West, there are certain steps that can be taken now.

Finally, if there is to be advanced any proposal designed to ease even by the smallest measure the tensions of today's world, what more appropriate audience could there be than the members of the General Assembly of the United Nations?

I feel impelled to speak today in a language that in a sense is new – one which I, who have spent so much of my life in the military profession, would have preferred never to use.

That new language is the language of atomic warfare.

The atomic age has moved forward at such a pace that every citizen of the world should have some comprehension, at least, in comparative terms, of the extent of this development, of the utmost significance to every one of us. Clearly, if the peoples of the world are to conduct an intelligent search for peace, they must be armed with the significant facts of today's existence.

My recital of atomic danger and power is necessarily stated in United States terms, for these are the only incontrovertible facts that I know. I need hardly point out to this Assembly, however, that this subject is global, not merely national, in character.

The fearful potentials

On July 16, 1945, the United States set off the world's first atomic explosion.

Since that date in 1945 the United States of America has conducted 42 test explosions.

Atomic bombs today are more than 25 times as powerful as the weapons with which the atomic age dawned, while hydrogen weapons are in the range of millions of tons of TNT equivalent.

Today the United States stockpile of atomic weapons, which, of course, increases daily, exceeds by many times the explosive equivalent of the total of all bombs and all shells that came from every plane and every gun in every theater of war in all of the years of World War II.

A single air group, whether afloat or land-based, can now deliver to any reachable target a destructive cargo exceeding in power all the bombs that fell on Britain in all of World War II.

In size and variety, the development of atomic weapons has been no less remarkable. The development has been such that atomic weapons have virtually achieved conventional status with our armed services. In the United States, the Army, the

Navy, the Air Force, and the Marine Corps are all capable of putting this weapon to military use.

But the dread secret, and the fearful engines of atomic might, are not ours alone.

In the first place, the secret is possessed by our friends and allies, Great Britain and Canada, whose scientific genius made a tremendous contribution to our original discoveries, and the designs of atomic bombs.

The secret is also known by the Soviet Union.

The Soviet Union has informed us that, over recent years, it has devoted extensive resources to atomic weapons. During this period, the Soviet Union has exploded a series of atomic devices, including at least one involving thermo-nuclear reactions.

No monopoly of atomic power

If at one time the United States possessed what might have been called a monopoly of atomic power, that monopoly ceased to exist several years ago. Therefore, although our earlier start has permitted us to accumulate what is today a great quantitative advantage, the atomic realities of today comprehend two facts of even greater significance.

First, the knowledge now possessed by several nations will eventually be shared by others – possibly all others.

Second, even a vast superiority in numbers of weapons, and consequent capability of devastating retaliation, is no preventive, of itself, against the fearful material damage and toll of human lives that would be inflicted by surprise aggression.

The free world, at least dimly aware of these facts, has naturally embarked on a large program of warning and defense systems. That program will be accelerated and expanded.

But let no one think that the expenditure of vast sums for weapons and systems of defense can guarantee absolute safety for the cities and citizens of any nation. The awful arithmetic of the atomic bomb does not permit of any such easy solutions. Even against the most powerful defense, an aggressor in possession of the effective minimum number of atomic bombs for a surprise attack could probably place a sufficient number of his bombs on the chosen targets to cause hideous damage.

Should such an atomic attack be launched against the United States, our reactions would be swift and resolute. But for me to say that the defense capabilities of the United States are such that they could inflict terrible losses upon an aggressor – for me to say that the retaliation capabilities of the United States are so great that such an aggressor's land would be laid waste – all this, while fact, is not the true expression of the purpose and the hope of the United States.

To pause there would be to confirm the hopeless finality of a belief that two atomic colossi are doomed malevolently to eye each other indefinitely across a trembling world. To stop there would be to accept helplessly the probability of civilization destroyed, the annihilation of the irreplaceable heritage of mankind handed down to us from generation to generation, and the condemnation of mankind to begin all over again the age-old struggle upward from savagery toward decency and right and justice.

Surely no sane member of the human race could discover victory in such deso-lation. Could anyone wish his name to be coupled by history with such human degradation and destruction?

Occasional pages of history do record the faces of the "great destroyers," but the whole book of history reveals mankind's never-ending quest for peace and man-kind's God-given capacity to build.

It is with the book of history and not with isolated pages that the United States will ever wish to be identified. My country wants to be constructive, not destruc-tive. It wants agreements, not wars, among nations. It wants itself to live in freedom and in the confidence that the people of every other nation enjoy equally the right of choosing their own way of life.

Proposal for joint atomic contributions

I therefore make the following proposals:

The governments principally involved, to the extent permitted by elementary prudence, to begin now and continue to make joint contributions from their stock-piles of normal uranium and fissionable materials to an International Atomic En-ergy Agency. We would expect that such an agency would be set up under the aegis of the United Nations.

The ratios of contributions, the procedures and other details would properly be within the scope of the private conversations I have referred to earlier.

The United States is prepared to undertake these explorations in good faith. Any partner of the United States acting in the same good faith will find the United States a not unreasonable or ungenerous associate.

Undoubtedly initial and early contributions to this plan would be small in quan-tity. However, the proposal has the great virtue that it can be undertaken without the irritations and mutual suspicions incident to any attempt to set up a completely acceptable system of worldwide inspection and control.

The Atomic Energy Agency could be made responsible for the impounding, storage, and protection of the contributed fissionable and other materials. The ingenuity of our scientists will provide special safe conditions under which such a bank of fissionable material can be made essentially immune to surprise seizure.

The more important responsibility of this Atomic Energy Agency would be to devise methods whereby this fissionable material would be allocated to serve the peaceful pursuits of mankind. Experts would be mobilized to apply atomic energy to the needs of agriculture, medicine, and other peaceful activities. A special pur-pose would be to provide abundant electrical energy in the power-starved areas of the world. Thus the contributing powers would be dedicating some of their strength to serve the needs rather than the fears of mankind.

The United States would be more than willing – it would be proud to take up with others principally involved the development of plans whereby such peaceful use of atomic energy would be expedited.

Of those principally involved the Soviet Union must, of course, be one.

Out of fear and into peace

I would be prepared to submit to the Congress of the United States, and with every expectation of approval, any such plan that would –

First, encourage worldwide investigation into the most effective peacetime uses of fissionable material, and with the certainty that they had all the material needed for the conduct of all experiments that were appropriate;

Second, begin to diminish the potential destructive power of the world's atomic stockpiles;

Third, allow all peoples of all nations to see that, in this enlightened age, the great powers of the earth, both of the East and of the West, are interested in human aspirations first, rather than in building up the armaments of war;

Fourth, open up a new channel for peaceful discussion and initiate at least a new approach to the many difficult problems that must be solved in both private and public conversations, if the world is to shake off the inertia imposed by fear; and is to make positive progress toward peace.

Against the dark background of the atomic bomb, the United States does not wish merely to present strength, but also the desire and the hope for peace.

The coming months will be fraught with fateful decisions. In this Assembly; in the capitals and military headquarters of the world; in the hearts of men everywhere, be they governors or governed, may they be the decisions which will lead this world out of fear and into peace.

To the making of these fateful decisions, the United States pledges before you – and therefore before the world – its determination to help solve the fearful atomic dilemma, to devote its entire heart and mind to find the way by which the miraculous inventiveness of man shall not be dedicated to his death, but consecrated to his life.

APPENDIX B

Treaty on the Non-Proliferation of Nuclear Weapons

THE STATES concluding this Treaty, hereinafter referred to as the "Parties to the Treaty,"

Considering the devastation that would be visited upon all mankind by a nuclear war and the consequent need to make every effort to avert the danger of such a war and to take measures to safeguard the security of peoples,

Believing that the proliferation of nuclear weapons would seriously enhance the danger of nuclear war,

In conformity with resolutions of the United Nations General Assembly calling for the conclusion of an agreement on the prevention of wider dissemination of nuclear weapons,

Undertaking to cooperate in facilitating the application of International Atomic Energy Agency safeguards on peaceful nuclear activities,

Expressing their support for research, development and other efforts to further the application, within the framework of the International Atomic Energy Agency safeguards system, of the principle of safeguarding effectively the flow of source and special fissionable materials by use of instruments and other techniques at certain strategic points,

Affirming the principle that the benefits of peaceful applications of nuclear technology, including any technological by-products which may be derived by nuclear-weapon States from the development of nuclear explosive devices, should be available for peaceful purposes to all parties to the Treaty, whether nuclear-weapon or non-nuclear-weapon States,

Convinced that, in furtherance of this principle, all Parties to the Treaty are entitled to participate in the fullest possible exchange of scientific information for, and to contribute alone or in cooperation with other States to, the further development of the applications of atomic energy for peaceful purposes,

Declaring their intention to achieve at the earliest possible date the cessation of the nuclear arms race and to undertake effective measures in the direction of nuclear disarmament,

SOURCE: 21 UST 438, Mar. 5, 1970.

Urging the cooperation of all States in the attainment of this objective,

Recalling the determination expressed by the Parties to the 1963 Treaty banning nuclear weapon tests in the atmosphere, in outer space, and under water in its Preamble to seek to achieve the discontinuance of all test explosions of nuclear weapons for all time and to continue negotiations to this end,

Desiring to further the easing of international tension and the strengthening of trust between States in order to facilitate the cessation of the manufacture of nuclear weapons, the liquidation of all their existing stockpiles, and the elimination from national arsenals of nuclear weapons and the means of their delivery pursuant to a treaty on general and complete disarmament under strict and effective international control,

Recalling that, in accordance with the Charter of the United Nations, States must refrain in their international relations from the threat or use of force against the territorial integrity or political independence of any State, or in any other manner inconsistent with the Purposes of the United Nations, and that the establishment and maintenance of international peace and security are to be promoted with the least diversion for armaments of the world's human and economic resources,

Have agreed as follows:

Article I

Each nuclear-weapon State Party to the Treaty undertakes not to transfer to any recipient whatsoever nuclear weapons or other nuclear explosive devices or control over such weapons or explosive devices directly, or indirectly; and not in any way to assist, encourage, or induce any non-nuclear-weapon State to manufacture or otherwise acquire nuclear weapons or other nuclear explosive devices, or control over such weapons or explosive devices.

Article II

Each non-nuclear-weapon State Party to the Treaty undertakes not to receive the transfer from any transferor whatsoever of nuclear weapons or other nuclear explosive devices or of control over such weapons or explosive devices directly, or indirectly; not to manufacture or otherwise acquire nuclear weapons or other nuclear explosive devices; and not to seek or receive any assistance in the manufacture of nuclear weapons or other nuclear explosive devices.

Article III

1. Each non-nuclear-weapon State Party to the Treaty undertakes to accept safeguards, as set forth in an agreement to be negotiated and concluded with the International Atomic Energy Agency in accordance with the Statutes of the International Atomic Energy Agency and the Agency's safeguards system, for the exclusive purpose of verification of the fulfillment of its obligations assumed under this Treaty with a view to preventing diversion of nuclear energy from peaceful uses to nuclear weapons or other nuclear explosive devices. Procedures for the safeguards

required by this article shall be followed with respect to source or special fissionable material whether it is being produced, processed or used in any principal nuclear facility or is outside any such facility. The safeguards required by this article shall be applied on all source or special fissionable material in all peaceful nuclear activities within the territory of such State, under its jurisdiction, or carried out under its control anywhere.

2. Each State Party to the Treaty undertakes not to provide: (a) source or special fissionable material, or (b) equipment or material especially designed or prepared for the processing, use or production of special fissionable material, to any non-nuclear weapon State for peaceful purposes, unless the source or special fissionable material shall be subject to the safeguards required by this article.

3. The safeguards required by this article shall be implemented in a manner designed to comply with article IV of this Treaty, and to avoid hampering the economic or technological development of the Parties or international cooperation in the field of peaceful nuclear activities, including the international exchange of nuclear material and equipment for the processing, use or production of nuclear material for peaceful purposes in accordance with the provisions of this article and the principle of safeguarding set forth in the Preamble of the Treaty.

4. Non-nuclear-weapon States Party to the Treaty shall conclude agreements with the International Atomic Energy Agency to meet the requirements of this article either individually or together with other States in accordance with the Statute of the International Atomic Energy Agency. Negotiation of such agreements shall commence within 180 days from the original entry into force of this Treaty. For States depositing their instruments of ratification or accession after the 180-day period, negotiation of such agreements shall commence not later than the date of such deposit. Such agreements shall enter into force not later than eighteen months after the date of initiation of negotiations.

Article IV

1. Nothing in this Treaty shall be interpreted as affecting the inalienable right of all the Parties to the Treaty to develop research, production and use of nuclear energy for peaceful purposes without discrimination and in conformity with articles I and II of this Treaty.

2. All the Parties to the Treaty undertake to facilitate, and have the right to participate in, the fullest possible exchange of equipment, materials and scientific and technological information for the peaceful uses of nuclear energy. Parties to the Treaty in a position to do so shall also cooperate in contributing alone or together with other States or international organizations to the further development of the applications of nuclear energy for peaceful purposes, especially in the territories of non-nuclear-weapon States Party to the Treaty, with due consideration for the needs of the developing areas of the world.

Article V

Each Party to the Treaty undertakes to take appropriate measures to ensure that, in accordance with this Treaty, under appropriate international observation and through appropriate international procedures, potential benefits from any peaceful applications of nuclear explosions will be made available to non-nuclear-weapon States Party to the Treaty on a nondiscriminatory basis and that the charge to such Parties for the explosive devices used will be as low as possible and exclude any charge for research and development. Non-nuclear-weapon States Party to the Treaty shall be able to obtain such benefits, pursuant to a special international agreement or agreements, through an appropriate international body with adequate representation of non-nuclear-weapon States. Negotiations on this subject shall commence as soon as possible after the Treaty enters into force. Non-nuclear-weapon States Party to the Treaty so desiring may also obtain such benefits pursuant to bilateral agreements.

Article VI

Each of the Parties to the Treaty undertakes to pursue negotiations in good faith on effective measures relating to cessation of the nuclear arms race at an early date and to nuclear disarmament, and on a treaty on general and complete disarmament under strict and effective international control.

Article VII

Nothing in this Treaty affects the right of any group of States to conclude regional treaties in order to assure the total absence of nuclear weapons in their respective territories.

Article VIII

1. Any Party to the Treaty may propose amendments to this Treaty. The text of any proposed amendment shall be submitted to the Depositary Governments which shall circulate it to all Parties to the Treaty. Thereupon, if requested to do so by one-third or more of the Parties to the Treaty, the Depositary Governments shall convene a conference, to which they shall invite all the Parties to the Treaty, to consider such an amendment.

2. Any amendment to this Treaty must be approved by a majority of the votes of all the Parties to the Treaty, including the votes of all nuclear-weapon States Party to the Treaty and all other Parties which, on the date the amendment is circulated, are members of the Board of Governors of the International Atomic Energy Agency. The amendment shall enter into force for each Party that deposits its instrument of ratification of the amendment upon the deposit of such instruments of ratification by a majority of all the Parties, including the instruments of ratification of all nuclear-weapon States Party to the Treaty and all other Parties which, on the date the amendment is circulated, are members of the Board of Governors of the International Atomic Energy Agency. Thereafter, it shall enter into force for any other Party upon the deposit of its instrument of ratification of the amendment.

3. Five years after the entry into force of this Treaty, a conference of Parties to

the Treaty shall be held in Geneva, Switzerland, in order to review the operation of this Treaty with a view to assuring that the purposes of the Preamble and in the provisions of the Treaty are being realized. At intervals of five years thereafter, a majority of the Parties to the Treaty may obtain, by submitting a proposal to this effect to the Depositary Governments, the convening of further conferences with the same objective of reviewing the operation of the Treaty.

Article IX

1. This Treaty shall be open to all States for signature. Any State which does not sign the Treaty before its entry into force in accordance with paragraph 3 of this article may accede to it at any time.

2. This Treaty shall be subject to ratification by signatory States. Instruments of ratification and instruments of accession shall be deposited with the Governments of the United States of America, the United Kingdom of Great Britain and Northern Ireland and the Union of Soviet Socialist Republics, which are hereby designated the Depositary Governments.

3. This Treaty shall enter into force after its ratification by the States, the Governments of which are designated Depositaries of the Treaty, and forty other States signatory to this Treaty and the deposit of their instruments of ratification. For the purposes of this Treaty, a nuclear-weapon State is one which has manufactured and exploded a nuclear weapon or other nuclear explosive device prior to January 1, 1967.

4. For States whose instruments of ratification or accession are deposited subsequent to the entry into force of this treaty, it shall enter into force on the date of the deposit of their instruments of ratification or accession.

5. The Depositary Governments shall promptly inform all signatory and acceding States of the date of each signature, the date of deposit of each instrument of ratification or of accession, the date of the entry into force of this Treaty, and the date of receipt of any requests for convening a conference or other notices.

6. This Treaty shall be registered by the Depositary Governments pursuant to article 102 of the Charter of the United Nations.

Article X

1. Each Party shall in exercising its national sovereignty have the right to withdraw from the Treaty if it decides that extraordinary events, related to the subject matter of this Treaty, have jeopardized the supreme interests of its country. It shall give notice of such withdrawal to all other Parties to the Treaty and to the United Nations Security Council three months in advance. Such notice shall include a statement of the extraordinary events it regards as having jeopardized its supreme interests.

2. Twenty-five years after the entry into force of the Treaty, a conference shall be convened to decide whether the Treaty shall continue in force indefinitely, or shall be extended for an additional fixed period or periods. This decision shall be taken by a majority of the Parties to the Treaty.

Article XI

This Treaty, the English, Russian, French, Spanish and Chinese texts of which are equally authentic, shall be deposited in the archives of the Depositary Governments. Duly certified copies of this Treaty shall be transmitted by the Depositary Governments to the Governments of the signatory and acceding States.

In witness whereof the undersigned, duly authorized, have signed this Treaty.

Done in triplicate, at the cities of Washington, London and Moscow, this first day of July one thousand nine hundred sixty-eight.

PARTIES TO THE NON-PROLIFERATION TREATY (NPT) AS OF APRIL 1977

102 states which are parties to NPT

Nuclear-weapon states[1]

Union of Soviet Socialist Republics	United Kingdom	United States

Non–nuclear-weapon states

Afghanistan	Haiti	Panama
Australia	Holy See	Paraguay
Austria	Honduras	Peru
Bahamas	Hungary	Philippines
Belgium	Iceland	Poland
Bolivia	Iran	Republic of South Vietnam
Botswana	Iraq	
Bulgaria	Ireland	Republic of Surinam
Burundi	Italy	
Cambodia	Ivory Coast	Romania
Canada	Jamaica	Rwanda
Central African Republic	Japan	San Marino
	Jordan	Senegal
Chad	Kenya	Sierra Leone
China, Republic of	Korea, Republic of	Singapore
Costa Rica	Laos	Somalia
Cyprus	Lebanon	Sudan

---

[1] For purposes of the NPT, a nuclear weapon State was defined as one which has manufactured and exploded a nuclear weapon or other nuclear explosive device prior to January 1967.

SOURCE: ERDA.

Czechoslovakia
Dahomey
Denmark
Dominican Republic
Ecuador
El Salvador
Ethiopia
Fiji
Finland
Gabon
Gambia
German Democratic
    Republic
Germany, Federal
    Republic of
Ghana
Greece
Grenada
Guatemala

Lesotho
Liberia
Libyan Arab Republic
Luxembourg
Madagascar
Malaysia
Maldives
Mali
Malta
Mauritius
Mexico
Mongolia
Morocco
Nepal
Netherlands
New Zealand
Nicaragua
Nigeria
Norway

Swaziland
Sweden
Switzerland
Syrian Arab
    Republic
Thailand
Togo
Tonga
Tunisia
United Republic of
    Cameroon
Upper Volta
Uruguay
Venezuela
Western Samoa
Yugoslavia
Zaire

States which are not parties to NPT

Nuclear-weapon states

China   France

Nonnuclear-weapon states

Albania
Algeria
Argentina
Bahrain
Bangladesh
Bhutan
Brazil
Burma
Cape Verde
Chile
Comoros
Congo
Cuba
Democratic People's
    Republic of Korea

Democratic Republic
    of Vietnam
Equatorial Guinea
Guinea
Guinea-Bissau
Guyana
India
Israel
Liechtenstein
Malawi
Mauritania
Monaco
Mozambique
Niger
Oman

Pakistan
Papua New Guinea
Portugal
Qatar
Sao Tome and
    Principe
Saudi Arabia
South Africa
Spain
Uganda
United Arab
    Emirates
United Republic of
    Tanzania
Zambia

States that have signed NPT, but not yet ratified

Barbados	Indonesia	Turkey
Colombia	Kuwait	Yemen
Democratic Yemen	Sri Lanka	
Egypt	Trinidad & Tobago	

States outside NPT that have some, but not necessarily all of their nuclear facilities under safeguards

Argentina	India	Portugal
Brazil	Indonesia	South Africa
Chile	Israel	Spain
Colombia	Pakistan	Turkey

APPENDIX C

Executive Order 11902 by President Gerald R. Ford: procedures for an export licensing policy, February 2, 1976

THE Energy Reorganization Act of 1974 transferred to the United States Nuclear Regulatory Commission the licensing and related regulatory functions previously exercised by the Atomic Energy Commission under the Atomic Energy Act of 1954, as amended.

The exercise of discretion and control over nuclear exports within the limits of law concerns the authority and responsibility of the President with respect to the conduct of foreign policy and the ensuring of the common defense and security.

It is essential that the Executive branch inform the Nuclear Regulatory Commission of its views before the Commission issues or denies a license, or grants an exemption.

Now, therefore, by virtue of the authority vested in me by the Constitution and statutes of the United States of America, including the Atomic Energy Act of 1954, as amended (42 U.S.C. 2011 *et seq*.), and as President of the United States of America, it is hereby ordered as follows:

SECTION 1. (a) The Secretary of State is designated to receive from the Nuclear Regulatory Commission a copy of each export license application, each proposal by the Nuclear Regulatory Commission to issue a general license for export, and each proposal by the Nuclear Regulatory Commission for exemption from the requirement for a license, which may involve a determination, pursuant to the Atomic Energy Act of 1954, as amended, that the issuance of the license or exemption from the requirement for a license will, or will not, be inimical to or constitute an unreasonable risk to the common defense and security.

(b) The Secretary of State shall ensure that a copy of each such application, proposed general license, or proposed exemption is received by the Secretary of Defense, the Secretary of Commerce, the Administrator of the United States Energy Research and Development Administration, hereunder referred to as the Administrator, the Director of the Arms Control and Disarmament Agency, hereinafter referred to as the Director, and the head of any other department or agency

SOURCE: F.R. Doc. 76–3382. Filed Feb. 2, 1976.

which may have an interest therein, in order to afford them the opportunity to express their views, if any, on whether the license should be issued or the exemption granted.

SEC. 2. Within thirty days of receipt of a copy of a license application, proposed general license, or proposed exemption, the Secretary of Defense, the Secretary of Commerce, the Administrator, the Director, and the head of any other agency or department to which such copy has been transmitted, shall each transmit to the Secretary of State his views, if any, on whether and under what conditions the license should be issued or the exemption granted.

SEC. 3. The Secretary of State shall, after the provisions of section 2 of this order have been complied with, transmit to the Secretary of Defense, the Secretary of Commerce, the Administrator, the Director, and the head of any other department or agency who has expressed his views thereon, a proposed position of the Executive branch as to whether the license should be issued or the exemption granted, including a proposed judgment as to whether issuance of the license or granting of the exemption will, or will not, be inimical to or constitute an unreasonable risk to the common defense and security.

SEC. 4. If the heads of departments and agencies specified in section 2 of this order are unable to agree upon a position for the Executive branch, the Secretary of State shall refer the matter to the Chairman of the Under Secretaries Committee of the National Security Council in order to obtain a decision. In the event the Under Secretaries Committee is unable to reach a decision, the Chairman of that Committee shall refer the matter to the President for his decision.

SEC. 5. The Secretary of State, after taking the actions required by this order, shall notify the Nuclear Regulatory Commission of the position of the Executive branch as to whether the license should be issued or the exemption granted, including the judgment of the Executive branch as to whether issuance of the license or granting of the exemption will, or will not, be inimical to or constitute an unreasonable risk to the common defense and security. The Executive branch position shall be supported by relevant information and documentation as appropriate to the proceedings before the Nuclear Regulatory Commission.

Gerald R. Ford

The White House
February 2, 1976

APPENDIX D

Nuclear policy statement by President Gerald R. Ford, October 28, 1976

WE HAVE known since the age of nuclear energy began more than 30 years ago that this source of energy had the potential for tremendous benefits for mankind and the potential for unparalleled destruction.

On the one hand, there is no doubt that nuclear energy represents one of the best hopes for satisfying the rising world demand for energy with minimum environmental impact and with the potential for reducing dependence on uncertain and diminishing world supplies of oil.

On the other hand, nuclear fuel, as it produces power also produces plutonium, which can be chemically separated from the spent fuel. The plutonium can be recycled and used to generate additional nuclear power, thereby partially offsetting the need for additional energy resources. Unfortunately – and this is the root of the problem – the same plutonium produced in nuclear powerplants can, when chemically separated, also be used to make nuclear explosives.

The world community cannot afford to let potential nuclear weapons material or the technology to produce it proliferate uncontrolled over the globe. The world community must ensure that production and utilization of such material by any nation is carried out under the most stringent security conditions and arrangements.

Developing the enormous benefits of nuclear energy while simultaneously developing the means to prevent proliferation is one of the major challenges facing all nations of the world today.

The standards we apply in judging most domestic and international activities are not sufficiently rigorous to deal with this extraordinarily complex problem. Our answers cannot be partially successful. They will either work, in which case we shall stop proliferation, or they will fail and nuclear proliferation will accelerate as nations initially having no intention of acquiring nuclear weapons conclude that they are forced to do so by the actions of others. Should this happen, we would face a

SOURCE: *Public Papers of the President*, 1976, document 987, pp. 2763–78.

world in which the security of all is critically imperiled. Maintaining international stability in such an environment would be incalculably difficult and dangerous. In times of regional or global crisis, risks of nuclear devastation would be immeasurably increased – if not through direct attack, then through a process of ever-expanding escalation. The problem can be handled as long as we understand it clearly and act wisely in concert with other nations. But we are faced with a threat of tragedy if we fail to comprehend it or to take effective measures.

Thus the seriousness and complexity of the problem place a special burden on those who propose ways to control proliferation. They must avoid the temptation for rhetorical gestures, empty threats, or righteous posturing. They must offer policies and programs which deal with the world as it is, not as we might wish it to be. The goal is to prevent proliferation, not simply to deplore it.

The first task in dealing with the problem of proliferation is to understand the world nuclear situation.

More then 30 nations have or plan to build nuclear powerplants to reap the benefits of nuclear energy. The 1973 energy crisis dramatically demonstrated to all nations not only the dangers of excessive reliance on oil imports but also the reality that the world's supply of fossil fuels is running out. As a result, nuclear energy is now properly seen by many nations as an indispensable way to satisfy rising energy demand without prematurely depleting finite fossil fuel resources. We must understand the motives which are leading these nations, developed and developing, to place even greater emphasis than we do on nuclear power development. For unless we comprehend their real needs, we cannot expect to find ways of working with them to ensure satisfaction of both our and their legitimate concerns. Moreover, several nations besides the United States have the technology needed to produce both the benefits and the destructive potential of nuclear energy. Nations with such capabilities are able to export their technology and facilities.

Thus, no single nation, not even the United States, can realistically hope – by itself – to control effectively the spread of reprocessing technology and the resulting availability of plutonium.

The United States once was the dominant world supplier of nuclear material equipment and technology. While we remain a leader in this field, other suppliers have come to share the international market – with the U.S. now supplying less than half of nuclear reactor exports. In short, for nearly a decade the U.S. has not had a monopoly on nuclear technology. Although our role is large, we are not able to control worldwide nuclear development.

For these reasons, action to control proliferation must be an international co-operative effort involving many nations, including both nuclear suppliers and customers. Common standards must be developed and accepted by all parties. If this is not done, unrestrained trade in sensitive nuclear technology and materials will develop – with no one in a position to stop it.

We in the United States must recognize that interests in nuclear energy vary widely among nations. We must recognize that some nations look to nuclear energy because they have no acceptable energy alternative. We must be sure that our efforts to control proliferation are not viewed by such nations as an act to prevent them from enjoying the benefits of nuclear energy. We must be sure that all nations recognize that the U.S. believes that nonproliferation objectives must take precedence over economic and energy benefits if a choice must be made.

Previous action

During the past 30 years, the U.S. has been the unquestioned leader in worldwide efforts to assure that the benefits of nuclear energy are made available widely while its destructive uses are prevented. I have given special attention to these objectives during the past 2 years, and we have made important new progress, particularly in efforts to control the proliferation of nuclear weapons capability among the nations of the world.

In 1974, soon after I assumed office, I became concerned that some nuclear supplier countries, in order to achieve competitive advantage, were prepared to offer nuclear exports under conditions less rigorous than we believe prudent. In the fall of that year, at the United Nations General Assembly, the United States proposed that nonproliferation measures be strengthened materially. I also expressed my concern directly to my counterparts in key supplier and recipient nations. I directed the Secretary of State to emphasize multilateral action to limit this dangerous form of competition.

At U.S. initiative, the first meeting of major nuclear suppliers was convened in London in April 1975. A series of meetings and intensive bilateral consultations followed. As a result of these meetings, we have significantly raised international standards through progressive new guidelines to govern nuclear exports. These involve both improved safeguards and controls to prevent diversion of nuclear materials and to guard against the misuse of nuclear technology and physical protection against theft and sabotage. The United States has adopted these guidelines as policy for nuclear exports.

In addition, we have acted to deal with the special dangers associated with plutonium.

– We have prohibited export of reprocessing and other nuclear technologies that could contribute to proliferation.

– We have firmly opposed reprocessing in Korea and Taiwan. We welcome the decisions of those nations to forego such activities. We will continue to discourage national reprocessing in other locations of particular concern.

– We negotiated agreements for cooperation with Egypt and Israel which contain the strictest reprocessing provisions and other nuclear controls ever included in the 20-year history of our nuclear cooperation program.

– In addition, the United States recently completed negotiations to place its civil nuclear facilities under the safeguards of the International Atomic Energy Agency – and the IAEA has approved a proposed agreement for this purpose.

New initiatives

Last summer, I directed that a thorough review be undertaken of all our nuclear policies and options to determine what further steps were needed. I have considered carefully the results of that review, held discussions with congressional leaders, and benefited from consultations with leaders of other nations. I have decided that new steps are needed, building upon the progress of the past 2 years. Today, I am announcing a number of actions and proposals aimed at:

– strengthening the commitment of the nations of the world to the goal of nonproliferation and building an effective system of international controls to prevent proliferation;

– changing and strengthening U.S. domestic nuclear policies and programs to support our nonproliferation goals; and

– establishing, by these actions, a sound foundation for the continued and increased use of nuclear energy in the U.S. and in the world in a safe and economic manner.

The task we face calls for an international cooperative venture of unprecedented dimensions. The U.S. is prepared to work with all other nations.

Principal policy decisions

I have concluded that the reprocessing and recycling of plutonium should not proceed unless there is sound reason to conclude that the world community can effectively overcome the associated risks of proliferation. I believe that avoidance of proliferation must take precedence over economic interests. I have also concluded that the United States and other nations can and should increase their use of nuclear power for peaceful purposes even if reprocessing and recycling of plutonium are found to be unacceptable.

Vigorous action is required domestically and internationally to make these judgments effective.

– I have decided that the United States should greatly accelerate its diplomatic initiatives in conjunction with nuclear supplier and consumer nations to control the spread of plutonium and technologies for separating plutonium.

Effective nonproliferation measures will require the participation and support of nuclear suppliers and consumers. There must be coordination in restraints so that an effective nonproliferation system is achieved, and there must be cooperation in assuring reliable fuel supplies so that peaceful energy needs are met.

– I have decided that the United States should no longer regard reprocessing of used nuclear fuel to produce plutonium as a necessary and inevitable step in the nuclear fuel cycle, and that we should pursue reprocessing and recycling in the future only if they are found to be consistent with our international objectives.

We must ensure that our domestic policies and programs are compatible with our international position on reprocessing and that we work closely with other nations in evaluating nuclear fuel reprocessing.

– The steps I am announcing today will assure that the necessity [sic] increase in our use of nuclear energy will be carried on with safety and without aggravating the danger of proliferation.

Even with strong efforts to conserve, we will have increasing demands for energy for a growing American economy. To satisfy these needs, we must rely on increased use of both nuclear energy and coal until more acceptable alternatives are developed. We will continue pushing ahead with work on all promising alternatives such as solar energy but now we must count on the technology that works. We cannot expect a major contribution to our energy supply from alternative technologies until late in this century.

To implement my overall policy decisions, I have decided on a number of policies that are necessary and appropriate to meet our nonproliferation and energy objectives.

– First, our domestic policies must be changed to conform to my decision on deferral of the commercialization of chemical reprocessing of nuclear fuel which results in the separation of plutonium.

– Second, I call upon all nations to join us in exercising maximum restraint in the transfer of reprocessing and enrichment technology and facilities by avoiding such sensitive exports or commitments for a period of at least 3 years.

– Third, new cooperative steps are needed to help assure that all nations have an adequate and reliable supply of energy for their needs. I believe, most importantly, that nuclear supplier nations have a special obligation to assure that customer nations have an adequate supply of fuel for their nuclear powerplants, if those customer nations forego the acquisition of reprocessing and uranium enrichment capabilities and accept effective proliferation controls.

– Fourth, the U.S. must maintain its role as a major and reliable world supplier of nuclear reactors and fuel for peaceful purposes. Our strong position as a supplier has provided the principal basis for our influence and leadership in worldwide nonproliferation efforts. A strong position will be equally important in the future. While reaffirming this Nation's intent to be a reliable supplier, the U.S. seeks no competitive advantage by virtue of the worldwide system of effective nonproliferation controls that I am calling for today.

– Fifth, new efforts must be made to urge all nations to join in a full-scale international cooperative effort – which I shall outline in detail – to develop a system of effective controls to prevent proliferation.

– Sixth, the U.S. must take new steps with respect to its own exports to control proliferation, while seeking to improve multilateral guidelines.

– Seventh, the U.S. must undertake a program to evaluate reprocessing in support of the international policies I have adopted.

– Finally, I have concluded that new steps are needed to assure that we have in place when needed, both in the U.S. and around the world, the facilities for the long-term storage or disposal of nuclear wastes.

Actions to implement our nuclear policies

In order to implement the nuclear policies that I have outlined, major efforts will be required within the United States and by the many nations around the world with an interest in nuclear energy. To move forward with these efforts, I am today taking a number of actions and making a number of proposals to other nations.

I. Change in U.S. policy on nuclear fuel reprocessing

With respect to nuclear fuel reprocessing, I am directing agencies of the executive branch to implement my decision to delay commercialization of reprocessing activities in the United States until uncertainties are resolved. Specifically, I am:

– Directing the Administrator of the Energy Research and Development Administration (ERDA) to:

● change ERDA policies and programs which heretofore have been based on the assumption that reprocessing would proceed;

● encourage prompt action to expand spent fuel storage facilities, thus assuring utilities that they need not be concerned about shutdown of nuclear reactors because of delays; and

● identify the research and development efforts needed to investigate the feasibility of recovering the energy value from used nuclear fuel without separating plutonium.

II. Restraint in the transfer of sensitive nuclear technology and facilities

Despite the gains in controlling proliferation that have been made, the dangers posed by reprocessing and the prospect of uncontrolled availability of plutonium require further, decisive international action. Effective control of the parallel risk of spreading uranium enrichment technology is also necessary. To meet these dangers:

– I call upon all nations to join with us in exercising maximum restraint in the transfer of reprocessing and enrichment technology and facilities by avoiding such sensitive exports or commitments for a period of at least 3 years.

This will allow suppliers and consumers to work together to establish reliable means for meeting nuclear needs with minimum risk, as we assess carefully the wisdom of plutonium use. As we proceed in these efforts, we must not be influenced by pressures to approve the export of these sensitive facilities.

III. Assuring an adequate energy supply for customer nations

– I urge nuclear suppliers to provide nuclear consumers with fuel services, instead of sensitive technology or facilities.

Nations accepting effective nonproliferation restraints have a right to expect reliable and economic supply of nuclear reactors and associated, nonsensitive fuel. All such nations would share in the benefits of an assured supply of nuclear fuel, even though the number and location of sensitive facilities to generate this fuel is limited to meet nonproliferation goals. The availability of fuel-cycle services in several different nations can provide ample assurance to consumers of a continuing and stable source of supply.

It is also desirable to continue studying the idea of a few suitably-sited multinational fuel-cycle centers to serve regional needs, when effectively safeguarded and economically warranted. Through these and related means, we can minimize incentives for the spread of dangerous fuel-cycle capabilities.

The United States stands ready to take action, in cooperation with other concerned nations, to assure reliable suppliers of nuclear fuel at equitable prices to any country accepting responsible restraints on its nuclear power program with regard to reprocessing, plutonium disposition, and enrichment technology.

– I am directing the Secretary of State to initiate consultations to explore with other nations arrangements for coordinating fuel services and for developing other means of ensuring that suppliers will be able to offer, and consumers will be able to receive, an uninterrupted and economical supply of low-enriched uranium fuel and fuel services.

These discussions will address ways to ensure against economic disadvantage to cooperating nations and to remove any sources of competition which could undermine our common nonproliferation efforts.

To contribute to this initiative, the United States will offer binding letters of intent for the supply of nuclear fuel to current and prospective customers willing to accept such responsible restraints.

– In addition, I am directing the Secretary of State to enter into negotiations or arrangements for mutual agreement on disposition of spent fuel with consumer nations that adopt responsible restraints.

Where appropriate, the United States will provide consumer nations with either fresh, low-enriched uranium fuel or make other equitable arrangements in return for mutual agreement on the disposition of spent fuel where such disposition demonstrably fosters our common and cooperative nonproliferation objectives. The United States seeks no commercial advantage in pursuing options for fuel disposition and assured fuel supplies.

Finally, the United States will continue to expand cooperative efforts with other countries in developing their indigenous nonnuclear energy resources.

The United States has proposed and continues to advocate the establishment of an International Energy Institute, specifically designed to help developing countries match the most economic and readily available sources of energy to their power needs. Through this Institute and other appropriate means, we will offer technological assistance in the development of indigenous energy resources.

IV. Strengthening the U.S. role as a reliable supplier
If the United States is to continue its leadership role in worldwide nonproliferation efforts, it must be a reliable supplier of nuclear reactors and fuel for peaceful purposes. There are two principal actions we can take to contribute to this objective:

– I will submit to the new Congress proposed legislation that will permit the expansion of capacity in the United States to produce enriched uranium, including the authority needed for expansion of the Government-owned plant at Portsmouth, Ohio. I will also work with Congress to establish a framework for a private, competitive industry to finance, build, own, and operate enrichment plants.

U.S. capacity has been fully committed since mid-1974 with the result that no new orders could be signed. The Congress did not act on my full proposal and provided only limited and temporary authority for proceeding with the Portsmouth plant. We must have additional authority to proceed with the expansion of capacity without further delay.

– I will work closely with the Congress to ensure that legislation for improving our export controls results in a system that provides maximum assurance that the United States will be a reliable supplier to other nations for the full period of agreements.

One of the principal concerns with export legislation proposed in the last Congress was the fear that foreign customers could be subjected to arbitrary new controls imposed well after a long-term agreement and specific contracts for nuclear powerplants and fuel had been signed. In the case of nuclear plants and fuel, reliable long-term agreements are essential, and we must adopt export controls that provide reliability while meeting nonproliferation objectives.

V. International controls against proliferation

To reinforce the foregoing policies, we must develop means to establish international restraints over the accumulation of plutonium itself, whether in separated form or in unprocessed spent fuel. The accumulation of plutonium under national control, especially in a separated form, is a primary proliferation risk.

– I am directing the Secretary of State to pursue vigorously discussions aimed at the establishment of a new international regime to provide for storage of civil plutonium and spent reactor fuel.

The United States made this proposal to the International Atomic Energy Agency and other interested nations last spring.

Creation of such a regime will greatly strengthen world confidence that the growing accumulation of excess plutonium and spent fuel can be stored safely, pending reentry into the nuclear fuel cycle or other safe disposition. I urge the IAEA, which is empowered to establish plutonium depositories to give prompt implementation to this concept.

Once a broadly representative IAEA storage regime is in operation, we are prepared to place our own excess civil plutonium and spent fuel under its control. Moreover, we are prepared to consider providing a site for international storage under IAEA auspices.

The inspection system of the IAEA remains a key element in our entire nonproliferation strategy. The world community must make sure that the Agency has the technical and human resources needed to keep pace with its expanding responsibilities. At my direction, we have recently committed substantial additional resources to help upgrade the IAEA's technical safeguards capabilities, and I believe we must strengthen further the safeguard functions of the IAEA.

– I am directing the Secretary of State and Administrator of ERDA to undertake a major international effort to ensure that adequate resources for this purpose are made available, and that we mobilize our best scientific talent to support that Agency. Our principal national laboratories with expertise in this area have been directed to provide assistance, on a continuing basis, to the IAEA Secretariat.

The terrible increase in violence and terrorism throughout the world has sharpened our awareness of the need to assure rigorous protection for sensitive nuclear materials and equipment. Fortunately, the need to cope with this problem is now broadly recognized. Many nations have responded to the initiatives which I have taken in this area by materially strengthening their physical security and by cooperating in the development of international guidelines by the IAEA. As a result of consultations among the major suppliers, provision for adequate physical security is becoming a normal condition of supply.

We have an effective physical security system in the United States. But steps are needed to upgrade physical security systems and to assure timely international collaboration in the recovery of lost or stolen materials.

– I have directed the Secretary of State to address vigorously the problem of physical security at both bilateral and multilateral levels, including exploration of a possible international convention.

The United States is committed to the development of the system of international controls that I have here outlined. Even when complete, however, no system of controls is likely to be effective if a potential violator judges that his acquisition of a nuclear explosive will be received with indifference by the international community.

Any material violation of a nuclear safeguards agreement – especially the diversion of nuclear material for use in making explosives – must be universally judged to be an extremely serious affront to the world community, calling for the immediate imposition of drastic sanctions.

– I serve notice today that the United States will, at a minimum, respond to violation by any nation of any safeguards agreement to which we are a party with an immediate cutoff of our supply of nuclear fuel and cooperation to that nation.

We would consider further steps, not necessarily confined to the area of nuclear cooperation, against the violator nation. Nor will our actions be limited to violations of agreements in which we are directly involved. In the event of material violation of any safeguards agreement, particularly agreements with the IAEA, we will initiate immediate consultations with all interested nations to determine appropriate action.

Universal recognition of the total unacceptability of the abrogation or violation of any nonproliferation agreements is one of the most important steps which can be taken to prevent further proliferation. We invite all concerned governments to affirm publicly that they will regard nuclear wrongdoing as an intolerable violation of acceptable norms of international behavior, which would set in motion strong and immediate countermeasures.

VI. U.S. nuclear export policies

During the past 2 years, the United States has strengthened its own national nuclear export policies. Our interests, however, are not limited to controls alone. The United States has a special responsibility to share the benefits of peaceful nuclear energy with other countries. We have sought to serve other nations as a reliable supplier of nuclear fuel and equipment. Given the choice between economic benefits and progress toward our nonproliferation goals, we have given, and will continue to give priority to nonproliferation. But there should be no incompatibility between nonproliferation and assisting other nations in enjoying the benefits of peaceful nuclear power if all supplier countries pursue common nuclear export policies. There is need, however, for even more rigorous controls than those now commonly employed, and for policies that favor nations accepting responsible nonproliferation limitations.

– I have decided that we will henceforth apply new criteria in judging whether to enter into new or expanded nuclear cooperation:

• Adherence to the nonproliferation treaty will be a strong positive factor favoring cooperation with a nonnuclear weapon state.

• Nonnuclear weapons states that have not yet adhered to the nonproliferation treaty will receive positive recognition if they are prepared to submit to full fuel cycle safeguards, pending adherence.

• We will favor recipient nations that are prepared to forego, or postpone for a substantial period, the establishment of national reprocessing or enrichment activities or, in certain cases, prepared to shape and schedule their reprocessing and enriching facilities to foster nonproliferation needs.

● Positive recognition will also be given to nations prepared to participate in an international storage regime, under which spent fuel and any separated plutonium would be placed pending use.

Exceptional cases may occur in which nonproliferation will be served best by cooperating with nations not yet meeting these tests. However, I pledge that the Congress will not be asked to approve any new or amended agreement not meeting these new criteria unless I personally determine that the agreement is fully supportive of our nonproliferation goals. In case of such a determination, my reasons will be fully presented to the Congress.

– With respect to countries that are current recipients of U.S. nuclear supply, I am directing the Secretary of State to enter into negotiations with the objective of conforming these agreements to established international guidelines, and to seek through diplomatic initiatives and fuel supply incentives to obtain their acceptance of our new criteria.

We must recognize the need for effective multilateral approaches to nonproliferation and prevent nuclear export controls from becoming an element of commercial competition.

– I am directing the Secretary of State to intensify discussions with other nuclear suppliers aimed at expanding common guidelines for peaceful cooperative agreements so that they conform with these criteria.

In this regard, the United States would discuss ways of developing incentives that can lead to acceptance of these criteria, such as assuring reliable fuel supplies for nations accepting new restraints.

The reliability of American assurances to other nations is an asset that few, if any, nations of the world can match. It must not be eroded. Indeed, nothing could more prejudice our efforts to strengthen our existing nonproliferation understandings than arbitrary suspension or unwarranted delays in meeting supply commitments to countries which are dealing with us in good faith regarding effective safeguards and restraints.

Despite my personal efforts, the 94th Congress adjourned without passing nuclear export legislation which would have strengthened our effectiveness in dealing with other nations on nuclear matters.

– In the absence of such legislation, I am directing the Secretary of State to work closely with the Nuclear Regulatory Commission to ensure proper emphasis on nonproliferation concerns in the nuclear export licensing process.

I will continue to work to develop bipartisan support in Congress for improvements in our nuclear export laws.

VII. Reprocessing evaluation program

The world community requires an aggressive program to build the international controls and cooperative regimes I have just outlined. I am prepared to mount such a program in the United States.

– I am directing the Administrator of ERDA to:

● Begin immediately to define a reprocessing and recycle evaluation program consistent with meeting our international objectives outlined earlier in this statement. This program should complement the Nuclear Regulatory Commission's (NRC) ongoing considerations of safety safeguards and environmental requirements for reprocessing and recycling activities, particularly its Generic Environmental Statement on Mixed Oxide Fuels.

• Investigate the feasibility of recovering the energy value from used nuclear fuel without separating our plutonium.

– I am directing the Secretary of State to invite other nations to participate in designing and carrying out ERDA's reprocessing and recycle evaluation program, consistent with our international energy cooperation and nonproliferation objectives. I will direct that activities carried out in the U.S. in connection with this program be subjected to full IAEA safeguards and inspections.

VIII. Nuclear waste management

The area of our domestic nuclear program dealing with long-term management of nuclear wastes from our commercial nuclear powerplants has not in the past received sufficient attention. In my 1977 Budget, I proposed a fourfold increase in funding for this program, which involves the activities of several Federal agencies. We recently completed a review to determine what additional actions are needed to assure availability in the mid-1980's of a federally-owned and managed repository for long-term nuclear wastes, well before significant quantities of wastes begin to accumulate.

I have been assured that the technology for long-term management or disposal of nuclear wastes is available but demonstrations are needed.

– I have directed the Administrator of ERDA to take the necessary action to speed up this program so as to demonstrate all components of waste management technology by 1978 and to demonstrate a complete repository for such wastes by 1985.

– I have further directed that the first demonstration depository for high-level wastes which will be owned by the Government be submitted for licensing by the independent NRC to assure its safety and acceptability to the public.

In view of the decisions announced today, I have also directed the Administrator of ERDA to assure that the waste repository will be able to handle spent fuel elements as well as the separated and solidified waste that would result if we proceed with nuclear fuel reprocessing.

The United States continues to provide world leadership in nuclear waste management. I am inviting other nations to participate in and learn from our programs.

– I am directing the Secretary of State to discuss with other nations and the IAEA the possibility of establishing centrally located, multinationally controlled nuclear waste repositories so that the number of sites that are needed can be limited.

Increased use of nuclear energy in the United States

Even with strong conservation efforts, energy demands in the United States will continue to increase in response to the needs of a growing economy. The only alternative over the next 15 to 20 years to increased use of both nuclear energy and coal is greater reliance on imported oil which will jeopardize our Nation's strength and welfare.

We now have in the United States 62 licensed nuclear plants, providing about 9 percent of our electrical energy. By 1985, we will have from 145 to 160 plants, supplying 20 percent or more of the Nation's electricity.

In many cases, electricity from nuclear plants is markedly cheaper than that produced from either oil or coal-fired plants. Nuclear energy is environmentally preferable in a number of respects to other principal ways of generating electricity.

Commercial nuclear power has an excellent safety record, with nearly 200 plant-years of experience (compiled over 18 chronological years) without a single death from a nuclear accident. I have acted to assure that this record is maintained in the years ahead. For example, I have increased funds for the independent Nuclear Regulatory Commission and for the Energy Research and Development Administration for reactor safety research and development.

The decisions and actions I am announcing today will help overcome the uncertainties that have served to delay the expanded use of nuclear energy in the United States. While the decision to delay reprocessing is significant, it will not prevent us from increasing our use of nuclear energy. We are on the right course with our nuclear power program in America. The changes I am announcing today will ensure that we continue.

My decisions today do not affect the U.S. program of research and development on the breeder reactor. That program assumes that no decision on the commercial operations of breeder reactors, which require plutonium fuel, will be made before 1986.

Conclusion

I do not underestimate the challenge represented in the creation of a worldwide program that will permit capturing the benefits of nuclear energy while maintaining needed protection against nuclear proliferation. The challenge is one that can be managed only partially and temporarily by technical measures.

It can be managed fully if the task is faced realistically by nations prepared to forego perceived short-term advantages in favor of fundamental long-term gains. We call upon all nations to recognize that their individual and collective interests are best served by internationally assured and safeguarded nuclear fuel supply, services, and storage. We ask them to turn aside from pursuing nuclear capabilities which are of doubtful economic value and have ominous implications for nuclear proliferation and instability in the world.

The growing international consensus against the proliferation of nuclear weapons is a source of encouragement. But it is certainly not a basis for complacency.

Success in meeting the challenge now before us depends on an extraordinary coordination of the policies of all nations toward the common good. The United States is prepared to lead, but we cannot succeed alone. If nations can work together constructively and cooperatively to manage our common nuclear problems, we will enhance our collective security. And we will be better able to concentrate our energies and our resources on the great tasks of construction rather than consume them in increasingly dangerous rivalry.

Remarks by President Jimmy Carter on nuclear power policy, April 7, 1977

The President's Remarks Announcing His Decisions Following a Review of U.S. Policy and a Question-and-Answer Session With Reporters. April 7, 1977

THE PRESIDENT. Good morning, everybody.

I have two items to discuss with you this morning. Then I'd like to answer a few questions.

Economic stimulus package

One relates to the economy and the need for continuing emphasis on the stimulation package. Based on the best information available to us now, we'll have an accumulated spending shortfall for this current fiscal year, fiscal year 1977, plus revenue collections in excess of the anticipated amount, of about $10 billion. In other words, we have collected about $10 billion more from the American taxpayers than we anticipate spending in 1977.

I feel very strongly that this money should go back to the American taxpayers. We need it for the economy to maintain its present strength. And the only equitable way that I see is through the already prepared tax refund which would average about $50 per person which, as I have said before, would be about 30 percent of the 1976 income taxes paid by a family making about $10,000 a year.

Nuclear power policy

The second point I'd like to make before I answer questions is concerning our Nation's efforts to control the spread of nuclear explosive capability. As far back as

SOURCE: Presidential Documents – Jimmy Carter, 1977, vol. 13, no. 15, Apr. 18, 1977

30 years ago, our Government made a proposal to the United Nations that there be tight international controls over nuclear fuels and particularly those that might be made into explosives.

Last year during the Presidential campaign, both I and President Ford called for strict controls over fuels to prevent the proliferation – further proliferation of nuclear explosive capability.

There is no dilemma today more difficult to address than that connected with the use of atomic power. Many countries see atomic power as their only real opportunity to deal with the dwindling supplies of oil, the increasing price of oil, and the ultimate exhaustion of both oil and natural gas.

Our country is in a little better position. We have oil supplies of our own, and we have very large reserves of coal. But even coal has its limitations. So, we will ourselves continue to use atomic power as a share of our total energy production.

The benefits of nuclear power, particularly to some foreign countries that don't have oil and coal of their own, are very practical and critical. But a serious risk is involved in the handling of nuclear fuels – the risk that component parts of this power process will be turned to providing explosives or atomic weapons.

We took an important step in reducing this risk a number of years ago by the implementation of the nonproliferation treaty which has now been signed by approximately a hundred nations. But we must go further.

We have seen recently India evolve an explosive device derived from a peaceful nuclear powerplant, and we now feel that several other nations are on the verge of becoming nuclear explosive powers.

The United States is deeply concerned about the consequences of the uncontrolled spread of this nuclear weapon capability. We can't arrest it immediately and unilaterally. We have no authority over other countries. But we believe that these risks would be vastly increased by the further spread of reprocessing capabilities of the spent nuclear fuel from which explosives can be derived.

Plutonium is especially poisonous, and, of course, enriched uranium, thorium and other chemicals or metals can be used as well.

We are now completing an extremely thorough review of our own nuclear power program. We have concluded that serious consequences can be derived from our own laxity in the handling of these materials and the spread of their use by other countries. And we believe that there is strong scientific and economic evidence that a time for a change has come.

Therefore, we will make a major change in the United States domestic nuclear energy policies and programs which I am announcing today.

We will make a concerted effort among all other countries to find better answers to the problems and risks of nuclear proliferation. And I would like to outline a few things now that we will do specifically.

First of all, we will defer indefinitely the commercial reprocessing and recycling of the plutonium produced in U.S. nuclear power programs.

From my own experience, we have concluded that a viable and adequate economic nuclear program can be maintained without such reprocessing and recycling of plutonium. The plant at Barnwell, South Carolina, for instance, will receive neither Federal encouragement nor funding from us for its completion as a reprocessing facility.

Second, we will restructure our own U.S. breeder program to give greater priority to alternative designs of the breeder other than plutonium, and to defer the date when breeder reactors would be put into commercial use.

We will continue research and development, try to shift away from plutonium, defer dependence on the breeder reactor for commercial use.

Third, we will direct funding of U.S. nuclear research and development programs to accelerate our research into alternative nuclear fuel cycles which do not involve direct access to materials that can be used for nuclear weapons.

Fourth, we will increase the U.S. capacity to produce nuclear fuels, enriched uranium in particular, to provide adequate and timely supplies of nuclear fuels to countries that need them so that they will not be required or encouraged to reprocess their own materials.

Fifth, we will propose to the Congress the necessary legislative steps to permit us to sign these supply contracts and remove the pressure for the reprocessing of nuclear fuels by other countries that do not now have this capability.

Sixth, we will continue to embargo the export of either equipment or technology that could permit uranium enrichment and chemical reprocessing.

And seventh, we will continue discussions with supplying countries and recipient countries, as well, of a wide range of international approaches and frameworks that will permit all countries to achieve their own energy needs while at the same time reducing the spread of the capability for nuclear explosive development.

Among other things – and we have discussed this with 15 or 20 national leaders already – we will explore the establishment of an international nuclear fuel cycle evaluation program so that we can share with countries that have to reprocess nuclear fuel the responsibility for curtailing the ability for the development of explosives.

One other point that ought to be made in the international negotiation field is that we have to help provide some means for the storage of spent nuclear fuel materials which are highly explosive, highly radioactive in nature.

I have been working very closely with and personally with some of the foreign leaders who are quite deeply involved in the decisions that we make. We are not trying to impose our will on those nations like Japan and France and Britain and Germany which already have reprocessing plants in operation. They have a special need that we don't have in that their supplies of petroleum products are not available.

But we hope that they will join with us – and I believe that they will – in trying to have some worldwide understanding of the extreme threat of the further proliferation of nuclear explosive capability.

I'd be glad to answer a few questions.

Questions

Q. Mr. President, in the last administration there was some proposal to have regional reprocessing centers which seem, to some people, to put the emphasis on the wrong thing. Does this mean that you are going to not favor regional reprocessing centers? And, secondly, would you be prepared to cut off supplies of any kind of nuclear material to countries that go nuclear?

THE PRESIDENT. Well, I can't answer either one of those questions yet. I have detailed discussions with Prime Minister Fukuda, with Chancellor Schmidt, and also with Prime Minister Callaghan, for instance, just in recent days about a joint approach to these kinds of problems.

Obviously, the smaller nations, the ones that now have established atomic powerplants, have to have someplace either to store their spent fuel or to have it reprocessed. And I think that we would very likely see a continuation of reprocessing capabilities within those nations that I have named and perhaps others.

We in our own country don't have this requirement. It's an option that we might have to explore many, many years in the future.

But I hope that by this unilateral action we can set a standard and that those countries that don't now have reprocessing capability will not acquire that capability in the future. Regional plants under tight international control obviously is one option that we would explore. No decision has been made about that.

If we felt that the provision of atomic fuel was being delivered to a nation that did not share with us our commitment to nonproliferation, we would not supply that fuel.

Q. Mr. President, this carries an assurance, which you had said earlier, for an assured and adequate supply of enriched uranium to replace the need for plutonium. Do you foresee any kind of price guarantees also for underdeveloped and poorer countries so that the supply would not only be assured but at a reasonable price in case lack of reprocessing drove prices up?

THE PRESIDENT. I don't know what the future prices of uranium might be. At the present time, of the enriched uranium that we produce, about roughly a third of it is exported, roughly a third of it is used for our domestic needs, and about a third of it is put in storage.

There has been an attenuation in recent years of the projected atomic powerplant construction in our own country. Other nations, though, are moving more and more toward atomic powerplants. But I can't tell you at this point that we will guarantee a price for uranium fuel that's less than our own cost of production, and that would be a matter of negotiation, perhaps even on an individual national basis.

I think that a standard price would probably be preferable, but then we might very well give a particular nation that was destitute or a very close friend of ours or who cooperated with us in this matter some sort of financial aid to help them with the purchase.

Q. You also said last year a couple of times that you hoped to call a world energy conference to discuss this as well as a lot of other things. Do you foresee that happening any time in the near future?

THE PRESIDENT. The item of nuclear powerplants and the handling of spent nuclear fuels and the curtailment of the possibility of new nations joining us in their capability for explosives will be on the agenda in the discussion in London early in May. And this will be a continuing process for us.

I might add that Secretary Vance also discussed this question with the Soviet authorities on his recent visit to Moscow and asked them to join in with us in enhancing the nonproliferation concept. Their response was favorable. But it will entail a great deal of negotiation, and I can't anticipate what the results of those negotiations might be. We obviously hope for it to apply to all the nations in the world.

Q. Mr. President, does your change in the domestic program mean that you will not authorize building the Clinch River breeder reactor in Tennessee?

THE PRESIDENT. The Clinch River breeder reactor will not be terminated as such. In my own budget recommendations to the Congress, we cut back – I can't remember the exact figure – about $250 million out of the plutonium breeder reactor – the liquid metal fast breeder reactor program.

I think that we would continue with the breeder reactor program on an experimental basis, research and development, but not move nearly so rapidly toward any sort of commercial use.

We also, obviously, are concerned about the adverse economic impact of these changes. And in the areas that would lose employment that was presently extant, as we increase our capacity for producing nuclear fuels, even using new techniques, other than gaseous diffusion, like centrifuge and laser beam use, then we would try to locate those facilities over a period of time – it's a very slow-moving process – in areas like Clinch River where they might be adversely affected.

Q. Mr. President, does this mean that Canada selling nuclear power equipment to France and others, and France selling to others – does this mean that we will supply those other countries so that they won't make more power?

THE PRESIDENT. Well, I might say that the two countries that most nearly share our commitment and even moved ahead of us in this field have been Canada – perhaps because of their unfortunate experience with India – and Australia. Both those countries, along with us, have substantial supplies of nuclear fuel themselves.

I would hope that we could develop an interrelationship with other countries to remove the competitive aspect of reprocessing itself. There is obviously going to be continued competition among our own Nation, Canada, France, Germany, England, in the selling of atomic powerplants themselves. It ought to be a clearly drawn distinction between the legitimate and necessary use of uranium and other enriched fuels to produce electricity, on the one hand, and a prohibition against the use of those fuels for explosives.

It would be impossible, counterproductive, and ill-advised for us to try to prevent other countries that need it from having the capability to produce electricity from atomic power. But I would hope that we and the other countries could form an alliance that might be fairly uniform in this respect. I know that all the other countries share with us this hope.

The one difference that has been very sensitive, as it relates to, say, Germany, Japan, and others, is that they fear that our unilateral action in renouncing the reprocessing of spent fuels to produce plutonium might imply that we prohibit them or criticize them severely because of their own need for reprocessing. This is not the case. They have a perfect right to go ahead and continue with their own reprocessing efforts. But we hope they'll join with us in eliminating in the future additional countries that might have had this capability evolve.

Q. Mr. President, is it your assessment, sir, that some of the smaller nations that are now seeking reprocessing technology are doing so in order to attain nuclear weapon capability as well as or in addition to meeting their legitimate energy needs?

THE PRESIDENT. Well, without going into specifics – I wouldn't want to start naming names – I think it's obvious that some of the countries about whom we are concerned have used their domestic nuclear powerplants to develop explosive capability. There is no doubt about it.

India, which is basically a peaceful nation, at least as far as worldwide connotations are concerned, did evolve an explosive capability from supplies that were given to them by the Canadians and by us.

And we feel that there are other nations that have potential capacity already for the evolution of explosives. But we are trying to make sure that from this point on that the increasing number of nations that might have joined the nuclear nations is attenuated drastically.

We can't undo immediately the mistakes that have been made in the past. But I believe that this is a step in the right direction.

Just one more question.

Q. Mr. President, are you willing to trade off your scrapping of 30 water projects or even some of them in exchange for a tax rebate package?

THE PRESIDENT. Well, I am not much of a trader. That is one of my political defects for which I have been criticized a great deal. We will be receiving the report on the analysis of water projects about April 15. I am not sure if that exact date will be met. And I'll assess each one of those projects on its own merits. And I would hope that the $50 tax refund will also be assessed on its own merits.

I know enough about politics to realize that we will lose some votes perhaps within the Congress because of water projects that we don't advocate. I also realize that there might be water projects that would be completed, I think ill-advisedly, against my inclinations. I don't have the final say-so about it. So there will have to be some interrelationship there. I wish and hope there is little, if any. But I can't prevent that.

But I am not inclined at all to trade a water project that's not needed or my approval of it in return for a vote on the tax refund which I think is needed for every Member of Congress and the people that look to that Congress Member for leadership.

Q. What's your forecast on the passage of the tax rebate?

THE PRESIDENT. I don't know yet. Majority Leader Byrd and Senator Cranston, Senator Humphrey, and others had a meeting I believe on Tuesday. They had additional meetings yesterday.

They are working very hard on this vote. I talked to Senator Byrd this morning, and he gave me a report on the progress that he thought we were making. And also the Vice President and I are contacting some of the Members of the Senate to let them know about our arguments on why the tax refund should be given back to the American people.

This morning I drafted about a 1½ page summary of the arguments in favor of the tax refund to the American people, including the shortfall in spending and the over-collection of taxes which is a recent development. I think that prospects still look good.

Thank you very much.

REPORTER. Thank you, Mr. President.

Nuclear power policy

Statement by the President on His Decisions Following a Review of U.S. Policy, April 7, 1977

There is no dilemma today more difficult to resolve than that connected with the use of nuclear power. Many countries see nuclear power as the only real opportunity, at least in this century, to reduce the dependence of their economic well-being on foreign oil – an energy source of uncertain availability, growing price, and ultimate exhaustion. The U.S., by contrast, has a major domestic energy source – coal – but its use is not without penalties, and our plans also call for the use of nuclear power as a share in our energy production.

The benefits of nuclear power are thus very real and practical. But a serious risk accompanies worldwide use of nuclear power – the risk that components of the nuclear power process will be turned to providing atomic weapons.

We took an important step in reducing the risk of expanding possession of atomic weapons through the Non-Proliferation Treaty, whereby more than 100 nations have agreed not to develop such explosives. But we must go further. The U.S. is deeply concerned about the consequences for all nations of a further spread of nuclear weapons or explosive capabilities. We believe that these risks would be vastly increased by the further spread of sensitive technologies which entail direct access to plutonium, highly enriched uranium, or other weapons usable material. The question I have had under review from my first day in office is how can that be accomplished without forgoing the tangible benefits of nuclear power.

We are now completing an extremely thorough review of all the issues that bear on the use of nuclear power. We have concluded that the serious consequences of proliferation and direct implications for peace and security – as well as strong scientific and economic evidence – require,

– A major change in U.S. domestic nuclear energy policies and programs; and

– A concerted effort among all nations to find better answers to the problems and risks accompanying the increased use of nuclear power.

I am announcing today some of my decisions resulting from that review.

First, we will defer indefinitely the commercial reprocessing and recycling of the plutonium produced in the U.S. nuclear power programs. From our own experience, we have concluded that a viable and economic nuclear power program can be sustained without such reprocessing and recycling. The plant at Barnwell, South Carolina, will receive neither Federal encouragement not funding for its completion as a reprocessing facility.

Second, we will restructure the U.S. breeder reactor program to give greater priority to alternative designs of the breeder and to defer the date when breeder reactors would be put into commercial use.

NOTE: The President spoke at 11:20 A.M. in the Briefing Room at the White House.

Third, we will redirect funding of U.S. nuclear research and development programs to accelerate our research into alternative nuclear fuel cycles which do not involve direct access to materials usable in nuclear weapons.

Fourth, we will increase U.S. production capacity for enriched uranium to provide adequate and timely supply of nuclear fuels for domestic and foreign needs.

Fifth, we will propose the necessary legislative steps to permit the U.S. to offer nuclear fuel supply contracts and guarantee delivery of such nuclear fuel to other countries.

Sixth, we will continue to embargo the export of equipment or technology that would permit uranium enrichment and chemical reprocessing.

Seventh, we will continue discussions with supplying and recipient countries alike, of a wide range of international approaches and frameworks that will permit all nations to achieve their energy objectives while reducing the spread of nuclear explosive capability. Among other things, we will explore the establishment of an international nuclear fuel cycle evaluation program aimed at developing alternative fuel cycles and a variety of international and U.S. measures to assure access to nuclear fuel supplies and spent fuel storage for nations sharing common non-proliferation objectives.

We will continue to consult very closely with a number of governments regarding the most desirable multilateral and bilateral arrangements for assuring that nuclear energy is creatively harnessed for peaceful economic purposes. Our intent is to develop wider international cooperation in regard to this vital issue through systematic and thorough international consultations.

APPENDIX F

President Jimmy Carter's message to Congress on the proposed Nuclear Non-Proliferation Act, April 27, 1977

THE need to halt nuclear proliferation is one of mankind's most pressing challenges. Members of my Administration are now engaged in international discussions to find ways of controlling the spread of nuclear explosive capability without depriving any nation of the means to satisfy its energy needs. The domestic nuclear policies which I have already put forward will place our nation in a leadership position, setting a positive example for other nuclear suppliers as well as demonstrating the strength of our concern here at home for the hazards of a plutonium economy. Today I am submitting to the Congress a bill which would establish for the United States a strong and effective non-proliferation policy.

This bill relies heavily upon work which the Congress has already done, and I commend the Congress for these valuable initiatives. I look forward to working with the Congress to establish a strong, responsible legislative framework from which we can continue strengthened efforts to halt the spread of nuclear weapons.

Among our shared goals are: an increase in the effectiveness of international safeguards and controls on peaceful nuclear activities to prevent further proliferation of nuclear explosive devices, the establishment of common international sanctions to prevent such proliferation, an effort to encourage nations which have not ratified the Non-Proliferation Treaty to do so at the earliest possible date, and adoption of programs to enhance the reliability of the United States as a supplier of nuclear fuel.

This bill differs from pending proposals, however, in several respects:

1. It defines the immediate nuclear export conditions which we can reasonably ask other nations to meet while we negotiate stricter arrangements. The proposals currently before Congress would impose criteria that could force an immediate moratorium on our nuclear exports, adversely affecting certain allies whose cooperation is needed if we are to achieve our ultimate objective of non-proliferation.

2. It defines additional nuclear export conditions which will be required in new agreements for civil nuclear cooperation. In particular, we will require as a continu-

SOURCE: Presidential Documents – Jimmy Carter, 1977, vol. 13, no. 18, May 2, 1977.

ing condition of U.S. supply that recipients have all their nuclear activities under IAEA safeguards. I view this as an interim measure and shall make it clear to all potential recipients and to other nuclear suppliers that our first preference, and continuing objective, is universal adherence to the Non-Proliferation Treaty.

3. For the near future, it attempts to tighten the conditions for U.S. nuclear cooperation through renegotiation of existing agreements to meet the same standards as those we will require in new agreements. I believe that this approach will better meet our non-proliferation objectives than will the unilateral imposition of new export licensing conditions.

4. It increases the flexibility we need to deal with an extremely complex subject. For example, instead of requiring countries that want our nuclear exports to foreswear fuel enrichment and reprocessing for all time, it allows us to draft new agreements using incentives to encourage countries not to acquire such facilities. It also permits me to grant exceptions when doing so would further our basic aim of non-proliferation. All new cooperation agreements would, of course, be subject to Congressional review.

This bill is intended to reassure other nations that the United States will be a reliable supplier of nuclear fuel and equipment for those who genuinely share our desire for non-proliferation. It will insure that when all statutory standards have been met, export licenses will be issued – or, if the judgment of the Executive Branch and the independent Nuclear Regulatory Commission should differ, that a workable mechanism exists for resolving the dispute.

Since I intend personally to oversee Executive Branch actions affecting non-proliferation, I do not think a substantial reorganization of the responsibility for nuclear exports within the Executive Branch is necessary. This conclusion is shared by the Nuclear Regulatory Commission.

The need for prompt action is great. Until domestic legislation is enacted, other countries will be reluctant to renegotiate their agreements with us, because they will fear that new legislation might suddenly change the terms of cooperation. If the incentives we offer them to renegotiate with us are not attractive enough, the United States could lose important existing safeguards and controls. And if our policy is too weak, we could find ourselves powerless to restrain a deadly worldwide expansion of nuclear explosive capability. I believe the legislation now submitted to you strikes the necessary balance.

Jimmy Carter

The White House, *April 27, 1977*

APPENDIX G

Fact sheet on the proposed Nuclear Non-Proliferation Act, April 27, 1977

THE Nuclear Non-Proliferation Policy Act of 1977, the domestic nuclear policies announced by the President on April 7, and the additional policy decisions included in this fact sheet, are key components of the administration's nuclear non-proliferation policy. The President's policy decisions include:

– New conditions we will require for the granting of nuclear export licenses;
– Additional new conditions we will require in new U.S. Agreements for Cooperation. These agreements are the formal, bilateral undertakings which form the basis for civil nuclear interactions with other nations;
– Policies the executive branch will follow in making recommendations to the Nuclear Regulatory Commission on the export of sensitive items such as plutonium and highly enriched uranium (the weapons usable form of uranium, known as HEU);
– Policies the executive branch will follow in deciding whether to approve a request by another nation to retransfer U.S.-supplied fuel to a third nation for reprocessing;
– Policies to improve U.S. reliability as a nuclear fuel supplier by introducing greater clarity and predictability into the export licensing process.

Together, all these policies will place the United States in a leadership position among nuclear suppliers, and will establish a strong and effective non-proliferation policy. These policies have been developed, and must be evaluated, as a complete package. They are intended as a delicately balanced blend of:

– *Denials* for those items, such as reprocessing plants, which we believe create such a large risk that their export should be avoided whenever possible;
– *Controls* over those items and technologies, required by ongoing programs, where improved safeguards and conditions for physical security will substantially reduce the risk. These controls will be backed up by stiff sanctions which would be imposed on violators;
– *Incentives* – the United States fully recognizes that there is no such thing as an

SOURCE: Presidential Documents – Jimmy Carter, 1977, vol. 13, no. 18, May 2, 1977.

effective unilateral non-proliferation policy. We must gain the support of other nations – both suppliers and recipients – if we are to reach our common goal of limiting the spread of nuclear weapons. Hence the administration's program includes substantial elements of incentives, particularly in the areas of: uranium resource assessment; guaranteed access to non-sensitive, low enriched uranium (LEU) nuclear fuel; and spent fuel storage.

The following are key features of the Nuclear Non-Proliferation Policy Act of 1977, and related administration policies.

1. The bill establishes for the first time a statutory requirement forbidding the independent Nuclear Regulatory Commission (NRC) from granting a license to export nuclear materials or facilities until it has been notified by the executive branch of its judgment that the issuance of a license "will not be inimicable to the common defense and security." This judgment will be reached by the Departments of State, Defense, Commerce, the Arms Control and Disarmament Agency, and the Energy Research and Development Administration.

In arriving at these judgments, the executive branch will adhere to the following policies not detailed in the act;

– Continue to embargo the export of enrichment and reprocessing plants;
– Avoid new commitments to export significant amounts of separated plutonium except for gram quantities for research and analytical uses;
– Avoid new commitments to export significant quantities of highly enriched uranium (HEU) except when the project is of exceptional merit and the use of low enriched fuel or some other less weapons usable material is clearly shown to be technically infeasible;
– Require direct Presidential approval for any supply of HEU greater than 15 kilograms (the approximate amount needed for a bomb);
– Undertake efforts to identify projects and facilities which might be converted to the use of LEU instead of HEU;
– Take steps to minimize inventories of weapons usable uranium abroad.

2. The bill defines the immediate nuclear export conditions which we can reasonably expect other nations to meet while we negotiate stricter agreements for cooperation. These conditions include:

– A requirement for International Atomic Energy Agency (IAEA) safeguards on all exported items and on any other plutonium or enriched uranium that might be used in the exported facility or produced through its use.
– A requirement that no U.S. export be used for research or production of any nuclear explosive device.
– A requirement that no U.S. export be retransferred by a recipient nation to any other nation without the prior approval of the United States.
– A requirement that no fuel exported from the United States be reprocessed without the prior approval of the United States.

These criteria differ from proposals currently before Congress which include criteria that could force an immediate moratorium on U.S. nuclear exports. Such a moratorium would seriously damage U.S. relations with certain allies whose cooperation is essential if we are to achieve our non-proliferation objectives.

3. The bill defines additional nuclear export conditions which will be required in new agreements for cooperation. These include:

– A requirement, in the case of non-nuclear weapons states, that IAEA safeguards cover all nuclear materials and equipment regardless of whether these have been supplied by the United States. Fulfillment of this requirement will be a condition of continuing U.S. nuclear supply.

The President has also directed that this requirement be viewed only as an interim measure, and that the United States' first preference, and continuing objective, is universal adherence to the Non-Proliferation Treaty.

– The stipulation that United States cooperation under the agreement shall cease if the recipient detonates a nuclear device or materially violates IAEA safeguards or any guarantee it has given under the agreement.

– A requirement for IAEA safeguards on all U.S.-supplied material and equipment for indefinite duration, whether or not the Agreement for Cooperation remains in force.

– The U.S. right of approval on retransfers extended to all special nuclear material produced through the use of U.S. equipment.

– The U.S. right of approval on reprocessing extended to all special nuclear material produced through use of U.S. equipment.

4. For the near future, the bill proposes to tighten the conditions for U.S. nuclear cooperation through the renegotiation of existing agreements to meet the same standards as those we will require for new agreements (as specified in 3 above). This approach will better meet U.S. non-proliferation objectives than would an attempt to impose unilaterally new export licensing conditions.

5. The bill provides the flexibility needed to deal with the many different situations and nations involved. For example, it makes the necessary exceptions for licenses under existing multilateral agreements. It also establishes an efficient mechanism for the President and Congress to review cases where the executive branch and the independent NRC differ on the granting of a proposed export license. And it permits the President to grant exceptions from the stiff new conditions required for new agreements for cooperation, if he considers that this is in our overall non-proliferation interest.

6. The bill creates sanctions against the violation of nuclear agreements by providing that no nuclear export shall be granted to any non-nuclear weapons state that, after enactment of this legislation:

– Detonates a nuclear explosive device;

– Terminates or abrogates IAEA safeguards;

– Is found by the President to have materially violated an IAEA agreement or any other guarantee it has given under an agreement for cooperation with the United States;

unless the President determines that such a cutoff would hinder the achievement of U.S. non-proliferation objectives, or would jeopardize the common defense and security.

7. The legislation proposes the establishment of an international Nuclear Fuel Cycle Evaluation Program, aimed at furthering the development of alternative, nuclear fuel cycles which do not provide access to weapons usable material, as announced by the President in his April 7 statement.

8. As an essential element of the international evaluation program, the legislation proposes a number of policies to assure that adequate nuclear fuel supply will be available to all nations as a non-proliferation incentive. These include:

– A policy to assure adequate U.S. uranium enrichment capacity;

– A policy assuring that nuclear exports will be licensed on a timely basis once statutory requirements are met;

– U.S. initiatives to promote international consultations to develop multilateral means for meeting worldwide nuclear fuel needs.

The bill further requires the President to report to the Congress on the progress of these discussions and to propose any legislation he may consider necessary to promote these objectives.

9. The bill commits the United States to work with other nations to strengthen the International Atomic Energy Agency (IAEA) through: contribution of technical resources, support and funding; improving the IAEA safeguards system; and, by assuring that IAEA receives the data needed for it to administer an effective, comprehensive international safeguards program.

APPENDIX H

International Fuel Cycle Evaluation: working groups

Working Group 1 – Fuel and Heavy Water Availability
            (Co-Chairmen: Canada, Egypt, India);
Working Group 2 – Enrichment Availability
            (Co-Chairman: France, Federal Republic of Germany, Iran);
Working Group 3 – Assurances of Long-Term Supply of Technology, Fuel and
            Heavy Water and Services in the Interest of National Needs
            Consistent with Non-Proliferation
            (Co-Chairmen: Australia, Philippines, Switzerland);
Working Group 4 – Reprocessing, Plutonium Handling, Recycle
            (Co-Chairmen: Japan, United Kingdom);
Working Group 5 – Fast Breeders
            (Co-Chairmen: Belgium, Italy, USSR);
Working Group 6 – Spent Fuel Management
            (Co-Chairmen: Argentina, Spain);
Working Group 7 – Waste Management and Disposal
            (Co-Chairmen: Finland, Netherlands, Sweden);
Working Group 8 – Advanced Fuel Cycle and Reactor Concepts
            (Co-Chairmen: Republic of Korea, Romania, USA).

SOURCE: Final Communique of the Organizing Conference, International
Nuclear Fuel Cycle Evaluation, Oct. 1977.

Guidelines for nuclear transfers, the Nuclear Suppliers' Group

In a document dated 21 September 1977 but released only in early 1978, the Nuclear Suppliers' Group, an informal body representing 15 countries with nuclear export industries,* has defined principles for safeguards and export controls on nuclear transfers to non-nuclear-weapon states. This is the first public statement of the Group, which was convened in February 1975, with the aim of complementing the rules of the Non-Proliferation Treaty by a practice of agreed export constraints for the major suppliers of nuclear installations.

1. THE following fundamental principles for safeguards and export controls should apply to nuclear transfers to any non-nuclear-weapon state for peaceful purposes. In this connection, suppliers have defined an export trigger list and agreed on common criteria for technology transfers.†

Prohibition on nuclear explosives

2. Suppliers should authorize transfer of items identified in the trigger list only upon formal governmental assurances from recipients explicitly excluding uses which would result in any nuclear explosive device.

Physical protection

3. (a) All nuclear materials and facilities identified by the agreed trigger list should be placed under effective physical protection to prevent unauthorized use and han-

---

*   Belgium, Britain, Canada, Czechoslovakia, France, East Germany, West Germany, Italy, Japan, the Netherlands, Poland, Sweden, Switzerland, USA and USSR.

†   The full text will be published in early February 1978.

SOURCE: International Institute for Strategic Studies, *SURVIVAL* 20, no. 2 (March/April 1980), documentation.

dling. The levels of physical protection to be ensured in relation to the type of materials, equipment and facilities, have been agreed by suppliers, taking account of international recommendations.

(b) The implementation of measures of physical protection in the recipient country is the responsibility of the government of that country. However, in order to implement the terms agreed upon amongst suppliers, the levels of physical protection on which these measures have to be based should be the subject of an agreement between supplier and recipient.

(c) In each case special arrangements should be made for a clear definition of responsibilities for the transport of trigger list items.

Safeguards

4. Suppliers should transfer trigger list items only when covered by IAEA safeguards, with duration and coverage provisions in conformity with the GOV/1621 guidelines. Exceptions should be made only after consultation with the parties to this understanding.

5. Suppliers will jointly reconsider their common safeguards requirements, whenever appropriate.

Safeguards triggered by the transfer of certain technology

6. (a) The requirements of paragraphs 2, 3 and 4 above should also apply to facilities for reprocessing, enrichment, or heavy water production, utilizing technology directly transferred by the supplier or derived from transferred facilities, or major critical components thereof.

(b) The transfer of such facilities, or major critical components thereof, or related technology, should require an undertaking (1) that IAEA safeguards apply to any facilities of the same type (i.e. if the design, construction or operating processes are based on the same or similar physical or chemical processes, as defined in the trigger list) constructed during an agreed period in the recipient country and (2) that there should at all times be in effect a safeguards agreement permitting the IAEA to apply Agency safeguards with respect to such facilities identified by the recipient, or by the supplier in consultation with the recipient, as using transferred technology.

Special controls on sensitive exports

7. Suppliers should exercise restraint in the transfer of sensitive facilities, technology and weapons-usable materials. If enrichment or reprocessing facilities, equipment or technology are to be transferred, suppliers should encourage recipients to accept, as an alternative to national plants, supplier involvement and/or other appropriate multi-national participation in resulting facilities. Suppliers should also

promote international (including IAEA) activities concerned with multi-national regional fuel cycle centres.

Special controls on export of enrichment facilities, equipment and technology

8. For a transfer of an enrichment facility, or technology thereof, the recipient nation should agree that neither the transferred facility, nor any facility based on such technology, will be designed or operated for the production of greater than 20 per cent enriched uranium without the consent of the supplier nation, of which the IAEA should be advised.

Controls on supplied or derived weapons-usable material

9. Suppliers recognize the importance, in order to advance the objectives of these guidelines and to provide opportunities further to reduce the risks of proliferation, of including in agreements on supply of nuclear materials or of facilities which produce weapons-usable material, provisions calling for mutual agreement between the supplier and the recipient on arrangements for reprocessing, storage, alteration, use, transfer or retransfer of any weapons-usable material involved. Suppliers should endeavour to include such provisions whenever appropriate and practicable.

Controls on retransfer

10. (a) Suppliers should transfer trigger list items, including technology defined under paragraph 6, only upon the recipient's assurance that, in the case of (1) retransfer of such items, or (2) transfer of trigger list items derived from facilities originally transferred by the supplier, or with the help of equipment or technology originally transferred by the supplier, the recipient of the retransfer or transfer will have provided the same assurances as those required by the supplier for the original transfer.

(b) In addition the supplier's consent should be required for (1) any retransfer of the facilities' major critical components, or technology described in paragraph 6, (2) any transfer of facilities or major critical components derived from those items, (3) any retransfer of heavy water or weapons-usable material.

SUPPORTING ACTIVITIES

Physical security

11. Suppliers should promote international cooperation on the exchange of physical security information, protection of nuclear materials in transit, and recovery of stolen nuclear materials and equipment.

Support for effective IAEA safeguards

12. Suppliers should make special efforts in support of effective implementation of IAEA safeguards. Suppliers should also support the Agency's efforts to assist member states in the improvement of their national systems of accounting and control of nuclear material and to increase the technical effectiveness of safeguards.

Similarly, they should make every effort to support the IAEA in increasing further the adequacy of safeguards in the light of technical developments and the rapidly growing number of nuclear facilities, and to support appropriate initiatives aimed at improving the effectiveness of IAEA safeguards.

Sensitive plant design features

13. Suppliers should encourage the designers and makers of sensitive equipment to construct it in such a way as to facilitate the application of safeguards.

Consultations

14. (a) Suppliers should maintain contact and consult through regular channels on matters connected with the implementation of these guidelines.

(b) Suppliers should consult, as each deems appropriate, with other Governments concerned on specific sensitive cases, to ensure that any transfer does not contribute to risks of conflict or instability.

(c) In the event that one or more suppliers believe that there has been a violation of supplier/recipient understandings resulting from these guidelines, particularly in the case of an explosion of a nuclear device, or illegal termination or violation of IAEA safeguards by a recipient, suppliers should consult promptly through diplomatic channels in order to determine and assess the reality and extent of the alleged violation.

Pending the early outcome of such consultations, suppliers will not act in a manner that could prejudice any measure that may be adopted by other suppliers concerning their current contacts with that recipient.

Upon the findings of such consultations, the suppliers, bearing in mind Article XII of the IAEA Statute, should agree on an appropriate response and possible action which could include the termination of nuclear transfers to that recipient.

15. In considering transfers, each supplier should exercise prudence having regard to all the circumstances of each case, including any risk that technology transfers not covered by paragraph 6, or subsequent retransfers, might result in unsafeguarded nuclear materials.

16. Unanimous consent is required for any changes in these guidelines, including any which might result from the reconstruction mentioned in paragraph 5.

Notes

CHAPTER 1. INTRODUCTION

1 Oppenheimer's recitation from the Bhagavad-Gita: "If the radiance of a thousand suns were to burst at once into the sky, that would be the splendor of the Mighty One . . . I am become death, the destroyer of Worlds."

2 The history of civilian nuclear power and the aspirations that propelled it are recorded with insight in the knowledgeable account of Irvin C. Bupp and Jean-Claude Derian, *Light Water: How the Nuclear Dream Dissolved* (New York: Basic Books, 1978).

3 The routinization of magic is the norm for human societies. Its custody and manipulation falls first to prophets and shamans; then to castes of priests who regulate its dispensation and define its powers – even while nurturing the aura of mystery that perpetuates fascination, and purports to provide protection for the devotees. In today's secular culture the process of routinization and conventionalizing has been more thorough. The move to apply nuclear knowledge and technology to virtuous civilian ends has meant divining away most of the magic, leaving behind only a thin potion that encourages special effort and heightens the feeling of high endeavor. Care for the nuclear totem indeed passed to institutions (the AEC, its supporting labs, and ancillary divisions of the private nuclear industry) whose members were unusually solidaristic, and who shared a pool of common beliefs and values. Their job has been to manage the nuclear "white" magic, while the castes of statesmen and warriors occupied themselves with the nuclear "black" magic.

4 For a full account of the Non-Proliferation Treaty, and an agonized examination of its limitations, see William Epstein, *The Last Chance: Nuclear Proliferation and Arms Control* (New York: Free Press, 1976).

5 The seminal work is Graham Allison's *Essence of Decision* (Boston: Little, Brown and Co., 1971). See also Morten H. Halperin et al., *Bureaucratic Politics and Foreign Policy* (Washington, D.C.: Brookings Institution, 1974). The definitive critique of bureaucratic politics and related theory is by Robert J. Art: "Bureaucratic Politics and American Foreign Policy: A Critique," *Policy Sciences* 4, no. 4 (1973): 267–90.

CHAPTER 2. THE IMPASSE ON ENRICHMENT
SERVICES

1   As reported in Atomic Energy Commission, *Annual Report to Congress, 1974* (Washington, D.C.: Government Printing Office). See AEC Press Release, July 2, 1974.

2   These developments are examined by Paul L. Joskow, "The International Nuclear Industry Today: The End of the American Monopoly," *Foreign Affairs* 54, no. 4 (July 1976): 788–803.

3   The impact of the 1973 OPEC actions on the world energy outlook is considered in Raymond Vernon (ed.), "The Oil Crisis: In Perspective," *Daedalus*, Fall 1975.

4   The term "nuclear establishment" is convenient shorthand for those private and public organizations that have collaborated in putting civilian nuclear power on the rails, and who share a deep belief in its bountiful promise: the AEC; corporations engaged in reactor manufacture, construction, and related functions; and the now defunct Joint Committee on Atomic Energy (JCAE). Though such a label can connote a solidarity of interest that distorts a more complex reality, the term does accurately describe the degree of concert that characterized the thinking and actions of those who committed their talents and careers to the cause of atomic power.

5   AEC estimates, and those of other bodies, are cited and reviewed in the Atlantic Council of the United States, *Nuclear Fuels Policy*, Report of the Atlantic Council's Nuclear Fuels Policy Working Group, Washington, D.C., 1976. See also the projections of the Atomic Industrial Forum made before the JCAE, *Hearings on AEC Authorization, FY 1973*, 92d Cong., 2d sess., 1972.

6   There is no single history or analytical study that captures the full flavor of the Atomic Energy Commission's institutional personality and ethos. Some of its character comes across in the critical work of Irvin C. Bupp and Jean-Claude Derian, *Light Water: How the Nuclear Dream Dissolved* (New York: Basic Books, 1978).

7   Some backers of nuclear power were anxious to avoid having the country's nuclear fuels program fall victim to such an ideological confrontation. Various ideas were floated for the creation of quasi-public corporations that would take positions somewhere between the AEC's support of a continued government monopoly and the administration's vision of privatization. Commissioner Clarence E. Larson was the persistent booster of a proposal originally sketched by Philip Sporn, president of the American Electric Power Company, for a consortium of utility companies, already operating power-generating reactors, to build and manage the next generation of enrichment plants. (Sporn's views about the government's role in the electric power field were developed in his book, *The Social Organization of Electric Power Supply in Modern Societies* (Cambridge, Mass.: MIT Press, 1971.) See U.S. Atomic Energy Commission, Office of Planning and Analysis, "Nuclear Power Growth," 1974-2000, WASH-1139 (74) (Washington, D.C.: Government Printing Office, February 1974). Conceived as a public corporation financially independent of the U.S. Treasury, it would relieve the government of the financial responsibility for capitalizing multibillion dollar enrichment projects,

insuring that they would be seen on commercial principles and involving consumers directly in the planning and operation of any new facilities. A related scheme
was designed by Representative Craig Hosmer, senior minority member of the
JCAE. Dubbed the U.S. Enrichment Corporation, it was a nearly exact replica of
TVA. Without ties of ownership or management to utilities or other private corporations, it would be freshly constituted as an autonomous corporate entity sanctioned by Congress, but otherwise self-reliant. Neither proposal to organize the
enrichment services gained much support. Caught between the implacable resistance of the AEC to any incursion on its domain, and the unswerving Nixon
administration commitment to removing enrichment from the public sphere entirely, they suffered the fate of reasonable compromises outmatched by the political
clout of their antipodal contenders, each enjoying its philosophical high ground.

8   These steps are described and skillfully placed in the context of the
United States' nuclear diplomacy by Edward F. Wonder, *Nuclear Fuel and American
Foreign Policy Multilateralization for Uranium Enrichment* (Boulder, Colo.: West-
view Press, 1977).

9   Wonder (ibid.) provides the definitive account of this episode.

10   Ibid., p. 27.

11   If sentiment in the executive branch ran strongly against an accommodating approach to the Europeans, it was at least matched by the views of
the Joint Committee on Atomic Energy. To JCAE members, cooperation smacked
of a giveaway. Already inclined to look skeptically at the practice of offering enrichment services at concessionary rates, they were utterly opposed to yielding technology and markets as well.

12   President Richard M. Nixon, Message to the Congress on a Program to Insure an Adequate Supply of Clean Energy in the Future, June 4, 1971.

13   Henry A. Kissinger, Talk to the Washington Energy Conference,
February 11, 1974.

14   If the JCAE needed any outside support to confirm the wisdom
of its opposition to privatization, it received some from the electric utility industry
– the owners and operators of LWRs. The industry trade association, the Edison
Electric Institute, contracted with the Arthur D. Little Corporation to look at the
idea of utility participation in privatization consortia, following the lead of the
proposal made by Phillip Sporn and Commissioner Clarence E. Larson. They concluded that the venture was financially very risky. Assessments made in conjunction
with the study underscored the uncertainties of rates and of natural uranium supply
and thereby raised grave doubts about the profitability of fully commercial enrichment enterprises. On the basis of this evaluation, electric utilities became, on the
whole, tacit opponents of privatization, out of concern for the viability and reliability of private ventures deprived of government backing. Arthur D. Little, Inc.,
"A Study of Base-Loan Alternatives for the Northeast Utilities System: 1981–1984."

15   Report in *Nucleonics Week*, June 4, 1972.

16   Paraphrase offered by a senior Nixon administration official.

17   For an account of the shifting premises of U.S. foreign economic
policy, see Stephen D. Cohen, *The Makings of United States International Economic
Policy* (New York: Praeger Publishers, 1977).

18   U.S. Congress, JCAE *Hearings on AEC Authorization, FY 1973*.

19   "The AEC Announces Details of New Contracting Arrangements for Uranium-Enriching Services," AEC Press Release R-26, January 22, 1973. Its terms are discussed in Vince Taylor (for PanHeuristics), "The Myth of Uranium Scarcity," Los Angeles, Calif., April 25, 1977.

20   Ford Foundation Nuclear Energy Policy Study Group and Mitre Corporation Report, *Nuclear Power Issues and Choices* (Cambridge, Mass.: Ballinger Publishing Co., 1977), p. 360.

21   Atomic Energy Act Amended, 1954, sec. 1612.

22   38 Federal Register 12 180.

23   AEC Press Release P-421, December 8, 1972, quoted in Wonder, *Nuclear Fuel*, p. 33.

24   AEC, Annual Report, *The Nuclear Industry 1973*, WASH 1174-73, p. 49.

25   In defense of their enrichment policy, administration officials later would argue that they were concerned about the back-end of the fuel cycle, which they felt had been neglected by the AEC (shunted off to private industry *prematurely*) because it lacked glamour, was not rewarded with career advancement, and was tangential to maintenance of the organization's position and power. To get work going on perfecting reprocessing, and solving the disposal problem, meant – to their mind – freeing resources tied up in AEC enrichment operations. According to this argument, problems at the back-end of the fuel cycle were largely a budgetary matter, so privatization was in the end an environmental and safety virtue.

26   AEC, *Annual Report to Congress*, 1974.

27   Dixy Lee Ray, Testimony before U.S. Congress, JCAE, Hearings, August 3, 1974.

28   The AEC's internal organization below the commission level was exceptionally tolerant of lapses in the attention and wisdom of commissioners, and it did little to compensate for them. Full and constructive cooperation from commission officials would not be taken for granted. Two features of AEC bureaucracy worked against help and support from below: (1) the abiding belief of old hands that they knew more about nuclear affairs than anyone else, and that the best results could be achieved by letting them get on with running the shop; and (2) the AEC's structure, built around semiautonomous divisions that offered multiple opportunities for strong-willed, highly independent executives to delay, divert, and discourage. Often it was a tenacious insistence on correct procedure, backed by mastery of nuclear matters, that served bureaucratic power. As one former commissioner has remarked, in commenting on the agency's keepers of the nuclear faith, "They told you when to pray, how to kneel, and looked askance at those who didn't know the routine, even if they were believers who wanted to worship at the alter of atomic power." Under such circumstances, the level of cooperation reached between appointed commissioners and permanent officials necessarily depended on two things: the compatability of personalities and the degree of convergence between the policy preferences of the political leadership and the established interests of the bureaucracy. Given the irregular contact between the commission and senior directors of operating divisions, which was partly the result of the general manager's

buffering role, there was little in the way of informal and easy exchange among the major players in AEC policy making. A plural executive unable to act in concert, and lacking in political astuteness, found it difficult to enlist the support of the bureaucratic barons in enterprises of uncertain design and of dubious value to the organizations they led.

When the commissioners were inclined and sufficiently unified to exercise leadership in setting AEC objectives and defining programs, they were handicapped by the depth of their staff. A proficient staff is a vital asset for appointed agency heads seeking to direct a large, technically oriented bureaucracy. With it, they are in a position to determine the kinds of information (financial, administrative, technological) needed to pass judgment on major policy issues; to evaluate the material flowing up to them from the bureaucracy; and to make provision for independent assessments where there is evidence of vested organizational interest biasing information and analysis. Without competent staff, appointed leadership is hostage to the goodwill and philosophic congeniality of permanent officials with a stake in program decisions and policy outcomes that often diverge from its own. The value of an able staff sensitive to the thrust of central policy and committed to achieving its objectives is most evident when there is an attempt to shift policy out of its well-established traces. Inadequacy of staff support is one reason why the commissioners proved themselves so inadequate as overseers of AEC operations – whether those determined by the powerful internal baronies or those dictated by the White House. (It is also why the White House made sure to stock the critical Planning and Analysis Division with its own people.)

29   An example of the contribution that might have been made by an incisive general manager's office would be a critical examination of the projections being done by the Office of Planning and Analysis. As part of their forecasting responsibilities, officials there routinely surveyed utilities to ascertain what their estimated needs would be. The results were conveyed without passing the data through an interpretive analysis. A conscientious review at the general manager's level would have discounted the figures emerging in spring 1974 by taking into account two caution factors: the exaggerated statement of demand requirements forced by new contracting procedures, and the temporary, unsustainable swing to nuclear power by utilities frightened by the oil embargo. That kind of assessment was never made, nor was the meaning for anticipating the crisis and dealing with the effects extracted from it.

30   There was only one, insubstantial, effort to introduce the international political component into the enrichment debate. It took the form of a low-key NSC staff study to ferret out the fuller implications of the stop–go dialogues with the Europeans. With terms of reference drawn to encompass the uncertainties surrounding enrichment capacity, an interagency working group to study the issue was organized in late 1973. Direction was shared by Benjamin Huberman, deputy director for program analysis, and David Elliott, a staffer responsible for scientific and technical affairs. The project was soon stymied by lack of cooperation on all sides. The AEC under Dixy Lee Ray balked at any politically minded review and offered only pro forma collaboration. State, for its part, saw the exercise more as a continuing threat by the NSC to extend its control over foreign policy than as a chance to gain some intellectual and bureaucratic leverage over nuclear energy

issues. The discord over jurisdiction meant that the working group would prove unable to produce a good, tight options paper stating clear alternatives or to force a searching look at the new direction of nuclear export policy.

31   The cause of Dixy Lee Ray's bitterly hostile attitude toward the State Department has been traced to an incident in her career as a marine biologist. As the story is recounted, she on one occasion found herself at odds with an unidentified government within whose province she was conducting her scientific investigations. Being asked to leave the country, an action that would terminate suddenly a project representing a substantial scholarly investment, she appealed for help to the local U.S. embassy, but to no avail. Believing that the embassy had failed to get properly exercised at an affront to an American scientist, and that it was staffed by lazy incompetents, she carried away from the affair a deep resentment of the striped-pants set. Such is the stuff of which interagency politics are made.

32   Reported in *Nucleonics Week*, July 4, 1974.

33   See assessment made in ibid.

34   Ibid.

35   Ibid.

36   Congress, too, was a victim – if not an entirely innocent one – of the ploys of the administration and the AEC officialdom. The change in contracting modes had been presented to the JCAE as a business measure warranted on economic grounds. It conformed with the members' own opposition to the "subsidization" of foreign utilities. No hint was given of ulterior purposes. In early 1974, as the committee became aware of a possible enrichment bottleneck, it held hearings to determine if there was reason to be anxious about a dangerous shortfall appearing. Under hard questioning, former Chairman Schlesinger acknowledged a possible problem but offered assurances that the capacity of the three existing plants (buttressed by the CUP addition) would tide the United States over. The testimony of agency officials, although differing in accent and stresses, did little more to enlighten the congressmen about the storm ahead. See U.S. Congress, JCAE, Hearings, February 1974.

37   At the end of May 1974, Ray was embroiled in a related dispute over the AEC's granting of an export license for a fuel shipment to the Indian Tarapur reactor (see Chap. 3). In a routine procedure undisturbed by the explosion, the commission officials sanctioned the delivery – a judgment in which State's Indian desk just as routinely joined. The action was blocked by David Elliott, the NSC staffer who was gradually assuming responsibility for the council's late-dawning interest in proliferation. Working with Sisco, he succeeded in forcing a letter to the New Delhi government stating that in the light of recent events this would be the last such shipment unless India subsequently accepted IAEA safeguards and a moratorium on further explosions.

38   *Nucleonics Week*, August 1, 1974.

39   President Dwight D. Eisenhower, Executive Order 10841.

40   As for plutonium recycling, it proved to be a dud. The outlook on commercial reprocessing was too cloudy for any reasonable estimates to be made of the LWR fuel demand to be met through plutonium recycling. Furthermore, the outstanding legal and regulatory obstacles to reprocessing precluded an unequivocal governmental commitment to expediting commercial development.

41   Dixy Lee Ray, Testimony before JCAE Hearings, August 3, 1974.

42   President Richard M. Nixon, Statement made August 6, 1974, reported in *Nucleonics Week*, August 10, 1974. This statement declared: "The President wishes to lay to rest uncertainties which have recently arisen concerning the assurance of an adequate supply of enriched uranium. The President assures holders of conditional contracts that the United States will, in any event, fulfill the fuel requirements in those contracts from United States supply sources. The President affirms that assured and timely availability of enrichment services is of paramount importance to those countries, including the United States, that have selected nuclear power as a major source of energy for the coming decades. Non-discriminatory access to such services and reliability in supply . . . will be essential features of the United States policy in the future as they have in the past."

CHAPTER 3. A NEW LOOK AT PLUTONIUM

1   The major share of the responsibility for the casualness with which the proliferation issue was treated can be placed at the door of Henry Kissinger, who wore two hats during this period, first as national security advisor and later as secretary of state. From both positions he dominated the United States' foreign policy to an unprecedented degree. No action of consequence could be taken without his personal approval; no significant decision could be made by others except as mandated by a delegation of his authority. Kissinger did use subordinates, and often very effectively. But the delegation of power and responsibility was not institutionalized. It was ad hoc, of limited duration, and subject to being overriden or withdrawn. He never created a system for the direction, concentration, and monitoring of all the major facets of U.S. foreign relations. Those subjects whose importance he denigrated (such as nuclear proliferation) or could not comprehend (international economics, for example) he simply neglected. They were tended by the custodial departments or bureaus that followed pat formulas and precedent, or they were left unattended altogether. In either of those latter circumstances, important developments could occur without arousing the high-level attention that they warranted. The Kissinger foreign policy style has been intensely scrutinized. Among the more insightful critiques of his NSC system is I. M. Destler, *Presidents, Bureaucrats, and Foreign Policy* (Princeton, N.J.: Princeton University Press, 1972). See also the ungenerous yet penetrating account of former NSC staffer Roger Morris: *Uncertain Greatness* (New York: Harper and Row, 1977). Kissinger's own voluminous memoirs, *White House Years* (Boston: Little, Brown and Co., 1979), reveal much of his general thinking about world affairs; less of his methods.

2   The changing face of the international market in civilian nuclear power in the early and mid-1970s and its implications for regulating the spread of technology were reviewed in Paul L. Joskow, "The International Nuclear Industrry Today: The End of the American Monopoly," *Foreign Affairs* 54, no. 4 (July 1976):788–803. Further exploration of the commercial situation in civilian nuclear power was offered by Steven J. Baker, "Monopoly or Cartel?" *Foreign Policy*, no. 23, Summer 1976, pp. 205–18.

3   Estimates based on discussions with U.S. government officials and independent experts.

4   Research and Policy Committee of the Committee for Economic Development, *Nuclear Energy and National Security* (Washington, D.C.: 1976), p. 38.

5   Reported in *New York Times*, May 19, 1974.

6   Indian–American nuclear exchanges before and after the nuclear explosion are discussed at length by Onkar Marwah in Onkar Marwah and Ann Schulz (eds.), *Nuclear Proliferation and the Near-Nuclear Countries* (Cambridge, Mass.: Ballinger Publishing Co., 1975).

7   The explosion itself should not have come as a surprise: The United States was forewarned in early 1972 – by remarks of the secretary of the Indian Atomic Energy Authority made to U.S. officials and duly recorded – that India was preparing for a peaceful nuclear explosion (PNE). ACDA tried to get interest in a preemptive U.S. action, but was frustrated at State, the NSC, and the AEC. At that time, proliferation and ACDA were both marginal to Washington's power centers.

8   ACDA understandably had pushed the hardest for a harsher response. Its director, Fred Ikle, was becoming the administration's most ardent, if largely uninfluential, antiproliferationist. His energetic remonstrances urging a tougher stand were lent a deaf ear by the secretary. Kissinger found the agency's line of reasoning unconvincing. Beyond the difference of viewpoint there was a basic clash of styles and philosophies. The secretary's anti-ACDA bias inclined him to give its views short shrift and, over time, turned into a personal hostility toward Ikle. In the end, the agency director was denied all access to Kissinger. (It is a commentary on the personalized politics at the upper reaches of government that Kissinger often voiced a nostalgic preference for Ikle's predecessor, Gerard Smith, even though Kissinger had been instrumental in forcing Smith out of office in the purge of all those most closely involved with SALT I – itself an odd act in the light of the administration's self-congratulation on achieving the treaty.) Ikle's ostracization by the secretary of state did little to enhance ACDA's already unimpressive status within the executive branch. In truth, the agency's estrangement probably meant little for the evolution of Kissinger's thinking on nuclear proliferation.

9   The distinction between peaceful nuclear explosions and the testing of a warhead is purely one of nomenclature. The idea of using nuclear energy in large excavation projects was born in the AEC, and pushed by scientists at the Lawrence Livermore Laboratory in California. It was inspired by the general desire to promote nuclear power, and by the laboratory's particular interest in winning support for a program in which it had an organizational stake. The confusion created by contriving a separate category of peaceful explosions hampered efforts to develop an airtight safeguards system. As Ikle would complain to Congress: "From an arms control point of view, peaceful nuclear explosions are a diabolical invention. They pretend to make a distinction where there can't be one and make it easier for governments to move in the direction that could lead to weapons production." Quoted in William Epstein, *The Last Chance: Nuclear Proliferation and Arms Control* (New York: Free Press, 1976), p. 177.

10   Abraham S. Friedman and Myron B. Kratzer, "Visit of Indian AEC Chairman and Thorium and Accelerator Teams," Atomic Energy Commission memorandum, Setpember 1966.

11   NSSM 202 was to be the first systematic look at proliferation since an NSC study prepared in 1969, which focused on implementation of the then recently signed NPT. That review had done little more than reaffirm the treaty's virtue and spell out steps to be taken to win its approval. In keeping with the thinking then prevalent in the White House, it concluded that no special effort should be made to twist arms in the interest of ratification.

12   Committee for Economic Development, *Nuclear Energy and National Security*, New York, September 1976, p. 25.

13   ACDA, *Annual Report*, 1976.

14   From William D. Metz, "Reprocessing: How Necessary Is It for the Near Term?" *Science Weekly*, April 1, 1977, p. 41.

15   NRC, "Environmental Survey of the Reprocessing and Waste Management Positions of the LWR Fuel Cycle," NUREG-0116.

16   Irvin C. Bupp and Jean-Claude Derian, *Light Water: How the Nuclear Dream Dissolved* (New York: Basic Books, 1978), p. xii.

17   The AEC technical assistance program is scathingly criticized in an article by Congressman Clarence E. Long: "Nuclear Proliferation: Can Congress Act In Time?" *International Security*, 1, no. 4 (Spring 1977): 52–79.

18   Indirect encouragement for development was also provided by the AEC's extreme dilatoriness in perfecting waste-storage techniques and by its failure to build disposal facilities: The United States never exercised the option of repatriating spent fuel from U.S.-built reactors that was written into general agreements of cooperation.

19   Myron E. Kratzer, Testimony before U.S. Congress, Senate Committee on Government Operations, *Hearings on Export Reorganization Act of 1976*, 94th Cong. 1st sess., January 29, 1976.

20   Herbert H. Brown, Testimony, *Hearings on Export Reorganization Act of 1976, January 29, 1976*.

21   Ford Foundation Nuclear Energy Policy Study Group and Mitre Corporation Report, *Nuclear Power Issues and Choices* (Cambridge, Mass.: Ballinger Publishing Co., 1977), p. 386. Cited hereafter as Ford/Mitre.

22   Robert Seamans, Testimony before U.S. Congress, Senate Committee on Government Operations, *Hearings on Export Reorganization Act of 1975* 93d Cong., 1st sess., April 30, 1975.

23   Ford/Mitre.

24   Quoted by Robert S. Ingersoll, in answers to written questions from Senator Glenn, appearing in *Hearings on Export Reorganization Act of 1976*, p. 739.

25   Administration backing of the license followed on the heels of an earlier decision to provide India with further deliveries of heavy water, conditional only on guarantees of no diversion to unsafeguarded facilities. Although the terms of the agreement provided for inspection and safeguards, no controls on non-U.S. facilities were required, as they are for NPT signatories and as U.S. policy generally demands.

26   Decision recorded in II Nuclear Res. Rep., 30,080.10 (June 21, 1976).

27   Marcus A. Rowden, Testimony, *Hearings on Export Reorganization Act of 1975*, April 29, 1975. Victor Gilinsky's position was succinctly stated a year later in "Plutonium, Proliferation, and Policy," *Technology Review* 79, no. 4 (February 1977):58–65.

28   President Gerald Ford, Executive Order 11902, Nuclear Export Procedure, February 18, 1976.

29   The flood of proposed legislation is chronicled and examined by Michael A. Bauser, "United States Nuclear Export Policy: Developing the Peaceful Atom as a Commodity in International Trade," *Harvard Law Review* 18, no. 2 (Spring 1977):227–72.

30   Taylor's definitive and most influential writing was a book he coauthored with Mason Willrich, *Nuclear Theft: Risks and Safeguards* (Cambridge, Mass.: Ballinger Publishing Co., 1974). Prior to publication, it was serialized in the *New Yorker*, where it was something of a cause célèbre.

31   Bauser, "United States Nuclear Export Policy," p. 246. The Symington cutoff was imposed on Pakistan in early 1979 and rescinded on the urgent request of President Carter a year later.

32   Congress's strong views about the European export program were registered by another activist antiproliferation senator, Abraham Ribicoff, in an article entitled "A Market-Sharing Approach to the World Nuclear Sales Problem," which appeared in *Foreign Affairs* 54, no. 4 (July 1976):764–787. There the senator chastised France and Germany for selling sensitive fuel-fabricating facilities and proposed a cutoff of LEU fuel if they continued in their obdurate ways. Were the U.S. threat to put them in a more cooperative mood, the United States should offer to divide up the global reactor market with its commercial competitors in order to remove the incentive for offering reprocessing or enrichment technology as a lure. See also the article by Senator Adlai E. Stevenson: "Nuclear Reactors: America Must Act," *Foreign Affairs* 55, no. 1 (October 1976), pp. 63–76.

33   William O. Lowrance, "Nuclear Futures for Sale: To Brazil from West Germany, 1975," *International Security* 1, no. 2 (Fall 1976): 24.

34   Committee for Economic Development, *Nuclear Energy and National Security*, p. 18.

35   Baker, "Monopoly or Cartel?" p. 211.

36   Secretary of State Henry Kissinger, "From Coexistence to World Community," Address to the United Nations General Assembly, September 23, 1974.

37   Secretary of State Henry Kissinger, Address to the Wisconsin Institute of World Affairs, Milwaukee, Wis., July 14, 1975.

38   *New York Times*, January 28, 1976.

39   The agreement is summarized and assessed in the report of U.S. Congress, Office of Technology Assessment, *Nuclear Proliferation and Safeguards* (New York: Praeger Publishers, 1977), pp. 220–3.

40   Secretary of State Henry Kissinger, Address to the United Nations General Assembly, September 22, 1975.

41   The Barnwell facility is discussed in detail in "The Fri Review," later in this chapter.

42   See Albert Wohlstetter et al., *Moving toward Life in a Nuclear Armed Crowd?* (Los Angeles: PanHeuristics, 1976).

43   Nuclear Regulatory Commission, *Final Generic Environmental Statement on the Use of Recycled Plutonium in Mixed Oxide Fuel in Light-Water Cooled Reactors*, NUREG–002.

44   Committee for Economic Development, *Nuclear Energy and National Security*, p. 27.

45   The pair, Connor and Schleede, were already in harness pushing Ford's struggling privatization bill. The Nixon–Ford interregnum had left as one of many orphans the plan for governmental support and encouragement of the two private enrichment consortia. Finding the matter lying dormant, aware of the need to act on expansion of existing capacity, and personally committed to the principle of privatization, Schleede and Connor relaunched the campaign and drafted the enabling legislation. Both men were strong apostles of the Ford administration's bracing free-enterprise philosophy. And Schleede, for his part, was point man in the White House's last-ditch resistance to the strip-mining bill supported by the Democrats, a bill it viewed as overly restrictive and anti–energy growth. These biographical facts are of ironic interest in the light of their subsequent role in pushing the Fri Report toward a position that bode ill for commercial reprocessing.

46   President Gerald Ford, Uranium Enrichment Message, June 26, 1975.

47   President Gerald Ford, Statement on Nuclear Policy, October 28, 1976.

48   Prominent among them were Columbia University Law Professor John Palfrey, a former AEC commissioner who was active in the NPT negotiations, and Albert Carnesale, a nuclear engineer who was associate director of Harvard University's Program on Science and International Affairs.

49   Jimmy Carter, Address on Nuclear Policy to the United Nations, May 13, 1976.

50   Jimmy Carter, Election Speech, San Diego, Calif., September 25, 1976.

51   President Gerald Ford, Statement on Nuclear Policy, October 28, 1976.

CHAPTER 4. MAKING THE CARTER NUCLEAR POLICY

1   Jimmy Carter, Address on Nuclear Policy to the United Nations, May 13, 1976.

2   Ford Foundation Nuclear Energy Policy Study Group and Mitre Corporation Report, *Nuclear Power Issues and Choices* (Cambridge, Mass.: Ballinger Publishing Co., 1977). Cited hereafter as Ford/Mitre.

3   Ibid., p. 2.

4   Ibid., p. 4.

5   John Palfrey, "The Plutonium Connection: Nuclear Power and Nuclear Weapons," unpublished manuscript, July 1977, p. 17.

6   Ford/Mitre, p. 24.

7   Ibid., p. 29.

8   Ibid., p. 74.

9   Michael Nacht, "Nuclear Energy and Nuclear Weapons," Report of the 1975 Aspen Workshop on Arms Control, p. 3.

10   Ford/Mitre, pp. 30–1.

11   Ibid., p. 31.

12   Ibid., p. 33.

13   Ibid., p. 3.

14   Quoted, without attribution, *Washington Post*, April 9, 1977.

15   *New York Times*, April 28, 1977.

16   Quoted by Edward Wonder, "Nuclear Commerce and Nuclear Proliferation: Germany and Brazil, 1975," *Orbis* 21, no. 2 (Summer 1977).

17   On the matters of fuel assurances and assistance in the management of reactor waste, reticence was also called for. No precise programs had emerged in PRM–15. Moreover, OBM – once it had gotten a crack at the new policy – strongly urged that Washington should not undertake any commitments whatsoever until there was a clearer idea of the costs. Deputy Director James McIntyre drafted a memo laying down procedures for budgetary review of any proposals to be made to foreign governments. No commitment could be made without prior OMB authorization. As of April 1977, nobody had a firm understanding of what would be included in a fuel-assurance package or how the United States would go about organizing the storage and/or disposal of radioactive materials from civilian reactors; so references on the incentive side of the president's policy were to be intentionally vague.

18   President Jimmy Carter, Statement on Nuclear Power Policy, April 7, 1977.

19   Ibid.

20   Ibid.

21   They had seen as a particularly bad omen the Carter administration's decision to delay indefinitely the delivery of high-enriched uranium (HEU) earmarked for research laboratories in Europe. The delay, which had been urged by the State Department, was not, however, meant as a signal of any sort, and certainly not as the forerunner of a general fuel embargo. It simply seemed to make sense to hold off the shipment while the administration worked out the terms of its overall export policy. In Europe the matter was viewed much more gravely. Although a secondary issue, it did exacerbate relations by contributing to fears of a confrontation provoked by U.S. intransigence. In the French view (shared by other Europeans), the United States was bound by treaty to permit members of the European Atomic Energy Community (Euratom) to make use of U.S.-supplied fuels as they saw fit, so long as the materials were not applied to military purposes or transferred out of the community. Under the terms of an agreement of cooperation signed with Euratom in 1960, the United States had relinquished the power of prior approval on future reprocessing. That accord now seemed in danger of unilateral abrogation.

22   The White House Fact Sheet, Nuclear Non-Proliferation Act of 1977, April 27, 1977.

23   *New York Times*, April 9 and May 17, 1977.

24   In fact, the new administration's review of the project had been on a separate track with a shorter lead time than PRM–15. Clinch River was evaluated by a task force centered in the Executive Office, in which OMB played a leading role. The preliminary budget inherited from the Ford administration had called for a large outlay to finance the next step in the plant's construction. A decision had to be made quickly. The technical and economic arguments against a continuing commitment to Clinch River were compelling in the eyes of Carter administration officials who opposed the proposed quarter of a billion dollar allocation.

25   Quoted in *Nuclear News*, May 1977.

26   Ibid.

27   *New York Times*, April 28, 1977.

28   Ibid., April 22, 1977.

29   *Washington Post*, April 1, 1977.

30   Ibid., April 24, 1977.

31   Senator Frank Church, "Arms, Energy and the Atom: The Lethal Dilemma," Address at MIT, May 2, 1977.

32   *New York Times*, November 8, 1977.

33   The singular resiliency of the project, and the fantical devotion of its congressional supporters, owed something to the formidable and relentless lobbying efforts made in its behalf. In the spring and summer of 1977, the Capitol was flooded by industry representatives, by allies in the AFL–CIO who were concerned about the threat to jobs and who rose to challenge what they saw as the environmentalist no-growth forces, and even by representatives of the American Petroleum Institute, who saw the issue less as a matter of support for the competing energy source than as a test of a broader principle, i.e., whether the emerging energy legislation and the nation's answer to its energy needs would concentrate on conservation or on exploitation of old and new resources. The strenuous lobbying campaign was abetted by the equivocal position of ERDA officials, who retained considerable authority as technical experts on matters of nuclear technology, even though their agency had suffered a loss of credibility because of its manifest shortcomings in dealing with safety and export questions. Schlesinger himself gave lukewarm support to the president's position; he could not fail to do so when other officials were prepared to offer circumspect aid to the backers of Clinch River. (Lee Gosick, head of the Reactor Safety Division, for example, testified to the security of the site in retort to the finding of a consulting firm, Burns and Roe, that it was geologically unstable.) In the traditional manner of relations between agency and legislative allies, technical data favorable to the project were funneled to congressional sympathizers and damaging data were not volunteered. Moreover, some senior officials lent the weight of their positions to the pro-breeder forces by making known private views contrary to official administration policy. This common practice was defended by pointing to the requirement that they respond frankly to direct congressional queries.

34 Quoted in *Washington Post*, June 15, 1977.

35 See the account in *Nucleonics Week*, May 5, 1977.

36 Ibid.

37 Ibid.

38 See the illuminating account of Irvin C. Bupp and Jean-Claude Derian, *Light Water: How the Nuclear Dream Dissolved* (New York: Basic Books, 1978), pt. 1.

39 Robert O. Keohane and Joseph S. Nye, "Transgovernmental Relations and International Organizations," *World Politics* 27, no. 1 (October 1974): pp. 39–62. Their concept of transgovernmental activity derives from their more general theory of transgovernmental politics; see Robert O. Keohane and Joseph S. Nye (eds.), *Transnational Relations and World Politics* (Cambridge, Mass.: Harvard University Press, 1972), pp. 43–4.

40 Joseph S. Nye, Jr., Statement at the International Conference on Nuclear Power and Its Fuel Cycle, Salzburg, Austria, May 2, 1977.

41 This section draws heavily on my article, "Carter's Nonproliferation Strategy: Fuel Assurances and Energy Security," *Orbis* 22, no. 2 (Summer 1978):333–56.

42 Joseph S. Nye, Jr., Testimony before U.S. Congress, House Committee on International Relations, the Subcommittee on International Economic Policy and Trade, October 3, 1978.

43 Joseph S. Nye, Jr., Address to the Atomic Industrial Forum, New York City, October 23, 1978.

CHAPTER 5. THE CARTER STRATEGY

1 Joseph S. Nye, Jr., Address to the International Conference on Nuclear Non-Proliferation and Safeguards, New York City, October 23, 1978.

2 Gerard Smith, Remarks before the International Fuel Cycle Evaluation Conference, Washington, D.C., October 18, 1977.

3 President Jimmy Carter, Opening Address to the International Fuel Cycle Evaluation Conference, Washington, D.C. October 17, 1977.

4 International Nuclear Fuel Cycle Evaluation, Final Communiqué of the Organizing Conference, October 21, 1977.

5 Atlantic Council Nuclear Fuels Policy Working Group, *Nuclear Power and Nuclear Weapons Proliferation* (Boulder, Colo.: Westview Press, 1978), p. 45.

6 Ibid., p. 88.

7 Ted Greenwood, Harold Feiveson, and Theodore Taylor, *Nuclear Proliferation: Motivations, Capabilities, and Strategies for Control* (New York: McGraw Hill, 1977), p. 175.

8 Coprocessing and "spiking" techniques certainly had enough value as antiproliferation measures that their neglect by civilian nuclear authorities can properly be added to the sins of misfeasance committed by the AEC in its heyday as promoter of nuclear power. The commission's commitment to PUREX as the technologically and economically preferred method had left little room for serious

consideration of adaptions or alternatives. Ironically, one reason for the early un-
hesitating acceptance of PUREX for the civilian program was that the technology
for obtaining the high-grade plutonium appropriate for the agency's military program already had been perfected. Excessively low cost estimates for the Barnwell
facility owed much to the failure to appreciate the difference between the operating
modes demanded for producing reactor-grade fuel and those needed for obtaining
weapons-grade fuel. The technology's military origins also help to explain the high
risk of diversion associated with PUREX, because the separated material contains
a large proportion of the isotope plutonium-239, the prime bomb-making substance.

Coprocessing as an alternative mode of fuel recovery was not a technical innovation. The idea had been bandied about among engineers, industrialists, and AEC
bureaucrats for years. It had been rejected as the technological basis for the reprocessing of spent fuel for two fundamental reasons. First, it raised the estimated cost
by a moderate amount, roughly 10–15 percent, because of the somewhat more
elaborate process involved. That cost increment was considered too high a price to
pay at the time when the connection between the use of plutonium as a civilian
power fuel and weapons proliferation was not being made. Second, it simply was
easier – as a matter of technical congruence – to build on existing technology and
existing knowledge than to chart new routes. The inertial factor in decision making
on issues involving sophisticated technology should not be ignored. The technical
and organizational momentum that had built up behind plutonium recycling,
abroad as well as in the United States, was a constraining fact of life for U.S.
officials engaged in the fuel-cycle review. The cumulative decisions made over the
years by officials on whom considerations of technological compatibility had exercised a dominant influence made acceptance of structural modifications an uphill
struggle.

       9   Atlantic Council, *Nuclear Power and Nuclear Weapons Proliferation*,
p. 88.

      10   David C. Gompert, Introduction to Greenwood, Feiveson, and
Taylor, *Nuclear Proliferation*, p. 6.

      11   Atlantic Council, *Nuclear Power and Nuclear Weapons Prolifera-
tion*, p. 88.

      12   CIVEX was conceived jointly by Walter Marshall, deputy direc-
tor of the United Kingdom Atomic Energy Authority, and Chauncy Starr of the
Electric Power Research Institute, the U.S. electric utilities' collective research and
development organization. Unlike the PUREX procedure, the CIVEX method
never completely separates the plutonium from its waste products, which serve as
contaminants. The prospects for the CIVEX process are discussed by Charles K.
Ebinger in *International Politics of Nuclear Energy*, The Washington Papers, vol. 6,
no. 57 (Beverly Hills and London: Sage Publications, 1978).

      13   Victor Gilinsky, "Plutonium, Proliferation and the Price of Re-
processing," *Foreign Affairs* (Winter 1978–79):374–86.

      14   Karl Kaiser, "The Great Nuclear Debate," *Foreign Policy*, no. 30,
Spring 1978, pp. 83–110.

15   Declaration of the Nuclear Suppliers, January 1977.

16   Ibid.

17   Richard Burt, in *New York Times*, April 3, 1980.

18   U.S. Congress, House Committee on International Relations, *Hearings on the Nuclear Antiproliferation Act of 1977*, 95th Cong., 1st sess., p. 348.

19   Ibid., p. 162.

20   Ibid., p. 233.

21   Ibid.

22   Frederick Williams, "The Nuclear Non-Proliferation Act of 1978," *International Security* 3, no. 2 (Fall 1978):45–50.

23   Ibid.

24   42 USC 2112.

25   Ibid., sec. 128 f- (1).

26   Williams, "Nuclear Non-Proliferation Act," p. 49.

27   Sec. 123 (2).

28   *Washington Post*, April 16, 1978.

29   Quoted in *Christian Science Monitor*, April 4, 1978.

30   Ibid., April 14, 1978.

31   *Washington Post*, April 16, 1978.

32   An ironic sidelight to the strained relations with Euratom was offered by the quarrel that broke out between Bonn and Paris in the spring of 1979. At issue was France's refusal to return to Germany plutonium it had recovered from the reprocessing of spent German reactor fuel at La Hague. The French demanded guarantees that it be used only for peaceful purposes. The Germans found the demand both insulting and a violation of Euratom rules on free transfer of nuclear materials. Apparently, the action was a step in a French campaign to amend the Euratom Treaty to insure France's total control over its own civil and military nuclear programs. A spin-off of the dispute was to complicate Washington's efforts at renegotiating its agreement with Euratom. See *New York Times*, May 14, 1979.

33   Atomic Energy Act of 1954, sec. 131, as amended by Nuclear Non-Proliferation Act of 1978.

34   313 (B) (2).

35   Joseph S. Nye, Jr., Testimony before U.S. Congress, House Committee on International Relations, Subcommittee on International Economic Policy and Trade, October 3, 1978.

36   Ibid. Nye's testimony reiterated the administration position he had first enunciated on June 12, 1978, in a speech at the Uranium Institute (London). There he had declared: "Certainly, the way the U.S. will respond to requests for transfer for reprocessing of U.S. origin spent fuel will depend on the extent to which other countries have made serious efforts to recognize and take proliferation concerns into account. At the same time, we are ready to take their energy security concerns into account." Nye's words, approved by President Carter, reflected the victory of the moderates in the internal debate over policy toward foreign reprocessing that dated back to the early days of the administration.

37   Ibid.

38   Ibid.

39   Gilinsky, "Plutonium, Proliferation and the Price of Reprocessing," p. 375.

40   Ibid., p. 385.

41   *Washington Post*, April 4, 1978.

42   Ibid.

43   *New York Times*, April 9, 1978.

44   Ibid., April 11, 1978.

45   Ibid., June 14, 1978.

46   Ibid., June 25, 1980.

47   Ibid., June 26, 1980.

48   References are to the *Summary and Overview: A Report of the Technical Co-ordinating Committee to the Final INFCE Plenary Conference*, Washington, D.C., February 1980.

49   Ibid., p. 18.

50   Ibid., p. 14.

51   Ibid., p. 23.

52   Ibid., p. 45.

53   Ibid., p. 34.

54   Ibid., p. 35.

55   George W. Rathjens, Deputy U.S. Special Representative for Non-proliferation Matters, Remarks to Japan Atomic Industrial Forum, March 13, 1979.

56   The promise and problems of truly multinational facilities are analyzed by the contributors to Abram Chayes and W. Bennett Lewis (eds.) *International Arrangements for Nuclear Fuel Reprocessing* (Cambridge, Mass.: Ballinger Publishing Co., 1977). The IAEA has undertaken an exhaustive study of multinationally organized regional centers covering the back-end of the nuclear fuel cycle. Its report appeared in spring 1977 as *Regional Nuclear Fuel Cycle Centers* (Vienna: International Atomic Energy Agency).

57   The IAEA study of a possible plutonium storage system began as a political device to satisfy Dutch concerns about the Netherlands' participation in the URENCO consortium. Upset by West Germany's nuclear deal with Brazil, the Dutch parliament demanded that the internationalization of sensitive fuels be seriously explored before it would support continued participation.

58   John Palfrey, "The Plutonium Connection: Nuclear Power and Nuclear Weapons," unpublished manuscript, July 1977.

CONCLUSION

1   Joseph S. Nye, Jr., Statement at the International Conference on Nuclear Power and Its Fuel Cycle, Salzburg, Austria, May 2, 1977.

2   Irvin C. Bupp and Jean-Claude Derian, *Light Water: How the Nuclear Dream Dissolved* (New York: Basic Books, 1978), p. 188.

3   Carter probed into the possible technical adaptations to plutonium separation while the overriding issue of the amount of reprocessing by allies that

could be tolerated was the object of interminable bureaucratic wrangling. He personally detailed elements of a fuel-assurance package, but by not deciding how he wanted the program organized or who should run it, left its fate to oversized and undermanaged interagency committees.

4   A related response to the problem of excessive numbers and over-consultation is *the creation of informal networks among subordinate officials*. Although the interagency working group or its equivalent is maintained as the formal facade, actual responsibility for policy analysis, option writing, and review is passed to a group of intellectually and personally compatible officials. They maintain their own lines of communication, meet in less structured settings, and (with the approval of their superiors – a vital condition) make policy recommendations. This was the nature of the network that pushed the Ford administration toward a more skeptical position on plutonium recycling. The drawbacks of devolving policy planning and execution onto such an unstructured group are as noteworthy as the expedient ends the practice serves. Informal networks lack decision-making authority, are impermanent and normally issue-specific. They do not bind their agencies as more formal procedures should, and are inadequate vehicles for implementing a broadly cast policy when the network succeeds in winning administrative approval for any proposal its members might agree on.

Index